D1612931

AFRICA AND EMPIRE

UNIVERSITY OF LONDON
INSTITUTE OF COMMONWEALTH STUDIES
*

COMMONWEALTH PAPERS

General Editor

PROFESSOR SHULA MARKS

25

AFRICA AND EMPIRE

W. M. Macmillan,
*Historian and Social
Critic*

AFRICA AND EMPIRE

*

W. M. Macmillan,
Historian and Social Critic

EDITED BY
HUGH MACMILLAN
AND
SHULA MARKS

PUBLISHED FOR THE
INSTITUTE OF COMMONWEALTH STUDIES
BY TEMPLE SMITH

Published by

Temple Smith
Gower Publishing Company Limited
Gower House
Croft Road
Aldershot
Hants GU11 3HR
England

Gower Publishing Company
Old Post Road
Brookfield
Vermont 05036
USA

ISBN 0 566 05494 9

Printed and bound in Great Britain at
The Camelot Press plc, Southampton

CONTENTS

INTRODUCTION

HUGH MACMILLAN

THE first of October 1985 marked the centenary of the birth of William Miller Macmillan, one of South Africa's foremost thinkers on historical and social issues, and a leading critic of empire. To mark the occasion, the Institute of Commonwealth Studies, London, held a small symposium. The object of the meeting was not only to look at Macmillan's life and work, but also to take stock of subsequent developments in the fields which he pioneered. A unique feature of the meeting was the bringing together of scholars, three generations of the Macmillan family, and some of his younger contemporaries who were able to contribute valuable oral testimony and vivid memories of his personality. Most of the essays in this volume were first presented on that occasion, and are published here in revised form.

Macmillan's life (1885–1974) bridged the years from the 'scramble' for Africa to the end of metropolitan empires. The impact of imperialism and the need for decolonization were central to his concerns. Growing up in South Africa at the height of empire, he shared in many of the preconceptions of his contemporaries. What is remarkable was the extent to which he was able to free himself from many of their limitations. The tension between the liberal and radical elements in his thought has led to an ambiguity in his intellectual legacy, with scholars of different persuasions claiming him as their intellectual ancestor. Some of these ambiguities are represented in this collection: we have not tried to iron out the contradictions or impose any single viewpoint on our contributors.

Macmillan's greatest contribution was to the understanding of South African society, both in the past and in his own time. His present-day relevance is perhaps most striking in his conceptualization of South Africa as a single society. To see South Africa as 'a whole' was, in 1930, no mean achievement, but he began to move beyond this view towards the vision, however tentative, of South Africa as not only a single society but as a common society. In so doing he put an increasing distance between himself and most of his nominally liberal contemporaries. So unpopular were his views that he soon felt compelled to leave South Africa, as did his student and close friend, C. W. de Kiewiet, who, in his *History of South Africa, Social and Economic* (1941), was later to bring many of his ideas to a wider audience. It was only after the Second World War that these historians were given any recognition even in the English-speaking universities of South Africa. The relationship between them and their contribution to South African historiography is sympathetically portrayed in the piece by Christopher Saunders below.

There is a clear link between Macmillan's political concerns and his historical writing. In the context of the heightened debate on segregation in the 1920s, Macmillan saw his historical work as having immediate political purpose. The papers of Dr John Philip which provided the bulk of the material for his major historical works, *The Cape Colour Question* (1927) and *Bantu, Boer, and Briton* (1929), also illuminated his critique of Hertzog's 'Native' policies. There is, indeed, some evidence that Macmillan came to the Philip papers in 1920 with a preconception of the use to which they might be put, both in the rehabilitation of Philip's reputation and in the argument against segregation. In Macmillan's view, Philip had, in his own day, seen South Africa as 'a whole' and had argued for a separation of the races under overall British control at a time when the Xhosa still had most of their land. Thus an equitable division of the country was 'more possible' then than in the 1920s.[1] Writing in 1929, however, about Cradock's attempted clearance of the Zuurveld in 1812, he made clear his view that even at that date a policy of segregation was fundamentally impractical.

In the years that followed, some such clear-cut plan of 'keeping the races apart' has often had its champions; it appeals as the obvious way of escaping the entanglements of a mixed community in which advanced and backward peoples are thrown together. Had the segregation adumbrated in frontier policy at this early stage been realized in 1812 and 1819, it might have cost us much of the light as well as the shade in the story of the last hundred years. But the plan broke down at its first attempt because it ignored the fact that relationships had already been established. Even in those days of small things, the problem that the segregationists evaded was the crux of the matter, that fitting relationships must be maintained between white and coloured people in so far as they have already come to live and work together.[2]

Macmillan and many other historians of South Africa, both liberal and radical, have been censured for using the past to fight the battles of the present. It is not a charge which Macmillan would have taken very seriously, for, given his political commitment, it is improbable that he would have written history at all if he had not been able to see its political objectives.

However, Andrew Ross, in his essay in this collection, provides a new, and possibly surprising, twist to an old charge. He suggests that there was a rather different disadvantage to those usually advanced in Macmillan's use of history for political purposes. Thus Ross argues that Macmillan's treatment of Philip, primarily in *The Cape Colour Question*, not only fails to take sufficient account of his Scottish background, and of early nineteenth-century radical evangelicalism as an international movement, but also deliberately plays down Philip's commitment to racial equality. There is, indeed, evidence that Macmillan did tone down his original manuscript, on the advice of a well-intentioned reader, for what can only be called tactical reasons.

These tactics have to be understood in the context of white racial attitudes in the 1920s. It is not always recognized that in writing against segregation and for his view of 'One South African Society'[3] Macmillan was waging a war on two fronts. He was seeking to convert not only segregationists of the full-blooded racist variety, but also liberal segregationists whose ranks in the 1920s included Edgar Brookes, J. D. Rheinallt Jones, and the Hoernlés. While protesting their own commitment to racial equality, liberal segregationists clung to views of racial purity, were shocked at any suggestion of 'miscegenation', and maintained that blacks needed segregation for their own protection.

Some of the ambiguity in Macmillan's writings at this time stemmed from the fact that, in advance of almost all his liberal contemporaries, he was in the process of freeing himself from many of their preconceptions. These included a belief in the necessity of 'parallel institutions' and 'trusteeship', as well as in the desirability of an industrial colour bar. A similarly painful, though largely separate, journey was being made at much the same time by a handful of radical socialists.[4] It is hardly surprising, therefore, that Macmillan felt constrained to pull his political punches for fear that too forthright a statement of his own, or even Philip's, views would alienate readers who might be able to accept a part, but not the whole, of his message. A similar charge can be sustained against the concluding passages of both *Bantu, Boer, and Briton* and *Complex South Africa*, where his pleas for the recognition of the political · claims of the emergent black intelligentsia and middle class are qualified by reference to their small numbers, and the impossibility of their acquiring a 'swamping' vote in the foreseeable future.

While Andrew Ross sheds new light on Macmillan's interpretation of John Philip, Robert Ross also takes the treatment of Philip as his starting-point. In drawing attention to the links between Africa and the West Indies at the time of the debate on slave emancipation, Ross touches on a theme which Macmillan was to rediscover in the context of colonial development and decolonization in the 1930s. In the 1830s, James Cropper saw the example of the exploitation of nominally free 'Hottentot' labour in South Africa as a 'warning *for* the West Indies' of the dangers of exploitation of former slaves. A hundred years later Macmillan was to see in the decayed state of the Caribbean islands a 'warning *from* the West Indies' to Africa of the inadequacy of the colonial policy of 'trusteeship' and of *laissez-faire* economics.

The theme of the post-emancipation Cape is taken up in greater detail by John Marincowitz in an essay which fills a major gap in the existing historiography. He looks at the emergence of a 'Coloured' proletariat and at the appearance of class and racial differentiation in the mid- and later nineteenth century — the period which lies between that covered in *The Cape Colour Question* and *The South African Agrarian Problem and its Historical Development* (1919). He demonstrates that, while Macmillan underestimated the degree of 'Coloured' resistance in this period, he was more conscious than some later writers of the discontinuities between the pre- and post-emancipation eras. As we shall see, neither the strengths nor the limitations of Macmillan's account are accidental. Here, as elsewhere, his vision as a Fabian perhaps tended to alert him to the real changes wrought by reform and led him to underestimate the significance of class struggle.

If the history of the western Cape in the second half of the nineteenth century has been much neglected since Macmillan wrote about it in the 1920s, much the same can be said of the history of eastern Cape. This may partly explain the major gap in this collection: the absence of any reconsideration of Macmillan's best-known historical work, *Bantu, Boer and Briton*. It was a lasting disappointment to Macmillan that his reinterpretation of South

African history, which was completed in the later 1920s, had little or no influence in his lifetime on what was taught in South African schools. It has still not done so, but, despite the contemporary purposes for which it was written, his historical work has remained surprisingly undented by later revisions. The best known of these, even where they differ from him in emphasis, or occasionally invert his arguments, work largely within a framework which he laid down.

Perhaps the most polemical, least academic, yet arguably most influential, revision of *Bantu, Boer, and Briton* was Nosipho Majeke's *The Role of the Missionaries in Conquest* (1952). Written under a pseudonym by an English woman, Dora Taylor, on behalf of the Non-European Unity Movement, this purported to present a radical, Africanist, and Marxist view of the missionary factor. It is for the most part a rewrite of *Bantu, Boer, and Briton*, using its data to portray Dr John Philip as 'an agent of imperialism' masquerading as a 'friend of the natives'. It presents Philip, as Macmillan never did, as a twentieth-century liberal, and is in essence an attack on liberalism, and, beyond that, any white involvement in African political movements. While it cannot advance upon Macmillan's view of competition for land and labour as the prime determinant of events on the frontier, the book harks back to Theal and Cory in its view of Philip as ardent 'politician' and 'arch-meddler'.[5] While following Rosa Luxemburg in equating the British with capitalism, and the Boers with a more primitive mode of production, it notes that the Africans tended, and were encouraged, to ally themselves with the more 'progressive' force but were repeatedly betrayed.[6]

The distance between this position and that of Macmillan is not so great. One of his fundamental arguments was that the British 'abandonment' of the interior in the 1850s sowed the seeds of later conflict by allowing the triumph of the more reactionary segregationist ideology of the north over the integrationist ideology of the Cape. His charge against British imperialism was that it had failed both in its historic duty of protecting African interests and in its modernizing role, by forming an opportunist, but doomed, defensive alliance with the 'Boers' against the African people.[7] His view of the modernizing duty of British imperialism was not entirely incompatible with that of Luxemburg, nor indeed with Karl Marx's own view of the role of the British in India, although they would never have anticipated anything other than catastrophe for the 'natives' in the short run. The fundamental flaw in the Majeke–

Taylor pamphlet was an essential racism which made no distinction between the views and interests of different missionaries, different colonists, nor even different historians, seeing all from Theal to Macmillan as representatives of the *herrenvolk*.[8]

Attack from a different quarter came in 1963 from J. S. Galbraith, who, in *Reluctant Empire*, attempted a more academic revision of *Bantu, Boer, and Briton*. In a book which, for the most part, followed Macmillan's framework year by year, chapter by chapter, and, at times, page by page, though referring only once or twice to the object of revision, he sought to set the history of the Cape frontier in the context of imperial history, and to explain the workings of 'the official mind'. Galbraith's argument was essentially that Macmillan had exaggerated the importance of Philip, the coherence of the missionary factor, and the clash of economic and humanitarian considerations within 'the official mind'.[9]

Galbraith's preoccupations with 'retrenchment' as the guiding principle of imperial policy, and with the official concern for 'order', made his book more conservative in tone, and even less sensitive to the internal dynamics of African societies than Macmillan's had been a quarter of a century previously. In Galbraith's work there is a marked shift away from Macmillan's explanation of events on the frontier in terms of land and labour — that is, from expropriation and exploitation — towards the official concern with 'order' and 'disorder' — the latter stemming from the alleged propensity of the 'natives' to steal cattle. In his attempt to rehabilitate Sir Benjamin D'Urban, Galbraith contrived not to mention the British murder of the Xhosa king, Hintŝa — a remarkable omission which was to be repeated a few years later in the first volume of the *Oxford History of South Africa*.[10] The shift away from Philip and the humanitarians also involved a shift away from the African point of view, at least in so far as they had sought to represent it.

Undoubtedly the central weakness of *Bantu, Boer, and Briton* is its lack of insight into Xhosa culture and the internal workings of Xhosa society. In *The House of Phalo*, written in the 1970s and published in 1981, Jeff Peires attempted to redress the balance. In Peires' view the 'liberal' historians, especially Macmillan, though sympathetic to the Xhosa, still have white colonists as their historical focus. 'Instead of rapacious Xhosa depriving peace-loving colonists of their cattle, they tended to depict rapacious colonists depriving peace-loving Xhosa of their land. But even on this view the Xhosa were more acted against than acting.'[11] Yet, in some ways, Peires does not seem to have moved far beyond Macmillan in his conclusions.

Peires' work does, of course, provide a great deal more material on Xhosa history and society than Macmillan ever could. Writing in an era in which the techniques of exploring African history and the imperatives for doing so had been greatly refined, Peires used recorded oral traditions — such as those of J. H. Soga which were published a year after *Bantu, Boer, and Briton* — and traditions collected by himself in the 1970s, as well as the work of social anthropologists, to present a far more accurate and detailed account. Although influenced by Macmillan's awareness of the movement of the Xhosa into a single South African society, *The House of Phalo* is not immune from dangers which Macmillan associated with the rise of social anthropology and the study of 'culture contact'.[12] These include a tendency towards a rather static view of the pre-colonial past as a 'golden age', and a kind of relativism which sees the effect of 'total' war on the frontier as 'reviving the already blurring division between the two cultures' and re-emphasizing 'their irreconcilable differences'.[13] In his treatment of Xhosa religion and economy, there are elements of both cultural and economic dualism.[14] Peires also still slips into passages which portray the Xhosa as mere victims of colonial rapacity.[15]

In *The House of Phalo*, Peires is primarily concerned with the history of the Xhosa people 'in the days of their independence' and the book ends in 1850. Although he cannot avoid discussion of the frontier he only includes it because he maintains that neither Macmillan nor Galbraith dealt adequately with settler expansionism. He therefore found it necessary 'to consider settler society in rather more detail than would otherwise be appropriate'.[16] Nevertheless, his work does not set out to provide a reconsideration of the history of the frontier 'as a whole'.

For a more thorough-going attempt to re-examine the history of the 'frontier', it is necessary to turn to Martin Legassick's essay on 'The frontier tradition in South African historiography'. Written and circulated in 1970, and published in 1980, it was the first and still remains the most wide-ranging attempt to relate the historiography of the period to changes in the political climate in the twentieth century. In particular Legassick saw that there were links between the historical treatment of the frontier and the shift from liberal segregationism to liberal integrationism. He was above all disposed to counter the suggestion that the genesis of twentieth-century racial conflicts could be traced to slavery, Calvinism, and the frontier, without reference to the later impact of capitalist development, industrialization, and competition in the labour market. He sought to apply to South Africa 'the argument that race relations are at bottom a class question'.[17]

Legassick began his essay with a quotation from Eric Walker's 1930 lecture on 'The frontier tradition in South African history'. He went on to look at the contribution of H. M. Robertson whose articles of 1934–35 stressed that the frontier was as much or more a place of cooperation as of conflict. He credited I. D. MacCrone with the formulation 'in detail', in 1937, of the view of the frontier which perceived racial prejudices developed in the Cape in the seventeenth and eighteenth centuries as underlying the attitudes of white South Africans in the twentieth century. It was MacCrone who brought to the study of the frontier the psychological notions of 'group' consciousness and identity, ideas which he used to combat 'scientific' racism, but which were later to be exploited by others in most illiberal ways. Legassick identified three main strands in the 'frontier tradition'. These were the idea of the frontier as a place of isolation and regression, as a place of conflict over land and labour, and as a place of interaction and cooperation. He was, of course, aware that both Macmillan and de Kiewiet had written of the frontier in all three of these aspects. Elsewhere he has written of Macmillan's 'ambivalent' role as a founder of the 'Liberal School' of South African historians with its stress on cooperation as against conflict.[18] He does not, however, seem to have been fully conscious of the extent to which Macmillan was the progenitor, at different times, of all three views of the frontier, nor of the extent to which he had anticipated Legassick's own concern with the origins of twentieth-century race attitudes, and their relationship to questions of class.

In *The South African Agrarian Problem* Macmillan had emphasized the isolation of the frontier as explaining the peculiarity and 'backwardness' of the 'Boers', a view which Legassick and others have come to contend.[19] In his later historical works his major emphasis was on the frontier as a place of conflict between Xhosa and settler over land and labour, rather than, as in the view of Theal and Cory, a place of conflict between 'civilization' and 'savagery'. But he was equally aware of the elements of interaction which had begun to make the Cape, including its frontier zone, a single society in the

14

early nineteenth century. Macmillan would have had no real quarrel with Legassick's assertion that 'trade and war, therefore, were but two sides of the same coin: so-called co-operation and conflict both entered simultaneously'.[20]

Macmillan did not go as far as Legassick's categorical assertion that the frontier was in no way the source of twentieth-century racial attitudes and conflicts. His work is, however, peppered with references, not only to the gradual emergence of white racial enmity towards blacks on the frontier in the course of the nineteenth century, but also to its intensification under the stress of industrial competition in the twentieth century. Macmillan fully shared the aversion of Legassick, and of Genovese, to the use of race in itself as an explanatory concept. He had noted the propensity, as Legassick was to do later, of frontier 'ruffians' such as Coenraad Buys and Louis Trichardt to make alliances with African chiefs, as well as that of Grahamstown merchants to run guns to the Xhosa. He commented that 'to the colour prejudice of later times such a charge seems well-nigh incredible' but drew the inference that 'the modern "instinct" for whites to sink their differences and stand together against the black man is not inborn, but a product of the many wars of the nineteenth century'.[21] Elsewhere he wrote that

... white prejudice against the black has unfortunately grown with the complexities of South African life: it was greatly embittered by the wars and conflicts of the last century, and threatens to reach a climax under the stress of the even more acute economic competition of today.[22]

Macmillan's view of the emergence of racial prejudice is, at the very least, thoroughly historical and dynamic. It contains no trace of MacCrone's notion of the passive inheritance in the twentieth century of a characteristic acquired two centuries previously.

Although he did not attribute its origin to Macmillan, Legassick was correct in seeing a link between the new emphasis on cooperation and the reaction against liberal segregationism. Macmillan developed the theme in order to emphasize the impossibility of segregation, whether in the early nineteenth or twentieth centuries, in so far as it failed to take account of the extent to which the lives of black and white had already become inextricably intertwined. But to him there was no contradiction between his primary emphasis on the conflict over land and labour and his

15

secondary emphasis on interaction. For he saw clearly that conquest and dispossession increased both interaction and dependence.[23] There was a tendency for some later liberals to reverse this relationship, deliberately to play down the elements of conflict, and to see them as incidental to an underlying harmony of interests. This was perhaps a reflection of the functionalism which had such a strong influence on both economists and social anthropologists in the 1930s, and through them, on later historians. Nothing could have been further from Macmillan's position or intention. He was inclined to deplore the emphasis upon the individual frontier wars, as distracting attention away from what he saw as the endemic nature of frontier conflict.[24]

Macmillan's later protestations that he had neither talent for, nor inclination towards, the study of theory tend to conceal the extent to which he used theoretical tools and believed in the power of ideas.[25] Running throughout his historical and sociological work is a profound interest in the processes of class formation and the actuality of class relations, although his reaction to revolutionary class struggle was far from enthusiastic. While his interest in class helped to make his work acceptable to an earlier generation of Marxist scholars, it has also continued to intrigue a later generation who are sometimes surprised to find that, writing sixty years ago, he shared some of their present-day preoccupations. The source of Macmillan's interest in, and knowledge of, class analysis is a little obscure. It need not, of course, have come from the reading of Marx. Gustav Schmoller, whose lectures he attended in Berlin in 1910, and to whom he always acknowledged a great debt, was a socialist and a materialist who lectured on class, but rejected the suggestion that class struggle, or any other phenomenon, could provide a single motor force for history. His most famous pupil, Max Weber, accepted much of Marx's class analysis, including his view of proletarianization, but deplored what he saw as his neglect of ideology as an engine of change.

While Macmillan frequently gave credit in both speech and writing to the influence of Schmoller he was not so mindful of the influence of another of his Berlin lecturers, Franz Oppenheimer, the pioneer sociologist and advocate of agricultural producer cooperatives. Oppenheimer, whom Macmillan did remember as daring to describe the Prussian Junkers as 'fighting cocks', strongly believed that the tendency towards what he called 'land monopoly', and the consequent inequitable distribution of land, was the primary cause of both rural exodus and urban unemployment. He noted that rural emigration was not always a factor of over-population but often came from areas of low population density. A concern with such issues was to be central to much of Macmillan's earlier 'sociological' work.[26] It is tempting, however, to speculate that Macmillan may have learned more outside the lecture room in Berlin than he was to recall when he wrote his memoirs sixty years later. He then remembered that, by contrast with the contemporary drama of the House of Lords crisis in Britain, political life in Germany seemed 'very slack and inactive'. He did not recall that he arrived in Berlin early in May 1910 in time for the climax of a serious political crisis over Prussian electoral reform. This coincided with the major pre-war industrial crisis — a nationwide lock-out in the building industry. Macmillan, who did remember that he 'schooled himself' to read a variety of newspapers, including *Vorwärts*, the daily paper of the then predominantly Marxist Social Democratic Party, must have been aware that this crisis split the radical Marxist wing of the party.

Rosa Luxemburg first saw the combination of political and industrial crisis as a revolutionary opportunity, and called for 'mass strike' action as a prelude to the overthrow of the monarchy. However, Karl Kautsky, the editor of *Vorwärts*, and leader of the 'Marxist centre', regarded the political and economic spheres as separate, and in an article on the Roman general, Fabius Cunctator, deplored Luxemburg's 'rebel's impatience' which would 'drive towards socialist revolution as rapidly as possible without regard to the objective limitations of the political scene'. It is surely plausible to see in this forgotten experience of a revolutionary moment, and the debates which accompanied it, a major formative influence on Macmillan's thought. For he joined the Fabian Society in the following year and, throughout his time in South Africa, remained committed to the gradualist road to socialism. He also retained, throughout his life, a tendency to keep economic and political factors separate in analysis.[27]

If nothing else, Macmillan probably acquired a basic familiarity with the theory and language of Marxism in Germany. He must have been exposed also to the increasing debate in radical circles on imperialism and militarism — a debate in which Schmoller himself was implicated if only as the butt of Luxemburg's sarcasm. This may have influenced what he later described, with characteristic, but misleading modesty, as his 'indeterminate and unsatisfactory' attitude

17

to the First World War, during which he resisted considerable social pressure to enlist. The only occasion on which he seems to have used such an explicitly Marxist phrase as 'class consciousness', or referred to what he called 'the terrible doctrine' of 'class war' in print, was in an anonymous article written in the aftermath of the Rand Revolt of 1922. He argued then that the international socialism of the 'Reds' had been subverted by Afrikaner nationalism, and while seeking to hold the middle ground between capitalists and 'Reds', he accused the bourgeoisie of Parktown and Yeoville of a more extreme and un-thinking advocacy of 'class war' than that of the workers themselves.[28] The formative influences on Macmillan's political thought, his ap-proach to class struggle and his response to the 1922 strike are discussed in a provocative and stimulating piece by Jeremy Krikler in this collection. Looking at Macmillan from the vantage point of the contemporary struggles in South Africa, Krikler is critical of what he sees as Macmillan's failure to identify with those actively involved in the revolutionary workers' movement. He argues that this was an inevitable consequence of Fabian élitism, and led to Macmillan's failure to achieve a new social order in South Africa. It is, however, debatable whether such an identification in the 1920s could have produced the desired result in view of the nature of the radical political movements in the period and the forces ranged against them.

In the event, Macmillan's contribution was to be in his empirical analysis of South African society. Whatever his political and theoretical standpoint, it is possible to find in Macmillan's writings some consideration of almost all the varied forms of master and servant relationship from master and slave, landlord and tenant, owner and sharecropper, to company and peasant producer; nor was he unaware of the rise of the African middle class, and the status of the intelligentsia. Above all, however, he was profoundly concerned with what Legassick described as a distinct 'type' of race relations — the competition in industrial conditions between black and white workers. The assertion that this phenomenon could be analysed in class terms would not have surprised Macmillan because he had himself attempted to do it. He was well aware that the possibility of survival outside the industrial economy, lower economic expect-ations, or 'the compulsions of the sub-subsistence sector' might either enable or compel black workers to accept lower wages than white. He would not have objected to the statement that this could be treated as 'a *structural* fact determined by previous history'.[29]

Macmillan himself noted that it was the 'dispersed Natives — the direct result of congestion in the Ciskei, and of more gradual extrusion elsewhere — [who] are the crux of the problem'. The Land Act of 1913 and wartime inflation had forced more and more 'Natives' off the land and into competition with unemployed whites. He observed that

> ... now the wheel has come full circle, and the essence of the 'Native' problem of today is that an exodus of starving unskilled Poor Whites from imperfectly developed European farms is brought into violent competition for unskilled labour with the still cheaper overflow of Natives from farms and from congested 'Reserves'. The foundations of economic life could hardly be more unsound than in modern South Africa.[30]

The greatest virtue of Macmillan's analysis was his realization that black and white workers were the product of similar and related pressures of proletarianization. In his analysis of the reserves he realized that while the better endowed could be seen as providing a form, however inadequate, of poor relief for the old and unemployed, they also provided a subsidy on wages which enabled some labourers 'to accept a rate of wages that disastrously lowers the standard for those others, a growing class, who have no such home base'. In other words the facts of differing degrees of proletarianization, and differing economic expectations, underlay not only the competition between black and white but also between black and black, and, in some parts of the country, between white and white.[31]

Macmillan's interest in issues of class was, of course, closely related to his central concern with the study of poverty — a study which both preceded, and ran parallel with, his historical work. His investigations of poverty greatly influenced his view of South Africa as a single society, and contributed to the formation of his belief that 'colour economically is a mere accident'.[32] His first book, *The South African Agrarian Problem*, was largely devoted to white impoverishment but even it displayed an explicit awareness of the need to see South Africa as a unity. Starting with the acute problems of 'poor whites', he went on to study poor blacks and came to see the interdependence of black and white poverty. By the time he published *Complex South Africa* in 1930 he had an enlarged and clarified vision of South Africa as a single political economy. The transition is illuminated by the essays of Jeffrey Butler and William Beinart in this volume.

These essays deal in some detail with Macmillan's approach to both agrarian and urban poverty. Butler shows how he was able to see, as early as 1919, that the problems of the 'poor whites' were not, as many then believed, a consequence simply of their own inadequacy but were the result of the commercialization of agriculture, and of unregulated rural transformation. While Butler is primarily concerned with 'poor whites' in the small country towns of the eastern Cape and the Karoo, Beinart looks at the analysis of rural change. He is especially concerned to trace Macmillan's influence, through such work as the 'sample survey' of Herschel district, on the radical historiography of the 1970s. In Beinart's view, Macmillan's later preoccupation with economic causation sometimes blinded him — as it did his successors, Legassick included — to less tangible cultural factors.

If Macmillan's use of a type of class analysis and his interest in poverty give a modern ring to his work, his treatment of culture may appear more dated. In the 1920s when social anthropologists such as A. R. Radcliffe-Brown and Winifred Hoernlé were introducing to South Africa Franz Boas's view of plural cultures, Macmillan clung to the older concept of a single culture. To some extent he looked back towards the views of Matthew Arnold and E. B. Tylor, but he also drew upon the contemporary universalism of Rabindranath Tagore, whose writings were known to him through their mutual friend, C. F. Andrews, best known as the close associate of Mahatma Gandhi.[33]

An awareness of the changes in meaning which were affecting the concept of culture led Macmillan to prefer the term 'civilization', a word which has fared particularly badly in the intervening years. While Macmillan succeeded very largely in freeing himself from contemporary white notions of 'savagery' and 'barbarism', he continued to see one of the elements of the South African problem as the juxtaposition of 'advanced' and 'backward' peoples in a single society. He saw people, and peoples, as existing with differing 'levels of culture', and as progressing towards 'civilization', although his view of 'civilization' was never racially defined. He saw it as neither 'white' nor 'dual', but as universal, and representing the best achievement of mankind.[34]

Although Boas' view of multiple cultures and of cultural relativism had been developed as part of a liberal response to Social Darwinist evolutionism and 'scientific' racism in the United States, Macmillan was quick to see the illiberal uses to which it could be put in South Africa.[35] His own view of 'civilization' had, at least, the merit of placing all people on a single cultural continuum. He sought to use historical analogies drawn from medieval Germany, Elizabethan England, or eighteenth-century Scotland, as well as from the English Industrial Revolution, to demonstrate that the African people of South Africa were simply passing through, rather more rapidly than may have been ideally desirable, processes of change which were universal. There were vestigial elements of assimilationism, evolutionism, and, perhaps, in relation to the 'poor whites', of eugenic 'degenerationism' in his thought, but these did not detract from his conviction that the African people of South Africa were, as he had noticed as early as 1911 in the slums of Johannesburg, 'on the upgrade', and would inevitably rise towards political power. For, as he wrote in 1930,

By our own act the blacks are part of us and segregation is impossible. Sheer domination may serve for a season — for twenty, fifty years, haply for more — though in the twenty years since Union Native self-consciousness has grown as it never did in a century preceding. The blacks must have a secure place in the country, peacefully and easily at once, or later by violent contention.[36]

His own antipathy to racism led him to regret the introduction from the United States of the very concept of 'race relations' as diverting attention away from more material considerations. While he was contemptuous of attempts to 'understand the native mind', he suggested that it was the 'European mind' which was in greater need of investigation. The Jungian associations of the title of his book, *Complex South Africa*, were not accidental for he came to see South Africa's white rulers as suffering from a psychological disorder, the most obvious feature of which was an irrational fear of, mingled with contempt for, the black majority.[37]

Macmillan differed from the majority of liberals in his certainty that there was no evidence for either racial inferiority, or superiority, and no need for further investigation of the topic. His own personal knowledge of, and friendship with, such outstanding African leaders as R. V. Selope Thema, D. D. T. Jabavu, Clements Kadalie, and Selby Msimang, convinced him that there was no question as to the

21

intelligence and educability of black people. He may have received some 'scientific' support for his views in the later 1920s from his friendship with Lancelot Hogben, the radical zoologist and critic of racial theory, who was for a time a professor at Cape Town. But his efforts to shift even liberal public opinion, let alone Hertzog's government, towards his view of the necessity of immediate, if mild, political reform along integrationist lines were unsuccessful. He came to believe that the influence of social anthropology, and the exponents of 'Bantu Studies', were undermining his efforts. He resented 'their alliance with and patronage from Gen[eral] Hertzog and the Union government which finds anthropology useful "proof" of [the] theory of inherent [African] inferiority'.[38]

My essay examines in detail the relationship between Macmillan and the social anthropologists. It endeavours to show that his hostility towards the static approach of the early functionalists stemmed not only from intellectual distaste for an approach which rejected history, but also from a realization of the political use which could be, and eventually was, made of their view of the multiplicity of cultures. Many of his criticisms were accepted by a younger generation of South African anthropologists such as Max Gluckman, Hilda Kuper and Monica Wilson who were to adopt a much more dynamic approach to social change, and to the interaction of 'cultures'.

Paul Rich, in his essay, also touches on Macmillan's relationship with the social anthropologists. He examines in detail his growing isolation from the mainstream of liberal opinion in the 1920s. He also looks at his relationship with the establishment imperialists of the 'Round Table' group, as well as with practising colonial administrators such as Philip Mitchell, and radical critics of empire such as Lord Olivier and Norman Leys. He illuminates some of the internal pressures and external attractions which contributed to Macmillan's decision to leave South Africa — a decision which was not finally made until 1933. By that time he had, as he told his friend, S. H. Frankel,

... about come to the end of my tether in Johannesburg. 'Bantu Studies' was getting rather too much for me! and, more particularly, I am sure I am right that the future is African more than *South* African — and African developments can be watched rather better a little out of the 'maelstrom' of Union Affairs.[39]

INTRODUCTION

The essays by Mona Macmillan and John Flint deal largely with Macmillan's travels, writing, and propagandist activities in the years between his departure from South Africa and the outbreak of the Second World War. Mona Macmillan's essay looks at the making of *Africa Emergent* (1938) in which her husband surveyed the whole of British Africa and expressed most forcefully his critique of 'indirect rule', his view of the inadequacy of 'culture contact' as an explanatory concept, his realization of the growing strength of African nationalism within emergent élites, and the danger of their exclusion and alienation by the anti-democratic trend of colonial policy. As he pointed out, the new intelligentsias had reason to see in 'indirect rule' a colonial version of South Africa's segregationist policies. It was also in *Africa Emergent*, which he described as an 'ecological' study, that he first formulated, in relation to Africa, his critique of the colonial economic policy of *laissez-faire*, emphasizing the 'absolute' and intrinsic poverty of much of the continent, and the need for new attitudes and policies towards African development.

John Flint also deals with the impact of *Africa Emergent*, and Macmillan's relationship with members of both the establishment and anti-establishment imperial pressure groups which were active in the 1930s. In addition, he considers the impact on Macmillan himself of his visit to the Caribbean as a consequence of which he wrote *Warning from the West Indies* (1936). It was this book, subtitled 'a tract for Africa and the empire', which, of all his works, was to have the greatest influence on colonial policy. It was circulated within the Colonial Office and contributed to the shifts in policy which culminated, under the stress of war in 1940, in the passing of the Colonial Development and Welfare Act. In *Warning from the West Indies* he expressed more forcefully than anywhere else his critique of the dominant orthodoxies, *laissez-faire*, trusteeship, and Lugard's notion of 'the dual mandate'. The book stressed the need for political as well as economic development in the West Indies, and was critical of the influence on policy both there and in Africa of settler minorities. These were criticisms which he tended to forget, or to suppress, in the changed political environment of the post-war world.

These essays point rather obliquely to significant changes in Macmillan's approach to empire and 'imperialism' which emerge from his two major books on colonial policy, as well as from his Heath Clark lectures on West Africa which were published in 1940,

23

his Fabian lecture on 'Freedom for colonial peoples' which was given in the same year, and his slightly later pamphlet, *Democratise the Empire*, (1941).[40]

The experience of the wider Africa which he gained as a result of extensive travels in the 1930s led him to modify his views on 'economic imperialism'. In his studies of poverty in South Africa he had seen the country's problems as lying essentially in black and white poverty resulting from landlessness, proletarianization and unregulated agrarian transformation. While never writing specifically about the development of capitalism in South Africa, he pointed to the historical analogies of the transition from feudalism in medieval Europe, and of the Industrial Revolution in nineteenth-century Britain. He had always at the back of his mind his knowledge of Scotland's Highland 'clearances' about which Marx himself had written with such eloquence and power. He had also applied to the study of the South African economy a modified version of Hobson's 'underconsumption' theory, stressing the need to consider the 'native' as both consumer and producer.

After years of fighting what he called 'the stock-pattern evils of imperialism' in South Africa it came as a shock to him, he recalled in 1940, to find in parts of Africa where there was neither land alienation, proletarianization, nor even, in some parts, direct taxation, a poverty 'every whit as abject as that induced by landlessness in South Africa'.[41] At the same time he produced an analysis of the cocoa-producing regions of the Gold Coast, which Polly Hill was later to describe as uniquely perceptive on the role of 'strangers' as entrepreneurs. In it he pointed to developments by apparently spontaneous African initiative, with little or no assistance or regulation by government. He argued that these processes had produced a 'derangement of tribal machinery' and 'social upheaval' which was at least comparable 'to any disturbance caused elsewhere by the capitalist exploitation of African mineral resources'.[42]

The orthodox view of 'economic imperialism', as formulated by Hobson and Lenin seemed to him, therefore, to be doubly complicated by the existence in some areas of intrinsic poverty and 'undevelopment' (which he contrasted with 'induced' poverty or 'underdevelopment') and elsewhere by processes of class formation and differentiation which appeared to have been more or less spontaneously generated. At the same time he argued, in the context of the pre-war debate on the return of Germany's former colonies, that the origins of African empires were as often military and strategic as purely commercial. He appears to have concluded that while the orthodox theory could and did explain black and white poverty in South Africa, and might have relevance in more commercially developed areas such as China, it did not apply with equal force in those parts of Africa which had suffered a shortage rather than an excess of capital investment, and whose contribution to world trade was still minimal. Such areas were the victims, he argued, not so much of 'economic imperialism' as of 'the dominant bourgeois economics' and its doctrine of *laissez-faire*. He went on to argue that the colonization of Africa was as much the consequence of its own weakness and 'backwardness' as of capitalist aggression. Even of South Africa he argued that it was white weakness and 'backwardness' rather than capitalist strength which lay at the root of the contemporary move towards segregation though, by implication, he saw that weakness as itself 'induced' by economic pressures.[43]

While his arguments foreshadowed much later debate on 'modernization', 'development' and 'underdevelopment', Macmillan had neither claims nor pretensions as a theorist of empire. He had, as was usual with him, a pressing political purpose. He was prompted and emboldened to mount this critique of the Hobson–Lenin theses at least in part by frustration with what he came to see as an unconstructive and essentially negative anti-imperialism prevalent in left-wing and Labour circles. He deplored the ignorance and lack of concern of most of the Labour movement about colonial issues, and felt that the rhetoric of anti-imperialism served as a substitute for necessary thinking about developmental issues in the 'backward' regions of the world.

In all probability Macmillan's strictures made little impact on the theory of 'economic imperialism', although rather similar arguments surfaced at a much later date in the writing of more conservative critics such as D. K. Fieldhouse, Ronald Robinson and Jack Gallagher. They did, however, bear some more immediate fruit in the establishment, a few months after his 1940 Fabian lecture, of the Fabian Colonial Bureau which was, by his own account, at least partly a response to it.[44] His ideas may also have had some influence on the Labour Party's document on post-war policy towards the African and Pacific colonies which was produced in 1943 and which is said to have been more concerned with practical problems than previous statements.[45] He may also have had some influence on the thinking of Arthur Creech-Jones, later Colonial Secretary, who in his introduction to the important volume of *Fabian Colonial Essays* wrote in 1944 that 'practical achievements depend on knowledge, technical skill and hard thinking; escapism into the philosophy of Lenin or socialist monasticism will not bring better nutrition or the rearing of cattle in the tsetse forest belt'.[46]

Macmillan's attempted revision of the orthodox theory stemmed not only from his experience of the difficulty of interesting the Left in developmental issues but also from his growing realization of the formidable barriers to 'progress' in Africa presented by 'natural' factors. While he warned of the danger of 'wholly materialist' explanations, he was particularly impressed by the work published during the 1930s, culminating in an official report on 'Nutrition in the Colonial Empire' of 1939, on dietary deficiency. He was acutely conscious of Africa's insatiable need not only for capital but for 'funds' for development in the fields of health, education, agriculture and basic infrastructure. In somewhat visionary passages in his Fabian lecture of 1940 he foresaw the need in the post-war world for international development agencies and corporations, for schemes involving voluntary service overseas, as well as for federations and free trade areas to overcome the barriers created by Africa's absurdly artificial colonial boundaries. In the same lecture he called for direct representation of the more important African colonies in the British parliament as a means of increasing public consciousness of colonial needs.[47]

His experience of governmental inertia and of the dead hand of the Treasury led him to doubt the ability of the colonial government, or governments, to deal with Africa's varied problems. He saw a need for 'controlled' private capital investment but doubted that the Colonial Office had the capacity to deal on equal terms with, for instance, sophisticated multinational mining companies. He was impressed by the professionalism and expertise of these large corporations and saw in South African mining law, with its provision for mineral leasing and progressive taxation, a model for their profitable control. He noted that it was the extreme scarcity of capital investment in much of Africa which led colonial governments to treat capitalists with an exaggerated respect and deference. He had doubts, also, as to the viability of 'the essentially non-socialist ideal of peasant proprietorship' as the basis for agricultural development, and thought in terms of 'controlled' plantations, as well as calling

26

attention to the 'new and at least highly constructive example of the Soviet State's dealings with primitive peoples'.[48] His position was, perhaps, summarized in the statement that 'the exclusive concern with capitalist "exploitation" makes Labour tilt in any particular case at a windmill of "economic imperialism", overlooking the underlying tragedy that Africans are open to exploitation just because they have so little to offer except their labour and their ambition'.[49]

It was only the outbreak of war, with the consequent loosening of Treasury controls on expenditure, which made possible some beginning in the implementation of the developmental policies for which Macmillan had campaigned. For the first time he was himself involved in the making and implementation of policy. The pre-war Colonial Office had kept him very much at arm's length but, as a member of its Advisory Committee on Education from 1940–43, he participated in the drawing up of a variety of plans for educational expansion. He was a signatory of the Channon Report which laid down the guidelines for the post-war development of African universities, and of the report on mass education which provided the blueprint for the setting-up of adult education and extension services. In the Empire Intelligence section of the BBC in London from 1941–43 he was involved in the establishment of what eventually became the African Service of the corporation. As the Senior Representative of the British Council in West Africa from 1943–45 he supervised the inauguration of the first effective network of public libraries, and initiated scholarship schemes which were intended to pave the way for the Africanization of the local civil services.[50]

After the war he was made a member of the Colonial Office Labour Advisory Committee which encouraged the establishment of trade unions and, from 1947, was Director of Colonial Studies at the University of St Andrews — a post which was, with some difficulty, created for him. The post-war Labour government, of which he was a natural supporter, made most conspicuous use of him on the Observer Mission to Bechuanaland to enquire into the events surrounding the banishment of Tshekedi Khama. Even then, he was not, as Michael Crowder shows in his lively and entertaining essay in this volume, the first choice of the Colonial Office, some of whose functionaries feared that he might not be relied upon to take the 'correct' line. For someone who had been a lifelong opponent of South African policy there was some irony in his being called upon to participate in a vain attempt to extricate a Labour government from an embarrassing *imbroglio* which had been created by its excessive sensitivity to South African pressure over Seretse Khama's marriage to a white woman. Nevertheless, he was able to use this opportunity to make positive recommendations for the future administration and economic development of the Protectorate.

There is, perhaps regrettably, no contribution in this volume on the post-war development in Macmillan's thought on African nationalism, decolonization and development. His views on these issues are largely contained in the revised edition of *Africa Emergent*, which was published by Penguin Books in 1949, and reached a very wide audience, as well as in his less successful, though not uninteresting, final statement, *The Road to Self-Rule: a study in colonial evolution* (1959), which combined history, reminiscence and contemporary analysis.

If Macmillan had been one of the first writers to draw attention to the rise of African nationalism, and to champion the cause of the emergent intelligentsias, his experiences in West Africa during the war appear to have contributed to an early disenchantment. Even before the war he had stressed the need in the Gold Coast, which he saw as probably 'the most hopeful of all African colonies', for further political education. He felt that the Gold Coast middle class displayed an unhealthy preoccupation with legal and constitutional issues and insufficient interest in what he saw as economic 'essentials', including the living and working conditions of their own migrant labourers from the Northern Territories.[51] Wartime experience tended to confirm these doubts. In 1947 he wrote that West African newspapers displayed 'more zeal for a vague African nationalism than for actual Nigerian or Gold Coast reconstruction, and most for the class interests of their civil servant, trader, teacher readers and their claims to places in Africanized services'. He regarded as 'obscurantist' the failure of Gold Coast politicians to take a lead in the campaign for the eradication of swollen-shoot disease in cocoa, as well as their opposition to the nationalization of mineral rights.[52] He seems also to have concluded that, in the changed circumstances of the post-war world, the emergent West African middle class was no longer the 'underdog' and was on the verge of real political power.

Macmillan was not entirely alone in foreseeing the danger of transferring power to the possibly exploitative representatives of an indigenous petite bourgeoisie. Leonard Barnes made a similar point in his book, *Empire or Democracy?*, in 1939.[53] But there is a sense in

which Macmillan's greatest intellectual strengths undermined his
ability to appreciate the force of nationalism in post-war Africa. His
fundamental antipathy to the very concept of 'race', and his
conviction that 'colour' was no more than an accident which gained
political significance only as a result of economic and social
inequality, led him to dismiss as emotional appeals which appeared
to be based in racial or colour consciousness. By 1947 he had
concluded that the battle for 'the rights of colour' was practically won
and that, outside of South Africa, a colour bar had 'no possible
future'.[54] His long-held distrust of exclusive nationalisms which had
been born of bitter personal experience of the Anglo-Boer War and
reinforced by two world wars, led him at times to equate Afrikaner
and African nationalism, and to see in both a rejection of the
uitlander.[55] At the same time his tendency to place greater stress, in
the final analysis, on economic than on social and political factors, his
conviction as to the poverty and 'backwardness' of the African
continent, and his concern with 'the condition of the people
question', made him unsympathetic to political appeals which
appeared to him to ignore economic realities. The slogan popularly
attributed to Kwame Nkrumah, 'seek ye first the political kingdom',
was anathema to him, for he detected in it an irresponsible populism.
He had long held the contrary view that 'considerations of political
freedom do not touch the oppression of poverty'.[56]

His wartime sojourn in West Africa seems to have convinced him
that sounder economic foundations had been laid in the 'mixed' or
settler colonies of East and Central Africa, where governments and
people were more concerned, in his view, about basic issues. His
support for the establishment of the Federation of Rhodesia and
Nyasaland put some distance between him and the more progressive
British Africanist pressure groups, the leadership of which had, by
the early 1950s, in any case passed to a new generation of activists.
This support stemmed partly from his conviction of the need for a
counterpoise to the northward spread of South African influence,
especially after 1948, partly from his view of the educational value for
South Africa of a demonstration of interracial cooperation and
'partnership', but also from a gut feeling that a project which
appeared to be economically rational ought also to be politically
correct.

At times his interest in the Federation brought him into apparent
alliance with the reactionary supporters of settler interests. There

may, indeed, have been some regression on his part towards the paternalist 'trusteeship' with which he had broken earlier. He seemed at times to have forgotten his own strictures on the segregationist trend of Southern Rhodesian policy in the early 1930s, and his assertion in the West African context later in the decade that solutions could not be imposed upon the emergent African élites. He had then written: 'It may be fatal even to try.'[57]

But Macmillan was painfully aware that in the late 1950s, after less than fifteen years of post-war developments of the type for which he had ceaselessly campaigned, the existing infrastructure was still sadly deficient. While he agreed that experience would be the best teacher he was fearful of the damage that might be done, especially to the rural masses of the population, by a process of trial and error. He was characteristically prescient in foreseeing the inadequacy of nationalist ideologies, and the fragility of African economies, at a time when unquestioning support for nationalist aspirations was fashionable in British Africanist circles. He was impatient with what he came to see as a cynical policy of cost-cutting disengagement on the part of the British government. He was however too sanguine as to the practicality and benefits of a prolonged period of tutelage at a time when the metropolitan power had lost the inclination to govern, and subject peoples were increasingly restless under a system which they saw as paternalism at best, and imperialist exploitation at worst.

In the concluding paragraphs of his last major contribution on these issues he nevertheless put his finger with unerring accuracy on what was to prove a major weakness of many newly independent governments — namely their domination by small urbanizing élites often lacking in knowledge, experience or sympathy with the predominantly rural masses. He warned in 1959 that 'any government has its foundations in shifting sands unless its authority in rural districts is fortified by intimate knowledge and understanding of the people's needs and moods'. He warned those nationalists who believed themselves to be 'the successful leaders of a revolution' that

... the revolution is hardly yet begun. The foundations of the new Africa must yet be laid in each of the separate states that are. The very possibility of a true expression of the African spirit demands, first of all, that those who dream of such a future should make more humble acknowledgement of the Africa that is.[58]

In the late 1950s, such warnings were as unfashionable and unpopular as his earlier warnings on the rise of African nationalism, the need for developmental expenditure, and political education had been in the 1930s. By the 1970s and 1980s, however, disillusionment with nationalist ideologies, large-scale failures in rural development, widespread famines, and crushing burdens of debt created by the oil crisis and world recession made such views less exceptional in concerned metropolitan circles, as well as among the new and often more highly educated generation of African intellectuals.

It was, perhaps, the tragedy of the last years of Macmillan's long life that he was compelled to live through a process of decolonization, the necessity of which he had long foreseen, as a powerless spectator. Decolonization involved the transfer of power to small élites who were, in his view, insufficiently prepared as a result of decades of neglect. With a handful of others, he had fought this neglect, but the reforms, when they came, were too little and too late. He did not doubt the potential of African peoples to rule themselves and ultimately to find their own solutions, but he was more conscious than most of the great burden of responsibility which was being placed upon nationalist leaders partly in response to their own demands, and partly as a consequence of shifts in the global balance of power. His views in his latter years could be seen, and often were seen, as paternalist and condescending, but they were informed by an unusually farsighted historical imagination, and stemmed from a profound sympathy with, and love of, Africa and its people.

Macmillan's achievement was not wholly unrecognized in his lifetime. He received honorary degrees from the universities of Oxford (1957), Natal (1962), and Edinburgh (1974). It is, however, probably true to say that his reputation has tended to grow since the early 1970s when his work was rediscovered by a new generation of South African historians and social scientists. His work on Africa 'beyond the Union', and in the West Indies, has remained largely unrecognized. In his essay in this collection, for instance, Christopher Saunders suggests that obscurity of style accounts for the apparent failure of his work on South African history, to gain more immediate acceptance. But it was, perhaps, the originality and unfashionability of his thought, as much as or more than any obscurity of expression, which caused much of his work to have a seemingly delayed impact. As one of those present at the symposium commented on his early work on 'Poor Whites', it seemed at times as if his mind and thought were running ahead of the language and vocabulary available to him.

As many of the essays in this collection indicate, Macmillan regularly identified topics, and reached conclusions about them, years ahead of his contemporaries. He never courted popularity and neither followed academic fashions nor showed much interest in establishing them. He had a passionate concern for the 'underdog' and seldom, if ever, shared either the official establishment or the fashionable anti-establishment view. If a prophet is a person who has the ability to see what others are unable to see, or do not wish to see in the present, as much or more than the ability to foresee the future, then Macmillan had some claim to the title. His 'most acute critical faculty', upon which Lionel Curtis and Sir James Currie among others are said to have remarked, enabled him to do pioneering work in an impressive variety of fields.[59] His closest intellectual and political affinity was probably with such individualistic socialists as Lord Olivier, who thought that *Africa Emergent* was the most important book written on Africa since the partition, not excluding Lord Lugard's *The Dual Mandate*, and Norman Leys, who thought that the same book should be compulsory reading for all visitors to Africa.[60] But his academic and propagandist output was much wider in scope than that of either of theirs.

It is remarkable how often his original perceptions were absorbed at a later date into a new orthodoxy, in many cases without attribution or acknowledgement. His early work on 'Poor Whites', which was concluded in 1919, prefigured much that was to gain greater acceptability and publicity in the report of the Carnegie Commission in 1932. His work on the poverty of the South African 'reserves', carried out in the mid-1920s, inspired and was largely confirmed by the Report of the Native Economic Commission of 1932, and many later reports, although its implications were not fully realised. His attacks on the paralysis of 'functional' social anthropology were absorbed into Gluckman's critique of Malinowski, and internalized by a new generation of anthropologists. His view of South Africa as a single society, and of its history as necessarily involving the study of all its peoples, was given wider currency by de Kiewiet and contributed, at least in some measure, to the emergence of the vision of South Africa as a 'common society' which was incorporated after the Second World War in the Freedom Charter.

Macmillan's critique of 'indirect rule', his early championing of emergent nationalist élites, his rejection of the traditional *laissez-faire* approach to colonial economic policy, with its emphasis on fiscal self-sufficiency, and his advocacy of a more interventionist approach to development, contributed to real shifts of policy beginning with wartime legislation on 'development and welfare'. Some of his arguments were reflected, as John Flint shows, without acknowledgement and in less trenchant form, in Lord Hailey's *African Survey* (1938). He had a significant influence also on the important report of the Royal Commission on the West Indies of 1939, as well as on the establishment of the Fabian Colonial Bureau, and on Labour Party thought on colonial issues which was to be implemented after 1945.

His questioning of the total applicability of the conventional theory of 'economic imperialism' to Africa seems to have been reflected, or perhaps independently rediscovered, in the much later analyses of more conservative academics. His discussion also foreshadowed some of the later debate among radical scholars on 'development and underdevelopment'. His identification of the spontaneous development of an indigenous capitalism on the Gold Coast was acknowledged by Polly Hill, the authority on the subject, but was passed unnoticed by the most recent historian of 'the emergence of African capitalism'.[61] Even his final doubts as to the competence of nationalist ideologies to contend with real economic problems would now be more widely accepted by the Left as well as the Right. None would now disagree with his view that there can be no real political independence without economic strength.

W. M. Macmillan's varied academic and public career ended before either African, Commonwealth or Development Studies had received any significant recognition in British universities. From the time of his first appointment as lecturer in History and Economics in Grahamstown (where he was probably the first person to be appointed to teach Economics in a South African university) to his last full-time appointment in St Andrew's where his department of Colonial Studies fell under the joint jurisdiction of History and Political Science, he was never easily constrained within the confines of a single academic discipline. He followed his mentor, Gustav Schmoller, in seeing no real division between history, economics and sociology. In many ways he was a pioneer in interdisciplinary studies and yet, paradoxically, a strong believer in the value of the older established academic disciplines of history and philosophy.

Among his many contributions, those which have the greatest relevance today, and which we hope this collection of essays vividly demonstrates, are his commitment to a non-racial approach, especially in the South African context, his determination that Africa's peoples must be studied not in isolation but in the context of 'our wider humanity', and his faith in the ability of the historical imagination to 'recreate the past, relate it to the present, and apply it as a guide to the future'.[62] At a time when the practical value of history, and of historical training, is underestimated, and its usefulness for 'developmental' purposes is officially denied, it is salutary to be reminded of the way in which W. M. Macmillan was able to use it as the essential foundation for profound insights into the processes of change in Africa past and present.

1

WILLIAM MACMILLAN AND
THE WORKING CLASS*

JEREMY KRIKLER

WILLIAM Macmillan's contribution to South African historiography is a formidable and complex one. His *Cape Colour Question* and *Bantu, Boer, and Briton* demolished the historiography which preceded his own. Theal, the historian whose works dominated the study of history in early twentieth-century South Africa, and against whom Macmillan took up the cudgels, has only an ideological interest for the contemporary student. In Theal's endless tomes, ideology is dressed up in uncited documents and the analysis presented reads as no more than a pedantic apologia and justification for colonial dispossession. It was Macmillan who launched the decisive scholarly attack upon the historiography dominated by Theal. *The Cape Colour Question* and *Bantu, Boer, and Briton* were, in their time (the 1920s), forceful exposés of 'histories' which, through their unfettered ideological bias, distorted the historical record. The magnitude of Macmillan's achievement in this regard is best appreciated by surveying the historical literature that he was to consign to oblivion: judged by its scale, Macmillan appears a giant.[1]

Macmillan, however, performed another pioneering role, one directly germane to the subject of this study. Moving beyond the archives, he conducted researches into the origins and character of poverty in South Africa in the 1910s and 1920s. Study of the urban poor of Grahamstown, the rural dispossessed generally, and active involvement in the Witwatersrand labour movement led him to produce a rich series of studies dealing with the conditions of working people and, at times, their struggles. It was most probably these writings, concerns and involvements which so alarmed many South African liberals of his own day and impelled one of their leading lights, Edgar Brookes, to complain that Macmillan and his followers spoke 'the language of Johannesburg with the accent of Moscow'.[2] This statement, of course, tells us more about Brookes than Macmillan for the latter, as will be revealed, displayed an abiding antipathy to the Bolshevik Revolution. But, clearly, Macmillan's interests and concerns were unique amongst his fellow academics.

In fact, some of his comments have a surprisingly contemporary ring to them. Consider, for example, these lines:

> The South African history which is really important is that which tells about the everyday life of the people, how they lived, what they thought, and what they worked at ... what they produced and what and where they marketed, and the whole of their social organisation.[3]

Written seventy years ago, this sentence almost reads like a manifesto for 'people's history'. The concerns it expresses guided some of Macmillan's researches: hence the fact that his writings have provided insights and data for recent works of South African social and economic history.[4] Macmillan's contemporary relevance needs to be accounted for. This essay seeks to explain and characterize his concern with poverty in South Africa and his involvement in the labour movement there.

The formative years

Stellenbosch, 1891–1903

Born in 1885, the son of a minister–schoolteacher who emigrated to the Cape Colony, Macmillan arrived in South Africa early in his sixth year. His childhood and youth were marked by the financial insecurity of his family ('I was always well aware that the family pennies had to be counted....'): it was the sudden loss of work that led William's father, the Reverend John Macmillan 'to prospect' for a source of income at the Cape. This he ultimately found, as master of a College boarding house in Stellenbosch, but it was not to prove secure. For the sleepy colonial society of Stellenbosch was to be swept by the political storms that arose in South Africa in the closing years of the nineteenth century: in 1895 it was divided in two by the Jameson Raid as its Dutch- and English-speaking wings coalesced around the causes of Boer independence and British imperialism respectively. The Afrikaner 'ruling class in Stellenbosch' — as Macmillan was later to call it — very rapidly squeezed John Macmillan out of his position so that by the time William was 15 his family had no fixed income. By 1900, then, his father's 'financial situation' was already 'very difficult' and it was never to be retrieved: 'For the remaining years of his life he was increasingly short of funds.' It was only a grant and scholarship which enabled the young William to pursue his studies in Europe and even whilst a Rhodes Scholar at Oxford, he was already sending financial assistance home.[5]

Combined with the financial insecurity suffered by the young Macmillan was a certain cultural alienation. As a member of the small Scots community of Stellenbosch, fierce in its pride of the old country, he defined himself *against* the growing Afrikaner nationalism in the town and was 'chafed' by its historical mythology — standard fare in the classroom. Indeed, a comparison of the myths taught him at school in Stellenbosch with Macmillan's later historical work suggests that he may have been drawn to demythologizing certain aspects of the South African past precisely because of the character of the early teaching he received.[6] The sharp divisions that characterized colonial society at the Cape on the questions that were ultimately to be fought out in the South African War manifested themselves even amongst school students. For 'four years after the Jameson Raid', Macmillan was later to recall, 'I became one of a small minority at loggerheads with the great majority of my schoolfellows'. Macmillan himself considered this decisive for his future development, believing 'those years [to] have largely determined the course of my further story. Had things been otherwise, I might have been absorbed into Cape life as a loyal colonial'.[7]

Two final facets of Macmillan's Stellenbosch years need to be noted: his relationship to its predominantly 'coloured' working class and the importance of Christianity in his early formation. As the early chapters of his autobiography reveal, Macmillan inclined towards the British-inspired political tradition of the Cape, with its qualified but formally non-racial franchise. This inclination appears to have resulted partly from the placing of his minority Scots community in Stellenbosch's colonial society as the British Empire and the Boer Republics moved ever closer to open conflict after the Jameson Raid. Macmillan, quite obviously, was a member of a community which owed allegiance to the British Empire and which was likely to champion the Cape 'liberal' tradition against the more racist political philosophy of the Boer Republics. He is likely, however, to have also imbibed the Cape tradition from a second and far more intimate source — his parents. The Reverend John

Macmillan, whose great influence William was later to acknowledge, had once been a missionary in India and would doubtless have inclined to the paternalistic Cape tradition in whose forging missionaries (including the great Scottish missionary, John Philip) played an important role. Inspired by the Christianity of his father — of whose ministerial station William was intensely proud and which he 'strove to live up to' — the young Macmillan came to believe that 'religious instruction' ought to be undogmatic and 'adapting itself' to the times in which it was situated. The step from such beliefs to a 'socially relevant' religious practice was obviously not a great one. And it was a step Macmillan was later to take.[8]

Macmillan's early life, then, appears to have immunized him against the virulent forms of racism against coloured people that were characteristic of so many white South Africans of his day. None the less, his upbringing was of course still thoroughly colonial. He may later have drawn attention to the fact that the coloureds of Stellenbosch — the 'great working class section of the community' — were not subjected to the residential segregation of later years and that some of their number attended school with him; but he was also to recall that 'small boys', such as he was at the time, 'were of course not encouraged to visit their homes'. Nevertheless the young William's comparatively benign attitude to coloured people is manifest; and it must have been strongly reinforced by the fact that Stellenbosch's 'Coloured population was enthusiastically on our side' in the growing confrontation between Boer and Briton — a confrontation in which Macmillan was to lose an elder brother, killed in action whilst serving in a Cape unit fighting alongside the British.[9]

Europe, 1903–1910

His family's financial difficulties and his peculiar brand of Christianity were to prove important for Macmillan's political and intellectual development in Europe. He took up his Rhodes Scholarship at Oxford University at the age of 18. If the particularities of his situation in Stellenbosch alienated him from the majority of his schoolfellows, neither did it permit his assimilation into the dominating social stratum of the undergraduate world which he now entered. (Financial pressures dogged him in Europe; not only was he to send financial assistance home whilst an undergraduate, but his father insisted that he stretch the funds of his Scholarship, designed for three years, to cover a fourth.) The 'vast majority' of his fellow-students had come to Oxford from English public schools and his social discomfort with them was keenly felt and well-remembered. His College, Merton, was run by 'bloods' (those with an aristocratic lineage) 'and those with money enough to act as bloods'. They lived 'high' and 'fast' and 'ignored us humbler people'. Not surprisingly, Macmillan was 'relieved to have [his] first year in digs rather than in college'.[10]

In such circumstances, Macmillan's Christianity became something of a social refuge. As he was later to admit, during his first year at Oxford he was rather isolated from his college and 'mostly out of things'; consequently, he was drawn to Mansfield Chapel, finding it 'congenial' and the high calibre of sermons delivered there stimulating. Macmillan's Christianity, however, was one cut off from the Oxford Establishment (he was of the 'Scotch Church' and was regularly attending its services by the time he left Stellenbosch). For him and his co-religionists in Oxford — where the power of the Church of England was almost 'overpowering' — Mansfield College (with its Chapel) 'provided an important link and focal point', offering, the 'Scotch undergraduates ... weekly services conducted by the most eminent Scotch churchmen of the day'. The circles Macmillan now 'came to move in were well aware of the social questions in England — slum conditions and unemployment and the seamy side of English life': he and his friends were very soon in 'search of a practical application of Christian principles'.[11] The 'social questions' to which he alluded appear ultimately to have become this field of application. Whilst Macmillan's early life provides clear evidence of why he, in particular, found his way to the socially concerned Christian circles of Oxford, it does not explain how or why those circles found their way to the 'social questions' which agitated them. A brief excursus on the historical development of late Victorian and Edwardian England is necessary to account for this and, indeed, to describe the forces which were to be decisive, at least partly, in shaping Macmillan's attitude to working people.

The last decades of the nineteenth century were momentous ones for the working class. 'The protracted hiatus in the development of the [English] labour movement between the 1840s and the 1880s' had at last come to a close. This hiatus, in the decades following the decline of Chartism, is partly to be explained 'by the length and hesitancy of the transition between workshop and factory as modal types of industrial organisation in England'. These were the years during which the working class was recomposed, its structure altered 'at every level, as the figure of the *collective labourer* in an integrated work process was generalized'.[12] The foisting of the factory system upon the labouring population was of cardinal importance for three reasons: first, it made for the *real* as opposed to the merely *formal*, subsumption of labour under capital;[13] second — as noted above — it helped to plunge the working class into a period of radical social and political dislocation; and third, by breaking up crafts and concentrating immense numbers of unskilled and semi-skilled workers into single production units, it laid the basis for unprecedented gains in trade union membership and organization. Macmillan arrived in England at a time when this dislocation had ended and when the trade union gains were very much in evidence: in the years immediately following the great London Dock Strike of 1889, the number of unionized workers leaped to one and a half million; by 1900, this figure stood at more than two million and, by 1914, it was four million.[14]

The growing industrial strength of the working class was augmented by its burgeoning electoral power: franchise reforms in 1867 and 1884-85 made working people (or, more precisely, working *men*) a constituency which could no longer be ignored. However, it was a constituency rooted in a class which had ceased to be revolutionary — hence the willingness of 'the rulers of Britain', as Eric Hobsbawm has argued, to accommodate (partially) the 'mass agitations of the poor' by periodically widening the franchise: these rulers resisted a significant extension of the vote during Chartism's heyday precisely because at that time they 'believed ... democracy ... to imply social revolution'.[15] The decline of a revolutionary class-consciousness amongst English workers following the defeat of Chartism has been noted by conservative, radical and Marxist historians alike.[16] The broad mass of working people, chastened by the 'mass mobilization of force against Chartism' and demoralized by the failures of what Lenin called 'the revolutionary epoch of English labour', moved rapidly to support reformist and evolutionary methods for the improvement of their lives.[17] Their movement in this direction was facilitated by the significant liberalization of the British state which occurred in the mid-nineteenth century — a liberalization which was itself a response to the revolutionary pressures of the 1830s and 1840s.[18] These are the underlying historical reasons for a fact which is of particular significance for this study: the industrial and political power of the working class which was to exercise a gravitational pull upon intellectuals like Macmillan was a power for *reform*.

Another crucial development in late nineteenth-century Britain was the dissolution of *laissez-faire* economics and its associated political ideology . Their three most potent solvents were the onset of the Great Depression in 1873, the rise of new great industrial competitors (Germany and the USA), and the increasing power of the trade unions themselves: the latter's intervention in the market — to raise the price of labour-power through the collective action of its owners — was a *fait accompli* by the end of the nineteenth century.[19]

The dissolution of the hitherto dominant economic orthodoxy combined with the new mass struggles for better working and living conditions (centred on the efforts of an increasingly powerful reformist trade unionism) to draw many middle-class intellectuals into a typically late Victorian and Edwardian project: the 'scientific' study of 'the poor'. The findings of such study, they believed, could provide the basis for enlightened interventions by the state. The ideology attendant upon such a project became particularly deep-rooted because it could be implanted in a new social stratum then emerging in Britain. For, as Hobsbawm has pointed out, it was only in the thirty years before 1914 that there emerged in Britain that '*nouvelle couche sociale*' comprising the 'educated senior administrator or bureaucrat, the technologically or scientifically trained manager or businessman ... the office-worker, [the teacher in] ... a national system of primary, secondary and higher education'. The growing importance of this new stratum is manifest: between 1881 and 1911, the number of males employed in public administration rose from 100,000 to 300,000, whilst the number employed in the professions and their subordinate services increased by two-thirds in the same period. This new stratum initially found it difficult 'to find a firm place in the middle and upper-class structure of late Victorian Britain' and was therefore drawn to what Hobsbawm (perhaps mis-) designates 'middle-class socialism'.[20]

It was a combination, then, of the factors mentioned above which gave rise to the political and intellectual milieu which was to be decisive for Macmillan. This was the milieu of Booth and Rowntree's classic studies of poverty in London and York, of the Fabians (the self-proclaimed 'intellectual proletariat'), of Toynbee Hall — the pioneer social settlement in East London where people from the universities could live with the poor, study their conditions and attempt to improve the latter's lives and education. Their political objectives were clearly demarcated: a belief in the necessity for social change was to be inculcated in the ruling class through the collection and presentation of data which revealed the extent of poverty and the gains in 'efficiency' that would be achieved through the expansion of the state's powers; the existing institutions of society — and the modified versions of them produced by their subsequent evolution — were to be the agents of such change; and, finally, such change as was effected was to be incremental and gradual in nature — that is, evolutionary rather than revolutionary.[21]

The boundaries of this political culture were also to prove the limits of Macmillan's prescriptions for ending poverty in South Africa. Here, however, we need only note that it permeated Oxford University and the circles Macmillan came to move in. This permeation, however, was a recent phenomenon: in the late 1860s, the University had been sufficiently reactionary to drive Thorold Rogers (later to be a pioneer of 'people's history') from his professorship on account of the militancy of his anti-Tory opinions.[22] Nevertheless, the University could not entirely isolate itself from the historical developments in late nineteenth-century England mentioned above. In 1899, for example, Ruskin College was established with the express purpose of providing places at Oxford for working-class students. The College, of course, was the progeny of the reformist political and intellectual culture described above — a fact which was made patently clear in 1906 by the revolt of its students who characterized its teaching as 'a disguised propaganda in favour of the capitalist system'.[23]

Macmillan, however, was soon to be steeped in this culture. Toynbee Hall — that admixture of Christian charity (it had been founded by Canon Samuel Barnett in 1884) and Fabian study and activism — had a marked influence upon the socially concerned Christian undergraduates at Oxford. 'I constantly heard of Toynbee Hall', recalled Macmillan of his time at Oxford, 'and other such attempts to study and help' the poor: and at the very end of his life, he was still struck by its activities in Oxford: 'in my first summer term, on Whit Monday, the sponsors of Toynbee Hall and other such settlements brought up large parties of East-enders to disport themselves on or by the river.' Still more decisive for Macmillan's intellectual development was that part of the teaching he received at Oxford whose existence can be traced directly to the milieu described above: that course of lectures by A. L. Smith which dealt with political and social questions, and which, Macmillan later wrote, 'became part of my own history'. These lectures included analyses of such matters as 'population, poor law, federations, and notably the historical development of the socialist movement'. Smith's teaching was considered by the future historian to be crucial to his intellectual formation.[24]

As important as these influences in propelling Macmillan's inclinations and sympathies in the direction they were ultimately to go, however, was his direct experience of the social distress of Edwardian England and Scotland. His enforced frugality did not permit much of the continental travelling undertaken by the Rhodes scholars of his day. When the College closed for vacations he was forced, for six months of the year, into what he dubbed his 'double life' — penny-watching vacations during which he cycled across England. He was later to remark that it was through these trips that he

'became aware of the great varieties of English social life, and ... the tremendous divisions that existed. My interest in social conditions was enormously stimulated ... and this I suppose was an unconscious preparation for the social studies which ... became my life's work.[25]

Macmillan did not merely witness this social distress as would a sensitive student observing the suffering of people *external* to himself: it was made immediate to him through the social dislocation and economic need suffered by a broader community with which his own kith and kin had links — the Scottish crofters. For his uncle, Duncan Macmillan, was a tenant farmer upon the Balmacaan Estate of Glen Urquhart in the Highlands of Scotland, the very centre of the Scottish peasantry. A far more substantial tenant than the average crofter, Macmillan's uncle would nevertheless not necessarily have had different views on what the young William was to call 'the evils of landlordism', for Duncan's family had itself been evicted from their ancestral plot and placed upon inferior ground. In his undergraduate years, Macmillan visited his rural cousins and was so moved by the plight of the Scottish peasantry in general that he felt constrained to publicize its plight.[26] This he did in a paper delivered to the Broderick Club at Merton College in March 1906. This short study, memorable for its strong sense of social injustice buttressed by statistical evidence, is an impressive analysis (by an early twentieth-century Oxford undergraduate) of the socioeconomic vice which fastened upon the tenant farmers of the Scottish Highlands from the early nineteenth century onwards. Quite obviously a landmark in Macmillan's intellectual development, his paper — entitled 'Highland Deer Forest' — merits summary here.

'Crofter evictions began early last century when the Napoleonic wars created a mania for sheep-farming....' This 'mania' largely subsided after the American Civil War when 'this industry' began 'finally' to decline, at which point 'impoverished Highland landlords' began to convert 'a large & ... increasing area of the Scottish Highlands into a playground for English plutocrats & American millionaires....' That is to say, since 1872, a great swathe of territory had been converted into deer forests and 'the total acreage "under deer" had risen from 1 and ¾ millions to 3 m's in 1904'. This had brought catastrophe to the crofters whose customary rights to the glen were liquidated:

... not only is trespassing prosecuted with the severest rigour of the law but the crofters on these estates are forbidden to take lodgers; or if lodgers should inadvertently trespass on the sacrosanct forests the offence is visited on the head of the unfortunate native, his host.

A 'disastrous change' had thus been wrought in the lives of so many 'by the extinction or expulsion of the crofters and the conversion of the scanty remnant ... into a population of menials'. No doubt, the landlords had benefited from the conversion of crofter land into hunting ground

... but the point is that forests are detrimental to the happiness of the greatest number as even their predecessors the large sheep farms were which benefitted a few big men ... while crofters are left to starve on the moorland or to eke out a precarious existence by the sea.

Macmillan also referred to the chronic landlessness amongst crofters in the Hebrides, the extreme subdivision of landholdings there and the reduction of so many to 'squatting' in that region. In the Highlands of Scotland, Macmillan concluded:

... the evils of landlordism have put the people 'agin the landlords' at any price & made the most truly conservative people imaginable into the most ardent Radicals.... So we may well say with the suffering Gael ... — 'bas gha na feidh' — Death to the Deer![27]

Macmillan could not have penned these lines — with phrases such as 'a playground for ... plutocrats & ... millionaires' or 'the evils of landlordism' — had he not felt the crofters' plight so intensely and personally. And the essay, however immature it appears within the larger corpus of Macmillan's writings, reveals something of his quintessence as an intellectual. Beginning with a discussion of the values to be drawn from the analysis (in this case: that when 'the sacred rights of property [are] opposed to the best interests of the country', they have but 'the slightest claim to continued recognition'[28]), the 'Highland Deer Forest' goes on to provide an historical analysis of the origins of the contemporary crisis (using government commission reports as source material) and actually advances proposals for its resolution. Indeed, the essay is structurally not dissimilar to Macmillan's great study of the origins of South African rural poverty which was published more than a decade later.[29] This youthful and impassioned essay — with its weaving together of scholarship and social sensitivity, analysis and activism, documentary and field research,[30] past and present — foreshadows so many of the mature Macmillan's studies as to convince one that his historical preoccupations and methods of analysis, at least those of his South African years, were being definitively set during this time.[31]

Taking up his divinity studies in Aberdeen in 1906, he was already firmly Liberal in his opinions.[32] Although such a description of his views may appear misleading, it is in fact perfectly consistent with the milieu described earlier. It should be remembered that during the latter half of the nineteenth century, the Liberal Party was the political focus, not only of a great many social reformers but of most politically conscious workers as well: in the early twentieth century, many who supported the Liberals would later vote Labour.[33] By the end of his first winter in Aberdeen, following his own 'bent', Macmillan read to 'the theological society' an original composition which he was later to describe as 'more a Fabian tract on current affairs than a treatise on theology'. Studies at the König Wilhelm University of Berlin in 1910 lent intellectual rigour to his values and perspectives, but these were firmly held by this time. Shortly before he commenced his studies in Berlin, he was dismissed from his post at the Welsh public school at which he taught for political reasons.[34] In the school magazine, his students jested at his (Scottish) rendering of 'the ir-ron law of wages' — a cryptic pointer to the fact that he had based his teaching of the sixth form on the lectures he had himself received from A. L. Smith.

At the end of his life, Macmillan described his 'short summer semester in Berlin' as 'probably [having] had more influence [on his] later career than anything [he] learnt elsewhere'. Formally enrolling for a thesis on poor relief, drawn to the social historians and 'directed' to the famous economist Gustav Schmoller whose lectures he 'never missed', Macmillan's time in Berlin sharpened his skills as an analyst of poverty. When he returned to Britain afterwards, he was persuaded (and aided financially) by an aunt to complete his divinity studies, which he decided to do in Glasgow rather than in Aberdeen. It was in this city that he 'discovered ... an "East-end" university settlement along the lines I knew in London'. Joining the settlement, Macmillan lived on the very edge of the Cowcaddens — a notorious slum area of Glasgow. The view from his window was of 'chimney-pots and all-pervasive smoke such as the sun could never really penetrate'. His duties for the settlement took him into streets 'where the police only went in pairs'. And in 'great tenements [he] often found people crowded together so that they used the bed in relays — a night shift followed by a day shift'. Recalling the scenes more than half a century later, Macmillan wrote that he had 'never forgotten the experience'.[35]

Would Glasgow, with its slums, its large industrial working class, its political radicalism (it was the centre of the Socialist Labour Party), its militant workers of the Clyde — would this Glasgow have shifted Macmillan still further to the Left, beyond his 'social Christianity' and the Fabianism which he appears, perhaps only half-consciously, to have embraced? It is a question which should be posed, if only to stress that the (majority) reformist tradition of the British labour movement, which so influenced Macmillan and other intellectuals of his day, was counterposed to a minority (at times, revolutionary) tradition — a tradition whose influence produced a radically different type of intellectual. But this remains a hypothetical question. For in 1910, 'before [he] had got into anything like [his] stride in Glasgow' — he had only been there a few months — he 'received a telegram' which 'curtly' instructed him to report to

Grahamstown in South Africa. A little while before, Macmillan had 'unhopefully' applied for a job, in the newly created Department of History and Economics at the town's university. His application had been successful. At an annual salary of £340, he 'was to be lecturer in charge of the new dual Department'.[36]

The South African years

Grahamstown and the urban poor, 1911–1916

When he took up his post in Grahamstown in 1911, Macmillan's formative years were at an end. He was still to be subjected to the impact of events, some of them momentous, yet to unfold. But, by this time, his responses to them appear to have been set. A belief in the power of ideas buttressed by convincing evidence, in the need to achieve change through the reforming of existing institutions and policies, a distrust of revolutionary theory and method, a firm adherence to a socially concerned Christianity — these were Macmillan's guiding ideals during his South African years. They bore the lineaments of the political and intellectual tradition which nurtured him during that formative decade in Europe spent as student, journalist and teacher in England, Scotland, Wales and Germany. As his first two publications suggest — *Sanitary Reform for Grahamstown* and *A Study of Economic Conditions in a Non-Industrial South African Town*, both published in Grahamstown in 1915 — it is that tradition, and its influence upon him, which accounts for so many of his activities on his return to South Africa.

The second of these pamphlets seemed to crystallize his entire political and intellectual development in Europe. Based upon a firsthand knowledge of the conditions of the town's white poor acquired through personal investigation, the pamphlet is imbued with his social Christianity with quotations from the chapters of Romans, Bishop Gore ('the first charge on ... industry must be the life and welfare of its workers') and the prophet Jeremiah.[37] In calculating 'the poverty line', he drew upon Rowntree's study of York and some of what he had learned in Germany:[38] indeed, his analysis is informed and powerfully strengthened by a sophisticated statistical methodology. And the effects of Macmillan's experience of Scottish slums are manifest too, as is evidenced by his reference to 'the Cowcaddens of Glasgow'.[39]

47

A Study of Economic Conditions in a Non-Industrial South African Town provided a concentrated economic profile of Grahamstown and presented a programme for the relief of its poverty. At the national level, it proposed the creation of a Ministry of Labour to see to 'labour problems' and it stressed the necessity for 'far greater public vigilance and supervision in questions of Public Health' as well as 'more vigorous and intelligent control and direction of National Education'. Charity, warned Macmillan, would be entirely inadequate to the task of liquidating poverty: 'a serious national policy of *Prevention*' was needed.[40] At the local level, he stressed the role that the municipal council could play: improved sanitation and abattoirs were urgent requirements and he recommended them to the local town council; he suggested the creation of 'a central committee to coordinate the work' of the various voluntary agencies then providing assistance to the poor; the formation of 'a Labour Bureau or Exchange' was another of his proposals — this, he argued, would aid the unemployed to find work and employers to procure workers; more thorough training in skilled trades' and 'more guidance on the destiny of growing youths' as well as better education were also required if they were to be saved 'from the blind alley and the pit'. Finally, Macmillan urged the necessity for workers to combine into unions to improve their wages and conditions. And he gave particular advice to women workers: for too long they had 'acquiesced' to 'the scandalous sweating' of their labour 'owing to the ... pernicious pocket money theory'; now it was necessary for them 'to organise, to investigate, to lay the facts bare'. Macmillan's suggestions in this regard, however, should not be taken to be the fruit of a belief in the need for workers to combine to strengthen their position in the class struggle intrinsic to their existence. Conceptions of class struggle were alien to him, even as they were to the Fabians in the metropole, and nowhere in his writings or politics were they to find a place.[41]

In many ways, then, *Economic Conditions in a Non-Industrial South African Town* was a classically Fabian tract: the presentation of data as a spur to social action, the recommendation of reforms, and the emphasis on the role of local government (the municipalities were a favourite Fabian focus and Macmillan was to return to them in a subsequent pamphlet)[42] — all bear testimony to this. Little wonder that one of Fabianism's founding-fathers, Sidney Webb saw fit to give Macmillan's study of the white poor of Grahamstown 'a short notice' in the *New Statesman*, referring to it as being 'on Booth, Rowntree, Bowley lines'.[43]

Macmillan's study did, however, bear another more disturbing aspect of Fabianism. The Fabians' political horizons were always bounded by the status quo: they sought the modification of the *existing* structure of society and their propaganda was always directed at the *ruling* class — conversion not compulsion was their method. And Macmillan's essay constituted no break from this aspect of Fabianism. Tied to the status quo, he argued his case in the idiom —one might say with the prejudices — of his audience. His paper, for example, was overwhelmingly concerned with the white poor — in a colonial society, this was the only section of the poor deemed to have the right to remedial measures. Moreover Macmillan's pamphlet had its complement of phrases such as 'depressing our own race, making a healthy white South Africa impossible' or 'our white civilization'[44] — in short, the idiomatic stock-in-trade of a prejudiced colonial society. Indeed, his advice to the white working class sat nicely with their prejudices. The cheap, unskilled black workers, argued Macmillan, through their competition in the labour market, tended 'to degrade whites down to and below their level'; this, he suggested, was 'the solid basis of the native menace'. To counter it, there was 'need for organisation and co-operation by the [white working] men themselves and by the public'.[45]

To combat white poverty, then, Macmillan was, in effect, proposing that white workers and 'the public' (by which presumably he meant the white middle class) combine against the black working class. The argument was politically dangerous as well as intellectually weak. If, as Macmillan argued, much white poverty was caused by the depressing effect upon wages and conditions exercised by the presence of still more exploited workers below the whites, then the conclusion, logically, had to be different to the one he drew. Put simply, the elevation of the wages and conditions of the most exploited (that is, black) workers would end the 'undercutting effect' alluded to by Macmillan; there could be no 'native menace' where all workers worked under the same conditions and fought for their betterment together. The political and industrial answer was a combination of white and black workers against their exploiters not, as Macmillan suggested, a combination of the white working and middle classes against the black worker. The latter simply strengthened the antagonism between the white worker and the 'cheap' unskilled black; it did not attack what Macmillan saw to be a major problem — the depressing effect on the working class generally of the presence of a large body of 'cheap' labour.

Given the manifestly Fabian inspiration of Macmillan's Grahamstown studies, it is perhaps not surprising that it was during the years he was stationed there that he first made formal contact with the Fabians. Early in 1916, Macmillan journeyed to England and there made 'contact with Beatrice and Sidney Webb', experiencing at least once their 'famous Sunday afternoon tea in Grosvenor Terrace'. Sidney, in fact, encouraged Macmillan's efforts in Grahamstown and even attempted to find funds for him. Once established, Macmillan's links with the Fabians proved important. His private papers reveal that he maintained fairly close contact with them during his South African years and, during the 1920s, he 'never failed to make a date with Sidney Webb' when visiting London; ultimately he was to lecture in the Fabian Lecture series.[46]

On his return from England in 1916, Macmillan must have been fairly satisfied with the fruits of his labours on behalf of the poorest section of the white working class of Grahamstown. His article on sanitary reform had 'succeeded at least in getting the Town Council to set enquiries on foot'. One of his suggestions in the pamphlet on poverty in Grahamstown — the establishment of a Labour Bureau — appears to have been taken up. His efforts and investigations may also have been one of the spurs to the creation of the Grahamstown Social Welfare League in 1915, an association to which he became secretary in the following year.[47] At the end of 1916, Macmillan presented a report to the Grahamstown League which was to be published under the title *Poverty and Post-War Problems*. Seeking to locate Grahamstown's social problems in a national context, and paying particular attention to the difficulties returning soldiers might face, this pamphlet stressed the need for, *inter alia*, state aid for soldiers' families 'for some months after the end of the war', a comprehensive public works programme, a fuller development of South Africa's resources through the building-up of its economic infrastructure and a more efficient system of taxation. Stressing the need for 'heavier' taxes, Macmillan provided something of a moral critique of the lifestyles of the wealthy: 'We must learn that to meet the unparalleled scarcity, any undue private extravagance is wrong, and in the presence of squalid poverty a positive danger.'[48]

Poverty and Post-War Problems was to be the last publication of

Macmillan's years in Grahamstown. In 1917, he was to move to Johannesburg to take up the Chair of History at the university there. From this point onwards his imagination was captured by the problems and politics of the two basic segments of the South African working class: the rural dispossessed and the Witwatersrand proletariat, the largest and most militant in Africa.

Macmillan and agrarian working people

Macmillan's general interest in rural poverty had been kindled, as we have seen, by his experience of the plight of the Scottish highland crofters. But it was an *urban* phenomenon which led his searching intelligence in quest of the origins of what he termed the 'South African Agrarian Problem'. That phenomenon was the squalid, teeming slums of Johannesburg — the city in which he was based for the final fifteen years of his South African period — with their 'Afrikaans-speaking refugees from the country districts'. It was, as he was later to stress, 'this large and growing number of displaced white country-folk in Johannesburg [which] invited reresearch into the conditions in the backveld from which they came'.[49] The growing importance of 'poor whiteism' as a political question no doubt also drew his attention to the mechanics of its origins in the rural world.

The great work which ultimately evolved from these concerns was *The South African Agrarian Problem and its Historical Development* published in 1919. Initially delivered as a series of lectures, the study was based upon arduous personal investigation and field research which provided him with a firsthand knowledge and experience of the conditions of the Afrikaner rural poor.[50] Macmillan's *Agrarian Problem* has remained, to this day, a remarkable exercise of the historical imagination. The most serious survey of the historical literature on the South African rural world yet published has recently paid tribute to its insights.[51] Its lacunae, some of them major (for example, the absence of any real discussion of class struggle), do not detract from the fact that, in many ways, the essay remains the boldest attempt to consider a quintessentially South African agrarian economy in terms of its epochal experience. Scanning more than a quarter of a millenium, it focused upon the essential structure of the agricultural economy — with its fatal contradictions, the culture it supported — which the Boer colonists carried across the sub-continent.

A comprehensive analysis of the theory advanced by Macmillan in

51

this seminal work cannot be undertaken here. But certain aspects of his *Agrarian Problem* do require detailed assessment because of their relevance to his attitude to working people and capitalism. The first of these is the connection he drew between the accumulation of commercial agriculturalists on the one hand and the poverty and increasing landlessness of the Afrikaner rural poor on the other. Sketching the deep, underlying contradictions within pre-capitalist Boer agriculture, and how these were by themselves generating poverty and low productivity,[52] Macmillan turned to the effects of the sudden eruption into this world of the mineral revolutions of the nineteenth century. The sudden agglomeration of people into new industrial centres and the creation of new markets attendant upon these revolutions demanded that the subsistence-dynamic of much of Boer agriculture be replaced by a ruthlessly commercial one: the immense and terrible difficulties of adjusting to such an agriculture were, for Macmillan, at the root of the 'agrarian problem'.[53]

A sense of transition, a determination to integrate his analysis of the South African rural world into the wider patterns of world history, illuminates Macmillan's analysis. The profound 'transition' through which his generation was living, he wrote, 'is not unlike that which Europe underwent in centuries, in the passing of feudalism and the coming of industrialism'.[54] Commercial production in agriculture led landlords to bring more and more of their land under their direct control: consequently, their poor tenant farmers-on-the-half 'had to go'. According to Macmillan, even after the First World War, most Afrikaner agricultural working people remained within the clutch of the sharecropping system (he compared it to 'the métayage system of France and Italy'), but it was rapidly giving way 'at one end to tenant-farming, at a fixed rent, and at the other to the wage system....'.[55]

Macmillan's sense of this transition to capitalism, however, was a critical one. There can be little doubt that he believed the transition to have resulted in a degradation of human relationships. 'Merely human relationships', he wrote, were 'giving way, as they did in Europe in the 16th century, to a *cash nexus*.' The old moral economy of the agrarian world was being broken down by the advance of capitalism. For Macmillan, the great advantage of the 'shares system over that of day labour' was the security or 'fixity of tenure' which it could give the sharecropper. This was now evaporating with the advance of new norms in agriculture: 'competition' was breaking down 'custom'. Agricultural zones which had long been accustomed to commodity production, such as the Cape's 'ostrich belt', were precisely the areas in which the problems of poverty were most acute.[56] For Macmillan, then, the commercialization of agriculture in South Africa produced both wealth and poverty. And if the Afrikaner tenantry increasingly made for the towns, this was not because the industrial bright lights beckoned them but because those tenants were being rapidly ground down into a position of abject and absolute dispossession; the epigraph of the *Agrarian Problem*, it should not be forgotten, is Thomas Hardy's famous sentence on the centrality of compulsion to urbanization:

... the process humorously designated by the statisticians as 'the tendency of the rural population towards the large towns', being really the tendency of water to flow uphill when forced by machinery.[57]

Macmillan was later to recall that '*The South African Agrarian Problem* marked a turning-point in my life and work, a diversion from poor-whites to poor-blacks'.[58] There are four likely reasons for this shift. First, his field research amongst the Afrikaner rural poor, and his rural travels generally, probably brought him into contact with the still more intractable problems of agrarian distress amongst black people; second, the massive black proletariat on the Witwatersrand, with its poverty and struggles, may well have exercised a gravitational pull upon Macmillan's interests and studies forcing him to look into its rural origins as had the Afrikaner slumdwellers of Johannesburg so compelled him earlier; third, the inexorable advance of segregationist ideology and policies, which Macmillan doughtily opposed, is likely to have driven him to concentrate his research upon the social conditions of black working people so that he might be well armed, at least empirically, in the battles he was to fight so passionately; finally, as he himself was later to point out, his historical research in the 1920s led him into the field to witness at first hand the results of the policies and conflicts that he was tracking through the documents of the nineteenth century.[59] Whatever the reasons, however, Macmillan was now set to fill the lacunae in his earlier social studies — studies from which the great majority of working people in South Africa had been excluded.

The path-breaking studies which were to emerge from Macmillan's new interests were, once more, based upon arduous investigative travel. They were to yield some of his most fertile writings: *The Land, the Native and Unemployment* (1924) and, above all, *Complex South Africa* (1930). At the centre of Macmillan's analysis of the plight of the black rural population was its massive and sudden dispossession:

... the Bantu millions have had to face a prodigious social revolution. They have been called upon, in the space of three generations or less, to adapt themselves, somehow or other, to live on what may be put at a rough estimate at about one-fifth of the land they lately held.[60]

The analysis of conditions within the reserves — with their congestion, malnutrition, poverty and dependence upon the earnings of migrant labourers — remained unrivalled within the corpus of South African studies for almost half a century. No less pioneering was his detailed exposition of the condition of black farmworkers — their poverty, insecurity and subjection to draconian laws. Grappling with the concept of alienation, he argued that the 'wholesale insecurity' of these primary producers on the land was 'a fatal bar to progress' in South African agriculture. 'Squattery', he declared, had to be ended and replaced by 'security of tenure'.[61]

One of the most important facets of Macmillan's analysis of black rural producers lay in his analysis of the origins of the relationships of tenancy under which they lived on white farms. He was careful, for example, to place the word 'squatter' in inverted commas:[62] for the people so designated were, in most cases, merely utilizing land which their ancestral communities had used for decades before the imposition of private property upon the countryside. Macmillan — like Engels[63] in one of his analyses — saw the origins of 'squatting' (and the seigneurial relations which attended it) in the continuing encroachments of colonists upon the land of indigenous rural communities. Land was conquered and parcelled out under the very feet of its inhabitants who were now compelled to work for their new masters: 'This, of course, is the truth about ... native "squatting"....'[64]

Macmillan's prescriptions for ending agrarian distress were many and varied: a brake upon the accumulation of land by great magnates, a graduated land tax, 'fair' rents, minimum wages, improved education for the poor, even the ownership of their plots (by white tenants at any rate) and more land for black peasants were recommended by him at one time or another.[65] But his most constantly reiterated demand was for security of tenure for black and white tenants alike:[66] this, he believed, was the key to advancing agricultural productivity.[67] There can be little doubt that this was the most deeply-felt of the recommendations which he made, probably because of its familial source in the Scottish Highlands. At the end of his life, in his autobiography, Macmillan was to comment that he still believed that 'the tenants' lack of legal status ought to be remedied', and on the preceding page he made a significant submission: 'Perhaps a slight knowledge of crofting conditions in the Highlands made me concentrate on the question of land-tenure.'[68]

There is something conservative, in the best sense of the word, in Macmillan's proposed remedies for the ending of rural poverty. Appalled at the results of proletarianization — slums, insecurity, unemployment — he sought not the transcendence of its world, a decisive break towards a future society, but rather that steps be taken towards a rural idyll of prosperous, secure smallholders. Give the sharecroppers a bigger share of the produce they draw out of the earth,[69] make them secure on the land, he seemed to say, and all will be well with the tenants — they will not need to flock to the towns. A world of crofters — before their evictions, before the sheep and deer took their place on the land — seemed to him the most wholesome of all:

... the shares system in all districts must be put on a legal footing, regulated by independent land courts, and made the basis of the peasantry we desire to create. Then and only then — with fixity of tenure — cooperation and improvements in agricultural method will begin to have a fair chance, and crofter areas on the Scottish model may be made to supply that easier access to the land which it must be our policy to secure.[70]

By the time Macmillan penned these lines, the possibilities of creating such a peasantry in South Africa were being liquidated with ferocious rapidity. If there were to be a future of plenty and security for the primary producers on the land — or, indeed, in the towns —the means of attaining it would be radically different from those proposed by Macmillan, as would the world those means attained. In the first instance, it would have to be based upon the very existence of a proletariat and its potentialities and not on an impossible desire to create an idyllic version of the epoch preceding proletarianization itself.

Macmillan and the labour movement

One logical starting-point for an analysis of Macmillan's relationship to the South African labour movement is his *Agrarian Problem*, a work in which he clearly articulated certain socialist — or quasi-socialist — perspectives akin to those of an English thinker who was to have a fairly important influence upon him: the historian and social critic of 'industrialism', R. H. Tawney. For the *Agrarian Problem* provided a critique of accumulation for accumulation's sake, just as Tawney did. Describing the praise lavished upon the free-spending capitalist as 'stupid',[71] Macmillan passionately argued that:

It is true, though the twentieth century tends to forget it, that the production, and more especially the accumulation of wealth for its own sake, is, as Aristotle also wrote, 'contrary to nature'.[72]

The thread of such values is continuously interwoven with the scholarship of the *Agrarian Problem*. To take an example from its early pages:

It is necessary ... to insist, even dogmatically, that it is the prior necessity to combat poverty and bad conditions, and the vicious economic ideas and practices which result in moral as well as physical starvation, in order to create opportunity for the very beginnings of ... real liberty.[73]

Macmillan's comments clearly bear comparison with those of Tawney (he claimed that much South African poverty was the child of 'industrial civilization'[74] as Tawney might have attributed much of England's poverty to 'industrialism'). It was only in the year following the publication of *The Agrarian Problem* that Macmillan met Tawney for the first time: he well remembered the walks they enjoyed together and the large amount of 'lively inspiration' he received from the 'famous economic historian', as well as their 'common concern with the cause of workers' education' (Tawney was one of the founders of the Workers' Educational Association). And it was only in 1921 that Tawney's *The Acquisitive Society* appeared, a work which was to be of particular importance to Macmillan and which was an explicit critique of accumulation for its own sake. But despite the fact that Macmillan's essay in South African rural history predates both *The Acquisitive Society* and his meeting Tawney, the latter's influence is already manifest in Macmillan's work. Indeed, the very title of Macmillan's book was inspired by one of Tawney's: *The*

Agrarian Problem in the Sixteenth Century, a work published in 1912.[75] One may fairly assume that the intellectual tradition to which Tawney belonged — analysed so carefully by Raymond Williams[76] —played a significant role in the fashioning of Macmillan's perspectives as well.

One final feature of the *Agrarian Problem* needs to be stressed: Macmillan's integration of the values outlined above into the programme, as he saw it, of the labour movement generally. That movement, he argued, 'may have originated ... as a question of poverty' but it had become 'a good deal more' than this. The stronger trade unions had transcended the battle for a mere human existence for the working people and had now passed on to questions of 'profiteering' and the redistribution of wealth: 'to-day ... active unrest arises less from the problem of poverty than from a new consciousness of a *Problem of Wealth* or of *Property*.'[77]

Macmillan had written that line in 1919. He had, in fact, been in Johannesburg, centre of South Africa's working-class radicalism, since 1917 and from that point onwards, he had 'busily' set himself 'to understand the forces at work' there. Almost immediately, he made contact with the radical 'skilled artisans' employed by the municipality: 'very good men whose ... concerns got little attention from the so-called Labour Party' of the day.[78] Once on the Rand, he was very soon lecturing on labour relations and playing an active role in the Workers' Educational Association, becoming its president in the early 1920s and later extending his activities within it to black workers, especially those unionized by the Industrial and Commercial Workers' Union.[79]

Macmillan's involvement in the South African workers' movement and the talks which he delivered before working-class audiences guide us directly to the character of those of his perspectives which appear to have been socialist. There was nothing revolutionary in them. In a talk to the members of the Typographical Union in May 1924, he rejected the 'Bolshevik method' and unequivocally embraced what he seemed to view as a reformist English road to the 'New Social Order': 'Force', he declared, 'is *De*structive not *Recon*structive'.[80] But, as he stressed in a lecture to engineering workers, the key to improving the material condition of working people lay in '*organisation*'. This was the 'lesson of History' and, moreover, 'the only means' by which workers could train 'for wider control alike of Industry & the Fruits of Industry'.[81]

Another notable feature of Macmillan's values at this time is the degree to which they bore the lineaments of Tawney's influence. The notes which he made for both the lectures referred to above demonstrate this. In his talk to the engineering workers he defined the labour movement as 'a just protest' against the 'moral injustice' of a society structured as 'organised greed', and he went on to refer specifically to Tawney's *Acquisitive Society*, providing details of its publication and price. Indeed, in emphasizing to his audience the problems of the landless Afrikaner poor streaming off the land, he rejected — in a most Tawneyesque way — the idea that something called 'Industries' were the great panacea for socioeconomic ills: on the contrary, he argued, 'They make for *slums* and *exploitation*'. The 'sacred' rights of 'Property', he asserted, were 'hardly older' than the post-Reformation years: 'even Feudalism' had recognized no absolute right to it, as evidenced by its tying together of 'Land & Service'. And to the Typographical Union, he emphasized that a 'very strong section of University men everywhere' shared with workers an opposition to exploitation, 'greed' and 'acquisitiveness' and were 'in favour' of a 'New Social Order'.[82]

The reference to the shared values of workers and 'University men' was not accidental. There was nothing rhetorical in it: Macmillan was engaged in a sincere search for common ground between the universities and the unions. When, in 1922, Tom Mann, the famous British trade unionist, addressed an engineering workers' meeting on the Rand to which Macmillan was invited, the manner in which he introduced himself struck Macmillan as 'charming'. This was to take 'his bow to myself and the others' and address the meeting, 'Workers by brain and with hand'.[83] This was a formula Macmillan accepted with evident enthusiasm. In the same year that Mann delivered his speech Macmillan was referring, in a lecture to the Amalgamated Engineering Union, to the 'fellow suffering of Scientists fr. [om] Exploit. [ation] of Brains & Research'. And he began his talk to the typographical workers in a most comradely way: 'Fellow workers'.[84]

There was, of course, no real equivalence of the 'mental' and 'manual' labourers to which Macmillan referred. Quite obviously, he was not the 'fellow worker' of the people he addressed. Not only was his income, his job security (a tenured professor) and his ability to acquire property much greater than that of the average typographical worker, he certainly did not suffer from the 'exploitation of Brains and Research' to which he referred. And yet, notwithstanding this important reservation, we must still concede that Macmillan embraced the formula 'workers by brain and with hand' not in the way the Fabian aristocrat did — Beatrice Webb's diary reveals the way it could be used to signal an alleged superiority to workers — but in order to express his solidarity with working people.[85] For Macmillan came before workers, whom he considered the 'best of audiences', with neither the condescension of the cloistered academic nor the sentimentality of the romantic researcher. Considering it a 'privilege' to be able to address their meetings, which he sometimes did critically, his integrity and solidarity were immediately perceived by the working people with whom he came into contact.[86] A large proportion of the audience which assembled to hear Tom Mann speak, for example, was — as a trade unionist later confided to Macmillan — 'against professors being any use to the labour movement, and came to see the fun, but they left strong supporters of ... yourself ...'.[87]

However, Macmillan was more of an activist in the South African labour movement than the analysis so far suggests. Not only did he advise the Amalgamated Engineering Union on how it should structure itself (he believed it should combine features of both craft and industrial unions),[88] he also attempted to inculcate in white workers a consciousness of the ultimate identity of interests of *all* workers, black and white. In his WEA lectures, he was careful to hold the 'Exploited Natives' before his (white) audience[89] and, on at least one occasion, he enjoined it to consider 'the Natives [to be] still weaker & more exploitable workers'. Their problems, he asserted, were connected to those of the white poor and there could be 'No Remedy for either ... short of [a] new Social Order' which carried South Africa beyond the blights of 'Exploit^n & Acquisitiveness'.[90] In fact, one of Macmillan's last interventions before leaving South Africa in the early 1930s was on behalf of black workers: on 1 October 1931, at 'a conference of municipal workers' to which he had been 'invited as an observer', he 'harangued the assembly on the subject of passes' — a key issue for black workers but one which few white trade unionists ever took up.[91]

Macmillan's modest attempts to bring black and white workers together, or at least to engender in white workers a recognition of the still greater exploitation suffered by black workers, points towards the significant change in his thinking since his

Grahamstown years: in one of his publications of that time, he seemed to imply a necessity for the white working and middle classes to combine against the black proletariat. It was doubtless the realization of the dangers of such an approach, brought home to him by the advance of segregation (whose ideology promised the liquidation of white poverty through just such an alliance), that accounts for this shift in his perspectives. Once the danger became manifest to him, Macmillan — to his credit — began to muster powerful arguments against such a strategy. Some of their most cogent formulations are to be found in *Complex South Africa*, a book which was, in many ways, a scholarly and passionate intervention against the segregationists. In that work, he stressed that in those areas of the Cape where the 'Poor White' problem was most chronic, Africans were in a tiny minority and, therefore, the problem could *not* 'be attributed to Native complications'.[92] The nub of the problem in regard to the competition between white and black workers in the towns, argued Macmillan, lay precisely in the fact that the black worker was 'cheaper' than the white and consequently could be utilized to undercut the wages of the latter. The way out of this class quandary was not segregation but the raising of the condition of black workers. Once that was done, they could no longer be used to undermine the position of the white working class:

In the end ... the Poor Whites are little more than the 'reservoir' of unemployed to be found wherever Western industrialism has dislocated an old agrarian system. Yet the dread of Native competition with white derelicts distorts counsel, and leads away from the obvious deduction that if dependence on servile labour is indeed a factor in the making of Poor Whites the first remedy is the amelioration of the lot of these 'servile' natives ... the cry is for defensive measures, from an industrial Colour Bar onwards, which can only, and do all too effectively, make the natives poorer still, and to that extent an ever more real 'menace'.[93]

Colour, may be a peculiar social complication, but it is still only an accident, and in economics the blackness of the Native makes no difference. The problem he represents is in essentials that of 'dilution', familiar enough to workers in Europe when the war brought about an invasion of the skilled engineering trades by women.[94]

It would be well to conclude this analysis of Macmillan's involvement in the South African labour movement with an exploration of his attitude to workers in struggle. This may conveniently be done by focusing upon two militant strikes about which he wrote: the Johannesburg municipal workers' strike of 1919 and the Rand Revolt of 1922.

The 1919 strike was triggered by a retrenchment resolution of the Johannesburg Municipal Council which affected about thirty artisans at the power station. Ultimately, all municipal workers struck in solidarity with those threatened with unemployment, shutting down 'all municipal services of light, power and tramways' except those needed for emergencies. The next decisive step was the strikers' establishment of a Board of Control which cancelled the authority of the municipal council, and began to run and direct its services as well as collect its revenues into a trust account. Ultimately, the militancy of the (white) municipal workers was undermined — and, in this, their experience proved to be a microcosm of the tragedy of the white working class in South Africa generally — by their racist response to an outbreak of militancy by black workers over the issue of passes. Indeed, the early April editions of the *Rand Daily Mail* in 1919 reveal a directly inverse relationship between the militancy of these two groups of workers — the whites' declining as the blacks' ascended. (The editor of the newspaper, it should be noted, exploited the relationship, calling for a closing of white ranks and an end to the strike in face of the mobilization of black workers.) And Macmillan himself was under no illusions as to the fact that one of the 'main influences making for moderation' in the ranks of the municipal workers was 'apprehension of native unrest'. Ultimately, however, the strike forced nine councillors to resign, discredited the municipal council (even the *Rand Daily Mail* called for its temporary dissolution) and secured the withdrawal of the retrenchment resolution.[95]

One of the notable features of the strike was the militant socialism of many of the workers. (Perhaps, too, some of this socialism was not fatally flawed by racism for, at one of the mass meetings during the strike, the workers were addressed thus by one of their leaders: 'The time had come when every worker, white and black, would be entitled to a better and fuller life. They must be treated as human beings instead of profit-earning machines.') At the meeting at which the Council decided to proceed with the threatened retrenchments, workers issued threats from the gallery and, 'rising to their feet', sang the Red Flag. At a strikers' meeting in the Town Hall, 'the big organ' was decorated with the Red Flag whilst the banner of the International Socialist League was proudly displayed on the platform. One member of the Strike Committee, Mr McQueen, 'described the action of the workers as revolution', and the *Rand Daily Mail* noted that 'some of the strike leaders speak as if they regarded the Board of Control as a permanency ... as the first Soviet in this country ... What they preach is Bolshevism of the most evil kind....' The fears of middle-class South Africa were no doubt exacerbated by the fact that, as the drama of the strike unfolded, revolution and counter-revolution were in desperate combat in Central and Eastern Europe. Indeed, the editions of the *Rand Daily Mail* carrying news of the strike bore far more ominous tidings from afar: 'The Troubles of Germany', 'New Spartacist Outrage', 'The Revolution in Hungary', 'War Against the Bolsheviks', 'The Allies and Russia', 'Bolshevik Peril'.[96]

What, then, was Macmillan's attitude to the municipal workers' strike? He did, in fact, write an analysis of it, which was published in the *Rand Daily Mail* in April 1919.[97] One of its notable features is its opposition to what Macmillan termed the strike's initial 'revolutionary bias': those on the Board of Control who were, he wrote, 'pulling heavily in the direction of a Soviet, in the belief that The Revolution had come ... were irresponsible influences'. He insisted that the

... mass of workmen [did not] accept literally the common interpretation ... of Bolshevism, and are more interested in the much wider Labour movement. This wider movement appears to them a long-looked-for message of hope, and is quite divorced in their minds from war and revolution which have created chaos in Russia and a large half of Europe.

Having thus signalled his antipathy for revolutionary struggle, he also revealed a distaste for working-class militancy of any kind: he complained that the militant 'methods of the Power Station strike' of the preceding year 'deserve[d] the criticism even of the trade union movement, and helped to create the difficult situation out of which this trouble sprang'.

Chiding revolution and radical methods of struggle, Macmillan nevertheless was careful to point to the provocation constituted by the municipal council's retrenchment resolution. This was bound to lead to a struggle: 'The plain fact is that society is divided into two camps whose points of view are so widely different that misunderstanding is inevitable.' 'Rising [and] excessive ... prices and profits' were spurring the organization of workers and without 'adequate insurance against unemployment, the ... demand of Labour for shorter hours holds the field as the only attempt at a definite policy in the matter'. The 'wider labour movement', he pointed out, and here was a clear reference to himself and others like him, 'has captured the imagination and idealism of men in all classes who look toward the realisation of the new social order'.

Macmillan's article issued a warning apparently directed at the ruling class. He seemed to enjoin it to exercise moderation in its dealings with workers: 'widespread discontent like the present, reinforced as it is by ideas ... is among the mightiest of all revolutionary forces.' And then in a memorable line which mocked the municipal council, he continued:

That great force, even as manifested in one small corner like ours, is not to be damned back by the Dame Partington's mop of a municipal council that is resolved to 'stand firm'.[98]

The Rand Revolt of 1922, which erupted three years after the municipal workers' strike, was the first major workers' insurrection South Africa had known. During it, 'nearly all' of Macmillan's 'friends and acquaintances ... volunteered for service as special constables' against the strikers. Macmillan, however, 'was too involved with the workers to do this. I knew', he later recalled, 'that the best of the men had a case.' Remaining in Johannesburg for the duration of the crisis, he kept 'in touch with the constitutional trade union leaders' who had been so rapidly marginalized as the strike burnt along towards an insurrection. 'Without committing' himself, moreover, he 'made attempts at mediation'; he was also secretly aiding a 'moderate' trade unionist who was to be 'in hiding for several months' (Macmillan does not make clear the party — government or militant workers — from whom the man was hiding).[99]

Macmillan penned his reflections on the revolt of the white workers in two articles — 'War on the Witwatersrand', which he published under the pseudonym 'Z' in *The South African Quarterly*, and 'The truth about the strike on the Rand' which appeared in *The New Statesman* in England. The first of these articles, written during the very month of the insurrection itself, has not the analytical control or interest of the second. 'War on the Witwatersrand' is essentially a plea to the groupings which constituted what one might term 'respectable middle class opinion' in South Africa — a plea for moderation, for an understanding of the working people's position, a plea for the rectification of ignorance, an implicit plea (even to the mine-owners, it appears) to cease waging the class struggle.[100] Thus, whilst the article does contain some of the arguments which were to be stated with much greater force and coherence in the *New Statesman*, its chief significance is a 'symptomatic' one: it is classically Fabian in its politics.

'We are ... between the upper mill-stone of Capitalism weighted by Landlordism ... and the nether mill-stone of extreme Labour and the extreme narrowness of one side is the exact measure of the extreme on the other....' These sentiments, drawn from the very first paragraph of 'War on the Witwatersrand' find repeated reiteration: the 'Marxian doctrine of Class War' of 'the revolutionaries' was 'essentially the same' as the belief of the employers and others that bloodshed was necessary to settle the strike; or, again: '"Reds" and the Chamber alike have looked to force rather than to reason and the spirit of Christianity...'; both the revolutionaries' 'terrible doctrine of the class war' and the 'acute "class consciousness"' evinced in the wealthier suburbs were responsible for the 'disastrous quarrel'.[101] Macmillan here portrays class struggle not as an inevitable concomitant of capitalism but rather as an unfortunate and irrational excess. The insurrection could have been avoided, he implied, if only moderation had held sway in both camps: the workers 'were probably wrong or ill-advised to take up the challenge'; the mine-owners, meanwhile, might have 'cut the ground from under the feet of the revolutionaries' by some 'sympathetic gesture'. What remains unfortunate in such an analysis — given that Macmillan was the foremost South African historian of his generation — is its abdication of historical explanation. A gifted historian such as he should surely have perceived that an insurrectionary struggle cannot be explained by complaining of the implacability of the contending social forces that compose it. What determined the implacability of capitalists and workers alike? What made their clash so unremitting? An analysis which centred upon such questions was more likely to create the sympathy for the strikers which Macmillan, in his decency, sought to create. Such an analysis, however, would have required an emphasis upon the essential class nature of the fateful combat of March 1922. And it was precisely 'class struggle' from which Macmillan was taking flight. The class-consciousness which he discerned both amongst the militant workers and the inhabitants of Johannesburg's wealthy suburbs seemed to him an irrational phenomenon, one which prevented a rational moderation from prevailing. He called upon 'moderating liberal opinion to organise itself for the healing of the wounds of the nation'. Unable to prevent those wounds from being inflicted, could mere moderate opinion ever 'heal' the class fracture which gave rise to them incessantly?[102]

'The truth about the strike on the Rand' was published in the *New Statesman* in May 1922. A shorter study than Macmillan's *South African Quarterly* piece, it is more impressive in its analysis — perhaps because its theorization of the revolt is not continuously interrupted by the pleas which punctuate 'War on the Witwatersrand'. Curiously, this important contemporary analysis of the insurrection has remained almost entirely neglected for half a century. Its merits are best viewed in relief — that is, against the weaknesses and silences of a more recent analysis.

In *Class, Race and Gold*, Frederick Johnstone — using the indices of what could be called 'parliamentarism' — argues that 'the political position' of white workers was utterly different from that of black workers in the 1920s and that their rights made them 'politically free'.[103] Clearly, the white workers themselves took a different view: they were, for example, aware that their trade union rights did not guarantee them the elementary right to be heard by their employers. (Johnstone himself points out that the revolt was triggered by the Chamber of Mines' refusal to continue negotiating with union leaders whom the Chamber went on to insult as people of low 'mental calibre'.)[104] The right to vote, moreover, did not prevent white workers from feeling sufficiently alienated to join battle with the state's military and police forces: an insurrection — one put down by artillery bombardment and the storming of workers' districts, amongst other methods — cannot be said to be the response of people who feel themselves to be 'politically free'.

The striking originality (even today) of Macmillan's interpretation of the Revolt lies precisely in its emphasis upon the political unfreedom and alienation of the white working class and their importance in the detonation of the revolt. A fundamental cause of the strike, argued Macmillan, was the dictatorial attitude of the mine-owners in whose ranks 'panic and reaction' held sway: their deliberate refusal to negotiate with the leaders of the organized working class was, for the workers a more crucial issue than that of wages. And he placed this fact in the wider context of the poor political voice accorded working people by a bourgeois state:

The Union Parliament is truly representative in its middle-class, landlordly and capitalist outlook, and affords little encouragement for Labour to look to it for sympathetic redress of its grievances....

Indeed, working people could look forward to no more than 15 per cent of parliamentary seats in South Africa: 'Inevitably, therefore, South African Labour leans to the policy of "direct action"....' As to the violence of the strike, some of the responsibility for it 'must rest on the employers who determined to allow the strike to drift to a "settlement" by starvation, and whose attitude was *hubristic* to a degree', some of them openly calling for bloodshed. There was a clamour for martial law 'and probably many of the men started shooting because they thought the other side would inevitably shoot *them* — to drive them back to work'.[105]

Macmillan would have disagreed with another of Johnstone's judgements, his conclusion that the events of the Rand Revolt 'must be seen as the most dramatic ... manifestations of a struggle between ... mining companies ... and white workers over the determination of the precise mode of operation of the system of racial discrimination'.[106] Such views Macmillan rejected as superficial. The opposition of white workers to the repeal of the industrial colour bar, he believed, was no mere jockeying for racial privilege: 'what is involved is the whole question of their standard of life.' The root of their opposition lay in the mine-owners' attempt to destroy worker intransigence and the conditions of employment they brought about by flooding the mine-shafts with a wave of 'defenceless and exploitable' African workers.[107]

Macmillan, it should again be noted, appears to have written his analysis *against* the revolutionaries of the strike. He knew well enough the militant and vibrant socialist culture on the Rand — it was strong enough for the leaders of the insurrection to go to the gallows defiantly singing 'The Red Flag', and it was deep enough for a young Jeppe schoolboy to add Marx, Engels, Lenin and Daniel de

Leon to the pleiad of his childhood heroes.[108] In his *New Statesman* article, Macmillan curtly dismissed the views of the 'Marxian Socialists' of the South African labour movement as 'crude, violent and ... antiquated'; and he even tended a little to an 'agitational' theory of the insurrection in arguing that the recently proletarianized Afrikaner mineworkers with their strong (Boer) Republican sentiments and military traditions were, 'to the "Red" Internationals as clay to the hands of the potter ...'. On the other hand, he dismissed the 'theory of long premeditation and organisation' on the part of working-class leaders: if these had existed, he reminded his readership, nothing could have prevented 'the sacking of Central Johannesburg or the destruction of the mines' on 'March 10th or earlier' when the authorities had not yet mustered sufficient forces to quell an uprising. The idea, mooted in the British press, that the insurrection was the product of 'Russian machinations' was 'moonshine'.[109]

Macmillan's short analysis of the strike has its faults: he greatly underestimated the degree of collusion between the mine-owners and the state authorities; he dismissed the revolutionaries (although the revolutionary ideology of some of the workers and their leaders was surely crucial for transforming a strike into a rebellion); above all, he omitted black workers and white working-class racism from his main argument.[110] The latter is perhaps the most serious of Macmillan's silences. For the Rand Revolt, indelibly stamped with both proletarian insurgency and virulent racism, revealed the fatal limits placed upon a workers' movement by its exclusion of, and hostility to, the majority of the working class because it was black. A section of the working class separated from the major cohorts of the proletariat was one ultimately cut off from the real power of labour in South Africa. Without the presence of that magnet, the needle of white labour swung to the ultra-Right, transforming the political compass of the country as a whole. Its effects were soon to be felt by Macmillan himself as he witnessed the crucial role played by white workers and their organizations in consolidating segregation in South Africa. Macmillan, in his sensitivity, unquestionably lent dignity to the many victims of March 1922 ('the upheaval of the Ides of March' as he called it) by focusing on the class roots of the conflict: 'It remains that it was a strike against dictation, prolonged and embittered by the threat and fear of retrenchment and unemployment.'[111] Decent though the tone of this declaration is, it cannot capture the tragic ambiguities and contradictions of the insurrectionary strike that was aimed both at capital and the majority of the proletariat.

Conclusion

Even with all their limitations, Macmillan's views, and involvement in the South African labour movement reveal an impressive consistency and integrity. However, it would perhaps be fitting to conclude this analysis by pointing to the fundamental contradictions in his thought in relation to the workers' movement and its ultimate goals. His attitudes were, as we have shown, essentially a product of the reformist tradition of English Labour tempered by an anti-acquisitiveness. The somewhat contradictory mixture of Fabianism and 'anti-industrialism' that he embraced was shared by similarly placed intellectuals in Britain — for example, by the historians R. H. Tawney and Barbara and J. L. Hammond, all of whom had an influence on Macmillan.[112]

Nobody who has worked through the documents of his South African years will deny that, notwithstanding certain lapses, Macmillan desired an *ultimate* economic equality for all people. Abjuring revolution and class struggle (he commended the allegedly 'harmonious community of interest between owner and tenant' of pre-commercial sharecropping),[113] he sought to achieve this equality in the classically Fabian way — by presenting data and fashioning arguments of a logic superior to that of his conservative opponents. In this, he was similar to Tawney whose writings also sought to convert all to the collective project of creating an economy of equality. The error (one is almost tempted to write 'delusion') of such writings has been stated by Raymond Williams, with characteristic fineness of judgement:

It is difficult ... not to feel, as of much of the writing in this tradition, that although it recognises what Tawney calls 'the lion in the path' [i.e. those benefitting from, and prepared to fight to maintain inequality], it yet hopes that the path can be followed to the end by converting both traveller and lion to a common humanity. For Tawney [and we should add Macmillan here] ... the ... inequality and avoidable suffering of contemporary society are subject ... to a moral choice; when the choice has been made, it is only a matter of deliberate organization and collective effort [rather than class struggle].[114]

Those in power are seen to be 'his kind of men, and will understand his language: if they do not, he has only to say it again'.[115]

Thus Macmillan addressed all his major writings not to the oppressed (he was not seeking to rally them) but to those in power. Even his famous researches into the plight of the peasantry in Herschel were undertaken in order to spur the government into benevolent action on behalf of black peasants in general; his findings were presented to General Hertzog's government, the most segregation-minded one in South African history until after the Second World War. Not surprisingly, his discoveries — many of them startling — were completely ignored.[116] Addressed to those in power, like those of the Fabians elsewhere, Macmillan's writings inevitably gravitated towards the idiom and even the ideology of his opponents. Thus, even a book like *Complex South Africa* — one of the most important contemporary critiques of segregationist policy — reveals those confusing lapses which often marred the force of his arguments. In arguing for the extension to the Union as a whole of the Cape's formally non-racial franchise (which gave propertied blacks the vote) he wrote, for example:

We are indeed much more likely to get the attention needed for the Reserves — even to make them effective separate areas if we so wish — if we bind the handful of rising natives to us....[117]

And in addressing white trade unionists, he went even further. Here are his own comments on his lobbying those unionists to support development loans to the Reserves:

I found the approach ... that made most impression was to steal a little 'segregationist' thunder and to press to ease the situation [caused by the competition in the labour market between 'cheap' black labour and that of the whites] by organised development in the Reserves, offering openings for native artisans in native areas.[118]

Here the slippage from the 'New Social Order' to segregation is well-nigh complete and the dangers of Fabian strategy sadly manifest. It is not clear if Macmillan ever perceived those dangers although a comment at the end of his life suggests that he became acutely aware of its naïveté:

In my innocence ... I overlooked the fact that the ruling classes in South Africa have a genius for merely ignoring inconvenient facts, however accurate, and in all these years I never really succeeded in making the facts bite. It might have been better had I thrown caution to the wind, and worked for a straight fight.[119]

The characteristic honesty and the painful self-criticism of these words render them melancholy and even poignant.

Macmillan's approach to the attainment of what he saw to be the goal of the labour movement — a society without exploitation and acquisitiveness — was, in fact, profoundly unpolitical. That society was to be brought about without struggle, without the political mobilization of the rural dispossessed and the urban workers whose oppressions he so keenly felt. Economics and political struggle were, for him, radically divorced from one another, as is suggested by the following remark:

... my early reading and my researches in the field made me more certain that African problems were determined by economics, and I was inclined to put economic improvement before social and political, to an extent which made some of my students detect a neo-Marxist.[120]

Such an approach is, of course, antithetical to that of a Marxist for whom 'capitalism is, after all, a *politico*-economic phenomenon'[121] and for whom fundamental economic change can never be achieved without political struggle.

Macmillan's views on the political rights of black people (that is, most workers) during his South African years reveal the central fracture between politics and economics in his thought. Desiring an improvement in the economic condition of black working people, he still proposed to leave them voteless: the Cape franchise, cast across the Union, was all he pressed for in *Complex South Africa*. As for the masses, he did not feel them ready to be political actors: 'in the mass ... they [are] still ... incapable ... of full citizenship.' Or, still more stridently: 'The semi-barbaric masses are nowhere near ready to acquire a swamping vote.'[122]

To summarize, then, 'the realisation of the new social order', to which Macmillan signalled his allegiance in his article on the power workers' strike, was negated, from beginning to end, by his rejection of class struggle and his separation of politics (except in its most élitist forms) from the project to create economic equality. As a general rule, the goals of a political movement must be inscribed in its strategy. That, perhaps, is the central message of Macmillan's failure even to begin realizing 'the New Social Order' — a message made all the more powerful by the sincerity with which he desired that realization. 'He who wants the end', wrote Gramsci in a famous line, 'must want the means.'

2

'PARALYZED CONSERVATIVES':[1]
W. M. MACMILLAN, THE SOCIAL SCIENTISTS,
AND 'THE COMMON SOCIETY', 1923–48

HUGH MACMILLAN

W. M. MACMILLAN set his South African trilogy *The Cape Colour Question, Bantu, Boer, and Briton* and *Complex South Africa* in the context of the contemporary discussion of 'the World Race Problem' and of 'culture contact' but the underlying thrust of his work is actively hostile to the very concept of 'race' when equated with 'colour'. He saw 'colour' as an abstraction, an accident, which was used to divert attention away from real issues of economics and politics.[2] His greatest contribution was to teach that

For good or ill the country is made up of black as well as white, and to satisfy the complete needs of her varied population is the essential Native Problem. Civilization, being neither of the East nor the West, knows no Colour Bar.[3]

It was his contention 'that the fundamental interests of Black and White are one'.[4]

The trilogy was written under the shadow of Hertzog's plans for 'segregation'. Quoting Croce's then recent assertion that 'every true history is contemporary history', Macmillan sought to demonstrate that, while a form of protective segregation might have been possible in the early nineteenth century, it was quite impossible in the 1920s. By that time blacks and whites had become inextricably entangled in a 'common society'. In making this argument he was not only swimming against the political tide, but also against the intellectual current of his time.

While General Smuts is said to have told Macmillan that he might be honoured by future generations, in the South Africa of the early 1930s he found himself increasingly isolated intellectually and totally powerless politically.[5] On the one hand he looked back to a Cape ideal of actual legal equality and at least potential political equality. On the other, he looked forward to a non-racial South Africa in which neither race, colour, nor ethnicity would have political or economic significance. He would have had no quarrel in the 1920s and 1930s with the Freedom Charter of the 1950s which states that 'South Africa belongs to all who live in it, black and white', and that 'it will never be prosperous or free until all [its] people live in brotherhood, enjoying equal rights and opportunities'.[6]

In his vision of a 'common society', in his rejection of race and colour as the explanation of South Africa's problems; in his emphasis on the similarities rather than the differences between her peoples; in his emphasis on economics as politically explanatory; and in his belief in the power of history to give 'a better understanding of the past and a more certain knowledge of the present',[7] Macmillan found himself almost alone in the 'liberal' circles in which he moved. One reason for his isolation was the introduction of the concept of 'race relations' from the United States with the backing of the powerful Carnegie and Phelps-Stokes funds. Another was the introduction from Britain, also with American financial backing, of the new 'functionalist' brand of social anthropology with its static view of culture. Macmillan fought these two tendencies and their ambitions for control over the newly invented 'Bantu Studies'. He saw this battle as a reflection of the wider political drive for 'segregation' for he believed that the basic issue was 'whether the African people should be studied in the context of our common humanity or relegated to a special and inferior category'.[8]

He began his study of white, and then black, poverty in the belief that knowledge and the publication of the 'facts' would in itself stimulate change. He soon came to realize that South Africa was suffering from bad government and bad administration and that the remedy was political action 'to force reform of vicious legislation' rather than 'palliatives and amelioration'.[9] He was destined to lose the battle for academic territory to those whom he came later to describe as 'paralyzed conservatives' because his relentless probing of the origins of the 'Native Problem' and his assertion that it had its roots in the colonists' greed for land and labour were too subversive of the established order. This was better served by a new discipline which explicitly taught that knowledge of the past was unnecessary for the understanding of the present, or was even inimical to such understanding, and that society was composed of discrete cultures whose institutions were 'functional' to the maintenance of internal

73

harmony. The emphasis on the status quo as given, conveniently ignoring the facts of conquest and dispossession, and the stress on differences in either mentality or culture as the explanation of current poverty posed relatively little threat. These new approaches were eagerly seized upon by the more cautious and conservative 'liberals' such as C. T. Loram, J. D. Rheinallt Jones, Edgar Brookes, and Professor and Mrs Hoernlé.

Before considering the social scientific origins of the new 'liberal' orthodoxy, and its criticism of Macmillan's work, it is necessary to outline the development of his own views on such topics as history, race, culture and class. He shared the strengths and weaknesses of the teacher to whom he acknowledged his greatest debt, Gustav Schmoller, the founder of the 'younger historical school' of German economists. These were, on the one hand, a universalist multidisciplinary approach which made little distinction between history, economics and sociology, and, on the other hand, a distrust of theory. It was from Schmoller, who was also the teacher of Max Weber, Werner Sombart, and W. E. B. DuBois, that he acquired his interest in social and economic history, in land, labour and class formation. Schmoller has been variously described as a socialist and as a conservative social reformer and his school has been associated with the British school of social history which included the Webbs, the Hammonds, J. A. Hobson and R. H. Tawney. Macmillan came to know all of these and came broadly to share their Fabian political views.[10]

In his first major work on the 'poor whites' published in 1919, Macmillan stated that his subject was 'present-day sociological' and his approach was 'by methods of historical science'. Without some knowledge of social and economic history it would be impossible, he maintained, 'to set right what is visibly wrong with our social organization'.[11] He later stated that he did not believe that 'prophecy was [any] part of the function of an historian',[12] but he did hope that knowledge of the past could 'exorcise' the fear which he saw at the root of segregationist policies.[13]

In a key passage in *The Cape Colour Question* he quoted the view of the liberal legal historian, A. V. Dicey, that the emergence of scientific history in the course of the nineteenth century, in association with the growth of nationalism, had led to a new emphasis on the differences between peoples and cultures. He quoted with approval Dicey's question:

74

Could the Abolitionists, either in England or in the United States, have fought with success their desperate battle against oppression, had they not been strengthened by an unswerving faith in the essential similarity of all human beings, whether black or white?[14]

Conscious of this observation he went out of his way to demonstrate that world history, and especially medieval European history, could be used to show the essential similarity of the experience of peoples living in different places and at different times. He sought to counter contemporary racism, which he saw as a recent development, by reference to the not-so-distant backwardness of white ancestors, although he certainly did not believe in the necessity of all peoples to pass through the same historical stages.[15]

The 'backwardness' of Africans in South Africa could be explained, Macmillan believed, by the historical facts of the slave trade, and the colonists' greed for land and labour, without reference to any supposed, and unproven, difference in 'mentality'.[16] He believed that 'the weakness of the inferiority theory as the basis of a working policy is that it disastrously weakens the motives for raising coloured standards at all'. The force of the theory was, he felt, in any case weakened by panic legislation against black competition such as the Land Act of 1913 and the 'Colour Bar' Act of 1926, and by the rise of the Coloured people to recognised 'civilization'.[17]

Macmillan rarely, if ever, referred to 'civilization' as either 'white' or 'western', as did most of his 'liberal' contemporaries, and came in the later 1930s to define it as 'a synthesis of the best experience of all the human race' and as 'life more abundant for all'.[18] The word, for him, became more or less synonymous with 'modernization', and he was scornful of the relativism which would define 'any complex of superstitions rooted in ignorance of elementary physical facts ... not merely as culture, but as civilization'.[19] He questioned the right of any culture to preservation in its present form for he felt that progress had often come from the creative 'clash of cultures'. History, in any case, demonstrated the ability of weaker cultures to adapt themselves to and triumph over their supposedly stronger conquerors.[20]

He similarly saw class formation, 'dynamic differentiation', as part of 'an inexorable historical process' and something that was not in itself to be feared.[21] The emergence of a landless proletariat in South Africa could, perhaps, be delayed but it could not be stopped. It was vital to ensure that the process did not result in a 'rightless' serfdom.

75

The emergence of an African middle class with political aspirations was to be expected and welcomed; it should be incorporated into, rather than excluded from, the body politic.[22]

It was in 1923 that Macmillan made his first pronouncement on the subject of 'Native' as opposed to white poverty and gave some indication of the conclusions that he was beginning to draw from his detailed study of the Philip papers. It was in the same year, he later recalled, that he first became concerned about 'the rather doubtful doctrines the anthropologists were putting across on primitive peoples'.[23] There can be little doubt that a major source of these doctrines was A. R. Radcliffe-Brown, the recently appointed Professor of Social Anthropology at Cape Town. In that year, at Bloemfontein, he delivered what was in effect the first manifesto of the new 'functionalist' school, the birth of which has been dated to the publication in 1922 of his own *The Andaman Islanders* and of Bronislaw Malinowski's *Argonauts of the Western Pacific*.[24]

Radcliffe-Brown was determined to establish his own view of the new discipline and sought to distinguish 'functionalism' from historically oriented 'evolutionism' and 'diffusionism' on the one hand, and from psychology on the other. In his attack on the historical method, and on 'conjectural reconstructions', he followed Dicey in rejecting the study of origins but did not heed his warning as to the political dangers of a stress on the differences rather than on the similarities between peoples. Contrasting the historical and the inductive methods he insisted that history was not, and never could be, a social science. He distinguished between pre-literate peoples who could have no conception of history, and literate people who did, and maintained that history could only answer the questions: 'what happened?' and 'when?'. It could not answer the more important questions: 'how?' and 'why?'. He held that 'mere knowledge of the events of the past cannot by itself give any guidance in our practical activities. For what we need are not facts but generalisations based on the facts.'[25]

Radcliffe-Brown went on to make visionary claims for what could be achieved in the realm of social engineering once adequate 'laws of social development' had been worked out. There was a particular need for this new social science in South Africa in order to find a way in which

... two very different races, with very different forms of civilisation, may live together in one society ... without the loss to the white race of those things in its civilization that are of greatest value, and without that increasing unrest and disturbance that seem to threaten as the inevitable result of the absence of stability and unity in any society.[26]

While he spoke of 'one society' this was greatly weakened by his view of 'civilizations' as discrete units and by his emphasis on the differences between them. Perhaps the greatest difference between Radcliffe-Brown and Macmillan lay, however, in the former's total rejection of the practical value of history. Macmillan would also have disagreed with his assertion that 'the scientist must keep himself as free as possible from any considerations of the practical application of his results, and particularly so in a region of problems that are the subject of heated and often prejudiced discussion'.[27]

Radcliffe-Brown's claims for social anthropology in relation to the 'social control' of 'primitive' peoples aroused great interest in both 'liberal' and government circles. When he left South Africa in 1925 his academic mantle was inherited by Mrs Winifred Hoernlé who had herself studied under Haddon, Wundt and Durkheim and become a convert to the 'functional' approach. In 1923 she became the first lecturer in social anthropology at the University of the Witwatersrand.[28]

Mrs Hoernlé was a competent and inspiring teacher who attracted a number of very able students, but she was not an original thinker. In her own major theoretical statement in 1933 she closely followed the development of Radcliffe-Brown's ideas on 'structural functionalism', 'comparative sociology' and culture change.[29] With the establishment of the International Institute of African Languages and Culture in 1926 and the new interest in the 'changing African' Radcliffe-Brown had been forced to concede that cultures could be studied both synchronically and diachronically though he did not modify his earlier criticisms of the historical method. He rejected his earlier distinction between 'historic' and 'non-historic' cultures and asserted that 'the sociologist must study all cultures and by the same methods'. He acknowledged that sociologists might make use of historical data where these were available but he did not think that this would lead to competition or conflict with historians as 'the historian does not or should not seek generalisations. He is concerned with particular and generally chronological relations.'[30] In her own statement Mrs

Hoernlé made few concessions to history. Referring to Franz Boas' recent defence of the historical method in American cultural anthropology, she claimed that even he had been forced to concede that 'the functioning of a culture can be understood and must be studied without bringing in its history'.[31]

She showed a deep interest in social control and the ways in which 'law and order' were maintained in different societies. She repeatedly stressed the need to study cultures as 'wholes' and as 'going concerns' and derived from Durkheim the concept of 'equilibrium' — a word which was implied but not originally used by either Radcliffe-Brown or Malinowski. While stressing the value of 'applied anthropology' she insisted, of course, that it had nothing to do with 'the framing of policies and the working out of administrative details'.[32]

With their need to differentiate themselves from physical anthropology and psychology, and their shift away from 'evolutionism', the social anthropologists did provide some antidote to crude biological racism. Significantly, Radcliffe-Brown had almost nothing to say about race in 1923, though in 1931 he expressed some interest in 'the discovery of what differences in culture are the result of racial differences...'.[33] Mrs Hoernlé, on the other hand, stated that there was 'no essential connection between race and culture', although she continued to maintain a wide distinction between 'higher' and 'lower' cultures. By the mid-1930s cultural differences had become a more respectable justification for policies of segregation than racial differences.[34]

The anti-historical bias of the social anthropologists, and their interest in differences of either race or culture, provided the 'liberal' opponents of Macmillan's historical and economic work with a great deal of ammunition. J. D. Rheinallt Jones, who was Macmillan's friend, neighbour and colleague on the Johannesburg Joint Council, launched the first serious attack on his historical approach in 1926, a year before the publication of *The Cape Colour Question*. Jones attacked Macmillan for having revived the controversy on the 'Native Problem' between colonists and humanitarians through his rehabilitation of John Philip, and his portrayal of him as a protective segregationist. Claiming that political experience and historical knowledge had not provided 'the panacea for our racial difficulties' Jones lamented that 'the century-old controversy concerning the treatment of the Native races makes it impossible for either the politicians or the historians to agree upon a common basis for future policy'.[35] He went on to direct the attention of 'scientists' to the urgent need for work in 'the mental field of anthropological research'. He called for an answer to the question: 'is there evidence of qualitative differences between the European and Bantu mind?' He appeared rather tentatively to reject Levy-Bruhl's notion of 'primitive mentality', but in calling for further research as the prerequisite for the formulation of 'a sound policy in race relations', he implied that the question of 'mental' difference was still open.[36]

Macmillan's alleged disregard of psychological, cultural and social factors was the main burden of a later attack by another 'liberal', Edgar Brookes. Writing in 1933, he seemed to see in Macmillan and his 'economic' school a kind of crypto-Marxism, and held him primarily responsible for the emergence in student circles of 'communistic or semi-communistic' groups who 'speak the language of Johannesburg with the accent of Moscow'.[37] He acknowledged the value of this school in indicating points of unity between black and white, but it was

... the inexcusable failure to study the psychological basis of colour differentiation which constitutes [its] main weakness. There are social and cultural differences of some moment, and in spite of Karl Marx men are sometimes swayed more by non-economic than by economic motives.[38]

He recognized that the older anthropology had supplied the segregationists with 'a badly needed philosophy' but nevertheless praised the anthropological approach for 'keeping before the eyes of enthusiastic assimilationists certain inescapable facts of difference'. Macmillan was, of course, neither a Marxist nor, in the fullest sense of the word, an assimilationist. It is, however, true that his writings, with their emphasis on land, labour and poverty, did go some way to fill the gap caused by the lack of any sustained investigation or analysis of South African conditions from a Marxist perspective. He was at pains to defend himself against Afrikaner nationalist charges that he advocated 'miscegenation', not because he had any belief in 'race purity' but because he knew that, in South Africa, such charges were politically damaging.[39]

The essential difference between Macmillan and his 'liberal' critics was his rejection of their underlying assumption that, with white agreement, the 'Native Problem' could be solved. His historical vision and his distrust of theory led him to doubt the possibility of a permanent 'solution' to any problem, and to see the so-called 'Native Problem' as a national problem. He was certain that government would remain bad and selfish so long as the African population were not directly represented in every constituency on a common roll, and until parliament itself could hear the voices of the 'emergent' Africans whose eloquence and cogency in debate had so impressed him on the Johannesburg Joint Council.[40]

Macmillan did not, of course, advocate 'one man, one vote', and thought in terms of a limited franchise, but he differed from his 'liberal' critics in his refusal to compromise on his basic position that South Africa was, and should be seen as, 'a complex whole'. His hostility towards the concept of race made him deeply suspicious of any moves towards communal representation and he was aware of the disastrous consequences which this had had on the Indian sub-continent.[41] He never allowed himself even to toy with the idealist notion of 'total separation' as did so many 'liberals', black as well as white.

If Macmillan was so effectively isolated within the supposedly 'liberal' camp, apart from some support from former students such as Margaret Hodgson and S. H. Frankel, the question arises whether he could not have found allies from the Left. The labour movement, with which he had continuing contacts through the Workers' Education Association, was itself divided, with the Labour Party adopting a white chauvinist position and the Communist Party divided after 1928 on the issue of the 'Native Republic' and later weakened by expulsions. Macmillan was certainly in touch with such men as Bunting and Roux, but would have rejected the Comintern's policy of a 'Native Republic', as Bunting himself originally did, as a departure from the non-racial ideal, despite its recognition of the importance of emergent African nationalism. He would also have rejected the Party's advocacy of 'one man, one vote' but would have had little quarrel with the specific clauses on land and labour in its 1929 programme of action.[42] Perhaps significantly, his name was absent from an attack by the Party paper on the reactionary influence of the Joint Councils which singled out Jones, Pim, Ballinger and Brookes, but Macmillan in fact had little faith in the prospects of revolutionary politics. He observed that 'even in the seed-beds of the Rand Socialism, let alone Communism, is an exotic and has never flourished'.[43]

Macmillan outlined the main elements of his critique of 'the new fashion of Social Anthropology' in *Complex South Africa* in 1930. He argued that disintegration had already gone too far in South Africa to permit any 'simple refurbishing of the apparatus of tribal organization and custom', and that

undue stress on the different mentality of the Bantu [was] ... too often an excuse for shutting the eyes to the unpleasant fact that the Bantu are ordinary human beings, and that the bulk of them are inextricably entangled in and dependent on our own economic system.

The provision of 'bread, even without butter', was more urgent than 'the long quest to "understand the Native mind"'.[44]

Macmillan launched a more sustained and comprehensive attack after his departure from South Africa with the publication of *Africa Emergent* in 1938. The book was designed as an attack on the theory of 'culture contact' with its disregard of economics and politics and as a defence of the emergent African middle class which he saw as being excluded and embittered by the anti-democratic and authoritarian policy of 'indirect rule'. He noted that 'a good deal of energy is devoted to the study of the native mind, the native being taken to be "different", much less to our own influence in making life more difficult for people with dark skins'. He attacked the anthropologists for their 'microscopic' studies of particular tribes; their failure to carry out comparative research; and, turning the tables on Radcliffe-Brown, the inhibiting effect of their method on the ability to generalize. He also attacked 'cultural relativism' which he saw as a product of a false objectivity and argued that their work resulted in the 'apotheosis of the *status quo*'. He was especially critical of their tendency to reject the 'detribalized' and to contrast the worst urban slums with a pre-colonial 'Golden Age'.[45]

Some of Macmillan's strongest language was reserved for the advocates of segregation which was not 'of the realm of sane everyday politics' but was rather 'of the same genus as the racial decrees of Nazi Germany'.[46] In a damning passage he concluded that

The short truth is that the scientist, though shy of politics and inclined to mark out a distinct sphere of 'primitive' economics, arrives by a different road at a like conclusion to that of the segregationist politician, the scientist admires the black man and respects his institutions as complete in themselves; the segregationist, fearful that the black man may threaten

81

'white' civilization but with hardly veiled contempt for his institutions, rejoices at getting such respectable support for the view that it is best to leave him to them.[47]

The accuracy of this assessment is borne out by an examination of Malinowski's contributions to the study of 'culture contact' in relation to South Africa, as well as by Hoernlé's better known contribution on 'South African Native Policy and the Liberal Spirit'. Malinowski visited South Africa in July 1934 and gave two lectures on 'Native education and culture contact' which were revised to incorporate the fruits of experience gained by visits to his students in the field, who included Hilda Beemer (Kuper) in Swaziland, and Audrey Richards in Northern Rhodesia, and were published in 1936.[48]

His published article provides an almost perfect rationale for what was to become 'Bantu education' in the 1950s. Starting from a distinction between broad African education within the 'tribe' and narrow European 'schooling', and from the position that the colour bar was a given fact, he argued that it was wrong to provide people with a 'schooling' which they would then be prevented from using. It was dangerous to educate and then to discriminate, and it was therefore necessary for the 'Native' to be educated for his 'station in life'. In a key passage Malinowski maintained that

The Native has to receive schooling which will prepare him for his contacts and cooperation with the European section of society. He has to be taught subjects and skills which will make him as valuable as possible to his white employers and thus secure him the best possible economic and social situation. At the same time this schooling should be carried out in a manner which would produce the minimum of disintegration and which would keep him still in harmony with his own group.[49]

Foreshadowing later 'Bantustan' developments he warned that 'unless some sort of political scope is given to the African he will not be satisfied with anything less than equal political rights with the white settlers'. As the only justification for 'schooling' — as opposed to 'tribal' education — was preparation for cooperation with whites, Africans must be taught the language of the dominant group. 'English would, of course, be replaced by Afrikaans where the latter is spoken by the majority of Europeans'. 'Natives' must also be taught the nature of their legal disabilities so as not to develop in them 'the hope that through education [they] can become the whiteman's brother and his economic and political equal'.[50]

In a 'liberal' peroration which, he said, provoked 'hostile protests' at the time Malinowski called not for the end, but for the revision of, the colour bar, for the enlargement of the reserves, for better living conditions in the towns, and, significantly, for 'greater political autonomy'.[51] Malinowski, thus guided by his view of 'culture in relation to race', explicitly rejected the idea of a 'common society'. In a reworking of these lectures for a black American audience shortly before his death in 1942 he gave a qualified welcome to the Hertzog settlement of 1936 and discussed the possibility of 'equitable segregation' as a way of breaking the barriers of 'caste'. He came to the conclusion that 'there is a possibility of developing an equitable system of segregation, of independent autonomous development, which yet would have nothing whatsoever in common with the caste division'. Speaking as a Pole he maintained that 'oppressed and subject nationalities ... do not desire anything like fusion with our masters and conquerors'. While rejecting discrimination he saw 'differentiation' as totally compatible with 'the democratic structure of civilization'.[52]

There are obvious similarities between Malinowski's ideas and Hoernlé's later writings, and it is reasonable to assume a measure of cross-fertilization between them. Both started from the basic premise that race differences were in themselves the cause of 'ineradicable' prejudice, and that anything like racial, or even cultural, assimilation would be rejected by white and black alike. Writing in 1939 Hoernlé acknowledged his debt to Macmillan 'even where I do not see eye to eye with him', but saw the lesson of history in relation to the building of a 'common society' in South Africa as negative. He saw Philip's humanitarianism as an alien import and unsuited to 'frontier' conditions. It was the great failing of 'humanitarians of all kinds' that they underestimated 'the importance of differences of "race", and, to a lesser degree, of culture'. Liberals had been 'blind to the spirit of race-exclusivism', which he followed Macmillan in seeing as a relatively recent phenomenon.[53]

As is well known, Hoernlé concluded that 'total separation', though impracticable, was the 'ideal' solution. He saw the resistance of the peoples of the High Commission Territories to incorporation with South Africa as lending weight to this view. He argued that it would be no more difficult to convert the reserves, especially the

Transkei, into 'independent Native states' than to incorporate the three protectorates.[54]

With his new emphasis on the liberty of the group rather than the individual Hoernlé welcomed the moves by some of the 'keenest minds' among young Afrikaner intellectuals to apply the lessons of their own history as a 'volk' to the study of relations between black and white.[55] Among those keen minds were, one can assume, H. F. Verwoerd and W. M. Eiselen, Professors of Psychology and Social Anthropology at the University of Stellenbosch.

These two men, who became the leading ideologists of 'apartheid' in the 1940s and 1950s, were both of marginal Afrikaner ethnicity and had in the later 1920s participated in the annual meetings of the South African Association for the Advancement of Science where several of the previously quoted statements of sociological theory were first presented. They had certainly rubbed shoulders there with the Hoernlés, Rheinallt Jones, Isaac Schapera, S. H. Frankel, I. D. MacCrone and other liberals including Professor D. D. T. Jabavu and, possibly, Macmillan himself.[56] Eiselen contributed with the Hoernlés, Jones, and others to the two anthropological volumes edited by Schapera during the 1930s, *Western Civilization and the Native* and *The Bantu-speaking Tribes of South Africa*.[57]

Although Eiselen had apparently published a 'segregationist' pamphlet in 1929 there was not much in these early contributions to indicate that he would become not only the most plausible ideologist, but also the most respectable salesman, of apartheid.[58] His later apologies for this policy, and his creation of 'Bantu Education', evidently owed a great deal to Malinowski, though his debt to Hoernlé was made more explicit. He quoted with special approval Hoernlé's remarks on 'total separation' and sought to demonstrate that this was not unattainable. 'The sacrifice involved for both White and non-White is not too high a price to pay for deliverance from the evils of a caste society with its present bitter enmity which may one day lead to the destruction of many things that we hold dear.'[59] Following Malinowski he saw the admitted fact that the majority of 'Natives' favoured 'integration' as an unfortunate but avoidable consequence of their 'schooling'. Following Hoernlé he saw the resistance of the protectorates to incorporation as an argument for the development of Bantustans. Apartheid was a 'long-range programme', and its gradual realization need not lead to economic dislocation. The first stage would be strengthened influx controls to save the 'Bantu' from 'uncertainty and hardship in the towns'. The underlying justification of apartheid was, of course, 'the natural and not man-made differences existing between European and Native'. What was required was another Great Trek 'away from caste-society which is our undoing, and towards areas of liberty'.[60]

The above quotations come from a lecture given by Eiselen to the Institute of Race Relations in 1948. The Institute called in Mrs Hoernlé to reply to him, and presumably to refute the suggestion that her late husband had been an advocate of apartheid. In her response Mrs Hoernlé was a good deal more strident than Eiselen himself in her insistence upon the right and duty of every race to defend 'Western civilization'. While acknowledging that the races in South Africa were 'inextricably juxtaposed within one community' she thought that 'race purity' would best be preserved by 'mutual respect'. She saw the preservation of 'race purity' as a problem of social engineering similar to that which had given rise to the incest taboo.[61] Conceding that her late husband's classification of the alternatives facing South Africa as 'assimilation', 'parallelism' and 'total separation' was, perhaps, 'too rigid, too abstract', she settled for 'Christian trusteeship'. While she envisaged, and called for, continued 'cultural assimilation' and economic integration she recoiled from 'social assimilation' though she thought it salutary for South Africans to be reminded that it was taking place in the United States.

Her plea for 'the integration of all our races into our South African State' was, therefore, qualified by her insistence upon 'race purity', social separation, and 'the whiteman's right to demand guarantees from men of different cultures whom he admits to full citizenship in the State'.[62] The fact that she had moved, over fifteen years, from a protective view of African cultures as harmonious 'wholes' towards a positive advocacy of 'cultural assimilation' was, however, significant. This shift, reluctant though it appeared to be, can best be explained by her own encouragement of urban research and the influence upon her of the findings of her own students.

For there had developed within the British school of social anthropology in the 1930s an internal opposition composed almost entirely of South Africans, Isaac Schapera, Monica Hunter (Wilson), Hilda Kuper, Ellen Hellman, Meyer Fortes, and above all, Max Gluckman, who took issue with the prevailing orthodoxy on three main points. These were: the relationship between social anthropology and history; the position of cultures within a 'composite' or later 'plural' society; and the treatment of conflict as opposed to harmony within societies. The historical and political awareness of these South African anthropologists has been explained in more or less environmental terms.[63] But an important part of the intellectual environment which formed them was the conflict between the historical and anthropological approaches to South African society in which Macmillan had figured as a major protagonist. At least three of these anthropologists had studied history at the University of the Witwatersrand, if only briefly, and at least two of them remained very close to Macmillan. Furthermore their collective critique of social anthropology closely followed the lines laid down by Macmillan in *Complex South Africa* and *Africa Emergent*.

An opening shot in the internal debate on the role of history can be seen as early as 1929 in a review of *Bantu, Boer, and Briton* by Isaac Schapera. His reading of this book, and of de Kiewiet's first book, led him to conclude that 'the historical study of the native problem is thus a subject not merely of scientific and academic interest, but of immense practical importance'.[64] A similar point was made by the missionary anthropologist, Edwin Smith, in a review of *Complex South Africa* in 1931,[65] but the sparks did not really begin to fly until the mid-1930s when Malinowski's seminar turned its attention to culture contact. In 1935 he was forced to acknowledge that the omission of this from his own work was 'the most serious short-coming of my whole anthropological research in Melanesia'.[66] In his introduction to a collection of articles on the subject, Malinowski took issue with Monica Hunter, Isaac Schapera, and Lucy Mair for falling into the error of supposing that it was either necessary or possible to use historical methods to reconstruct in the past a 'zero-point' against which to measure culture change. Malinowski professed himself to be only interested in live traditions which could provide information about the present; he argued that 'to the student of culture change what really matters is not the objectively true past, scientifically reconstructed and all-important to the antiquarian, but the psychological reality of today'. Fieldwork could provide him with all the material that he needed.[67]

At the same time Malinowski took issue with Schapera and Fortes who had suggested that cultures in contact must be seen as forming a single social field. Fortes maintained that 'culture contact is a dynamic process and not a mechanical pitchforking of elements of culture, like bundles of hay, from one culture to another'. Schapera had written of the emergence of 'a specifically South African culture, shared in by both Black and White'.[68] These arguments seemed to strike not only at Malinowski's holistic view of culture but also at his view of the relationship of caste and culture in societies divided by a colour bar. In his view, culture contact was to be seen as involving three simultaneous phases: 'Old Africa, imported Europe, and the New Composite Culture.'[69] He accused Fortes and Schapera of painting a false picture of harmonious interaction but there was, of course, little room for conflict in his own view of cultures in equilibrium.

The most sustained and effective criticism of Malinowski's views came from Max Gluckman who opened his campaign with a series of articles which were collected as *Analysis of a Social Situation in Modern Zululand*. In this ambitious work he set out, in the tradition of Radcliffe-Brown, to produce theories of social change, and began by demolishing Malinowski's view of the social field. He pointed out that his view could not have been sustained in South Africa in the early 1930s where Macmillan in history, Frankel in economics, and MacCrone in psychology had all seen the country as a single society even if 'composed of heterogeneous culture groups'.[70] He went on to demonstrate that, in spite of the colour bar, the black and white inhabitants of Zululand formed a single community and that they existed in a 'temporary equilibrium' which was sustained as much by the force of government, and Zulu opposition to it, as by economic cooperation across 'the dominant cleavage' that lay between black and white. He then examined the history of Zululand to find out how this community had come into existence and to identify earlier periods of relative stability and of social change. He emphasized that his use of historical reconstruction was not to look for a 'zero-point' of change but for earlier examples of change, the processes of which must remain constant. He used his contemporary and historical material to develop some theories of change which took account of conflict, and could hopefully be applied in other contexts.[71]

Thirty years later Gluckman explained that the experience which influenced his presentation of these 'principles in analysis' was hearing Macmillan say 'If people worried about the next ten years, instead of the next fifty years, there would be some hope for South Africa.' Gluckman explained

This taught me that to look into the distant future, or to examine a society at its highest level of order and opposition, distracted important attention from immediate, short-run problems. It might well be that at some time in the future differential incorporation of the ethnic groups must produce, under the principle of the developing dominant cleavage, violent disturbance and radical change. In the immediate present my duty as a scientist was to see how the system worked at least in the short-run. Thirty years later it still works.[72]

Gluckman may, perhaps, have overstated his debt to Macmillan whom he saw as 'the great historian who first brought Africans and their societies into proper perspective in historical analysis.'[73] He may also have understated his debt to Marx, for he was close to the Communist Party of South Africa in the 1930s. It is not altogether surprising, however, that his attention should have been turned by Macmillan to the study of cooperation, conflict and change in a 'common society', for it was precisely the tendency of Macmillan's historical and economic analyses to expose the roots of present conflict which distinguished him from the social scientists and which so much alarmed his colleagues, Jones and Brookes. He frequently warned of the futility of speculation and prophecy on the basis of an incomplete knowledge of the present.[74]

Gluckman also documented in his work on Zululand a process which ran counter to most of Macmillan's direct experience but which he had foreseen as a consequence of the new emphasis on cultural differences — namely, the growth of ethnicity and the revival of custom. Noting that this was encouraged by the government as part of the policy of segregation, and that it had produced 'a social anthropology which records the vitality of Bantu culture without reference to its origins', he explained this vitality as a result of exclusion by, and reaction against, 'White civilization'.[75]

In a later critique of 'Malinowski's sociological theories' Gluckman went further along the trail which had been blazed by Macmillan in *Africa Emergent*. There is not space here to elaborate his arguments but his main lines of attack were on the neglect and misunderstanding of history; the denial of the single society; the avoidance of the study of conflict; the emphasis on the differences rather than the similarities between cultures; and the stress on their uniqueness and integrity. He concluded that Malinowski's approach resulted in 'the worst kind of practical anthropology; welfare work without morality, based on naive oversimplification'.[76]

When Macmillan revised *Africa Emergent* in 1947 he was able to leave out his strictures on the social anthropologists for it seemed that they were no longer relevant and 'points once calling for laboured argument now admit of blunt statement'.[77] Indeed, by a curious paradox, when South African historians finally turned their attention to African history in the 1960s — thirty years after the emasculation of Macmillan's department at Wits — they had to look to the anthropologists for guidance, for many of them including Gluckman himself, Schapera, the Wilsons, and Hilda Kuper, had done excellent historical work.[78]

Macmillan had therefore played a significant part in shifting the social scientists from their static view of unique cultures towards a broader view of conflict and change in a common or, at least, 'plural' society. Did his views have any wider political significance? In terms of white politics it could be claimed that he had some direct personal influence, and an indirect influence through his pupil and friend, S. H. Frankel, on the painfully slow progress of J. H. Hofmeyr towards acceptance of the 'common society' in the later 1930s.[79] But the Liberal Party emerged too late, and although Margaret Ballinger, one of its leaders, was a pupil, colleague and friend, it lacked cutting edge and attracted support from 'Africanist' members of the African National Congress (ANC), like Jordan Ngubane, whose rejection of Communism was stronger than their commitment to the 'common society'.

Of course, there was also, and there remains, a non-racial strand in the tradition of the African National Congress which found expression in the Freedom Charter of 1955. Macmillan was a friend of Dr A. B. Xuma who is said to have consulted him on the formulation of the ANC's first open and non-racial constitution in 1942, though his influence in that direction may only have been slight, and Xuma himself appears to have ended his days in the 'Africanist' camp.[80] The non-racial line was, perhaps, most eloquently represented by Professor Z. K. Matthews, whose belief — as expressed in response to Eiselen in 1949 — that 'Black and White are inextricably bound together' certainly matched Macmillan's earlier views but need not, of course, have been derived from them.[81]

It may well be that the influence on Macmillan from African sources was as great as, or greater than, his own influence in that direction. A great deal has been written and said about the moderating influence of the Joint Councils on radical blacks. Less attention has been paid to their radicalizing influence on moderate whites. Macmillan always believed that their greatest value lay in their educative impact on whites, and there is no reason to doubt that he spoke from his own experience. Macmillan was influenced by such men as R. V. Selope Thema, still in the early 1920s a radical journalist, Selby Msimang, a co-founder of the Industrial and Commercial Workers Union and the founder member of the ANC who took the greatest practical interest in the organization of labour, and Clements Kadalie himself. They awakened his interest in black poverty and oppression, and fuelled the anger and indignation which are the hallmark of his best writing: in 1926 he felt the need to guard against 'the danger of being driven by some hard facts of history to an almost blind negrophilism'.[82]

Macmillan regarded Selope Thema as the most impressive of the African participants in the Johannesburg Joint Council and acknowledged his contribution as an informant. As early as 1922 Thema had picked up a point which was to be one of the themes of Macmillan's historical work — that is, the argument that while segregation might have been possible along the line of the Fish river in the early nineteenth century, it was no longer possible in the twentieth. It is not entirely clear whether the idea came from Thema or Macmillan in the first place. More than thirty years later Macmillan could still recall how Thema had repeatedly stated that the African people were 'part and parcel' of the South African whole.[83]

Macmillan's attempts to bridge the divide between the intellectual and the political spheres were doomed to failure. His attempts to radicalize the Joint Councils and to use them as a political power base came to little, though they prompted Loram and Jones to establish the Institute of Race Relations in a largely successful attempt 'to draw the political sting from the study of African disabilities'.[84] Before he left South Africa in 1932, Macmillan had come to see the danger of usurping the place of African leadership noting that 'we have either repressed [the African] or demoralised him by doing any little that is done *for* him'.[85] It may, however, be said of the political thrust of his own work, as he himself said of the most 'trenchant' of the Joint Council memoranda, that while the drafting was the work of European members 'the substance was more often the Africans' contribution'.[86]

3

A LIBERAL DESCENT? W. M. MACMILLAN, C. W. DE KIEWIET AND THE HISTORY OF SOUTH AFRICA*

CHRISTOPHER SAUNDERS

W. M. MACMILLAN is usually seen as the founder of the liberal school of South African historiography while C. W. de Kiewiet is regarded as the most brilliant of his students.[1] Little attempt, however, has been made to tease out the relationship between the two men, or to assess how much their contributions to South African historiography had in common. In seeking to place them and their work in context, this chapter first considers their personal relationship, and then begins an assessment of their work. A full assessment would require a detailed examination of the wider intellectual milieu touched upon in some of the other papers in this collection.

The personal relationship

Three years after Macmillan became first Professor of History at the School of Mines in Johannesburg in 1917, Cornelis Willem de Kiewiet registered as an undergraduate at what had become the University College, Johannesburg, and from 1922 would be known as Wits.[2] Unhappy with the major course he began, and hearing of Macmillan's reputation for intellectual excitement, de Kiewiet switched to history. 'Pinkie', as Macmillan was to be known because of his complexion, but also for his views, had a crucial intellectual influence on de Kiewiet. His breadth of knowledge and lively mind made him an inspiring teacher. He lacked fluency and polish in his lecturing, but de Kiewiet thought this an advantage, 'because he kept you running and made you understand through the sheer force of the labor of following him'. He remembered that Macmillan stood out on the campus as 'one of the few really well-educated lecturers', able to call on a knowledge of Greek history, the German middle ages, or the ideas of such eminent contemporaries as R. H. Tawney and Harold Laski, both of whom he had met in England. From Macmillan, de Kiewiet learned how 'to hunt out information for myself, how to find the essential meaning, and [how to] set it down in clear English'.[3]

Before he completed his undergraduate degree, de Kiewiet was being asked to help mark essays and was one of those to whom Macmillan entrusted batches of documents from the papers of John Philip, to aid him in the research that would lead to *The Cape Colour Question* (1927) and *Bantu, Boer, and Briton* (1929). Macmillan asked his brightest students to find relevant information on a particular theme in the documents they were given, many of which were extremely difficult to decipher. In this way, de Kiewiet learned the excitement of working on manuscript sources.[4] Macmillan did his writing at home, and allowed de Kiewiet to use his university office. There for the first time he conversed on equal terms with an African visitor, someone interested in history, quite possibly R. V. Selope Thema. This was an important episode in his liberation from the narrow, prejudiced environment of his Johannesburg childhood.[5]

After completing his degree with distinctions in History and Dutch, de Kiewiet went to Cape Town to work in the archives for Macmillan. He also began research for an Honours long essay based on work he had done for his mentor on the Philip material. He then broadened this into an MA thesis, which he entitled 'Government, emigrants, missionaries and natives on the northern frontier 1832–1846'. In August 1924, after another month's work in the Cape archives, he completed the writing in Salisbury, Southern Rhodesia, where he had taken a teaching post to earn money to supplement the scholarship he had won from Wits for overseas study. When Macmillan received the thesis — no copy of which survives — he called it 'capital' and sufficient for the degree, but suggested he do more research to take the story to the annexation of the Orange River Sovereignty in 1848, or even to Britain's abandonment of that territory in 1854.[6] As de Kiewiet did not have the money to return to Cape Town, he did not follow his supervisor's advice. Although Eric Walker, the external examiner, agreed with Macmillan that de Kiewiet should not have stopped in 1846, he nevertheless recommended a distinction, duly awarded at the University of the Witwatersrand graduation ceremony in April 1925.[7]

De Kiewiet recalled that it was Macmillan who led him

... to see the historic tragedy of the colored folk.... Only some time later did the fullness of South African history come through, because he spoke of the black man as an economic phenomenon, and quietly and thoroughly dispelled the false mythology of 'Kafir wars'.[8]

De Kiewiet's letters from Rhodesia confirm the importance of Macmillan's influence. He not only joined his teacher in criticizing George McCall Theal's pro-settler *History of South Africa*, but also explicitly made clear his agreement with Macmillan's views on matters of contemporary concern. Were the reserves developed as Macmillan advocated, de Kiewiet told friends in Britain, fewer Africans would flock into the towns and enter into competition there with 'poor whites'.[9] By 1924, if not earlier, de Kiewiet shared the more liberal views on race which Macmillan acquired after moving to Wits,[10] and in Southern Rhodesia he began to follow Macmillan in giving practical expression to his views, taking the white high school boys he taught to an African school, and preparing evidence for a commission on 'Native education'.[11]

Such activity came to an end with de Kiewiet's departure from southern Africa. As he left for England in 1925, Macmillan advised him 'to go to [A.F.] Pollard if you can', adding:

As for Research — [Edgar] Brookes has a useful tract, but the History need not worry you — it is very sketchy for the most part and some of it is bad, or wrong. You must consider the London supply of material, and be guided so as to make good use of that ... you might find as good a subject as any the Attitude and Influence of His Majesty's Government towards or on Native Policy in SA over a term of years — thirties to fifties, especially 1852 and 54, or ... in some ways better still, after it left the Republics to go their own way, e.g. 1854–77. I think, in fact am sure, that is your cue.[12]

Macmillan was correct in anticipating that his star student would be constrained in his choice of topic for his doctorate by the source material in London. It was inevitable that he would use the Public Record Office, and all theses in imperial history completed at the University of London at this time investigated some aspect of the 'official mind' and the making of policy. A. P. Newton, Rhodes Professor of Imperial History at the University of London, naturally became de Kiewiet's supervisor and helped steer him in that direction.

Perhaps, too, he did not follow Macmillan's advice to focus on 'native policy' because of the work Agar-Hamilton had done.[13] He chose instead to look at British policy towards the Afrikaners in the interior until the discovery of diamonds and the return of British rule across the Orange. The doctorate, published in 1929 under the title *British Colonial Policy and the South African Republics*, was followed, some years later, by a successor volume, *The Imperial Factor in South Africa*, which took up where the earlier monograph had ended, and also focused on imperial policy.

Despite de Kiewiet's move overseas, Macmillan continued to play an important role in shaping his career. They kept in touch, with de Kiewiet, for example, giving Macmillan his impressions of the Anglo-American Historians' Conference held in London in 1926,[14] and compiling the index for Macmillan's second Philip book, which bore the title *Bantu, Boer, and Briton*. After completing his doctorate, he went to Paris, then to the University of Berlin, following in Macmillan's footsteps there.[15] It was while in Berlin that he received, 'out of the blue', an invitation to teach in Iowa. He had long been worried about finding a permanent post, and had told Macmillan some years earlier that he thought he might 'plunge into native work' and, to equip himself for this, might 'go to the States, do some rural sociology, administration and teaching. . .'.[16] In London he was blacklisted by the South African High Commission because, he believed, he had given 'the Macmillan line' at a lecture at the Royal Colonial Institute. For the same reason he felt official pressure was applied to have an invitation to him to go to Cape Town as leave replacement for Eric Walker withdrawn.[17] As he left for Iowa in 1929, Macmillan told him that the chair at Rhodes might soon fall vacant, adding: 'We want you back in this country, which needs all the enlightened youth it can produce.' But Macmillan then went on to describe the Nationalist government returned to power in the 1929 election as 'harder and narrower' than before, which was hardly an encouragement to the younger man to return.[18] Nevertheless, de Kiewiet did not plan to remain in the United States and, even after marrying an American, told Macmillan 'I shall have no difficulty in persuading her to leave the United States when the time comes.'[19]

An opportunity to return to a prestigious post in South Africa presented itself when Macmillan, having clashed with two government ministers and wanting to settle abroad, resigned his Wits chair in 1933. As Macmillan's leading protegé, de Kiewiet expected to be offered it: he was only thirty-two, but S. Herbert Frankel, another of Macmillan's students, had been appointed to an economics chair at Wits in 1931 at the age of twenty-eight. In the event, it was probably his association with Macmillan, who was seen as a radical, rather than his youth, that counted against him, and Leo Fouché, head of the History Department in Pretoria, who had support from Smuts, was awarded the post. Macmillan, who visited de Kiewiet in Iowa in the last months of 1934, doubted whether he really wanted the job or would have been happy and successful had he got it.[20] Nevertheless de Kiewiet still considered returning to South Africa. While on leave in London in 1936, he put in a late application for the Cape Town chair vacated by Eric Walker. Asking Macmillan for a testimonial, he joked that he should perhaps tell the University: 'If you have heard the awful news about the redness of Professor Macmillan, it is not true.'[21] Cape Town, like Wits, made a 'safe' appointment. De Kiewiet had not been sure that he wanted the job, and when Cape did not give him an early answer he withdrew his application. Soon after he became an American citizen.

From the end of the war, de Kiewiet became a full-time administrator, first at Cornell and then at the University of Rochester. He advised the Carnegie Corporation in 1948 to grant funds to enable Macmillan to return to South Africa, which he did in 1949.[22] The two men continued to correspond until Macmillan's death in 1974. Their friendship included close attention to each other's work. De Kiewiet wrote a favourable review of Macmillan's *Africa Emergent* for the *American Historical Review* in 1938, and in the same year Macmillan spoke highly of *The Imperial Factor* in the *New Statesman*.[23] When the Clarendon Press decided in 1937 to commission a new social and economic series on the dominions, and on Eric Walker's suggestion asked de Kiewiet to write the South African volume, they also sought Macmillan's advice on the project.[24] De Kiewiet agreed with Macmillan's various recommendations.[25] Two years later Macmillan read de Kiewiet's draft before publication. Over a quarter of a century later, de Kiewiet was to write a reflective foreword, much of it a tribute to Macmillan, for the re-issue of *The Cape Colour Question*.[26]

Thus, Macmillan did much to shape de Kiewiet's career: he led him into history, and gave him his first experience of the excitement of researching documents. That he became a professional historian — which he only decided in 1929 — he owed to Macmillan's encouragement as much as anything else. But, because their professional careers followed different paths, and because they came from different backgrounds, their historical work took somewhat different directions.

Both were born outside South Africa, but Macmillan remembered Scotland and grew up in South Africa feeling as an expatriate Scot.[27] De Kiewiet's alienation from South Africa had different origins; he wanted to escape from his narrow, restrictive family and social background and establish himself on new terrain. When he arrived in London he immediately felt 'at home'.[28] He later toyed with the idea of returning to South Africa, but Macmillan's decision in the early 1930s to cut his ties with the country probably helped influence him to remain in 'the wider world'. So both men settled abroad, one before he had done his major writing on South African history, the other after completing it.

Both men came from relatively poor family circumstances: Macmillan's father had to ask his son for a loan while at Oxford, de Kiewiet's father was a poorly paid railway construction supervisor, and both his parents were most unsympathetic to his efforts to further his education.[29] But while de Kiewiet followed what was becoming the regular academic path for intending professional historians — Honours in History, then master's and doctoral research — Macmillan had become a Professor of History by a less usual route. After growing up in the Cape before the South African War, he was able to go to Oxford where, by default, he read History, against his expectation to 'go through the straight classical mill'. His strong social conscience was evident at Oxford: he tells us in his autobiography that the circles he moved in there were well aware of 'slum conditions and unemployment and the seamy side of English life'. A few years later, while attending Divinity lectures in Glasgow, he experienced slum conditions in that city at first hand. When he went to the University of Berlin, he began, but did not get far with, a thesis on poor relief. Before moving to the Wits chair, he was joint lecturer in history and economics at Rhodes, and while he held that post his research was concerned with contemporary issues rather than historical problems. In the 1920s his active involvement in the Workers' Educational Association, the trade unions, and then the Joint Councils further fuelled his passionate concern for the social relevance of historical writing.[30] If the main theme of his work was the contemporary and historical causes of poverty, for de Kiewiet —writing about South Africa from another continent — that theme only became one among a number of threads in his historical writing of the 1930s, and much of what he said about it came directly from Macmillan.

The two men, moreover, wrote for different audiences: de Kiewiet's first book bore the marks of the thesis from which it emerged, while Macmillan's two classic works of history based on the Philip papers were in large measure designed to influence white public opinion in South Africa against Hertzog's segregationist policies. In the 1920s Macmillan was as much concerned with contemporary as with historical issues, and his extensive sociological research, which involved detailed investigation of the 'situation on the ground', resulted in *Complex South Africa* (1930). Although de Kiewiet travelled widely by bicycle in Rhodesia while teaching there, he did not remain in South Africa long enough to gain the detailed knowledge of the country which Macmillan's extensive travels gave him. De Kiewiet's imaginative gifts enabled him to include vivid descriptions of the country in *The Imperial Factor* and the *History*, but he could not draw upon detailed statistical information of the kind Macmillan collected on his field trips. Under Macmillan's influence he was, as a student, much concerned with contemporary South African issues but, after completing his Honours degree, he left the country — first for Rhodesia, then Europe — and never returned as a resident. It was not until the 1950s, when he began to make regular visits to South Africa, that he started publishing semi-journalistic articles on the contemporary scene, long after he had stopped doing original research on South African history. Those articles were very much those of an outside observer. The books he wrote in the 1930s were designed for a general reading public abroad, and not primarily for a specifically South African audience. Written outside the country, they inevitably mined the sources available there: first the Public Record Office, and then printed government reports, the main source for the latter chapters in the *History*.

The intellectual relationship

The central ideas in de Kiewiet's work all came from Macmillan. From him, de Kiewiet learned of the flaws both in the nature of contemporary South African society and in the then dominant interpretation of the country's history. Theal and George Cory had interpreted that history from the white viewpoint and wrote of the triumph of white power in crushing African peoples. Their history was self-satisfied, bland and unquestioning. Macmillan led de Kiewiet to see that 'the whole unhistorical architecture of Theal and Cory broke down, so that ... there really was no South African history. It had to be rewritten round a fresh architecture.'[31] Those amateur historians were wrong on two fundamental points: the role of British policy and relations between white and black. Theal and Cory, who had both come to South Africa as young adults and made the country their home, blamed Britain in their writing for many of its troubles. By the time de Kiewiet immersed himself in the official documents in the Public Record Office he was already in semi-exile, with a deep sense of affection for Britain.[32] In his early writing he stressed the inevitability of conflict and misunderstanding: no one group or country was responsible for South Africa's ills.[33] He claimed to have been more critical than Macmillan of the role of the London Missionary Society in South Africa in the early nineteenth century, more ready to blame the British government and Milner, its representative in South Africa, for the outbreak of war in 1899.[34] Only gradually becoming aware of the need to distance himself from the official sources in London, he wrote his first two books largely to show that Theal was wrong in his criticisms of the role of the 'imperial factor'.

In the opening pages of British Colonial Policy and the South African Republics he asserted that relations between white and black constituted the main theme in South African history; that theme was far more significant than relations between English and Dutch-speaking colonists. But the title of de Kiewiet's first book accurately reflected its subject-matter and so the text could not have black–white relations as its central focus. It was in his chapter on 'social and economic developments in Native tribal life' written for the eighth volume of the The Cambridge History — where it appeared alongside three much less original chapters by Macmillan — that de Kiewiet showed that he could transcend the theme of imperial policy, and even that of group relationships, and write with insight about such processes as immiseration and proletarianization.[35] These became sub-themes in his second monograph, The Imperial Factor.

In pioneering local social and economic history, Macmillan took South African historiography further than that of other British dominions. With the publication of British Colonial Policy and then

The Imperial Factor, South African historiography squarely entered its imperial phase, paralleling work being undertaken on Canada, Australia and New Zealand.[36] In *The Imperial Factor* de Kiewiet again argued that British policy had not been 'malign'.[37] Reviewing the book, Macmillan agreed with this: he shared the belief that, for all its faults, the British Empire had on balance been an agent for good, although he did point out that trusteeship had in fact counted for little.[38] Yet while set in the mould of other studies of imperial policy, *The Imperial Factor* was concerned with more than a purely imperial policy perspective. As in his *Cambridge History* chapter, de Kiewiet showed that he was not content merely to follow the established political and constitutional focus of imperial history, and that he was aware of the importance of social and economic change 'on the ground'. In the introductory pages of his book he again picked up ideas taken from Macmillan's writings of the 1920s —above all, that the distinctive theme of black–white relations was not conflict but rather was the development of a close economic association. The subtitle of *The Imperial Factor* was 'A study in politics and economics', and one of its chapters was devoted to the economics of war, with lengthy sections on the process of dispossession in the eastern Cape. In his review, Macmillan gave special praise to the way the book dealt with increasing landlessness, and drew attention to the congestion in African areas already existing by the 1870s.[39] His *Cambridge History* chapter apart, however, it was only in his general *History*, written in the late 1930s, that de Kiewiet's prime focus became social and economic history.

Neither Macmillan nor de Kiewiet successfully avoided Eurocentricity in their historical writing. Following Philip himself in this, Macmillan tended to dismiss African societies as backward and barbaric. In both the books he based on the Philip papers, he laid much stress on the Victorian dichotomy between the 'civilized' on the one hand, and the 'primitive' and 'uncivilized' others. 'The long series of Kafir wars' were 'mere stages in the triumph of the robust young colonial community over the forces of barbarism which hemmed it in.'[40] Martin Legassick has spoken of the 'tendency, from Theal and Cory to Macmillan, to focus on the

... remorseless advance of white agricultural colonisation occurring either in a vacuum or in the form of establishing domination over the indigenous population of South Africa. [Thus] ... structures of domination and conflict have been analysed in 'racial' terms and assumed to have developed historically along unambiguously 'racial' lines.[41]

De Kiewiet's Eurocentricity is seen, for example, in the way his *History* begins with the arrival of the Europeans, and speaks of South African society being 'complicated by the presence of other races'.[42] Yet he was not as dismissive as Macmillan sometimes was of pre-conquest African societies, nor did he write of 'child races'.

De Kiewiet's writing may be said to have surpassed Macmillan's in two other major respects: in its sparkling and extremely elegant style — sometimes carried too far, so that an epigram in effect said little or nothing — and its ability to present a succinct and lucid synthesis. When still his student, de Kiewiet was urged by Macmillan to improve his style[43] — though Macmillan himself never wrote easily, and his style was often far from lucid. It was in London that de Kiewiet learned from fellow students, and taught himself, the essential elements of good style. It is of course the *History* that above all shows de Kiewiet's masterly gift for elegant writing and synthesis. Macmillan had written in detail about the early nineteenth century, and about his own time, but had not attempted to link the two in a general narrative. His writings on South Africa after leaving the country tended to repeat his earlier work, or were lightweight. But it was on the foundations Macmillan laid that de Kiewiet built his general structure. In this, such themes as the origins of the migrant labour system and the emergence of the colour bar in industry fell into place in the overall history of the country. The text he completed in the first year of the war still survives as the best overall synthesis of the history of the country.[44]

Neither man wrote any major new work on South African history after 1940: de Kiewiet's *Anatomy of South African Misery* (1956) was a polemical set of lectures while, for his new edition of *Bantu, Boer, and Briton* (1963), Macmillan merely re-ordered the earlier material and added a new concluding section.[45] To the Africanist historians of the 1960s the work of the early liberal historians of the 1920s and 1930s clearly shared similar limitations. Their picture of pre-colonial African societies was usually a highly generalized one: they had not tried to see Africans as equal actors to whites, or to understand African societies from the inside. Blacks were really of interest only in relationship to whites. Some of what they wrote of African societies might have been found in a work in the settler tradition of South African historiography.[46] Despite their challenge to Theal and Cory, many myths — for example, that African agriculture was backward — remained intact in their pages.[47] In the past fifteen years many of their judgements have been shown to have been simplistic and wrong: for example, that the Khoi societies of the western Cape collapsed 'undramatically and simply', or that Africans in the nineteenth century were 'without initiative'.[48] They ignored the work of Bryant and other amateur scholars of African societies, and did not use such anthropological insights as were available when they wrote.[49] However, they did assert the importance of the black role in South African history and, compared to other contemporaneous historians of colonial Africa, they were far ahead in admitting the importance of the African side of South African history and in attempting to analyse structural issues.

As critics have pointed out, like later liberal historians, Macmillan and de Kiewiet emphasized individual motivation rather than social structure and were quick to moralize,[50] but they were both more keenly aware of the importance of economics than most of those who were to follow them. As already noted, Macmillan's first lectureship was in economics as well as history, and de Kiewiet always regretted his lack of formal training in economics. British and European economic historians had the most critical intellectual impact on both Macmillan and de Kiewiet.[51] Though influenced in the 1920s by a materialist interpretation of history, neither became economic determinists, and while not unmindful of the significance of class, race nevertheless remained more important in their overall interpretation of South Africa's past. At the same time, being strongly opposed to racism, both men denied that race had been as all-important as South Africans usually claimed.[52]

With hindsight one may point to the limitations of their work, but it can only be understood in the context of its time. In the 1920s and 1930s it constituted a profound challenge to the then dominant historiography. If Macmillan's writing had a more explicit political purpose, de Kiewiet nevertheless also saw his work as relevant to present concerns. His pages which spoke of South Africa in the 1870s and 1880s were 'also about to-day',[53] and in expounding Macmillan's view that the central theme in South African history was the evolution of a single society, he believed himself to be addressing contemporary policies in South Africa. As attempts at segregation had failed in the past, so they would fail again because they were contrary to the process of incorporation he charted. He claimed that segregation ran counter to economic growth — an argument advanced more explicitly in his later, more polemical work.[54] He was attacking the intensification of segregation at a time when secondary industry was expanding, and the job colour bar was being applied in manufacturing as well as mining.[55] Although both Macmillan and de Kiewiet predicted that segregationist policies would fail, their vision of the past was a gloomy one: unlike the Whig historians in Britain, they could not revere the past, but had to chronicle the failure to achieve liberal goals and the triumph of racism.[56]

De Kiewiet only worked closely with Macmillan for a brief few years in the early 1920s, but Macmillan had at that time, and continued to have, a profound influence on his work. Without Macmillan's teaching, wrote de Kiewiet in the copy of *British Colonial Policy* he sent his mentor, 'this book could hardly have been written'.[57] A close textual examination of de Kiewiet's *History* shows that it drew heavily on all Macmillan's major writings.[58] Macmillan was the pioneer, the first to make the break away from the Theal perspective, but de Kiewiet contributed a masterly style and a superb ability to synthesize. He popularized Macmillan's ideas as well as enlarged on them. His style and his gift for synthesis made his *History* a bestseller, which over the years reached a far wider audience than Macmillan's three books put together.[59]

Macmillan, then, was the pioneer, who, initiated the new way of looking at South African history. De Kiewiet built on and popularized, and so helped establish, that approach. Later historians — today called liberals — adopted their overall perspective and consciously saw themselves as belonging to the tradition begun by Macmillan and continued by de Kiewiet. The continuities we have noted that remained between Macmillan and Theal were overshadowed by the break Macmillan made with the old tradition. Influenced by Fabian socialism, Macmillan can justifiably be called 'an old radical',[60] but he was not a historical materialist, did not blame capitalism for South Africa's path of development, and was reformist in political outlook. With de Kiewiet he believed strongly in liberal values, and both men were eclectic in their historical writing. They were the key figures in establishing a new approach to South Africa's past, for which 'liberal school of history' still seems the most appropriate phrase.

4

W. M. MACMILLAN:
POVERTY, SMALL TOWNS AND
THE KAROO*

JEFFREY BUTLER

Between 1911 and 1920, W. M. Macmillan wrote several short studies of poverty among whites in South Africa. Within that period he began three important changes of focus: first, he shifted from part economist, part sociologist to social historian, breaking with a strong political and administrative tradition in such scholarship as there was. Second, he moved from a study of white poverty to a preoccupation with black poverty, and, third, he made the first scholarly assault on a predominant 'settler' view of history held by scholars as well as by whites generally. Despite the controversial character of his views in both white communities at the time, he is today admired by Afrikaans- and English-speaking historians.[1] Doubtless, African, Asian, and Coloured historians of the future will share that apparently inescapable judgement — the scale of his achievement was immense.[2] But it is not easy to discern why and how he came to these related shifts, nor has their nature been clearly delineated. Macmillan in his autobiography, like Alan Paton in *Towards the Mountain*, gives an incomplete account of a major event in his intellectual life.[3]

Using Macmillan's work before he began in the 1920s to exploit the papers of Dr John Philip, this paper examines Macmillan's early career, his study of Grahamstown, and his celebrated study of the 'agrarian problem'.[4] I shall concentrate on four major themes important to Macmillan: the ignorance and prejudice in South Africa in relation to poverty; white–black relations in the labour market and the necessity for intervention; urban–rural relations and the centrality of land policy; and the importance of regional variation. Finally, in the light of Macmillan's propositions about South African small towns, I shall examine his achievement as an urban historian.

103

I

Macmillan is a wonderful subject for a biography. His father had a struggling and unsuccessful career, not quite a minister, nor an established teacher, taking his young family from Scotland to Stellenbosch in 1891, to 'become in effect housemaster in charge of a residence of the Victoria College' (later Stellenbosch University).[5] Unfortunately, the elder Macmillan suffered from the anti-British feeling among Afrikaners engendered by the Jameson Raid, and even more by the South African War, and his position came to an end in 1900.[6]

In writing of his childhood years in Stellenbosch, Macmillan is nostalgic and he deplores the destruction of an anglicizing Cape Dutch society.[7] Caught in the cross-fire of Anglo-Afrikaner conflict, the young Macmillan apparently took no 'pro-Boer' stand; and his father was unlikely to have wanted to criticize British policy.[8] Macmillan's account is interesting because it is essentially as a certain kind of liberal would give it, emphasizing the importance of individuals and moral issues. When for example, one of his students, A. L. Geyer, later a distinguished Afrikaner historian and editor of *Die Burger*, became an important Afrikaner nationalist, Macmillan deplored the move. He explained the change by Geyer's loss of a close English-speaking friend, Harold Howse, in the First World War. The war, he says, denied young Afrikaners the liberalizing influence of their young white English-speaking South African contemporaries.[9]

It would be valuable to date from contemporary material Macmillan's perception of Afrikaner nationalism in its post-1913 form as a threat to an understanding of South Africa's problems. If the first set of influences on him were his relationships with family and young Afrikaners in the Stellenbosch of his youth, a second set can be found in his relations as a young man to religion generally and the Dutch Reformed Church (DRC) in particular. He tells us little about his religious life except that, between schools in Oxford in 1906 and going to Rhodes University College in 1911, he dithered over pursuing studies in divinity, and was unclear about whether he intended going into the Church, the United Free Church of Scotland.[10] When he returned to South Africa, to Rhodes, he seems to have made contact with the small but growing Afrikaner community in Grahamstown, which established its first Dutch Reformed

Church in 1914, and in 1916 invited him to attend the DRC conference on poor whites in Cradock, as one of the Grahamstown delegates.[11]

Although, as we shall see, he protested against the growing politicization of the poor white problem, he remained on sufficiently good terms with DRC churchmen to be invited to another DRC conference on the 'native problem' in 1923. In a most generous passage in his autobiography, Macmillan regretted his failure to speak Afrikaans to Afrikaners — he must surely have been reasonably fluent — or to use his contacts among leading Afrikaner intellectuals and officials, including A. L. Geyer, Dr W. Eiselen, and Dr J. Holloway. In 1920, he wrote, Geyer 'advised me, I am staggered to find, to have my papers translated into Afrikaans'.[12] But his estrangement from nationalist Afrikanerdom accelerated in the 1920s, especially in relation to General Hertzog after 1926, and to Oswald Pirow and E. G. Jansen after 1930.[13] It may be that there was an ethnic dimension to his leaving South Africa permanently in 1932: he may have felt that South Africa was hopeless politically, largely because it was dominated by Afrikaners. It was not only that he feared Afrikaner nationalism: as early as 1931 he seems to have concluded that little help was to be expected even from such Afrikaners in the opposition as Jan Smuts and Jan Hofmeyr.[14]

A third set of influences came from English and German intellectual life. He was one of the first Rhodes scholars because Toby Muller, the father of C. F. J. Muller, the distinguished Afrikaner historian, refused a scholarship with Rhodes' name on it.[15] In Oxford Macmillan took some time to find his feet, but he moved in circles where 'social questions' were discussed, and learned much from A. L. Smith who lectured on what he 'modestly called ... "political and social questions": for example population, poor law, federations, and notably the historical development of the socialist movement'.[16] He gained a second in the history schools and left Oxford for five years of *wanderjahre*, still unable to make up his mind about going into the church, but coming increasingly into contact with the British liberal and socialist Left, either through their work or personally.[17] In 1910, he went to Germany for a semester and there came under the influence of Gustav Schmoller who 'with his extraordinary gift for analysis of the conditions of living, became one of my lasting inspirations', and considered doing a thesis with a Dr Saring on poor relief, perhaps prompted by Sidney and Beatrice Webb's 'famous report'.[18] But his time in Germany was short and he returned to Glasgow to complete a course in divinity, where he became involved in a university settlement in the slums 'along the lines' of one he had known in London. He was already a keen Liberal, but like so many Liberals at the time, was moving to the left. He joined the Fabian Society in 1911.[19]

The real heritage of these European years was to convince him to become a man of action in the world outside the ivory tower as well as a scholar. For him, as for many intellectuals in Britain, scholarship became and remained an instrument of public life, a conviction already well developed when he returned to South Africa in 1911. Most of his work was only thinly disguised pamphleteering, or rather explicitly propagandist, directed to live current issues as the titles show: *The Agrarian Problem* (1919), *The Cape Colour Question* (1927) and, after he had left South Africa, *Warning from the West Indies* (1936), to name only three. In the works based on the papers of Dr John Philip, *The Cape Colour Question* (1927), *Bantu, Boer, and Briton* (1929), the contemporary world constantly intrudes. They were aimed at destroying a view of South African history which regarded white settlers as innocent, and missionaries and Africans as villains, a view he regarded as fatal to facing the problems of a multiracial society.[20]

Macmillan was aware of the political problem. He became an apostle of Ranke, he wrote, and 'curbed any temptation to denounce social evils but concentrated first and last on establishing the facts'.[21] He developed a British Fabian's belief in the capacity of information to persuade, but was soon to realize that political action was necessary. Later he expressed a wistful regret that he did not get into parliament: if there had been 'native representatives' he might have become one, but he opposed the separate representation of Africans in 1936. He left South Africa, partly because he disapproved of the direction of policy at the University of the Witwatersrand which he felt denied him opportunities for scholarship, and because he thought he had a better chance of 'doing something' in the British colonial empire. 'The next step' he wrote on 28 November 1931 'is to plan for a British Africa which will definitely turn away from the awful warning of the Union.'[22]

II

In 1911 he was appointed lecturer in History and Economics at the new Rhodes University College, founded in 1904 in Grahamstown, but he did not remain solely a teacher and scholar for long. In the middle of 1912 he became ill and made the acquaintance of another Scot, Dr Saunders, who in 1914 became Medical Officer of Health (MOH) for Grahamstown. Together they produced an anonymous pamphlet 'Sanitary reform in Grahamstown' using statistics to show that Grahamstownians paid 'a quite heavy rate for a wretchedly inadequate service'. This paper led the Bishop of Grahamstown to ask him to do a further paper on the 'wretched conditions' in much of Grahamstown.[23]

What started as a possible paper on poor relief, developed into a study of poverty and an attempt to inform South Africa's rulers. Following closely the method used in B. Seebohm Rowntree's classic work, *Poverty*, a *Study of Town Life* (London, 1901), modified by the work of an American, Dr Atwater, he drew a 'Poverty Line' of £10 a month for a family of five as a minimum for a 'decent standard of life and efficiency'. Applying this standard to the white population of Grahamstown, he concluded that '7 per cent or 9 per cent of our white townspeople are living in poverty'. At the time, that was controversial enough, but he went on to link poor health to poverty — 'the poorer classes [are] singularly liable to disease'. Obliquely he argued that disease knew no racial boundaries: '... the existence of such areas and classes even in the location [black township] is a standing menace to the health and efficiency of the rest of the community....'[24]

Macmillan was diplomatically advancing views that he was to hold far more strongly and publicly later. At the time he was determined to show that poverty was not a matter of 'vice' and 'laziness', rejecting out of hand that in Grahamstown it was due to liquor and to spending on the 'Bioscope' [cinema].[25] As important for him was the discovery that poor whiteism was not a problem thrust on Grahamstown from outside — the 'great majority are Grahamstown people'.[26] He was moving towards a more 'holistic' approach, an assertion of the common interests and interdependence of the whole. 'Cheap labour is inefficient ...' he wrote, 'Poverty ... is a direct impoverishment of the whole.'[27]

On the second major theme, the importance of white–black

divisions in the labour market, Macmillan acknowledged the existence of a 'menace'. It was not moral factors that were central: 'A much more serious problem is native competition.'

The solid basis of the native menace is the fact that the native provides a class of workmen, who, while satisfying their own needs relatively easily reduce the standard of life and tend to degrade whites down to and below their own level.... This is the peril; low wages and inefficiency are its roots in Grahamstown and elsewhere, and so long as we allow selfish unregulated competition to govern wages even in our public service, so long do we go on with our unholy work of depressing our own race, making a healthy white South Africa impossible, and degrading the black himself in the process.[28]

Although Macmillan was using the racist coinage of his time, he was also making a radical argument, not in acknowledging the 'menace', but in attacking a free market in labour. Later in the lecture, he took his interventionist argument further when considering the problem of the urban worker in any small town: 'There is no sufficiently continuous demand....' Sickness or irregular employment could be a 'short step' away from 'loss of self-respect and moral ruin ... a most serious menace to our white civilisation.'[29] To meet the 'menace' he urged better education, and 'greater public support of efforts as by the School Board to exercise more guidance on the destiny of growing youth...'.[30] These remarks were clearly in the context of white education: school boards at this time had no role in black education.

Macmillan was not prepared to rely only on the long-term processes of education.

... In the face of the competition of cheap native labour there is the need for organisation and cooperation, by the men themselves and by the public, to secure and defend a minimum standard of life and efficiency; to meet such competition by lowering the barriers still further is of all things most fatal.... The moral of increasing efficiency and better training for our workmen, and standard wages would seem to be obvious.[31]

He quoted the Webbs' *Industrial Democracy* with approval: 'Better pay means better work', he wrote, echoing the contemporary Fabian interest in efficiency; factory acts had led to changes which 'tend in the long run to increased efficiency and production, to more wealth, and more, not less employment'.[32] But, in an extended analogy between the introduction of machinery in eighteenth-century England and the competition of 'cheap native labour', he singled out the cobblers and paperworkers in England as having, by organization, become 'the best paid and most highly skilled aristocracy of their trades...'.[33] He did not, in this paper, face the racial implications of such exclusivist policies in South Africa.

On the third major theme, the relationship of town and country, Macmillan had begun his study of Grahamstown by establishing statistically the existence of white poverty, and had then considered the various classes of the poor in Grahamstown. He tentatively placed Grahamstown in the context of the poverty of small towns generally: it was like other small towns in having virtually no industries. It had already lost leather and jam factories, and was losing wagon-making and saddlery, retaining only printing, milling and brickmaking, the latter 'largely by native labour...'.[34] He then attacked the notion that shopkeeping was the path to wealth.

The shop depends ... on the production of the country districts round, and this at once explains the acuteness with which we feel the collapse of ostrich prices.... We are, at present at least, essentially a poor community.... But through ignorance there is this widespread delusion that a small shop is the first step on the high road to respectability and wealth.[35]

Placing this argument of urban dependency in a national context he argued: 'The stream of young life must be diverted more and more to developing the land.... We require to produce more wealth, by land development rather than by industry for which conditions are unfavorable.'[36]

Not only were the small towns economic deadends in his view, they were also places of poverty and wretched living conditions. Treading carefully in the face of the comfortable in Grahamstown, perhaps hoping to avoid offending their civic pride, he wrote: 'My considered judgement is that there are slums in Grahamstown, and an alarming amount of degrading and degraded poverty which cannot be explained either by the war or the ostrich feather slump....'[37] The existing towns were themselves a problem: in terms which would surely have gained assent from a dominee anxious about the fate of an Afrikaner poor white in a city slum, he argued that the city in a multiracial context was dragging both races down:

I shall not readily forget what I have seen in the slums of Johannesburg; in almost every case where whites and blacks live side by side, the blacks are on the upgrade, in the slums because there was no other place for them, clean and decent; but their children were growing up there, learning 'civilization' from white neighbours, squalid and filthy, the very dregs of society.[38]

Poverty among whites had turned them into 'dregs', and while the black adults were 'on the upgrade', the black children were not — a selective racial and generational process was at work. However, many dominees would have bristled at the notion that whites were dragging blacks down. Moreover, the whole problem was a structural one, not one based on temporary factors like a war or price levels.

At this stage, Macmillan was a sort of urban sociologist — he referred to this early work as 'my doings in social economics'.[39] There was no historical material in the Grahamstown study, but it was a pioneering piece, regrettably largely ignored later, applying to a South African town the statistical techniques which had been used by Rowntree in his study of York.[40] He collected material on incomes by consulting school authorities who applied means tests for access to free education; he examined material on house ownership, showing how many people were owners of a single house, questioning the benefits of ownership by suggesting that it contributed to immobility.[41] By looking closely at shopkeeping, he showed how women and girls were employed for long hours at low wages and gave the awful warning that such exploitation led inevitably to prostitution.[42] And he isolated an area in Grahamstown of poor housing and inadequate drainage, drawing attention in passing to the worse problems in locations.[43] This early urban study seems to have convinced him that works such as Rowntree's and his own were dealing with the consequences of a particular kind of economic process, rather than the process itself, which he saw as having its roots in the countryside.

He did not let the matter rest after giving the paper on Grahamstown, and he was soon given the chance to enunciate his conclusions in a much wider arena than a Grahamstown young men's church club. In Grahamstown he had come into contact with an Afrikaner community sufficiently large to establish a church in 1914: perhaps he worshipped there occasionally. In November 1916 he went, as one of the Grahamstown delegates, to Cradock to a conference on 'Het Arme Blanken Vraagstuk' (The Poor White Problem) arranged by the *Inwendige Zending Kommissie* (literally, 'Internal Mission Commission' but translated as 'Home Mission Committee' by Cradock's local paper *The Midland News*).[44] Macmillan's name appears on the official list of delegates in the official report as 'Professor W. N. Macmillan'; the other Grahamstown delegate, was the *Eerwaarde* M. C. Theron, to whom Macmillan had referred in the Grahamstown study as one of his 'indefatigable guides through some hidden parts of our city'.[45]

Macmillan was not one of the leading speakers. He spoke in English, and his remarks were included in the official report. He did not, however, make any reference to them in his autobiography: there he showed only how political the poor white question had already become when the conference was interrupted by a young contemporary from Stellenbosch waving a telegram announcing the liberation of all prisoners from the rebellion of 1914.[46] Macmillan spoke on the second day, after hearing a series of speakers discuss the problem as a peculiarly Afrikaner one, and raising all the major themes in the National Party programme: segregation, mother-tongue instruction, bilingualism in the civil service, and 'civilized labour'. Fortunately, *The Midland News* summarized his words, but unfortunately the reporter was unaware of the potential of the thirty-one-year-old 'professor', or he might have quoted him at length.[47]

This Congress had not as yet fully grasped the question. He showed how many classes of paupers there were. Social legislation, the education of the public in general, and money were necessary. In Grahamstown, 70 per cent of the poor whites were of English extraction. Factories etc. were all very well, but these could not be established without skilled instructors and managers. These must be obtained from England or elsewhere and thus money was essential. Provision on a practical basis must be made for the women folk. He advocated cooperation between all public bodies.[48]

The official report is almost identical except that the demand for expenditure of public money was given great emphasis: the public had to be educated 'te verstaan dat zij DE HAND IN TE ZAK moesten steken (to understand that it would have to put ITS HAND INTO ITS POCKET)'. And as far as social legislation was concerned, '*was Zuid Afrika het minst ontwikkeld van alle landen* (South Africa was the least developed of all countries)'?[49]

Some tentative conclusions about Macmillan at this stage of his career seem permissible. First, he accepted the premise of the Cradock conference — it was about white poverty, not poverty in general. He did not protest at racist remarks by several speakers who had demanded segregation, he attacked 'make work' projects by government and had referred generally to individual merit and character, and even asked for compulsion to work.[50]

Second, said Macmillan, there had to be intervention, — 'social legislation', and the expenditure of public money; he desired to educate the public into seeing that poverty was not due to moral failure. Third, he resisted the strong ethnic note in the proceedings at Cradock by pointing to the poverty — 70 per cent of his sample —in Grahamstown's English-speaking population, making the point explicitly as he had not done in the Grahamstown paper. Fourth, he was sceptical of the suggestions of industrialization made by several speakers, including Thomas Searle, a successful industrialist, whose family had established large tanneries in Great Brak River using poor white labour.[51] He was drawing attention to the rural, non-industrial character of South Africa, which lacked the basis for rapid industrialization, and particularly lacked it in relation to manpower, a line he had only hinted at in the Grahamstown paper.[52] South Africa's *whites*, he was saying, were economically underdeveloped, and needed expensive outside help in both technical and managerial fields.

III

By the end of 1916 Macmillan was already launched on his career as scholarly commentator and polemicist on public affairs, and had begun writing for newspapers.[53] He gave another public lecture in 1916 on 'Poverty and Post-War Problems' to the Grahamstown Social Welfare League, apparently written in the context of considerable local hostility to his refusal to join the forces.[54] On 8 January 1917, he heard that he had been appointed to the Chair of History at the new university in Johannesburg, and in September 1917 he gave his fourth public lecture, on 'The place of local Government in the Union of South Africa', an expansion of brief remarks in the Grahamstown study.[55] Then, in May and June 1919, he gave the ambitious series of lectures on 'The South African agrarian problem and its historical development', published in September, a considerable elaboration of the themes he had dealt with in the first study in Grahamstown. These lectures, he was later to claim, heralded something of a turning point for him, 'a diversion from poor whites to poor blacks', clearly meaning a permanent shift of interest and focus.[56]

The lectures do not, as we shall see, explain why he was 'diverted' from 'poor whites to poor blacks', and the autobiography, if it gives an explanation at all, suggests that the Philip papers, which he first saw in 1920, were a revelation to him, returning him to historical work and initiating a ten-year quest involving frequent visits to the eastern Cape and the Transkei.[57] The shift to Johannesburg brought him into a big-city, industrial world different from Grahamstown: he now saw African workers in large numbers, white trade unionists, and organizations like the Workers' Educational Association (WEA), institutions familiar to him from his years overseas, phenomena amenable to treatment by the socialist intellectual tradition of contemporary Britain. Yet Macmillan did not become a student of South Africa's growing cities or its industrial organization, nor did he ever return to the detailed study of small towns for which his Grahamstown paper showed he had great aptitude. Instead, the phenomenon of the urban white poor in Grahamstown led him to investigate their origins. This was partly due to prodding from John X. Merriman who, on reading the Grahamstown study, suggested that he look at the 'state of the country districts of the Karoo'.[58] We should examine *The Agrarian Problem* lectures, therefore, to see to what extent he was moving away from the perspectives of the Grahamstown study, and how he perceived urban and rural problems in other parts of the country.

The South African agrarian problem, as Macmillan and most of his contemporaries saw it, was a problem of white poverty — specifically, the existence of a new urban underclass forced off the land: he used as an epigraph to his lectures, an ironic quote from Thomas Hardy: 'The process humorously designated by statisticians as "the tendency of the rural population towards the large towns" being really the tendency of water to flow uphill when forced by machinery.'[59] There were five lectures: the first dealt with the definition and scale of poverty, placed it in the context of other 'problems' — religion, the native question and industry — and delineated the 'peculiarities of the South African poverty problem'. The second was historical, subdivided at 1834, highlighting slavery, land tenure, inheritance, and the advent of mining. The third, 'Rural

113

conditions I' was largely about the Karoo; the fourth, 'Rural conditions II' was supposedly on 'the Northern Districts' but really on the 'large farm' and *bywoners*; and the final lecture returned to the 'Problem as a whole', an examination of 'back to the land' policies, land settlement, production and training.

Dealing in turn with the four major themes I identified as important to Macmillan, we can see how these lectures were an elaboration of all the themes in the Grahamstown study. He hammered away at the ignorance of South Africa's rulers and wealthy classes, generalizing the problem of poverty to the society as a whole. Leaving Grahamstown — 'on the whole a poor town' — he went to other areas, and to the problems of their *bywoners*.[60] In addition he used statistics from Johannesburg relief organizations to trace the origins of the newly urban poor, and used the censuses of 1910 and 1918 to show those districts which were gaining and losing white population.[61] He was, in fact, appealing to English-speakers in the heart of South African industry and mining to see the problems of the Afrikaner poor, who, he said, made up between 8 and 15 per cent of the white population.[62] He not only emphasized the numerical scale but the nature of the process. 'Our difficulties are due not a little to influx into the towns of the poor untrained men for whom the rural struggle has proved too hard ... the children of the pioneers of civilization in this wide land.'[63] Once more, poverty was not a moral problem: it was due to a process which had produced a 'submerged twentieth' of 'permanent absolute poverty', a process which had to be controlled: '... We have to reconstruct society so as to prevent considerably more than another twentieth from being dragged ... down to the level of those submerged.'[64] It was not only a white problem: 'When in addition one bears in mind the very low standard of living of the native and coloured people ... we are faced by a state of affairs sufficiently serious to warrant close investigation.'[65]

Second, on white–black relations in the labour market and the necessity for intervention, he advanced more forcefully the propositions of the first study, although he seems to have been becoming increasingly aware of the 'native question' and of deep conflicts of interest. He repeated his remarks about the competition of black labour (though he dropped the term 'native menace'), and the degradation of black as well as white in the Johannesburg slums. There was keen competition among whites as well — native labour should not be blamed for everything:

... unless we are to bring on ourselves a problem of black poverty even more serious than that existing, as the tale of disease tells us, alike in locations and in Native Territories, what we have to do is to create new and better openings for all classes, white and black, to increase the 'national dividend'.[66]

Continuing and elaborating the argument of the Grahamstown study, he pressed for protection of white workers by insisting on a 'minimum standard wage', and changes in the law to increase the number of whites on the land. He was aware of difficulties:

Action on these lines may have the effect of inducing the wholesale eviction of the bijwoners who are now on the margin of subsistence, and their supersession by native and coloured men.

His response, however, was to state that 'it is worth taking some risks'. To those who said that such legislation could only succeed if accompanied by 'segregation' of natives, he replied:

It is the poverty and low standard of the native which makes his competition so formidable to the unskilled white, and therefore ... it is urgently necessary to improve agricultural methods in the Native Territories.... Nothing can be more suicidal than to look to economic pressure — starvation — to provide ... an increased supply of 'cheap' native labour. Our true aim must rather be higher standards all round.[67]

There had to be better use of the countryside for blacks as well as whites, *bywoners* transformed into prosperous smallholders, African farmers using better methods in their existing territories.

Returning to the urban labour market, he acknowledged the 'enormous difficulty of colour'.[68] With the already developing policy of 'civilized labour' in mind, he argued that it was 'against all first principles, and in itself unjust to look for the remedy of white poverty by the mere substitution of whites for blacks in *existing employment*'[69] (Macmillan's italics). He seemed to say that white labour in industry would have to be protected by denying to anyone, coloured or white, the advantage that his willingness to work for lower wages gave him:

Provided the employment of colour in industry is hedged about by adequate safeguards, the coloured man doing skilled work being required to get the minimum standard wage, the superior ability and experience of the white will be the best security against the danger of undercutting white rates by an inferior class of native. Further *additional* employment even of unskilled blacks must directly increase the demand for white employment in the work of supervision.[70]

But nowhere did he tackle the problem of how this was to be secured. He assumed that merit, perhaps racially as well as culturally determined, would be economically effective, that an invisible hand would secure the expanding employment of whites and blacks. Furthermore, he assumed that whites would continue to be supervisors, that enough whites would be hired to supervise to help eliminate the unemployment among whites with no skills other than those of supervisors of black labour.

Third, Macmillan elaborated on the interconnection between town and country and industrialization as he had done both at Cradock and in the Grahamstown study. South Africa had little potential for industrial growth, he said, arguing by implication that the small towns would remain economic deadends. For 'some 2000 boys leaving Rand schools annually there are in Johannesburg only some 700 vacancies in apprenticeships'. Nor was there much hope for the future: 'As unless for the bare possibility of a considerable development of iron industries, the land and its products are the real basis of any industries likely to prove strong and healthy.'[71] Even the big cities, he was saying, could not find jobs for their white youth, let alone for those in the countryside. Given this bleak picture, he naturally paid most of his attention to the countryside.

In his Grahamstown paper, Macmillan had given some attention to urban problems, to poor housing concentrated in a low-lying, poorly drained part of the town, to the necessity of a public health policy, and to better education[72]. But his principal attention had been urban employment, and particularly in puncturing the small-town belief in shopkeeping as a path to wealth.[73] In these lectures, however, he has virtually nothing to say about the cities — the techniques used in Grahamstown were not applied to another town, small or large. For example, there is no parallel study of, say, Vrededorp in Johannesburg, where the newly arrived Afrikaner poor were concentrated. Rather, he romanticized Grahamstown's past by arguing that the Great Trek had diverted the 'eastern towns from production and gradual development to the work of distribution', leading to violent opposition to the extension of railways, which he regarded as essential to growth. At first this seems an odd argument: it is doubtful if the productive activities in Grahamstown, or other small towns, such as they ever were, could have survived the coming of railways; indeed, one industry whose decline Macmillan deplored in the Grahamstown study, wagon-making, was in a losing competition with them. But Macmillan was really thinking in terms of agriculture, of 'the close intensive development of the Cape Coast', rather than 'sheep, goats ... [and] the ostrich, none of which is the best basis for a dense population'.[74]

If the towns did not represent the future of South Africa, the countryside remained to be reconstructed by reversing established trends. The poor white ought not to be a figure of contempt: Macmillan set out to inform his Johannesburg English-speaking audience about the virtues and difficulties of 'the Boers', whom he almost certainly knew far better than anyone in the audience. At one point he said tartly, '... Not even the well-to-do can escape the conclusion that the poor *bywoner* or the unemployed townsman is a direct burden on all who work.'[75] He spoke at some length about their strengths and weaknesses:

On the whole the veld has produced a strong and independent race, and pride of race, mistaken as it may sometimes be, is in itself a good thing. Indeed it will be a sorry day for South Africa when we have eradicated pride of race, and even of family.... The real danger which arises from that spirit of independence is something wider than that many of them haughtily refuse to accept the unrestricted hours of employment, and living at the private beck and call of a master or mistress which 'domestic service' may involve.

In a remarkable passage he went to the heart of the South African political problem — the tendency of its groups, and particularly of Afrikaners, to see their interests and those of others as basically irreconcilable:

As liberty passes into licence, so the independent spirit ... has certainly weakened the capacity of the Dutch race for collective action or for compromise, the power of making allowances for the different views and successful working of political institutions ... The growth of Freedom is the

117

sacrifice of Privilege, of the unrestrained licence of a class, in the interest of a wider whole.

Showing how deeply embedded he was in contemporary British politics he added:

... whether it be the curtailment of the privilege of a ruling caste, the surrender of the monopoly of an Established Church, or the growth of a spirit of tolerance and cooperation, the principle is the same. The highest type of the State, like the noblest individual, will be known by its readiness to sacrifice the smaller to the greater Independence — which is Freedom.[76]

This was stirring stuff, and predictive of much that was to happen within Afrikanerdom, but it ignored one crucial fact: part of the ruling caste in South Africa was *dood arm*, 'dead poor', and it was the powerful privilege that their white skins secured to them which was to be used by politicians substantially to eliminate their poverty. It is hard to see how such an appeal could have succeeded with the leaders of the Afrikaners.

Recognizing the limited prospects for urbanization, he turned to the institutions of the countryside and, particularly, to finding some virtues in them. He deplored the tendency to move from a *bywoner* system, where there had been some mutual rights and obligations, towards tenancy, farming on declining shares, or wage labour. The *bywoner* system had 'often secured a harmonious community of interest between owner and tenant ... the social union of classes which is a strong and good feature of Dutch rural life'. That was being eroded by competition. 'There is evidence of the growth of social castes, the landlord and the landless, to the considerable, if only half-conscious, aggravation I fully believe of political feuds.' He then came out with his own version of 'back to the land', or rather what may be called 'save a populous land', showing his hostility to the 'wage system', and resistance to the expansion of a farm-owning class at the expense of *bywoners*. The system

... does offer the more competent men a degree of independence quite lacking in the wage system ... We must at all costs avoid the mistake of pursuing a policy which has as its sole end the putting of farmers in the place of bijwoners, instead of striving to convert existing bijwoners into good and efficient farmers and husbandmen.[77]

Macmillan was not, however, a rural romantic, hoping to restore conditions capable of sustaining a jolly yeomanry, or peasantry. Given his knowledge of urban squalor, and his bleak assumptions about the future of industry, he hoped to arrest some, not all, of the influx into the cities by creating a countryside which would hold a larger population in decency and self-respect. It was a radical notion, involving a head-on assault on the freedom of large landowners to accumulate, consolidate, and do as they pleased with their labour, especially by moving in the direction of wage labour rather than maintaining tenancy or farming on equitable shares. But it was an approach that largely ignored the Coloureds and the Africans, who had been there all along and who remained labourers in the whole scheme. It was not really back to the land, because it could at best stem the flow — only 'the more competent' would be able to stay. But in relation to land, he was raising the central issue of the rights of 'capital', a new acute *Problem of Wealth* or of *Poverty*.[78]

In relation to our fourth theme, the importance of regional variation, Macmillan showed his wonderfully earthy respect for fact, a product of his long journeys by cart, Model T Ford, and on foot, in which he interviewed all kinds of people. He barely hinted at regional variations in the Grahamstown study, but now he set out to show how great they were. Leaving the relatively well-watered coastal areas of Albany, the south-west, and the north-east he looked at the Karoo, emphasizing the absolute limits on population growth there, and questioning the fashionable interest in irrigation from Karoo rivers:

Nothing but an adequate supply of permanent water will suffice to remedy these disabilities of Karoo life.... It is hard to see how as the first plank in a national policy we can hope to set out on a large scale to change the nature of the illimitable veld.... Policy ought to turn in the first instance where nature seems to suggest greater possibilities of supporting a reasonably dense population.[79]

Considering the southern coastal belt between Port Elizabeth and Cape Town, he deplored the distortion of development by mining which had diverted 'the spread of railways from following the natural lines of earlier colonisation'.[80] The Great Trek had led to the 'premature dispersal of the not very dense population',[81] and this process had moreover led to a survival of pastoralism rather than an

119

expansion of agriculture.[82] Re-emphasizing the necessity of training by specialists which he had expressed at Cradock, he advocated training of farmers so that a 'dense population' on 'small holdings' would be possible on the southern coastal belt.[83]

This was the essence of Macmillan's regional argument — rainfall was crucial in determining where dense populations were possible. His remarks on the 'northern districts', which he did not clearly define, were general: the north had felt the impact of mining and railways, rinderpest and war — 10,000 people had been left behind in the camps, unable to return to the land. In the Transvaal many of those looking for work 'in the town or on the irrigation works' had lost their land to bondholders, something no longer true in the Cape; the Transvaal was simply following in the Cape's path.[84] So the rest of a lecture, supposedly on the 'northern districts' was taken up with the *'general system'*, *bywoners* and the large farm, and most of the illustrations were from the Cape. Here, once again, Macmillan showed his respect for unavoidable fact, accepting the need for the 3,000–4,000 morgen farms (6,000–8,000 acres) in the Karoo, and drawing attention to the need for management which already existed in 'the supervising genius of large [sic] and capable owner managers'.[85]

It is here that Macmillan did not follow his argument through. Acknowledging that the Karoo could not support a dense population on small-holdings, he looked to the owners to provide the solution. The test of the 'owner managers', he wrote, would be whether they could give some incentive to those for whom

... like the peasants of France in the days of Arthur Young, it takes the magic of ownership to convert the dry land of the Karoo into gold. [The large farm] will be judged as it serves these men as a stepping stone to greater efficiency and ultimate independence.[86]

If the analogy with revolutionary France is to be taken seriously, the large Karoo farmer was to be somehow the agent for the redistribution of his own land. Macmillan did not address the political issues involved, and he made what might be an even more important omission: his remarks about the capacity of well-watered areas to support dense populations at rising standards of living could easily have been applied to the 'native territories' whose development he regarded as essential. It was only later, at the DRC conference on the 'Native Problem' in 1923, that he was to address the problem explicitly, and to add the necessity of increasing the amount of land in African hands.[87]

IV

In examining Macmillan's career as a scholar up to 1920, we see a man in his thirties of prodigious energy, ability and generosity of spirit who saw the amiable context of his youth destroyed by political conflict. In his education there was a tension also between a secular, liberal and increasingly socialist milieu at odds with the traditionally liberal, Presbyterian, free market values of his family. This conflicting set of influences and his youth in Stellenbosch gave him both easy contact with Afrikaners and sympathy with the scale and intensity of their poverty. But it also created dilemmas for him as he contemplated the position of Afrikaners in South African society, and their capacity to cooperate with others.

Within that changing political and social context, his intellectual development seems to have been as follows: his early work on Grahamstown was all 'social economics', and led him to a highly unpopular set of beliefs: first, South Africa was a poor country, even for whites; second, there was a great deal of white poverty in towns, some of it English-speaking. Urged to look at the Karoo, he found more of the same, mostly among Afrikaners in town and country. So he began to ask where the white poor in the big cities and small towns came from in two senses: (a) geographical, from which districts; and (b) what caused the drift to towns in the first place. It was the latter question that turned him to historical inquiry, from which he came up with another unpopular answer — the white poor had been *forced* to leave the land. But even while he was concentrating on the white poor, he was conscious of a total society and critical of approaches which involved the rescue of only one portion of it. This shift of interest from town to country, from Grahamstown to South Africa, from 'social economics' to history, prepared him for a major shift of focus and sympathy, from an interest in white poverty to an interest in black poverty, a shift taking place *before* he saw the Philip papers. However, he remained interested in poverty as a whole, a characteristic stance for liberal scholars who all argued for the essential unity of the South African

121

economy. The papers gave his interest a specific historical form: that in the 1830s it had not been a matter of virtuous white frontiersmen facing the rapaciousness of blacks and the misrepresentations of missionaries. Africans had had genuine grievances then, and had genuine grievances against, *and common interests with*, their white contemporaries.

From the beginning of his South African scholarly career, Macmillan held the view that poverty was in the interest of no one and that, for South Africa, greater opportunities for all, to ensure a greater national dividend, would be the best policy. This focus probably had its roots in a general humanitarianism and in contemporary liberal and socialist thought. But he was dealing with, and living in, a society in which few thought that way. He was a product of his time, used its racist vocabulary, and held its assumptions about the inheritance of superior capacity by whites. Thus, in dealing with labour problems, he believed that, given equal conditions in the market place, whites would have nothing to fear. But it seems that his mind was running ahead of the vocabulary available to him: he certainly did not believe that racial differences ought to be the basis of unequal treatment. Whatever his beliefs about race, they did not prevent him from arguing for better opportunities for all and equality of treatment. Poverty was not a matter of race or moral quality; it was a product of circumstance amenable to manipulation.

To increase the national dividend, he showed a strong bias against distribution and pastoralism and in favour of production and agriculture where appropriate. He was no free market liberal.[88] He used on South African problems all the tools of a British welfare state liberal or Fabian socialist of the turn of the century, talking about national plans, minimum wage legislation, and suggesting legal intervention in the countryside on behalf of *bywoners*. He went further and implied quite radical interventions in relation to large landowners and in setting wages. But he never made clear how the white poor could be persuaded that a move to equality was in their interests, or how unskilled and unemployed whites would be reconciled to it. He remained a liberal in arguing that some 'risks' had to be taken, that securing the jobs and wage rates of the *already employed* would be in the interests of all. In other words, he had not by this time reconciled the problems of white poverty on the one hand, and black poverty on the other; he had not become a student of poverty in general, but he had moved from being a partisan of one disadvantaged group to that of another, from a minority group to a majority one — hardly a trivial shift. But the political problem of creating a widely disseminated consciousness of common interest among all groups eluded him, as it has eluded everyone else.

In talking of practical remedies, Macmillan adopted a modified 'back to the land' approach, itself popular among many Afrikaner leaders before 1930. He did this because, with his pessimistic view of industry, he saw a limited future for whites as townsmen — South Africa was unlike European countries in having no industrialized economy to absorb the expelled rural poor.[89] He combined this view with an acute sense of locality and the unalterable ecological features of the South African countryside. So he deplored the unscientific, opportunistic, and political character of irrigation and railway policies. But he was not a purveyor of large capital schemes: just as he had been suspicious of loose talk about 'factories', so he said nothing about irrigation in areas with high rainfall. Generally, he wrote of the necessity to change social structure and institutions as the prerequisite of growth, rather than make capital available.

As to the cities, Macmillan regarded them as receptacles for the expelled in which social processes worked to drag both white and black poor even further down. He did not have any major solutions to offer, but he showed the political obstacles to such palliatives as public health and housing. In challenging the ignorance of South Africa's legistators and city councillors, Macmillan drew attention to the difficulty of persuading the comfortable of the very existence of poverty, let alone the adoption of expensive solutions. His experience in Grahamstown from 1911 to 1917 could have been paralleled in the 1920s in Cradock, and surely elsewhere. There was a persistent tendency for Cradock's town fathers, and some visiting Union officials, to play down the existence of white poverty generally, and specifically in relation to housing.[90] In 1928, prodded by the Union government's Central Housing Board, the town council proposed a scheme directed at potential middle-class owners. The Board turned the proposal down. The council then proposed another scheme of ten houses for poorer people which was accepted and carried out, but the council refused to build another ten houses, even though the money was available.[91] Only at the end of the 1930s were housing schemes revived, involving two major schemes for whites by 1942. From 1936 on there is a spate of questionnaires on housing to the local white community which gives some idea of the scale and nature of poverty, and the degree to which it had changed from the early 1930s.[92]

The revival of interest in urban housing for whites seems to have been due to a changing political context in which there was increased competition for the loyalties of low-income Afrikaners, now becoming increasingly urbanized. It seems that Afrikaner leaders in the small towns now saw, as they had not done before, that urbanization was irreversible, and that the urban white poor had votes worth competing for by offering improved housing. In addition, rehousing made possible piecemeal segregation. These leaders had, in fact, moved to accept an industrialized and urbanized future for South Africa in a way in which Macmillan had not done by 1920. He may not have foreseen a South Africa of a few large metropolitan areas, but he did foresee the costs of an effective 'back to the land' policy. South African scholarship may have lost an urban historian, but it gained its first social historian and first critic of the historical attitudes behind the policies of the major parties.

5

JOHN PHILIP: TOWARDS A REASSESSMENT

ANDREW C. ROSS

PROFESSOR MACMILLAN never wrote the biography of John Philip which he had planned. After he had worked through the massive collection of Philip papers at his disposal to write his two famous studies *The Cape Colour Question*, and *Bantu, Boer, and Briton*, these papers were destroyed in the notorious fire in the library at the University of the Witwatersrand. Deprived of this resource, he felt a biography was not possible. It may be, however, that he had decided to move on to other things anyway, and the fire made the move easier. It is by no means clear that John Philip interested Macmillan deeply. Philip was rather a convenient hook onto which Macmillan could hang a fundamental critique of the South Africa of his own day, together with suggestions for a policy that would lead to a better future.

His two books based on the Philip papers were, and are, still of great importance. They presented an alternative picture of John Philip to the virtual caricature that then existed of the missionary in South African historiography, and Philip's original words are quoted so extensively in both that these volumes do compensate, in some measure, for the loss created by the Wits fire.

Although no one writing about the South Africa of the first half of the nineteenth century can avoid mention of Philip, there has been no major study devoted to his life and work in English since Macmillan's work. There have been, however, a number of important articles in the last twenty years dealing with Philip, the most important and, in my view, the most perceptive, being Andrew Nash's 'Dr Philip, the spread of civilisation and liberalism in South Africa'.[1]

Macmillan's work is still of fundamental importance and anyone interested in Philip has to begin there — but it still is only a beginning. Macmillan, just as much as Theal and Cory before him, or Nash and others more recently, worked within a format that inhibited his ability to gain a full understanding of who John Philip really was.

This format has four main limiting features. First, these scholars are writing not primarily about the past, but specifically to affect the South Africa of their own day; this tends to be more important than seeing Philip for who and what he was.[2] Second, they have little knowledge of the Scotland of the late eighteenth century which so profoundly shaped Philip. Third, none of them has any knowledge of, nor apparently, any interest in the evangelical revival in Britain and the USA, of which Philip was an outstanding representative; and fourth, they consider Philip on the South African stage alone and thus fail to see him as participating in a worldwide conflict of ideas.

I would like to consider each of these four limiting factors in order to indicate a way towards the construction of a more accurate picture of John Philip — a picture that will be different from those hitherto accepted, on the 'right' or the 'left', in South African historiography.

Andrew Nash's article, already referred to, and that of Julius Lewin[3] are typical of what has been written about Philip recently. Both authors openly admit that their central concern is a critique of 'liberalism' in South Africa. John Philip is considered because of the tradition that sees him as the 'father' of South African liberalism. He is not discussed in his own right, but only in so far as he can be seen as responsible for strengths and weaknesses that have characterized South African liberalism until the present day.

Macmillan's innovative work on Philip also suffers from this inhibiting factor. Macmillan was not so much interested in developing a critique of South African liberalism as in trying to encourage liberalism among the South African whites of his day. By attacking Theal and Cory's understanding of Philip, and by using extensive quotations from, and paraphrases of, Philip's own words, he did go a long way to allowing his readers to arrive at a better understanding of the man. However, his primary concern was to change the minds of his readers about the South African government's policy towards the serious problems of land, race and rural poverty. These were entirely worthy aims, but they led him to omit those important aspects of Philip's life and work which did not fit readily into achieving this end. There are two prime examples of this: his treatment of Philip's views on racial equality and his treatment of Philip's relationship with James Read and his sons.

It is clear that Macmillan plays down Philip's relations with James Read and his sons (the latter were, in today's parlance, 'Cape Coloureds') to the point that their existence appears peripheral to any understanding of Philip. Yet Christopher Saunders, in his article in *The South African Outlook*[4] has drawn attention to Read's importance, which is there for all who care to go through the mass of Philip correspondence. Saunders justifiably complains of pro-Philip writers who play down Read in order to build up their hero.

Macmillan did not simply play Read down in order to build Philip up, however. It seems more likely that Macmillan felt that Philip's very close relationship with the Reads was an aspect of his life that it would be best to treat with circumspection. In the South Africa of his day it would not have helped his plea for a reasonable and sensible liberalism to have highlighted the fact that Read, the allegedly notoriously unbalanced negrophile,[5] and his 'Coloured' sons were among Philip's closest associates. The evidence of their close relationship is unmistakeable in the vast number of letters from the two Reads to Philip on eastern frontier matters, and in the many letters of Philip where their judgements are reflected in what he wrote.[6]

The relationship began soon after Philip's arrival at the Cape when, despite Read's having been placed under ecclesiastical discipline by his predecessors, Philip came to his own opinion of the man and placed him in charge at Bethelsdorp. The closeness between the two men grew from then on. It was Read, and, later also his son, James jr., who were Philip's companions on so many of the long treks he made throughout South Africa — treks on which he learned so much and which shaped his understanding of people and events. It was Read who was Philip's companion on the very important and very long trek of 1842 which took Philip through the lands on the eastern frontier and through a great deal of what is now Lesotho, the Free State, the northern Cape and southern Botswana. Philip felt that his understanding of South Africa and its possible future was confirmed by what he saw and learned on this journey.

Although Macmillan never denies that Read accompanied Philip on many treks and wrote to him often, he does not dwell on their association and the reader is given no chance of knowing of Read's role as key adviser to Philip, or that he was Philip's main link with the opinions of the Kat River people and other 'Kaapse Volk', as well as with the Xhosa — particularly with Maqoma and his people. Moreover, Macmillan fails to mention a number of situations in which Philip unambiguously demonstrated the closeness of his relationship with the Reads, the most important of these incidents being the occasion when Read and his family were bitterly attacked by a group of other missionaries of the London Mission Society (LMS) led by Calderwood. This matter looms so large in Philip's correspondence with the LMS that there is no way that Macmillan could have overlooked it inadvertently.[7]

Calderwood and his friends were furious with Read for having taken the word of two of his Kat River Church elders over that of a white missionary. Philip backed Read during a long and bitter series of meetings which generated a mass of letters to and fro between the parties. In summing up the situation to his fellow LMS Directors in London, Philip wrote:

The parties can never be brought to act together and the only thing we can do with them is to keep them from threatening each other and from open war. They are entirely different men and represent two different classes of missionary. What is esteemed and practised as a virtue by one, is viewed as a crime in the eyes of the other. You will find the key to this secret in the following passage in Calderwood's letter of 8 July, No 9 'We object to the kind of intercourse which he has with the coloured people as indicated by his letters'.... In order to raise the people James Read would treat them as brethren and to this Mr Calderwood says 'We object' and to this object 'for the sake of the people themselves'. Both systems have been tried and their fruits are before the public. The Hottentots were converted on the principle of love and those that treat them on the other principle cannot have their love and this creates the [illegible] of the complainants against the Hottentots and the jealousy lest the caffres should be 'spoiled' in the same way.[8]

The fact that Philip backed the Reads against Calderwood, Brownlee and other traditional missionary 'heroes' is totally omitted by Macmillan. Since the evidence of the close relationship between Philip and the Reads, and the similarity in their attitudes to the problems of their day, is so clear in the records, one is forced to conclude that Macmillan deliberately excluded this important area of Philip's life. He did so, it would seem, because he felt that to let this relationship appear as it really had been would hinder rather than help his attempt to persuade South African whites of the reasonableness of his 'liberal' case. This case mattered more than a full exposition of Philip's life and work.

Any discussion of Philip and the Reads leads straight on to a discussion of Philip's attitude to race and Macmillan's treatment of it.

What strikes one on reading Philip's letters and reports is that, of the numerous specific statements that clearly reflect Philip's deeply held belief in racial equality, Macmillan refers only to one, and then only to qualify it. This is on a long report that Philip wrote for William Wilberforce in 1824 in which he asserted that the Khoi were often enslaved by men who were their moral and intellectual inferiors. On this Macmillan commented:

This last suggestion, that individual Hottentots might be superior to some colonists, for the time when it was written is a startling hypothesis, and an instance of Philip's extreme views. It is, however, an isolated statement, and in fact, goes no further than to show his profound belief in the potential equality of the races.[9]

Yet Philip's statement was in no way 'a startling hypothesis' among radical evangelical circles in either the United Kingdom or the United States. The ignorance of this movement in South African historiography will be considered a little later. What is even more surprising is Macmillan's assertion that this was an isolated statement.

Macmillan must have known that Philip had asserted the same thing in a report to his fellow LMS Directors in 1821.[10] His whole campaign for full civil rights for all the King's subjects in the colony made no sense apart from such a belief in racial equality. When one considers these two reports alongside his preface to *Researches in South Africa* and his report to the American Board of Commissioners for Foreign Missions of 1833, then it is Macmillan's statement that is extraordinary.

The American Board had requested a report from Philip to help them decide whether or not to begin work in southern Africa. Philip prepared the report with great care, and it was published by the Americans in their journal *The Missionary Herald*.[11] There Philip wrote:

So far as my observation extends, it appears to me that the natural capacity of the African is nothing inferior to that of the European. At our schools, the children of Hottentots, of Bushmen, of Caffres [Xhosa] and of the Bechuanas, are in no respect behind the capacity of those of European parents and the people of our missionary stations are in many instances superior in intelligence to those who look down on them, as belonging to an inferior caste.

In their day, Philip's colonial critics were correct in perceiving that he was a believer in equality. Why then did Macmillan ignore so much evidence, a great deal of which was published and necessitated no searching of manuscripts? Again, one can only conclude that Macmillan did so because it did not fit with his objective in writing about Philip. He was not interested in exploring all the facets of Philip's life and work, but in influencing his South African contemporaries in favour of different social and political policies from those then being pursued. The profound impact of Social Darwinism on the English-speaking world was still so strong in the second and third decades of the twentieth century that any emphasis on Philip's ideas on race would have robbed him of credibility in the eyes of the public which Macmillan was seeking to influence.[12]

Evidence in Macmillan's papers confirms the view that attitudes of the day were such that Philip's views on race had to be played down if he wanted to influence the South African audience for whom he was writing. Macmillan was warned by Miss Gertrude Edwards[13] to tone down certain passages in the original manuscript. She advised him, for instance, to cut out the statement that 'the white man's burden is borne on black shoulders' and a reference to 'the offence of dark skins'.[14] Perhaps typically, she believed that there must be some black intellectual 'inferiority', and asked what contribution the 'Bantu' had made to the world. In justifying a 'softly, softly' approach, she quoted a Sesotho proverb to the effect that 'It is better to fight your enemy on the hill than to meet him in the village'.

The second element in the South African approach to Philip which has inhibited a full understanding, has been the general ignorance of the history of Scotland in the period during which Philip grew up.

One of the crudest examples of this occurs in the entry on John Philip in the *The Dictionary of South African Biography*. This refers to Philip's parents as having been members of the Church of England. One can only explain this by suggesting that, since a biographical fragment written by Philip's son and grandson reported that the Doctor's parents had been members of the Established Church, the author of the DSAB article did not realize that the Church of England neither was, nor is, the Established Church in Scotland.

Much more important, however, is the fact that South African writing on Philip, even that carried out by someone of Scottish origin, like Macmillan, reflects insufficient knowledge of, and reflection upon, the Scottish influences on Philip. Yet these influences, after all, were fundamental to the shaping of the man.

There were two influences of particular importance. The first was that, until well into the lifetime of Philip's parents, lowland Scots had had as their neighbours a warlike tribal society, speaking a totally different language, and whose way of life constantly threatened law and order in the lowlands. It was only in the bitter years after 1746 that this last major tribal society in Western Europe was destroyed. The life experience of the older generation among whom Philip grew up consequently had many features in common with the lives of the Cape colonists in the first decades of the nineteenth century. As he grew up, Philip saw the sons and grandsons of the warriors who went down to defeat at Culloden take their place in Scottish society as teachers, ministers, and lawyers, as well as in many 'humbler' occupations. If this could happen to the sons of Lochiel, why not to the sons of Ngqika?

The second important feature of Philip's Scottish background was that the years 1750–1815 saw a profound revolution in Scotland. As T. C. Smout has pointed out, the Scotland of 1750 was little different from the Scotland of 1650 or 1550 in terms of basic agricultural and economic structures.[15] After 1750 the agricultural and industrial revolutions transformed the country with extraordinary rapidity. In the period 1780–1815, particularly, the first textile wave of the industrial revolution, which was centred on the small burghs of Scotland and did not lead to massive urbanization, brought Scotland one of the very few periods of general economic prosperity that the country has ever seen. Moreover, this prosperity was shared by the skilled artisan as well as by the entrepreneur and the professional classes: John Philip himself started life as a weaver, a group that gained particular prosperity at that time. And this was a time which also saw the freeing of the Scottish miners and salt-workers from a legal status virtually indistinguishable from slavery.

To Philip, the Scotland he knew was living proof that Adam Smith's ideas worked. Freed from feudal inhibitions and slavery, the system of *laissez-faire* economics, when combined with just government and civil rights, brought prosperity to all and created a situation of social mobility which gave wide opportunities to people of talent. Philip, like so many of the early missionaries, belonged to the class which benefited so remarkably in this period — the skilled artisans. He did not see the subsequent developments in Scotland, when the next stage of the industrial revolution turned central Scotland into one of the great centres of heavy industry in the world, and made Glasgow one of the most desperate centres of urban deprivation in Europe.

Philip grew up, through youth and manhood, in a Scotland that appeared to be entering a new era of prosperity and justice. *Laissez-faire* economics, good government and civil rights could do the same for the Cape Colony and would enable the Kaapse Volk[16] to play the role of the Scottish working classes of his youth; the Xhosa and Mfengu could follow in the path of the Highland tribesmen. There would be opportunity to rise in the social scale for some and prosperity for all.

No Englishman of that era had had the same experience of life and, even in Scotland by the 1820s, the Highlands and the Highlander had become wrapped in the romantic haze that has only recently begun to be cleared away. This romanticism quickly erased the memory of the bitterly difficult situation of living with Highland warriors as neighbours, and that erasure diminished the achievement of the school and the Kirk in transforming warrior people into the men and women who played such a significant role in modern Scotland and the wider world. Philip grew up before this occurred and so came to South Africa with perceptions not shared by his English contemporaries or by Scots of a later generation. This Scottish dimension, which unfortunately cannot be fully developed in this brief paper, is totally absent from the existing literature on Philip. Yet it is essential if John Philip is to be understood.

The third limitation in the existing writing about John Philip is its lack of understanding of the nature of the particular evangelical tradition in which he stood. The social and political 'quietism' of the evangelical movement in the second half of the nineteenth century appears to have led historians into ignoring the radical element in earlier evangelicalism. In Britain, a large section of evangelicals led by Wilberforce understood the call of the Christian gospel as demanding that they attempt to transform the 'world', as well as to convert individuals. The reforms that Wilberforce deemed necessary do not seem all that radical to modern eyes, except for the abolition of slavery, which attacked the 'sacred rights' of property. Nevertheless, social and political structures were to be reformed and not simply regarded as natural evils which Christians had no

132

alternative but to endure. There were many less famous British evangelicals who were a good deal more radical than Wilberforce in their understanding of what was demanded by reform. In the United States, the very influential evangelical group led by Charles Finney and the Tappan brothers certainly were committed to a much more radical restructuring of society than anything he envisaged. However, the important thing that bound them all together, from the moderate Wilberforce to people like Gerrit Smith who advocated slave rebellion was their deep belief that the gospel message demanded the creation of a just society and not simply spiritual change in individuals.

C. W. de Kiewiet talks of the 'impact of city-bred liberalism' upon Cape society and makes clear that he sees the British administration and the missionaries as together forming the channel for this disturbing influence.[17] This is not typical of the attitude of historians writing on the history of the Cape in the first decades of the nineteenth century: de Kiewiet's approach dismisses as secondary the deep divisions between administrators and missionaries and concentrates instead on the fact that both were alien and both brought new ideas to the Cape. Officials and missionaries are both seen simply as parts of a single 'city bred liberalism'. This is an extraordinary concept since, at least until the 1840s, the British administrators were traditional Tories. They may have demanded a standard of law and order disliked by Cape frontiersmen but they were in no way 'liberals'. Indeed, they were drawn from a class hostile towards those they despised as 'enthusiasts'. De Kiewiet, in addition, paid no attention to the profound division between those missionaries who were essentially pietist, and those of the tradition in which Philip stood.

Even on the issue of the abolition of slavery, which all evangelicals agreed was a sinful institution, there was division about how far this truth committed Christians to political action in order to end it. A further division existed between those evangelicals who were willing to take political action against slavery, but without any real concern for black people or their human dignity, and those who saw the two as inextricably linked.

There has been a tendency in American historiography to see all evangelical abolitionists as indifferent to the interests of black people other than on the issue of slavery. The work of Sorin on the New York abolitionists, however, together with the writing of Duberman,

T. L. Smith, R. H. Abzug and others, has shown that there was a powerful group among American evangelicals who were committed, not only to the abolition of slavery, but also to the advancement of black people.[18]

John Philip stands clearly as one of the most articulate of the British contingent among these radical evangelicals. His attitude towards race chimes in with the views of the North American group, although he would have shied away from Gerrit Smith's advocacy of slave rebellion.[19] The thought of Theodore Weld, whom Brauer and others believe did more even than Garrison to popularize the radical abolitionist position,[20] is clearly linked with that of Philip. After a series of debates on slavery and the humanity of the black person, famous in American history as the 'Lane Debates', Weld created the Lane Anti-Slavery Society, a model of the new radicalism. The constitution of the new society has been summarized thus:

The society's object? 'Immediate emancipation of the whole coloured race, within the United States' — slaves from master and 'free coloured man from the oppression of public sentiment' — 'and the elevation of both to an intellectual, moral and political equality with the whites.' Why? because the black man was created by God as 'a moral agent, the keeper of his own happiness, the executive of his own power, the accountable arbiter of his own choice'.[21]

Weld, and the widespread movement which he initiated, called for black people to be free so that they could take their place within American civilization. This was also Philip's view. Christianity and civilization were inextricably linked in his, as in Weld's, thought. In 1833 the year before the 'Lane Debate', Philip wrote his carefully considered report to the American Board, already referred to above. In it he wrote:

The civilisation of the people among whom we labour in Africa is not our highest object; but that object never can be secured and rendered permanent among them without their civilisation.... The blessings of civilisation are a few of the blessings which the Christian religion scatters in her progress to immortality; but they are to be cherished for their own sake as well as for ours, as they are necessary to perpetuate her reign and extend her conquests.

Because multitudes in England and America have lost their religion, to which they are indebted for their civilisation, many pious people make light of civilisation as connected with the labour of missionaries: but it should never be lost sight of that if men may retain their civilisation after they have lost their religion, that there can be no religion in such a country as this without civilisation: and that it can have no permanent abode among us, if that civilisation does not shoot up into regular and good government.

This close interrelating of Christianity, civilization and good government linked what might be called the 'radical' evangelicals. Wilberforce's prominence and his conservatism on so many issues, other than slavery, has distracted attention from the parallel radicalism among British evangelicals. People like Robert Haldane,[22] for example, one of the founders of evangelicalism in Scotland and an important influence on the young Philip, was quite certain that the French Revolution was a great event in human history. Its aims were wholly good but, he insisted, the French failed in their noble enterprise because of their lack of Christian faith.[23] Of the same mould was Henry Joy McCracken, the founder of the Sunday School movement in Ireland and one of the many Presbyterian ministers executed or imprisoned by the British for their part in the rising of the United Irishmen in 1798.

This tradition of evangelicalism created a kind of 'evangelical package' in which civilization, civil rights, good government and evangelical Christianity were all bound together — and they were either presented as a package or not at all, since none of the elements could really survive on its own. Fundamental to this understanding was the belief that the 'package' was for all humanity, irrespective of race. This phenomenon has been characterized as 'conversionism' by Philip Curtin[24] who uses this word to contrast this view with that which dominated the second half of the nineteenth century, which he characterizes as 'trusteeship'. The latter attitude, profoundly shaped by Social Darwinism, led people, even those labelled negrophiles, to hold black people as inferior by nature. Negrophiles or 'liberals' of that era were distinguished from others by their insistence that these inferiors were to be protected from exploitation, and to be educated and trained in ways appropriate to their inferior abilities. Ideas of 'trusteeship' persisted well into the twentieth century.[25]

It is here that the third element in the restricted view of Philip overlaps with the fourth. Hitherto, consideration of Philip has always portrayed him simply as an actor on the South African stage. What has to be considered is that he was a representative of this radical evangelicalism which was conducting a campaign — if not worldwide, at least throughout the English-speaking world — to make its views effective in the United States and the British Empire. John Philip has to be seen not as an eccentric missionary in South Africa, nor as one figure among many in this vague 'city-bred liberalism', but, very specifically, as the leader in South Africa of an evangelical crusade that stretched from New York to New Zealand.[26] As Richard Watson, the most prominent of the radical preachers among the Methodists in England, put it, this crusade was designed to ensure 'that the purity, and justice and kindness of his (Jesus) religion shall influence all institutions of society;... that all public oppression and wrong shall be removed'.[27]

South African historiographical ignorance of this movement and of Philip's role in it may also account for the lack of comment on its defeat by a new philosophy of race, civilization and progress. When John Philip, by then a tired old man, retired to Hankey to live among his beloved Kaapse Volk, he took with him a terrible sense of defeat. He was quite clear that it was not the traditions of Cape society that had defeated him, nor the conservativism of the Afrikaner people, but the attitude of mind of the British settlers and officials. It was British settlers who brought to South Africa a new set of ideas, a new understanding of humanity and human history determined by racial hierarchy. This was an understanding just as foreign to South Africa as 'the city-bred liberalism' of de Kiewiet, Walker, de Klerk and others.

In the 1840s this new attitude to race began to wield an ever-wider influence in the English-speaking world and later, in the 1860s, in the form of Social Darwinism, it appeared to be blessed with the irrefutable confirmation of science and became the dominant understanding of race in the western world. This world-view associated civilization and inevitable progress with an hierarchic racial understanding of man. The superior race was civilized and the inferior races gave way before it and the inevitable advance of civilization from which they were excluded by nature.

In South Africa, the first signs of this modern racist philosophy were manifested by the English settlers of the eastern Cape, and not by the Afrikaners. These latter, whether Cape Afrikaner or Voortrekker, had firm beliefs about the relations of master and servant but no coherent racist philosophy. Indeed, they were still largely pragmatic in their approach to race. In the Cape, it was an alliance of the Cape Afrikaners with Stockenstrom, Fairbairn and the leaders of the Kaapse Volk that brought about the non-racial franchise of 1853. The Voortrekkers were willing to engage black allies to fight against other whites[28] and a Voortrekker hero, Louis Trichardt, was willing to live with his family and friends as an ally and client of the Xhosa chief Hintsa.[29]

It was in the speeches of the leader of the British settlers of the eastern Cape, J. M. Bowker, that we first find notes that resonate with the tone of the new racist philosophy. The savage must give way, literally, before the advance of civilization and civilized man. In many passages of his speeches and letters, it appears that the 'savage' might be allowed to stay and survive in some kind of peripheral and menial role. However, elsewhere, the new note of the predestined replacement of the inferior race by the superior is sounded. In his famous 'Springbok' speech,[30] Bowker argues that the Xhosa must disappear before the advance of civilization as had done the great herds of springbok. This is a different 'civilization' from that talked of by Philip or Weld.

Despite the fact that this entry of the new racism into South Africa was by way of the English, racism is still seen as a product of 'the frontier' or of Afrikaner Calvinism in much South African historiography.[31] Its British origin was identified at the time by William Porter, the Cape Attorney-General. This Ulsterman, with close family connections to the radical presbyterianism of the McCracken variety, wrote of the appearance of the new ideology of race and progress among the settlers of the eastern Cape:

... this profound contempt of colour, and lofty pride of caste contains within it the concentrated essence and odious principle of all the tyranny and oppression which white has exercised over black. But the Cape-frontier Englishman is not alone. A member of the British House of Commons, in one of the New Zealand debates, has lately said, that the brown man is destined everywhere to disappear before the white man, and *such is the law of nature*.[32]

From the late 1830s onward, Philip had complained that it was the British settlers, not the Afrikaners, who most bitterly opposed all his policies for the indigenous people. For a long time he was able to comfort himself with his deeply held belief that the imperial government would always uphold equal rights for all its subjects. In the 1840s things changed. The behaviour of two governors, first Pottinger and then Smith, disturbed him deeply. As he came to appreciate exactly what were the attitudes of the new Colonial Secretary, Earl Grey, he concluded that his faith in Whitehall was now worthless. His disillusion was made complete by the attitude of the officers sent by Grey to South Africa. One of them, William S. Hogge, an Imperial Commissioner sent to aid Sir Harry Smith, wrote:

The history of the Cape is already written in that of America, and the gradual increase of the white race must eventually, though slowly, ensure the disappearance of the Black. Providence vindicates this its unalterable law by rendering all the philanthropic efforts that have been made to avert such a destiny subservient to its fulfilment.[33]

Philip did not live to see it, but the non-racial franchise, won despite the opposition from the British settlers, was the only important victory for the beliefs to which he had dedicated his life. So much else that he had worked and hoped for appeared to have been frustrated, although there is still a great deal of necessary work to be done on analysing what fruitful seeds, if any, his policies sowed in South Africa's soil.

A key point of this paper is that the defeat of Philip's ideas was one episode in the conflict, throughout the English-speaking world, between one perception of humanity and history and another. The radical evangelical 'conversionist' approach towards history and humanity was defeated by the new racism in those areas dominated by Britain. Despite the great influence of evangelical abolitionists in the United States, after the end of the Civil War the new racism triumphed there also.[34] This new racism, then, was not a notion rooted in Cape history, nor was it to be found growing out of Afrikanerdom; it was something that entered South Africa from outside — from Britain and the United States.

John Philip can only begin to be understood when he is seen as an important actor in this conflict over race: as a Scot, produced by a specific period of Scottish history; and as a leading figure of the radical tradition among evangelicals. He will not be understood, and consequently some of the conflicts in this period of South African history will not be understood, if his life and work are approached within the narrow limits in which it has hitherto been constrained.

Despite the constraints under which he worked, W. M. Macmillan's two studies, *The Cape Colour Question*, and *Bantu, Boer, and Briton* remain of fundamental importance. They are the beginning of modern historical study of the period of South Africa's history spanned by Philip's life. They are also vital sources of primary material no longer available in any other form. Perhaps most importantly, they give the reader insight into a brilliant and honest mind struggling with the problems of South Africa in the inter-war years as well as with the problems of writing history.

6

JAMES CROPPER, JOHN PHILIP AND THE
RESEARCHES IN SOUTH AFRICA

ROBERT ROSS

IN 1835 James Cropper, a prosperous Quaker merchant living in Liverpool and one of the leading British abolitionists, wrote to Dr John Philip, the superintendent of the London Missionary Society in South Africa, offering to finance the republication of the latter's book, *Researches in South Africa*, which had been issued seven years earlier. This offer was turned down.

This exchange was recorded by William Miller Macmillan in his first major historical work, *The Cape Coloured Question*,[1] which was primarily concerned with the struggles of Dr John Philip on behalf of the so-called 'Cape Coloureds'. These resulted in Ordinance 50 of 1828 and its confirmation in London, which lifted any civil disabilities for free people of colour. The correspondence on which it was based, in John Philip's private papers, was destroyed in the 1931 fire in the Gubbins library, Johannesburg, and I have not been able to locate any copies at Cropper's end. Any explanation as to why these letters were written must therefore remain speculative. Nevertheless, even were the correspondence extant, it is unlikely that it would contain a satisfactory explanation of what at first sight might seem a rather curious exchange. The two men had enough in common with each other, and knew each other's minds well enough, for them merely to give their surface motivation, and not to be concerned with deeper ideological justification. And the former level can be reconstructed fairly easily.

Cropper, it may be assumed, saw South Africa as a 'warning for the West Indies', which was especially timely in 1835 as the British Caribbean was having to adjust to the emancipation of its slaves.[2] The *Researches* gave many examples of how the nominally free could still be maintained in effective servitude, and Cropper undoubtedly hoped that this pattern would not be repeated. The slaves should not be free in name only, but free enough to allow the West Indies to prosper as a free market economy — the only way, in Cropper's eyes, that they possibly could. Philip, we know, did not wish to exacerbate old sores — not surprisingly since the initial publication of the *Researches* had caused a storm at the Cape and had led to an expensive libel suit, as Cropper well knew.[3] Moreover, by 1835 he was more concerned with the events on the Cape Colony's eastern frontier than with the status and oppression of the Khoikhoi, who had been the main subject of the *Researches*.[4] Underlying these reasons, however, there would seem to be a number of hitherto unrecognized connections between the two parts of the British Empire, and a number of ideological concerns, mainly to do with the meaning of freedom, which I hope to elucidate in the course of this paper.

I

John Philip was the archetype of the 'turbulent priest', an intermittently recurring figure in South African history, who does not keep to his cloth but who rather meddles in 'politics' — that is, one who speaks out in opposition to the established order. Similarly, *Researches in South Africa* was the first clear South African example of a campaigning book, written not merely to inform but rather as a call to action. It is a book which mirrors the tension that Philip himself must have felt about his role. He had come to South Africa as a convinced Tory, and had to a certain extent owed his appointment as superintendent of missions to this fact. The Director of the LMS considered that this would ease his relations with the colonial government and allow the healing of the rifts that emerged in the past years between the rigid Toryism of successive governors and the campaigning evangelism of, notably, James Read. Philip was also concerned, by virtue of his function, primarily with the organization of evangelization. Nevertheless, he became embroiled in open conflict with the colonial authorities, over the freedom of the press, over the position of the Khoikhoi within the colony and, later, over the policy to be followed with regard to the Xhosa and the northern frontier. To a contemporary governor he was 'more a *politician* than a missionary',[5] and historians of the settler persuasion were to be more stringent in their strictures.[6]

Philip himself recognized, at least subconsciously, the contradiction between his spiritual calling and his temporal activities. The last chapter of the *Researches*, whose tone is somewhat discordant with what precedes it, is an almost apologetic assertion of the centrality of the Protestant religion for material progress as well as for salvation. 'The Word of God', he wrote, 'is the only instrument adequate to the regeneration of the world.'[7] In the very last words of the book he stressed how the missionaries were working to accelerate 'the approach of that moral revolution which will shortly usher in the kingdoms of this world as the Kingdoms of our Lord and of his Christ'.[8] On the other hand, Philip did not place any emphasis on the kernel of the evangelical message — the salvation of individual souls. This was a characteristic, if surprising, omission, which was perhaps the result of either his lack of involvement in day-to-day pastoral work, or of his age (a generation older than most missionaries) or perhaps of his own lack of an emotional conversion.[9] In time this trait was to lead to conflict with those missionaries, notably Robert Moffat, for whom the individual gospel was far more important than the social.[10]

Philip, then, chose in the *Researches*, and in his work in general, to concentrate on the 'secondary blessings which "Christianity scatters in its march to immortality"'.[11] The reason for this emphasis is perhaps best exemplified in the report he wrote in 1825 on that much maligned mission station, Bethelsdorp in the eastern Cape, near Port Elizabeth, and which he reprinted in his book. He commented on the considerable consumption of British-made goods among the people of the station. This had reached 20,000 Rix-dollars (about £1,500) in 1822 and had probably increased since then.[12] Numerous stone houses were being built, which allowed the young women to keep their clothes, on which they spent much money, in a reasonable state, and thus to maintain their respectability. At the same time books could be kept in these houses without their coming to grief and, as Philip argued elsewhere, the habit of reading, much stressed by Protestantism anyway, was the first requirement of an inquiring and improving mind.[13] The number of 'native mechanics', was also steadily increasing.[14]

The justification for this emphasis on externals was, in the first place, propagandist. Philip had to counter the claim, as he reported it, that

You do not civilize the people; they are fit for nothing but slaves to the boers; you can never make them tradesmen, and you can never raise them above their present vitiated state, nor impart to them a taste for the decencies of life.[15]

It was, at the very least, a tactical necessity in his conflicts with the government to be able to point to the improvement in the manners and circumstances of the mission inhabitants. Later, when he was looking back over the struggles and writing with more sharpness than earlier, Philip would comment:

The question between us and the government was one of civilisation. The criterion of a people's civilisation with Lord Charles Somerset was whether the people used knives and forks.[16]

There was, though, a more fundamental reason for Philip's stress on the achievement of a respectable way of life. He believed that Christianity and savagery were incompatible, and conversely that Christianity and civilization were indivisible:

While I am satisfied, from abundance of incontrovertible facts, that permanent societies of Christians can never be maintained among an uncivilized people without imparting to them the arts and habits of civilized life, I am satisfied, upon ground no less evident, that if missionaries lose their religion and sink into mere mechanics, the work of civilization and moral improvement will speedily retrograde.[17]

The work of raising the material level of their charges was thus just as much a sacred task for the missionaries as was the preaching of the gospel. It was this equation which provided the mainspring for all Philip's political and missionary activity.

II

As Philip saw it, the achievement of such progress required independence or at least economic liberty. This vision derived from at least three separable, if interconnected, sources. First there was the general intellectual climate in Scotland.[18] Even though he never attended university — he owed his Doctor's title to the combined efforts of Columbia and Princeton, without his ever having set foot in America — Philip was well acquainted with the writings of the Scottish enlightenment, and with the political economists. As a long-term minister of an important church in the university city of

Aberdeen — where, incidentally, he had the good taste to marry a Miss Ross — this was only to be expected. Second, Philip was, in ecclesiastical terms, a convinced 'independent', deploring state intervention in Church matters and arguing against state subsidies for churches. He believed that the congregation itself should be responsible for the purity of its doctrine, the upkeep of its churches and the support of its minister. Third, there was his own background. In his early years, Philip himself had been the epitome of the craftsman who was able to raise himself from relatively humble origins to a respected social position by dint of his own sustained efforts. He had begun work as a weaver in his native Fife at the age of eleven, by the age of twenty he was works manager of a modern 'power' mill in Dundee, and shortly afterwards he became an independent weaver, with sufficient success that in 'six months [he] was doing well'. Only after this did he decide to train for the ministry.[19] This was the sort of career pattern which he saw as an ideal. 'The labourers and artisans ... in the manufacturing districts of North Britain'[20] were the reference group against whom he measured the Khoikhoi. It did not matter, as he recognized, that such success could not be achieved by everyone. It was the opportunity for advancement that was essential, for without it there was no incentive for the continual self-discipline inherent in a Christian life.

Given liberty in a society, material, intellectual and religious improvement were seen to be inevitable. In later life, Philip quoted with approval a speech by William Wilberforce in which he rather optimistically saw freedom as the palliative for all Africa's ills:

Africa will become the seat of civilisation, because the seat of liberty — the seat of commerce, because the seat of liberty — the seat of science, because the seat of liberty — the seat of religion, because the seat of liberty — the seat of morals because the seat of liberty — the seat of happiness, because the seat of liberty.[21]

This demand for freedom permeated all Philip's actions in South Africa. It united his earliest work as a declared opponent of what he saw as Lord Charles Somerset's tyranny with his later defence of the Khoi. In the miniscule society of English Cape Town, Philip could not fail to become aware of the highhandedness of the Governor, and quite soon after his arrival in South Africa he moved into opposition, both openly and covertly. His first actions, in alliance with Thomas

Pringle and John Fairbairn, were on behalf of the 1820 settlers and to bring about the freedom of the South African press.[22] He was also instrumental in having the Commission of Enquiry to the Colony in 1824, which would eventually lead to the major reorganization of the Cape government and the demise of Somerset's personal rule. To do this he had to. work secretly, through William Wilberforce and Steven Lushington, two evangelical members of the British Parliament; they were able to persuade the House of Commons to appoint the Commission without its true goal being apparent, especially as its terms of reference also included the affairs of Mauritius and Sri Lanka — presumably as camouflage. For this reason, Philip's role can only be gauged from his own reminiscences some twenty years later, not a particularly reliable type of source at the best of times, and certainly not when deriving from someone as convinced of his own importance as Philip was. Nevertheless, since there does not seem to be any other clear reason for the despatch of the Commission, his account may perhaps be accepted.[23]

Philip's first main work, though, was concerned with the relieving of the civil disabilities of the Khoisan. As evidenced by the first volume of the *Researches*, which was largely a campaigning book devoted to the removal of these disabilities, he saw these as deriving from three sources. The first was the 'Hottentot Code', promulgated by the Earl of Caledon, Governor of the Colony, in 1809. This was intended by its original authors to save the Khoi from the murderous oppression of the Dutch farmers, in particular in the eastern Cape. Indeed, by guiding exploitation within legal bounds, it may well have had that effect, and may have led to a reduction in the use of brute force against Khoi labourers.[24] Nevertheless, as Philip saw it, on the basis of considerable experience, it had the effect of maintaining the Khoi in the service of the farmers, or other Europeans, without the possibility of their escaping or even changing their level of employment. It did this in two ways. First, it required Khoi to have a fixed abode, which, since it was impossible for them to acquire land, virtually forced them to work for a farmer unless they could gain access to a mission station. It also demanded that any Khoi away from home carry a pass, made out by a European, on pain of being arrested and set to work for a neighbouring farmer. As a result, it was impossible for a Khoi to seek out the most advantageous employer and thus effectively obviated the need for competition for labour, to the great detriment of the employees.[25]

145

Second, Sir John Cradock's proclamation of 1812 allowed farmers to bind to them all Khoi children between the ages of eight and eighteen, theoretically to pay for the cost of their upbringing. Often this period could be surreptitiously extended, as it was difficult for Khoi to demonstrate that their period of service had ended. Moreover, it gave their parents the choice between staying with the children's master or breaking up their family, and thus tied them to the farmer.[26]

Third, and for Philip probably most significant, the administration of the law was one-sidedly in the hands of the farmers and their allies. At the local level the veldcornets, who were supposed to administer the codes initially set up for the protection of the Khoi, in fact invariably favoured their potential employers. These men therefore provided the Khoi with no escape from the oppression they experienced on the farms. Nor were the district magistrates much help. It was not merely that any Khoi lodging a complaint against a farmer would himself be put in gaol until the case was heard, often weeks if not months later, thus badly prejudicing the matter; but rather, the magistrates themselves acted as the first line of oppression, making it impossible for Khoi to escape from their bondage to the farmers. Often indeed the Khoi were forced to work for the magistrate himself at miserable rates of remuneration. The consequence was clear:

In a state of society where there is one law for the rich and another for the poor, and the sanctions of the law are borrowed to render the poor the victims of oppression, moral distinctions are confounded and the names of virtue or vice come to be regarded as exchangeable terms.... While the administration of justice is confined to one particular class of the community only, however that administration may be regarded for its equity, it is nothing better than the equity of a party of Bedouin Arabs, who make an equal distribution of the spoil they have taken from the unprotected caravan....[27]

What was necessary to remedy this situation was not merely a reform of the legal administration, and the institution of a system of laws which paid no account to racial status, but also the establishment of a free market in labour:

To allow the Hottentot the power of carrying his labour to the best market, is one of the first steps necessary in attempting to elevate the character of the coloured population, to undermine the system of slavery, to encourage the increase of free labourers, and to give a healthy stimulus to the industry of the colony.[28]

Philip was thus arguing for the application of the most modern principles of political economy to the Cape, and he did this explicitly. In the *Researches* he quotes Adam Smith extensively.[29] At one point he comments on colonial policy, as made in Britain as well as in South Africa, that 'things might have gone on in this way if Adam Smith, Ferguson, Malthus, Ricardo etc., had never blotted paper'.[30] Personal liberty was essential to a free economy, which in its turn was a necessary condition of material, and indeed of moral, progress for all the inhabitants of the Cape.

III

Philip's *Researches* were written, during 1827, in England whither he had come to campaign for the 'emancipation' of the Khoi. This campaign was largely conducted in cooperation with Thomas Fowell Buxton, who by this time was the major parliamentary spokesman and tactician for the abolitionists. At first, Buxton informed Philip that he could not help him because all his energies were absorbed by the struggle for the emancipation of slaves and the conflict with the West India interest, but Philip was eventually able to convince him that the two causes were inextricably intertwined. As he wrote to Buxton: 'If they aim at the abolition of slavery, is it to put freed slaves in the position of "free" Hottentots?'[31] For his part, Buxton may well have realized that the cause of the Khoikhoi could perhaps be used to extract statements of principle from the British parliament which could later be used in the West Indies, without the planter interest being aroused. This was indeed the case. On 15 July 1828 the House of Commons passed an unopposed resolution that:

... directions be given for effectually securing to all the natives of South Africa the same freedom and protection as are enjoyed by the free persons residing at the Cape, whether they be English or Dutch.[32]

Buxton's comment on this was simply 'These men do not know what they have done.'[33] In this he was right. Two days later, and thus in the strict sense independently, the Cape government passed Ordinance 50 which was very much of the same tenor.[34] When news of this came to England, Philip pressed that it be confirmed by Order in Council, with the proviso that it could not be amended or repealed without consent from London. The Colonial Secretary at the time, the Tory Sir George Murray, was a little fearful of the opposition this would receive from the West Indians, but it was pointed out to him that they had already had the opportunity to oppose the original motion. According to Philip's reminiscences, Murray then, more or less on the spur of the moment, decided to extend this order to all the British colonies.[35] Although this does not seem to be the strict truth, nevertheless a string of ordinances in the following years did extend the principle to the British West Indies, presumably following the precedent set for the Cape.[36] The full effect of these new regulations on the free black communities of those colonies cannot be judged with any accuracy, since slave emancipation followed only a few years later but it does seem reasonable to assume that they were of considerable importance in ensuring that no racially based measures were enacted to maintain the effective servitude of the ex-slaves.[37] In some colonies, other techniques were found, but that is another story.

IV

In addition to this exercise in political guile,[38] there was a more significant congruence between Philip and the abolitionists in Britain, namely at the ideological level. This is a field in which recent historiographic progress has been considerable, largely because of the failure of two previous attempts to explain the sudden rise of the movement to abolish the slave trade and slavery which occurred in Great Britain, and to a certain extent in North America, in the late eighteenth and early nineteenth centuries. To see it as deriving from a shift in religious sensibilities, without providing an explanation of that very shift itself, was clearly unsatisfactory.[39] Conversely, the argument, primarily associated with Eric Williams, that the slave trade and slavery were abolished because they were no longer functional for capitalism became untenable in the face of evidence that slavery and the slave trade were still thoroughly profitable at the moment of abolition and were not seriously inconveniencing the consumer in Britain or elsewhere.[40] All the same, there would seem, *prima facie* to be a flaw in an argument which does not link the growth of abolitionism, begun in Britain and exported to the rest of the world, with the capitalist Industrial Revolution, also begun in Britain and exported to the rest of the world at approximately the same time.

I have neither the space nor the competence to do full justice to the exceedingly subtle, and in my opinion satisfactory, solution to this paradox which has been articulated in terms of ideology. David Brion Davis has summarized both the basic tenets of the argument and the difficulties that it nevertheless contains. He wrote:

A causal explanation [of the antislavery conquest of European opinion] would ... have to relate the antislavery sensibility to the triumphant hegemony of a capitalist world view and particularly to capitalist views of labor, while avoiding any temptation to reduce the rise of abolitionism to the interests of an entrepreneurial class, a class which for the most part detested abolitionists.[41]

For the purpose of explication, perhaps the best place to begin is with Adam Smith and *The Wealth of Nations*, which Philip knew so well. According to a recent and most persuasive account, this work's engagement with economics was not so much a starting-point, but a solution. Its central concern, rather, was

... with the issue of justice, with finding a market mechanism capable of reconciling inequality of property with adequate provision for the excluded. Smith was simply transposing into the language of markets an ancient jurisprudential discourse ... about how to ensure that private individuation of God's dominion would not deny the propertyless the means of satisfying their needs.... The answer which Smith gave to this problem [was] that a system of competitive markets in food and labour could guarantee adequate subsistence to the labouring poor.... Smith's arguments were designed to show how an economy of abundance could be created in which this ancient jurisprudential antinomy between the needs of the poor and the rights of the rich could be transcended altogether.[42]

This was clearly an attractive argument to those who prospered during the Industrial Revolution. Much as they might be worried or shocked by the conditions of the labourers in the new factories, or feel guilty about their own wealth, they could take solace in the thought that, although things were not as they should be, they could be made as good as possible if men (and to a lesser extent women) both followed their own economic advantage and agitated for the removal of all limitations on economic freedom. Moreover, despite the horrors of early industrialization, the steady economic growth and general prosperity of Great Britain, the European country with the least economic regulation, probably seemed to confirm these men in their convictions.

There is an obvious corollary to this. If a free market in labour was not only economically advantageous but also morally right, it follows that slavery was both inefficient and therefore sinful. Middle-class Britons therefore attacked slavery with religious fervour, just as they attacked other trammels on the free economy, such as the Corn Laws. They could only justify their own prosperity by agitating against the causes, as they saw them, of other people's unnecessary misery. For this reason, anti-slavery became a major mass movement, probably the first modern political campaign in Britain.[43]

This certainly was how James Cropper saw his role in the world. A devout Quaker, he had had in his youth doubts about the legitimacy of his activities as a merchant until he read *The Wealth of Nations*, which for the rest of his life he treated almost literally as a second Bible. And, as one of the men who took the initiative in 1823 for the foundation of the Anti-Slavery Society, he was a key abolitionist and was certainly not considered an eccentric within that community.[44]

This is undoubtedly an oversimplified description of the mainsprings of abolitionist ideas. It can explain much, such as the contemporality of the abolition of slavery and the passing of the New Poor Law. Nevertheless, it was not of universal application. Ideally, though of course not in practice, the requirement of labour was limited to post-pubertal males. Economic liberalism and the economic restrictions of the ideal evangelical family found no difficulty in accommodating to each other, despite their apparent contradictions.[45] This explains, for instance, Philip's boast that he had decided to set up as an independent weaver master (in the 1790s) because of his abhorrence at the use of child labour in the factory where he then worked.[46] But his arguments in the *Researches* fell within the framework of Smithian liberalism, and this seems to have been why they were so easily accepted by the British government.

If this is the case, then the arguments put forward by Susan Newton-King, to the effect that Ordinance 50 was part of an attempt 'to increase the labour supply available to the colonists',[47] would not seem valid. Certainly in the early nineteenth century, not all the measures of the colonial government were in direct response to the demands of colonial landowners. As W. M. Macmillan had argued in *The Cape Colour Question*, the changes of Cape policy have to be seen within the context of the British Empire as a whole, and of the metropole in particular. He did not himself provide an explanation for the change in sentiment, which he considered to be crucial to the emancipation of the Khoi and the slaves, but the ideas which have been developed in the sixty years since *The Cape Colour Question* was written could be incorporated into his arguments without doing them fundamental damage.

V

In view of this, it is not difficult to understand Philip's refusal to acquiesce in the republication of the *Researches*. In the imperial context, the book still had its relevance, as the British West Indies began to adapt to a world without slaves, but in South Africa its role was finished. It had been a campaigning book, and the campaign had been won. Ordinance 50 of 1828, and its confirmation by the British government, which Philip saw as a more important measure (perhaps because he was personally involved in the decision-making process in this latter case), had given the Khoi freedom from legal discrimination. Submitting to a common human failing, Philip overestimated the importance of what he considered to be his major achievement. The Khoi had now been given the chance to make their own way in the labour market and it was up to them to take it. Philip was confident that many of them would succeed and that the failure of those who did not would be their own fault. Philip's sentiments were also shared by the earliest Cape liberals, who looked to him for leadership, as they viewed the emancipation not only of the Khoi but also of the slaves. Just before the ex-slaves acquired full control over their labour, with the end of the so-called apprenticeship in 1838, an editorial in the *South African Commercial Advertiser*, written by Philip's son-in-law John Fairbairn, stressed that, when the apprentices were free, 'it will be as other free men, *who depend on employment for food and upon character for employment*'.[48] If it was to work more efficiently, they felt, the labour market should be harsh but fair.

In the event, Philip came to realize that the fairness of the labour market had to be continually defended. In the 1830s he was one of those who were most instrumental in ensuring that a proposed Vagrancy Act was vetoed by the Colonial Office as in contravention of Ordinance 50.[49] Also, right at the end of his life, his last struggle was to maintain the position of the mission stations which he saw not just as religious institutions but as bases from which the labourers could defend their freedom by giving them some limited bargaining position. It was, he wrote, 'the old struggle under a new form ... to bring the people back to slavery by putting down the Institutions'.[50]

Philip's achievement in this regard should not be overestimated. Such research as has been done on the workings of Ordinance 50 would seem to suggest that its actual effect on day-to-day labour relations in the eastern Cape was fairly slight.[51] Nevertheless, perhaps Macmillan was right to argue that, by the 1920s, 'The Coloured People have no political grievance, are proud of their rights and, in spite of all disabilities, not only survive, but are definitely making upward progress'.[52] This was a result of the outlawing of legislation on the basis of colour in the Cape colony, and he hoped that similar action might yet save the Africans from the degradation with which they were threatened. This was the political message of The Cape Colour Question, and it was one that was signally not heeded. Not only were the civil disabilities of the Africans steadily sharpened, but, from the very moment at which he wrote, the rights and position of the so-called 'Cape Coloureds' were steadily eroded.[53]

7

FROM 'COLOUR QUESTION' TO 'AGRARIAN PROBLEM' AT THE CAPE: REFLECTIONS ON THE INTERIM

JOHN MARINCOWITZ

WILLIAM Miller Macmillan provides us with rare and valuable insights into Cape history during the nineteenth century. In his *The Cape Colour Question* and 'The problem of the Coloured people' he established the extent to which the colonial government succeeded in establishing a free market economy at the Cape by the middle of the nineteenth century.[1] After emancipation, the Cape was a 'colony whose dimensions no longer turned on colour policy',[2] but it was a colony in which legal equality 'tended to merge ... persons of colour ... into a composite mass — almost all of them equally resourceless and landless'.[3] In *The South African Agrarian Problem*, Macmillan also demonstrated the implications, for some rural inhabitants, of the intensified commercial land and labour relations that occurred at the Cape during the late nineteenth century as a result of South Africa's mining revolution. Macmillan forged his ideas from a range of official, unofficial and mission sources and began to move beyond the characteristic focus of traditional and general accounts on the themes of slavery, the Great Trek, the eastern frontier, Afrikaner nationalism and mining.[4] His work also transcended the preoccupation of some liberal and Afrikaner nationalist historians with the benefits or disadvantages of emancipation,[5] and it only partially shared the view of more recent work which stresses the continuity between pre- and post-emancipation society at the Cape.[6] Macmillan recognized the profound changes as well as the continuities that characterized social restructuring at the Cape after slavery.

Nevertheless, a longstanding gap in Cape historiography, which also characterizes Macmillan's work, concerns the experience of workers and peasants in the agrarian western regions during the years between emancipation and industrialization. That is the concern of this paper. It seeks to establish that Macmillan's assumption that

In the middle of the nineteenth century the affairs of the Coloured People, as they had now become known, ceased to be of any pressing importance ... yet this was a most critical stage in the history of the Coloured People demanding a degree of united action that was strangely lacking....[7]

was the converse of the truth. I shall argue that, during the decades after emancipation, social tensions grew steadily at the colony and culminated with the prospect of general insurrection. By 1851 regular and casual farm labourers and peasants had created considerable unity among themselves and made common cause with their Nguni, Khoisan and ex-slave counterparts in the eastern Cape and frontier region. This paper traces the social forces that were involved in this conflict and then moves on to an examination of aspects of race and class in the light of the mid-nineteenth century crisis and its aftermath. This expands upon Macmillan's *South African Agrarian Problem* which tended to trace rural poverty among whites to the era when diamond and gold mining developed, and dealt, for the most part, with differentiation and impoverishment among whites in isolation from other sectors of the rural poor. It also builds on Macmillan's analysis of Coloured poverty as an early problem of an urbanizing landless proletariat[8] by investigating responses of the rural poor to their predicament. These issues serve to develop ideas raised by Macmillan in the context of the neglected period between the years covered in *The Cape Colour Question* and *The South African Agrarian Problem*.

In the decade following emancipation roughly 7,000 of the 25,000 ex-slaves who worked the farms of the arable western Cape in 1838 moved to rural missions, villages and tracts of public land.[9] They, and those who remained on the farms as labour tenants, provided the casual and seasonal labour upon which agrarian employers became increasingly dependent. The autonomy that they derived in varying degrees from subsistence cultivation, and their mobility as casual and day workers, placed many proletarians in an unprecedentedly strong position in relation to their former owners and employers. Casual wages rose;[10] commercial farmers faced rising production costs; wheat farmers suffered a simultaneous drop in produce prices as a result of increased imports. Commenting on the problems of commercial farmers in September of 1848, the editor of the *Zuid Afrikaan* declared, 'a crisis, it would seem, has arrived'.[11]

By the late 1840s, commercial farmers in the western districts were growing increasingly impatient with a colonial government that opposed protective tariffs, a vagrancy law, and attempts to add a racial dimension to the Masters and Servants Law, on the grounds that these were artificial interventions in commodity markets. Farmers demanded the implementation of measures to effect the immediate and thorough proletarianization of the ex-slave labour-force that had settled on mission, private and public land. The 1849 Commission of Inquiry into the Masters and Servants Ordinance supported these coercive measures. Despite these recommendations, the Legislative Council members did not press for any stricter amendments to the Masters and Servants Law and took no steps to effect a vagrancy law because the British government was unlikely to grant the constitutionally requisite imperial sanction for such measures. The government was not altogether indifferent to the farmers' predicament, however. After some deliberation, the Legislative Council introduced a Bill on October 1851, 'to prevent the practice of squatting on government lands'. Farmers petitioned the government in support of the Bill and demonstrated 'in numbers' at Cape Town when the Squatters' Bill was read for a second time in the Legislative Council in mid-November. They also began to arm themselves and prepare to meet 'the hostile intentions towards them by the coloured people in reference to this Bill'.[12]

The proposed Squatters Bill was aimed at eliminating the autonomy of squatters, peasants, and casual labourers on public land. The total number of people who occupied public land at the Cape remains obscure, but the area involved comprised some 59 per cent of the land in the colony during the period 1841–55.[13] Several thousand people are likely to have been settled on public land in the arable western Divisions. Technically, the Bill also threatened the tenure of the nearly 9,000 people who occupied holdings at mission institutions which were established on land held by 'tickets of occupation' granted by the government to various mission societies.[14]

These proposals resulted in opposition from a very broad spectrum of people, including regular and casual farm labourers, harvest workers, and peasants in the western Cape, rebel Nguni in the eastern Cape and frontier, and defecting levies and inhabitants from missions in both regions. The land issue formed an important

and common element in both the Khoi-ex-slave 'Hottentot
Rebellion' and the Cape Nguni 'Eighth Frontier War'.[15] The crisis
developed into the 'bloodiest page in the whole history of the Cape
Colony',[16] and, for a time, elements of primary resistance to colonial
rule, incipient nationalism, and resistance to proletarianization
threatened to engulf much of the colony, both east and west, in civil
strife.[17]

There is clear evidence that the official deliberations over labour
policy which took place between 1848 and 1851 generated massive
rural discontent. Inhabitants and clergy on missions in the western
districts expressed concern at the ability of farmers to influence the
legislature. They warned the government of the dangers inherent in
constitutional proposals to grant legislative power to those interests,
'as represented in the Blue Book, documents ... concerning masters
and servants and [which] ... desire ... a vagrant law'.[18] A rumour
which prevailed in the eastern districts, '... that the government is in
contemplation to reduce them to a state of slavery', was 'very
industriously circulated by certain designing Hottentots'.[19] In
December 1850 a 'general rising' began in British Kaffraria. The
government declared martial law on the frontier districts and Sir
Harry Smith set off for the eastern Cape with a substantial
proportion of the military force that was normally stationed at Cape
Town. At the same time, farmers began to abandon farms on a
significant scale in parts of the eastern districts.[20] On 25 December
1850, 'the sky was red at night with the flames of burning farms of
the European settlers'.[21] A Moravian missionary reported:

In the course of a few short weeks, our three settlements to the Eastward of
the Great Fish River, Mamre, Goshen and Shiloh, have been abandoned to
the insurgent Caffirs ... the last-named — the oldest, largest and most
flourishing — has been reduced to a heap of ruins.[22]

The Kat River rebellion erupted in January 1851, and the mission at
Enon was deserted in February 1852.[23] By February 1851 it was clear
that:

... not only many of the Kat River Hottentots, but also others are joining in,
or in the eastern districts are going to join the Caffres.[24]

By June 1851 'most of the people at Theopolis institution had joined
the rebel party' and taken up arms against the government.

Contacts between peasants and workers on western-Cape missions and those of the eastern Cape and frontier developed in the late 1840s and early 1850s. Hundreds of mission occupants from the west settled on the newly established government-aided missions, or in 'frontier colonies of Hottentots' in the recently annexed district between the Keiskamma and the Kei Rivers.[25] Hundreds more served as levies in Kaffraria. The majority on each of the eastern-Cape missions, and a number of levies, joined the rebel cause as the hostilities progressed. By June 1851 there were reports that:

The great number of intelligent Hottentots now serving with the Caffres increase the difficulties by which the government is surrounded; they prolong the war and render it more bloody.[26]

Most levies did not defect. The majority returned home as soon as they could. Those who had 'discussed the taking away of the land' and the implications of the proposed Squatters Law with the rebels in the eastern region spread their views when they returned home to the western districts.[27]

Johannes Titus, a resident at Kat River during the early 1850s, was one of those who adopted and disseminated the rebels' views. He took part in the rebel attack on Fort Armstrong, was captured by the authorities, released, and returned home to his family at Zuurbraak in the western Cape. Once there, he joined up with the Old Party, which elicited growing support from disaffected inhabitants as the outrage at the Squatters Bill gained momentum. Titus apparently endeavoured to:

... spread sedition amongst the people here [Zuurbraak] by representing to them that the rebels under Uithaalder and others were fighting for the liberties of their nation — that it was only owing to their resistance that the Hottentots in the western Districts were not already enslaved or under Vagrant laws; that the people of Kat River had already driven away their missionary ... since they were sufficiently advanced to take care of their own interests ... that the people of other institutions ... had either already joined Uithaalder or were preparing to join him, and that he had come for the purpose of instructing people here to act their part in the revolution — and advised them to collect and take good care of whatever powder and lead they had or could get as a time would come when they might want it.[28]

Events in the eastern Cape found an echo in the west. In a letter that appealed to the government to investigate the situation in the western Cape, a trader at Napier village in Caledon reported:

... a general spirit of dissatisfaction, which shows itself as existing amongst the Hottentots of Genadendal and Elim and this place [who have] just returned from commando, or expressing itself in manners too numerous for me now to enumerate, but none so forcible as the general desire they evince of purchasing gunpowder. We have however in all cases decidedly refused to supply them ... threatening language has been used towards farmers and others. We are generally in a state of great alarm but I think we ought to keep it as secret as possible ... prevention is better than cure.[29]

In October 1851 a 'considerable body of [coloured] levies' from Clanwilliam Division disembarked at Cape Town after their terms of service on the frontier had expired. These armed men arrived at a time of intense debate leading up to the second reading of the Squatters Ordinance, and the farmers' demonstrations of 10 November 1851; the tension was further increased by news that the farmers were also arming themselves. In order to reach their homes, the levies passed through the Cape, Malmesbury and Koeberg districts, while resident and seasonal labourers worked at the harvest. As they proceeded, the levies reported to the harvesters 'that the farmers had gone to Cape Town to sign a paper to make slaves of them again'.[30]

The rural populace in the western districts prepared for armed confrontation. Women and children on farms in the Cape, Stellenbosch and Zwellendam Divisions gathered at particular venues, while the men formed armed patrols to guard the farms at night. In the more remote Clanwilliam Division some farmers abandoned farms and hired 'armed Europeans' as harvesters.[31] The measures which Field Cornet B. J. Duminy of Koeberg introduced in anticipation of the rebellion illustrate the urgency of the situation. He warned his 'fellow *burghers*' of the impending rebellion that was due to take place during the harvest; advised them to arm, arrange guards, and disarm the harvest workers; to disallow the customary shots to be fired at workers' harvest-home festivities; and to congregate at his farm if shots were fired or hostilities began. 'Be on your guard', he warned, 'we are surrounded by enemies quite as bad as the Kafirs.'[32]

There is evidence of extensive planning and organization for an uprising throughout the commercial farming districts of the western Cape. Meetings were held and there was widespread discussion about the form the rebellion would take and how people ought to respond: '... at Saron ... the common topic of conversation was on the intended outbreak of blacks ... their intention was to join the people of Groenekloof.'[33] Men from Genadendal circulated, with other itinerent casual labourers, among the harvest workers on the farms in Worcester and Piquetberg. They spread the word that, 'it was the intention of the people to rise'.[34] Two armed men patrolled the farms at D'Urban, while two men from Groenekloof held meetings in the vicinity of Paarl and '... incited the people in the area'.[35]

The general view was that regular, resident farm labourers would unite in rebellion with the casual workers drawn from the missions, rural villages and squatter settlements on public land. The uprising was to take place during the harvest when regular and casual workers were deployed in harvest gangs throughout the commercial wheat growing area. In the 1851–52 season, the labour force that harvested farms in the Zwartland alone amounted to nearly 4,000 people.[36]

The date for the mobilization is unclear. Local officials considered three possibilities most likely: 15 November when the harvest commenced; the anniversary of the emancipation from slavery on 1 December; or late December or early January at the end of the harvest.[37] One of the first targets was to be the convict station at Baine's Kloof where a number of the Kat River rebels, and others captured in the eastern Cape, were imprisoned.[38] Among those convicted for treason — some serving life sentences — were friends and relatives of residents in the western districts. A second phase in the rebellion would, by now, have been well under way. Parties operating from Zuurbraak, Zoar, Genadendal, and Elim were to attack, simultaneously, the villages of Zwellendam, Riversdale, Caledon and Bredasdorp.

Mission inhabitants prepared for armed struggle. Two wagons bound for Groenekloof carrying powder and lead, 'the property of the Hottentots at Groenekloof', were seized by farmers in the Zwartland.[39] People at the Elim mission purchased arms and ammunition.[40] A report from Tygerberg stated:

... the coloured people have possessed themselves of arms and ammunition to some extent ... parties of them go out occasionally for ball practice. This I have seen myself within the last eight to ten days, and during a residence of thirteen years in this Colony I have never seen it before and the language used on these occasions indicates hostile intentions and bad feelings.[41]

Some workers and peasants in Clanwilliam Division appear not to have possessed firearms. Instead they, 'were going about armed, some with their scythe blades fastened to straight sticks for their defence'.[42]

The heightened tensions prevailing in the western Cape in late 1851 and early 1852 were largely confined to the harvesters of the commercial farming heartlands. There is little evidence of widespread disaffection in the eastern Overberg and Midlands where labourers were, for the most part, settled on private land and were therefore not threatened by the Bill. There were reports of spasmodic clashes between squatters and settler-farmers in the pastoral interior and west coast region, but it was not until the 1860s that these escalated into war.[43]

By the end of 1851 the 'hostile designs and feelings of the coloured population' had intensified and created a 'panic' among farmers in the western districts. In an attempt to defuse the situation, the Legislative Council reversed its unanimous endorsement of the Squatters Bill of 10 October 1851, declaring it withdrawn on the grounds that:

... both parties requiring a total rest from strife and contention until their feelings of mutual hostility have had time to wear off ... the farmers as a class have upon this occasion exhibited absolute fear of the Coloured people and that the latter have in a similar ration gained confidence in their numbers and in their power.[44]

It seemed to the legislature under the circumstances,

... so absolutely essential to remove as completely as possible, any subject affecting or supposed to affect the coloured people or which could afford a pretext to designing parties for agitating them, that it is deemed imperative not merely to delay or postpone the measure but absolutely to withdraw it, without reference to its merits, in order to tranquilize the minds of both parties ... to pass a Bill now would be received by the coloured people as an act of oppression and by the farmers as a triumph and would thus tend to permanent estrangement.[45]

This view was endorsed by the Colonial Office, and is confirmed by other reports.

The Squatters ordinance is but a vagrant law, the dread of which I consider to be the principal cause of the Hottentot Rebellion ... at the present moment it would be as suicidal to the class of men who clamour for it, as it would be ruinous to its intended victims.[46]

The withdrawal of the Squatters Bill removed what a substantial sector of workers and peasants in the western Cape perceived to be an imminent and serious threat to the relatively independent lifestyles they had created after emancipation. With the removal of the most burning issue, dissatisfaction subsided and the harvesters' revolt did not materialize.

After 1838 it became quite clear that commercial farming in the western Cape could not depend solely on the 'free labour market'. Emancipation advanced proletarianization in so far as labour was 'freed' to enter a market in labour-power; but it was not yet 'freed' from all alternative means of survival. At a time when a colonial military force of between 9–10,000 men, including the bulk of those normally stationed in the western Cape, were engaged in the eastern districts,[47] the colonial government was unable to launch an assault on the partial autonomy of casual labourers and render them more dependent on wage labour. To achieve that would have required the systematic and forceful eviction of people from public land — an act of which the colonial state was incapable in 1851.

The notion that 'Coloureds' were politically passive during the period between emancipation and the 1890s is a longstanding myth.[48] Yet in the mid-nineteenth century, elements of primary resistance to colonial rule, proto-nationalism, and resistance to proletarianization threatened much of the colony with insurrection. Regular and casual workers and peasants in the western divisions forged considerable unity amongst themselves and their counterparts in the eastern Cape and frontier region. However, while ex-slave, Khoi and Cape Nguni inhabitants were generally sympathetic to the cause of rebellion, the role and attitudes of immigrant farmworkers from Europe and marginalized Dutch settler-farmers were less clear.

It is possible that some immigrant British labourers were also involved with the predominantly ex-slave and indigenous people's movement. During the late 1840s and early 1850s, perhaps 1–2,000 of these were scattered about the rural western Cape and were likely to have done some harvest day-work. They had either been shipped to the Cape as children during the 1830s, or were adult Irish and

English immigrant workers who arrived in the late 1840s. A number of immigrants were assimilated into the growing village and mission proletariat. English and Irish immigrants participated in the 1808 slave rebellion and in the demonstrations of opposition to the 1854 constitutional proposals.[49] The propertied classes also displayed considerable anxiety at the prospect of having convicted Irish rebels settle in the Cape countryside in 1849.

Generally, however, as social tension escalated in the western Cape in the late 1840s and early 1850s, most poor whites — and probably all poorer white small farmers and their sons — rallied with wealthier farmers against other sectors of the agrarian poor. Ties of kinship and friendship with established commercial farmers appear to have bound them to the status quo. Marginal and poor Dutch were the 'descendants of respectable landowners'. Cape inheritance laws rendered the birth certificate of a farmer's child a virtual title to land. None was threatened by the Squatters Law and relatively few were landless. Their earlier experience of a slave society probably also moulded race attitudes among poorer Dutch to some extent and engendered feelings of superiority that hindered the formation of non-racial class alliances among the rural poor.

Macmillan perceptively linked the intensification of racial feeling that followed emancipation with competition in the labour market.[50] Farmers generally demanded that ex-slaves be proletarianized and they often articulated their demands in racial terms. Racial prejudices that existed before emancipation developed a new function and meaning as capitalist labour relations intensified. A racial definition of the agricultural workforce was actively promoted after emancipation and was effectively implemented by the three Masters and Servants Laws of the early 1870s. These introduced, for the first time since emancipation, a distinct category of regulations for farmworkers. As such, they confirmed in law the extent to which 'regular farmworkers' had come to mean, both on the farms and in the official mind, workers who were neither British immigrants nor Dutch descendents — that is, 'European or white'.

At the same time, however, the position of marginalized whites in rural society grew increasingly ambiguous. Significant numbers of white casual labourers, sharecroppers and tenants had emerged in the western Cape by the late 1860s.[51] Inheritance laws guaranteed landholdings. But, as the generations turned over, they also broke holdings up into smaller parcels or concentrated increasing numbers of shareholders on farms which remained physically undivided. Their viability was often precarious. Droughts, soil exhaustion, economic depressions, and the commercialization of private farms and public property marginalized a growing number of small farmers. By the 1880s the definition and composition of the Cape's squatter population had changed, and now it included a considerable number of landless whites. At a time of acute farm labour shortage, a dilemma of central importance to the labour-policy formulators was whether they could proletarianize these squatters by coercive legislation. J. X. Merriman, Member of the Legislative Assembly, Treasurer of the Colony and Commissioner of Lands, Mines and Agriculture, put the problem quite succinctly:

Here are people saying that they are in want of labour ... if you have hundreds of white men squatting in idleness ... of course you have a scarcity of labour ... try and make your poor white people work.[52]

Many commercial farmers were not averse to employing poor whites as farm labourers, or to having them coerced into doing regular work.[53] In some cases, manipulations of race perceptions verged on justifying the proletarianization of whites. Statements about inter-familial marriages on subdivided farms having already 'lowered the race very perceptibly', or that 'a certain class of whites ... [were] more like blacks than Afrikaners', were not uncommon.[54] They suggest the extent to which employers and commercial farmers associated impoverished whites with the broader mass of the labouring poor.

Furthermore, an element of conflict had entered with the developing social distance between the wealthier middle-class farmers and their marginalized counterparts. An Oudtshoorn grain farmer complained of 'a class of whites whom you cannot trust'.[55] J. J. J. Fourie, who was named as being one of this 'class', revealed the resultant response:

... they [rich farmers] backbite and endeavour to underwork you by unfair means.... They may perhaps agree to pay you £25 or £30 a year, but when you have not been there two months they will ... drive you away as if you were a Hottentot. For five years I lived with a man for a little tobacco ... perhaps all those farmers are rich men, and they would naturally wish to keep the poor down.... I am of the poor people and mix with them. They discuss these things with me.[56]

The development of western Cape capitalism was increasingly skewed, however. Objectively, the relationships of the rural underclasses to the means of production did not correspond neatly with race. But neither did poor whites and Coloureds simply merge into a united working class. The ways in which poor whites perceived themselves, and how their landlords, employers and fellow labourers perceived them, illustrate something of the sociological and ideological complexity that constituted 'poor whiteism'.

... they [poor whites] regard it as a disgrace to work for another farmer. Many farmers nevertheless, would be glad to give them separate rooms and allow them to dine at table. Of course there are many respectable persons among the class. I think they could not do better than engage their services by the month.... [They occupy the land] ... of the farmers. One hires a farm and two or three occupy it. This occurs on my farm also. When I have spoken about it I am told that they assist one another. [Some 'on halves' and some not] ... they do not have any men but reap the harvests themselves.... No, not profit as far as I am aware.... It is true that when you get a white who does not mind working with the blacks, he assimilates with blacks in other ways. On the other hand the better class of black objects to working with the white man, because, he says, that gives him two masters....[57]

It is impossible to ignore the implications for agrarian relations of the continuity in a conservative tradition that originated from slave- and landholding structures where race did largely correspond with class. A persistent theme, and one which contrasted with the advocacy of a 'free labour market' for capitalist agricultural development, was the traditional solution of western-Cape commercial farmers to farm–labour problems; they consistently sought to conserve ex-slaves and apprentices as the agrarian labour force after emancipation.

Poor whites were often able to exploit the paternalism, kinship and conservatism that influenced the perception of commercial farmers as to who were the rightful members of the regular farm labouring class. In this way, they were often able to avoid regular resident wage labour. C. F. J. Muller, a Dutch Reformed clergyman of fourteen years' experience in George and Cape Town, outlined the relationship between marginalized whites and their employers and landlords.

Only a certain class would take service. They would much rather go into service with a respectable farmer. They like styling the farmer 'Oom' [Uncle] and the wife 'Tante' [Aunt]. As long as they can do that they know they are not regular servants, on a level with the native [coloured].... They are accustomed to be recognised as the offspring of respectable farmers in their own district ... a poor man will go up to a respectable farmer and shake hands with him and call him 'Oom'. The farmer again will give him a decent room to sleep in and not make him feel that he is a servant.[58]

Thus, impoverished whites could resort to a mode of resistance to proletarianization that was not available to other casual workers and peasants in the western Cape.

What gave such resounding echo to those factors differentiating 'poor whites' from 'the poor', and magnified them out of proportion to the immediate needs of capitalist agricultural expansion, was the fact that the emergent Afrikaner Bond, the political party of western-Cape agrarian capital, was in the process of carving out a constituency. This included those whom some commercial farmers would gladly have seen doing regular farm work, namely the poor whites, a very large number of whom were Afrikaners.

Perceptions about 'poor whites' were changing.[59] Many wealthy farmers were likely to have wanted to retain the support of those white sharecroppers or shepherds whose allegiance and identity were more closely affiliated to their landlords than the Coloured tenants or labourers. Without the support of this stratum, farmers were a good deal more isolated and vulnerable in the rural areas. Furthermore, the £25 property qualification was low enough to include a number of poor whites who, for example, may have held a share in an undivided farm. Regions which had concentrations of marginalized whites, such as the Midlands and Overberg, provided vital support to the Bond when it was based upon du Toit's programme in the early 1880s. J. H. Hofmeyr was unlikely to have wanted to jeopardize this by any uniform implementation of coercive measures aimed at increasing the supply of labour.

Indeed, an element in the process of consolidating Bond power, which depended on both Afrikaner commercial farmers and the Afrikaner poor, was the increased sense of urgency about the need to deny the remaining rural underclasses the franchise and education to ensure their more rapid proletarianization. Racial attitudes hardened as the labour crisis intensified. As one Midland farmer remarked:

If a servant approaches a master he must show respect in his salutations and say 'Dag Baas' (Good day Boss), and not 'how do you do'.... No, not slavery, but the line must be clearly defined.[60]

In fact, a clearer definition of 'the line' was in the process of being worked out during the daily struggles that took place in the rural western Cape.

The fact that emancipation preceded industrialization by some three decades meant that ex-slaveholders, unlike their counterparts in the American South, faced relatively little competition for labour from other sectors of the economy as a result of abolition. The labour shortages that plagued agrarian employers after emancipation arose, rather, as a result of the efforts of ex-slaves to reduce wage dependency. They did so by combining periodic casual work with varying degrees of autonomy as independent cultivators. Farmers' attempts to regularize casual work, and opposition from mission inhabitants, squatters, tenants, sharecroppers and the village proletariat, were a focal point in the struggles precipitated by emancipation. The dramatic events of the late 1840s and early 1850s, as well as the quiet, continuous and often equally effective opposition thereafter, suggest an active and influential role on the part of the rural underclasses in patterning the relations of production and shaping agrarian society.

The pressure of an increasing peasant population on scarce resources, the fragmentation of holdings, the privatization of public land, drought and soil exhaustion impoverished white and coloured smallholders in the period between emancipation and industrialization. But conditions in the western Cape were conducive to forms of differentiation and stratification that were simultaneously vertical and horizontal. By 1870 whites no longer formed part of the regular, resident labour force on farms. Furthermore, despite their occupations as casual workers, labour- and share- tenants, or squatters, they failed to merge with peasants and workers in general. In sum, there is a sense in which 'the agrarian problem' emerged soon after emancipation, and the 'colour question' assumed a new lease of life.

In his early work on agrarian poverty W. M. Macmillan wrote:

The story of South African economic development in the half century following the Great Trek has no doubt an interest and an importance of its own, but for our purpose here it has no significance until the changes that belong almost to our own generation.... Two of the prime factors in determining a country's economic life, its products, and its means of transport remain essentially unchanged, until the opening of the diamond fields in the years following 1869, and so far as the country districts are concerned later still....[61]

Yet Macmillan provided indispensable points of departure for a study of Cape agrarian history between emancipation and the mining revolution. He stressed the importance of the changes that distinguished pre- from post-emancipation society at the Cape. Official labour and immigration policies bear out his views. During the 1840s and 1850s, for example, the colonial government spent tens of thousands of pounds on importing British labourers to the Cape, and farmers employed them as regular farm hands. Macmillan also grasped the extent to which emancipation advanced proletarianization and suggested that, in some respects, racial tensions increased with the developing labour market. Again, official policies bear this out. By the 1870s regular, immigrant and local farmworkers were either 'Coloured' or 'black'. However, the full implications of these changes are best approached in the context of post-emancipation Cape society before urbanization and industrialization. This lacuna in South African historiography provides a unique opportunity for the study of developments in the dialectic between race and class in a society with intensifying and expanding commercial land and labour relations.

8

W. M. MACMILLAN'S ANALYSIS OF AGRARIAN CHANGE AND AFRICAN RURAL COMMUNITIES*

WILLIAM BEINART

W. M. MACMILLAN'S insights into agrarian change in South Africa in the late nineteenth and early twentieth centuries retained such freshness and trenchancy fifty years later that they could feed directly into the new radical historiography of the late 1960s and 1970s. He made a significant and innovative contribution in three major areas of analysis: the effects of the 'frontier' and the trekboer experience on later agrarian society; the 'agrarian revolution' on settler farms —and the accompanying process of accumulation and dispossession which he saw as analogous to the transition from feudalism in Europe;[1] and the impoverishment of the African reserves.

It is perhaps ironic that his work remained so innovative for so long, not least because subsequent historians failed to develop many of his key propositions. Whereas his formulation of the frontier thesis became a major and oft-repeated element in subsequent writings dealing with agrarian and broader issues, his investigations of changing patterns of production on the farms, and the deteriorating economic circumstances of the reserves, were to a significant extent lost. Why this was the case requires some explanation; and this would have to take account both of the general ideological climate in which historians of South Africa worked from the 1930s to the 1960s, and also the nature of the specific institutions and departments involved in studying and teaching history. In his introduction to the reprint of *The Agrarian Problem*, van Jaarsveld cites a number of historians, both English- and Afrikaans-speaking, working in this period whom he thinks were influenced by Macmillan. But the influence seems to have consisted in a very general acceptance of social and economic history as a significant field of study, rather than an exploration and development of Macmillan's analysis of change.

The central purpose of this paper, however, is not to discuss why Macmillan's work on agrarian questions was lost, but to look in some detail at the ideas he synthesized in the 1910s and 1920s and to suggest in very broad terms how his assumptions were reflected in the writing of those historians who did eventually pursue a similar line of analysis. The historical debates of the 1970s were of course influenced by many different intellectual currents, of which Macmillan's work was probably a rather weak one. Yet, insofar as he studied South Africa specifically and was part of a broader, if rather underrepresented, approach, his ideas might be considered to have wider influence than the footnotes indicate. It is perhaps timely then to re-engage with his works — particularly *The South African Agrarian Problem* (1919) and *Complex South Africa* (1930)[2] — to examine the logic of his arguments and to discover what he omitted.

The chapters in *Complex South Africa* dealing with the African reserves — including the 'sample district survey' of Herschel — are a useful baseline from which to work. They contain sensitive passages about the economic difficulties faced by the people of these areas; they deploy new material gleaned firsthand from fieldwork of a non-anthropological nature; and they are very revealing about Macmillan's attitudes to African society. Their importance has been emphasized, and their contents — not least on Herschel district itself — developed in Colin Bundy's writings on the peasantry which have been so influential in restimulating debates on agrarian history.[3]

Poverty, the inspiration of his industry

Macmillan succeeded in defining, more successfully than any of his contemporaries in the South African context, a specifically agrarian history and agrarian problem. The terminology is in itself important for it opened up a field for comparative insights and, in particular, could encompass the whole range of diverse rural societies and rural forms in the country. In his hands, it was a means of obviating the tendency to discuss different rural areas as discrete cultural, 'tribal' or racial units.

At the same time, his notion of agrarian society enabled him to consider the rural districts, whoever inhabited them, and under whatever social conditions, as part of a single larger unit of study. In a region where the great majority of people had, until shortly before he wrote, lived largely from or on the land, the concept of a rural part of society and an agrarian history depended very precisely on the growth of their urban industrial counterparts and a national state. Indeed, Macmillan's terminology derives not least from his commitment to the idea that there was one nation, and one economy for urban and rural people, black and white, in South Africa — a 'complex South African whole'.[4]

Some of the intellectual influences which contributed to Macmillan's analysis, as well as his research experiences in Grahamstown before he wrote *The Agrarian Problem*, have been touched on in other papers.[5] His notion of a common society was, of course, not entirely new; there are strong echoes throughout his writings of the old Cape liberal thinking, in which 'civilization' was to a certain extent conceived of as an attribute attainable regardless of colour. It was not least some of the inheritors of this tradition — churchmen and African leaders of the Eastern Cape — who began to draw attention to the deteriorating state of the reserves at about the same time as Macmillan. However, when his work on the agrarian economy is placed against that being produced by other intellectuals at the time, it stands out as distinctive. The small group of professional economists which emerged in the 1920s — some, like Frankel, strongly influenced by Macmillan — certainly shared the view that there was a national economy. But their concern was to study those features of investment, taxation and tariff policy, markets and transport which lent themselves to overarching statistical analysis. Research on agriculture, facilitated by the more systematic data published from 1918 in the national agricultural censuses, was largely concerned with economic and technical problems on white-owned farms.[6] Macmillan seems to have been the first to attempt a more comprehensive analysis and explanation of the interaction between the different sectors of the economy and the different rural regions, a synthesis which had important implications for approaches to African societies.[7]

Macmillan's ideas about the essential unity of the national economy provide the background for his concept of poverty —perhaps his central concern. The arguments in both *The Agrarian Problem* and *Complex South Africa* are structured around a demonstration, explanation, and analysis of poverty. It is a concept which in itself, and particularly in the way he deploys it, implies a single society, a single labour market and a single set of standards for judging wealth (or the capacity to survive). It is potentially unfettered by the cultural attributes which so many white South Africans believed enabled others to live at a lower margin of subsistence than themselves. His was not a completely culture-free notion of poverty, and his explanations, as will be illustrated, shifted through time. But especially in his later work, the concern with poverty as a general phenomenon was a quiet war cry against segregationist assumptions and solutions, against white protectionism, and against those liberals who were rediscovering the particularities of African societies and culture through the discipline of anthropology.

Undue stress on the different mentality of the Bantu becomes too often an excuse for shutting the eyes to the unpleasant fact that the Bantu are ordinary human beings, and that the bulk of them are inextricably entangled in and dependent on our own economic system.... At the present time it is more urgent that we see he is provided with bread, even without butter, than to embark on the long quest to 'understand the Native mind'.[8]

In *The Agrarian Problem* Macmillan stated quite explicitly that the eradication of poverty was one of his most fundamental aims. He expressed his concern in very general terms:

Poverty is thus the great enemy to human happiness, just because it makes the grosser bodily needs predominate, depriving its victim of his capacity for the highest life and of the power of realising the best that is in him.[9]

Indeed, it seems that it was through his concern with poverty that he initially developed his interest in agrarian change. His general concern had been shaped specifically by the growth of poor whiteism in South Africa, a phenomenon that had already been associated with rural problems, not least in the report of the Transvaal Indigency Commission (1908), which he regarded as 'something of a classic'.[10] But although he saw poverty, in abstract terms, as linked to a general state of unhappiness and as a stimulant to the baser instincts, he also saw it as corrupting society at large. In the South African context, this was not merely a moral corruption, but was expressed in the increasingly undesirable pattern of political life: a pattern of protectionism for poor whites and segregation for Africans.

Macmillan concentrated on white poverty in *The Agrarian Problem*, but by the time he wrote the essays which eventually made up *Complex South Africa* (in the second half of the 1920s), he, like some others of his contemporaries, had shifted his attention to recognize also the centrality of the 'Native problem'.[11] It is particularly interesting to note how he linked the two issues, not least because his conclusions were fundamental to the way in which he perceived the misdirected pattern of white opinion and state policy. The poor white problem, he noted, was often thought to be a result largely of the existence of a black working class which could undercut whites in the labour market. Macmillan was by no means convinced that this was the whole explanation: his analysis of agrarian accumulation and differentiation on the farms persuaded him otherwise. 'The Poor Whites are little more than the "reservoir" of unemployed to be found wherever Western industrialism has dislocated an old agrarian system.'[12] Be that as it may, he recognized that state policy was deeply shaped by the poor white problem and the demands for protecting poor whites in the labour market. Such an 'industrial Colour Bar' made the 'natives poorer still' and thus 'an ever more real "menace"'.[13]

But he had an alternative solution. The problem was as much black poverty as white poverty. He noted 'the disastrous effect even on the welfare of its European colonists of the poverty and backwardness of the native population'.[14] If this could be solved, and black living standards raised, then by implication the danger of undercutting would fall away; the undesirable features of job protection and segregation would be minimized. The solution to black poverty — which had to be recognized as such and not subsumed in assertions about cultural differences — was thus, in some senses, a prior problem: '... the only way of safety for white and black alike is to promote a general economic progress'; 'in the long run what is best for the Native is best also for the European'.[15]

These central tenets in Macmillan's writings, his intellectual and emotional antipathy towards segregation, his deep concern for welfare and his condemnation of poverty, link in with a variety of sub-themes which informed his approach. He dwelt on poverty largely, it seems, out of a welfarist concern but he also occasionally mentioned the political dangers, in the shape of social disturbances that it might cause. Improving the conditions of the poor, and extending further political influence to African spokesmen, would be an important way of containing such pressures. He also wrote of the need to increase production and improve national 'efficiency', and, like some of the liberal economists, saw the colour bar and job protection as inimical to this aim.[16] He had a clear perception of the linkages between a cheap labour policy, black poverty, the restriction of the internal market and the consequent constraints on expanding industrial production: 'the greatest drag on the industrial prosperity of the Union is the extreme poverty of the natives, and their trifling importance as a market.'[17] In some of these respects, his analysis went beyond that of the growing school of liberal economists. But he parted company with them especially in his conviction that the state had the power to, and should, intervene in the economic sphere, not merely by lifting segregationist restrictions but by actively promoting schemes for development and progress, thus alleviating poverty and distress. His lack of faith in a relatively unfettered 'free market', his whole analysis of the causes of poverty, his linkage of the process of accumulation to that of dispossession placed him closer to a Fabian, or social democratic, than a liberal position, although early twentieth-century British liberalism clearly envisaged a much expanded role for the state.

Explanations of poverty: economics and 'tradition'

At this stage in the argument, we should turn to examine more closely Macmillan's explanations of poverty, for it is in these passages that some of the contradictions or disjunctures in his analysis are revealed. The complexity and variety of his explanations are also important in discussing his legacy — that curious dual legacy which allowed part of his analysis to be appropriated by liberal historians, and another part, much later, by radicals. It will also be suggested that some of the assumptions which partly bedevilled his treatment of African society can be found — though they are sometimes hidden — in these explanations.

In *The Agrarian Problem*, Macmillan argues that the first cause of poverty amongst whites must be related to 'the changing conditions which have only comparatively lately given rise to the existence of an increasing number of the *landless*'. But, he goes on to suggest a cause 'of rather a different kind' — 'the effect of tradition in preventing ready adaptation to new conditions'.[18] The latter statement provides him with his text for an examination of the legacy of the trekboer experience; and he goes on to present elements of what came to be

173

called the 'frontier' thesis in a most eloquent and persuasive way. It was in 'the circumstances which made a "Trek-Boer"' in the years of company rule, and in the 'Boer character', that 'many of the particular ills which limit the capacity of our society for the best life' were to be found.[19] Opposition to any form of government, 'the old-standing cleavage between town and country', the 'nomadic life' and the '*Trek Geest*', dependence on hunting and on slave labour, aversion to manual labour, easy access to land, and redistributive inheritance patterns all contributed to forming this legacy. The result was an independent and sturdy 'race', but one which held deep racial feelings, which could not cope with change, and which could not work as a collectivity in a modern state.

At the same time, it is in this work that Macmillan advanced the analogy of a 'transition ... not unlike that which Europe underwent in centuries, in the passing of feudalism and the coming industrialism'.[20] His notions of the nature of accumulation on the farms were not yet developed, but he clearly detected the passing of a society in which 'human relationships' were predominant. It was being replaced by a system in which the 'cash nexus' took its inexorable toll and 'progressive' farmers ousted unwanted *bywoners* and tenants.[21] In proposing this line of explanation, Macmillan seems to come close to suggesting that lack of property, or lack of capacity to defend themselves against the process of dispossession, was of more importance than backwardness in shaping the expulsion of people from the rural areas. In implying that the more backward and less adaptive rural people were more likely to become landless, he does link the two explanatory themes. But his stress on the force of 'tradition', on the cultural traits which were formed by two centuries of 'pastoral habits of subsistence agriculture', seems to sit uneasily beside his materialist explanations of social change.[22]

It is nevertheless significant that Macmillan, at least in his earlier work, was not economistic in his approach and explored concepts of tradition, or what we might call culture, with some insight. The arguments about the trekboer legacy are briefly repeated in *Complex South Africa*, but they are not developed.[23] This may merely be because he felt that the ground had been covered in his earlier work; the focus of this book was in any case primarily on the contemporary context. But it may not be misleading to suggest that his approach to agrarian problems shifted during the 1920s. The analogy of the transition from feudalism is extended in *Complex South Africa* with perceptive comments on the nature of accumulation on white farms, and also on the changing forms of African as well as white tenancy. This book lays far more stress on the economic processes that produced dispossession, rural poverty, and migration to the towns.

One qualification must be made to such an argument: whereas Macmillan did not develop his ideas about the cultural traditions of rural whites, he did begin to explore the nature of African 'tradition' in *Complex South Africa*. He constantly stressed the fact that Africans had by and large been incorporated into the national economy, not least through the 'insatiable demand for native labour' and were 'very nearly a proletariat'.[24] But he was also well aware of the strength of rural conservatism. He found this phenomenon rather difficult to deal with in his general analysis. On the one hand, he was at pains to stress that African poverty should be judged according to the same criteria as white; on the other hand, he did not totally reject a 'cultural' dimension to poverty.

In Elliotdale, or Bomvanaland as it is called — a Native counterpart of Poor White Knysna — the most densely populated ... and by all accounts one of the most backward districts in the Transkei, robust pagans contrive to live fairly happily on what looks like the same bare minimum as that which drives their more advanced fellows of Herschel and Kingwilliamstown to active discontent and despair.[25]

Macmillan certainly did not suggest that what he considered as 'unmistakably backward tribes' like the Bomvana, Mpondo, or those in Natal and the Transvaal, were not poor. What he argues is that 'poverty in these parts may be less obtrusive', that customary sharing helped to offset its effects and that, because they had little incentive to 'better themselves', such communities could effectively survive on a smaller money income.[26]

There seems to be a variety of cross-currents in Macmillan's ideas on this question, perhaps because he did not try to work through the implications of his argument. While 'tradition' is deployed in earlier work to help explain more acute forms of white poverty, it seems in *Complex South Africa* to be a concept which helps explain why some Africans could escape the worst effects of poverty. The contrast implied, but not expounded, could be the basis for an important insight into the differences between white and black experiences of industrialism: that the greater pervasiveness of the 'cash nexus' in white, landed communities made the poor whites more vulnerable to dispossession and shortage of money than some of the poor blacks.

But there is another element in Macmillan's analysis of African society which should be mentioned, and which seems to indicate a further subtle shift in his thinking during the 1920s. Whereas he seemed to have some sympathy with the strengths of the Afrikaner cultural heritage in the *Agrarian Problem*, he had little time for African traditionalism. Culture became less an explanatory device and more an object of impatience in *Complex South Africa*. There is a distinct tone of hostility in his references to 'reactionary chiefs', or 'the shrewd old fellows dressed in blankets' or the patriarchal homestead head — 'my lord, the greybeard of the kraal' — who would supervise ploughing by young girls, a whip [for the cattle] in his hand.[27]

By contrast, he had clear sympathies with the more 'progressive' elements in African society. His praise for the missionaries was fulsome: 'the spread of civilization among the Natives of South Africa, and with it any progress they have made, as tribes or as individuals, has been all but exclusively the work of the Christian missionaries'.[28] Those who 'better themselves', who are prepared to forsake their preoccupation with 'useless cattle', who live in 'neat and tidy villages' are praised: he doubts that they have 'had a tithe of the attention and sympathy they demand'. They were hampered by the 'backwardness of the masses of their own people', the demands of kin and the congestion of the reserves, and they experienced great difficulties in a segregated society if they attempted to live up to 'civilized' standards. At the time, such sentiments were widespread amongst 'progressive' Africans themselves as well as amongst their white sympathizers. Macmillan firmly marked himself as a progressive: improvement for African society depended on greater incorporation into the complex whole, and greater opportunity within it. Change should be conceived in the image of the contemporary 'progressive' communities: 'In the long run the progress of the native population in civilization is the only hope for the well-being of South Africa.'[29] This conclusion resonated with Macmillan's increasing hostility towards the discipline of anthropology, and towards those liberals who explored segregationist ideas.[30] As will be illustrated, it also made it difficult for him to understand what was happening in districts such as Herschel.

Some of the elements of Macmillan's dual legacy to subsequent historians can perhaps be traced to these tensions and shifts in his explanations of poverty. Historians such as de Kiewiet, Walker, Hancock (in his earlier work) and P. J. van der Merwe became obsessed by the frontier as an area of study and a method of explanation, largely ignoring his ideas about accumulation.[31] In part, at least, their concern derived from their general understanding of segregation. By and large, they saw segregation as antithetical to the modern economic expansion of the country. It seemed to be the result of the racial attitudes and insecurity of the more backward elements in white society — Afrikaners, poor whites, and white workers — rather than those who controlled industry and commerce. Thus the Afrikaner mentality and the poor whites, rather than English-speakers or the pattern of capitalist growth, became the focus of study, and the frontier a means of approaching it. These societal features were what made South Africa different, particularly in the context of the other British settler dominions which were often used as a comparative matrix by English-speaking historians at the time. There were countervailing interpretations of the frontier even then, especially in Robertson's work on economic interaction.[32] But such currents were largely swept aside by the mainstream of historical writing which explored the frontier thesis as Macmillan had helped to define it, some eleven years before Walker. In regard to African society, a number of subsequent historians and economists saw the factors inhibiting African progress not least as the result of the nature of African society itself — thus echoing one rather subdued theme in Macmillan's work, but neglecting his concern with the larger economic processes which actively impoverished African communities.

The radical historians, however, largely rejected the frontier thesis and, with it, the cultural explanations of backwardness and impoverishment.[33] Stress was laid on the increasingly commercial nature of farming, the effects of land speculation, and the demise of *bywoners* because of capitalist agrarian growth. It was the process of accumulation, rather than any intrinsic cultural hangover, which explained Afrikaner impoverishment. The 'frontier', it was suggested, was as much a zone of interaction as of exclusion. Race attitudes, and the roots of the segregationist state, should be traced to the differentiated pre-industrial society of the Western Cape and to the forms of labour exploitation that developed in the period of industrialization, rather than to the frontier. In regard to the white-owned farmlands, Macmillan's insights into the changing forms of African tenancy during the process of commercialization were greatly extended. The metaphor of a transition from feudalism to capitalism was given more rigorous content, especially by Morris.[34] (Macmillan himself does not seem to have used the term 'capitalism' in this sense.)

But it was perhaps Macmillan's observations about poverty in the reserves in particular that were most directly taken up. His arguments that these areas had suffered from a long and calculated neglect were developed through the use of comparative insights from the study of other peasant societies, and from underdevelopment theory. State intervention had systematically shaped the reserves into labour reservoirs, or, when it appeared to take on a more developmentalist ethic in the 1930s, had largely done so in order to underwrite a migrant labour system threatened by a more comprehensive collapse of rural production. His stress on the fact that the African population had been deeply incorporated into the larger economy by the early decades of the twentieth century, or even before, was generally accepted. The internal structures of African communities after conquest — and the nature of their social and political responses were not given much space in these analyses —except in the sense that they could be used to restore 'tribalism' or assure some internal social security functions.

As in the case of Macmillan's later work, such analyses display a considerable sympathy with the progressive African communities who, for a time, successfully entered and competed in a common political and economic world. The improving peasant became one of the heroes of the new historiography. Although the analysis presented was in many ways materialist and Marxist, it was also deeply influenced by the older liberal incorporationist ideas that were to be found in Macmillan's work. Such analyses were informed by a particular perspective on African society which charted its experience by examining the objective economic processes of incorporation, rather than the response of the mass of rural Africans. It is an approach which, in the context of subsequent economic developments and subsequent attempts by the state to enforce apartheid policies based on separate 'nations' and cultures, remains highly persuasive; in some respects at least it is shared by those writing from a number of different ideological perspectives: Marxists and radical materialists, liberal incorporationists (but not the liberal segregationists of Macmillan's era), and African nationalists. It may not be entirely out of order to talk of a Cape-liberal-marxism as the defining characteristic of many analyses of the reserves.

Macmillan and Herschel district: discovering his hidden agenda

The significance of Macmillan's interpretations, and their linkages to more recent economic analysis of the decline of the reserves, will become clearer if the case study of Herschel is considered in more detail. So too, perhaps, will the critique being offered of some elements in such approaches.

The central purpose of the survey of Herschel was to investigate, by means of statistical evidence, conditions in an 'isolated' reserve district — to go beyond the material being collected for the annual agricultural censuses. In doing this Macmillan had the full cooperation of the Office of Censuses and Statistics and hoped that his methods would be used 'to obtain more reliable figures as to native production and consumption'.[35] But, given his broader preoccupations, it is not surprising that he demonstrated, in the words of the concluding sentence of a chapter in *Complex South Africa*, that 'a huge proportion of the community here depicted exists on the very lowest level of bare subsistence'.[36] Macmillan's argument is with those people who felt they 'know something about Natives',[37] who implied that 'tribal' Africans were not really poor, just different, that they worked for wages merely to supplement their rural productive activities. It was in many respects an argument against the idea that Africans were still 'tribal' — as will become clear in some of the propositions he advanced.

Although Macmillan did not openly criticize anthropologists and anthropological techniques in his chapters on the reserves, his method of study contrasted significantly with theirs. He was certainly not content to rely on material accessible in Johannesburg, and he visited Herschel district for about a month later in 1925. But he did not undertake many interviews with the African population, working instead through the magistrate, and collecting statistical material and general comment from government officers, traders and labour recruiters. The assumptions which lay behind his methodology were what later became known as 'formalist': by implication, Africans

179

were regarded as economic men in a shared national economy. He did not evince any research interest in the customs of local African communities, or in the way in which these had been affected by 'culture contact'. This systematic avoidance of anthropological preoccupations and 'functionalist' assumptions must be seen as one of his major contributions.

At the time Macmillan was researching and writing the chapters that made up *Complex South Africa*, he was reacting to the earliest development of professional anthropology in the country, under the guidance of a few individuals who espoused rather static notions of culture and advocated an explicitly ahistorical methodology. It would not be accurate to suggest that the anthropologists working shortly afterwards — from the early 1930s — and who wrote the classic southern African ethnographies were of entirely the same school. They were certainly not unaware of the problem of poverty, of the value of an historical approach, and of statistics. But it is important to stress that the academic product and assumptions even of these later anthropologists were significantly different from Macmillan's. Hellmann's pioneering study of an urban slumyard in Johannesburg confronted just such questions of urban poverty. But a good deal of her report — published some years later — was devoted to an analysis of 'culture contact'.[38]

In some of the rural anthropological studies the weight given to the impact of the broader economy on African people is less pronounced. Monica Hunter's *Reaction to Conquest*, which in fact included an earlier attempt to chart urban conditions, was one of the first, much quoted, ethnographic classics of the 1930s.[39] In her assessment of 'tendencies', she did come to the overall conclusion that 'famines are averted, and the standard of living of a minority has been raised, but for many there is a poorer diet, increasing poverty and no security of support during periods of unemployment'.[40] She found that the population on white-owned farms was particularly impoverished. However, Hunter referred very generally to other studies when discussing poverty in this national context. She did not weave such an analysis into her detailed rural material, and she used the terms rich and poor largely to refer to differences of wealth within African society, with the implication that there had always been such a division. Perhaps Macmillan himself would have had difficulty in applying his techniques to Pondoland, or mounting a critique of Hunter's research; as mentioned above, he saw the area as one of the more distinctly 'backward' and less incorporated regions, where poverty was 'hidden'. It may also be that Hunter was less conscious of poverty in Pondoland because the area may have experienced an upsurge of production in the late 1920s and had not yet been severely affected by the depression when she did her research.[41] Nevertheless, the differences between the kind of approach adopted by Macmillan in the 1920s, and that adopted by some of the key anthropologists of the 1930s — the most significant group of scholars who studied African rural communities at the time — is striking.

Macmillan's chapter on Herschel, then, was largely a statistical demonstration of poverty. He calculated, as carefully as he could with the available data, the value of agricultural production, of exports from the district, and of imports into it. His conclusion was that Herschel was by no means self-sufficient in grain and agricultural products. Cash income from the wages of migrant workers was therefore essential for purchases of food, as well as the large range of commodities needed for survival. But this income was not sufficient in itself to balance the notional accounts of the district. His was a telling argument against those who maintained that migrant labour was in any sense voluntary, or provided only a little topping up to an essentially subsistence economy.

Two succeeding magistrates in Herschel commented on Macmillan's report before it was eventually published in *Complex South Africa*: Munscheid in 1927 and Key in 1930.[42] Munscheid, a young magistrate sensitive to the political and economic problems of the area, emphasized the inadequacy of the quantitative data on which both he and Macmillan had to rely for their calculations. In some respects, the figures available for Herschel were even less adequate than those for Transkeian districts, and grain production figures, like those for other reserve districts, were largely based on estimates. As Munscheid noted, there was no compulsory dipping of cattle in Herschel — as there was in the Transkeian Territories —and therefore no reliable information even on this key element in the local economy. He mentioned that there were great differences in the numbers of stock recorded in census returns for different locations which could not easily be explained: 'very likely large numbers of stock are omitted, while other lots are shown twice over i.e. by the actual owner and by the man in whose charge they happen to be while grazing in the mountains.'[43] Nor had returns of purchases and sales by traders been systematically collected — as they were in the Transkei — until Macmillan did so. (Munscheid introduced a questionnaire for traders shortly after Macmillan's visit.)

Munscheid also suggested that it was misleading to talk of average landholdings, given the great variation between families. He despaired of obtaining any accurate figures on landlessness as the land registration system had hardly been implemented and headmen were likely to exaggerate the extent of the problem. Overall, he felt that Macmillan's figures probably underestimated the average size of arable plots and the value of meat as a 'consumption asset'.[44] He suggested that the figures for absentees were probably inaccurate, and he improved the system of collecting pass figures. While the figures that Macmillan used were of passes issued for those leaving 'in search of work', they seem also to have included some very short-term seasonal workers and some going on visits. The total number of people leaving the district was probably an underestimate, but some of the 11,649 passes issued in 1924 may have been for purposes other than long contracts. As Macmillan noted, this number was 'an amazing total for a population of barely 40,000'.

Key, in a much briefer comment, also felt that Macmillan had underestimated arable plot sizes. He estimated migration at about 75 per cent of adult males working outside the district for about six months in every year — a figure which Macmillan accepted and included in his final published chapter. But generally Key felt that the report was 'a fair statement of the economic position of the district and all my calculations and estimates go to proving its correctness'. Herschel was certainly 'not self-sufficient'.[45]

In retrospect, it does seem likely that Macmillan's figures, and calculations, may have led to an underestimate of the combined value of production and wage income. The comments by the magistrates at the time seem to suggest this, and they do not appear to have made an attempt to disguise local economic difficulties. It should be added that the general method of estimation of grain output in reserve districts at the time probably resulted in an understatement of actual production.[46] Figures available for the amount of grain bought and sold by traders in the later 1920s suggest a smaller gap between production and consumption than that estimated by Macmillan, although the magistrate reporting them noted that some grain was bought direct by local people from outside the district.[47] As in many later estimates of the value of reserve production, Macmillan did not include the value of such fixed assets as housing. While he assigned a value to pastoral products such as milk, hides, skins, wool and meat, he did not calculate the value of livestock at market prices as part of the district's fixed assets. (Many subsequent attempts to quantify the value of reserve output did include such a figure.)

While he may not have underestimated the number of people leaving the district for employment, it seems likely that he did underestimate the amount that they earned.[48] He calculated the deficit in the district budget at between £35,000 and £50,000 annually. He was able to record approximately £15,000 coming into the district from wage income and implies that much of the rest of the deficit was probably paid for from the same source. (Some of the deficit would carry over year by year in the shape of debts due to traders, but accumulated debts from previous years would have to be paid from cash income.) However, even if £40,000 were returned in cash to the district, that would have meant that each absentee accounted for roughly £5 or, at most, two months' wages. Against this possible general underestimation, however, must be set the very high value which Macmillan assigned to milk production — at nearly £84,000 it accounted for over half the total estimated value of production in his table.[49] This may have been a realistic amount given the importance of milk in the diet, but it seems to have been proportionately rather greater than figures calculated in subsequent economic surveys.

It is probably impossible to arrive at any very satisfactory critique of Macmillan's statistics, or to replace them with much more accurate figures. And even if upward adjustments were to be made, the evidence of very considerable poverty in Herschel district in the 1920s is clear. Poverty was particularly noticeable because so many of the district's population were deeply incorporated into the national economy as consumers and wage labourers. The people of the district themselves were certainly aware of their poverty, especially in the inflationary years after the First World War. This much can be accepted, and Macmillan's report represented a very significant advance in academic understanding at the time.

However, this section is not designed primarily as a critique of Macmillan's statistics. Rather, it is aimed at discovering his more hidden agenda, his assumptions about the nature of society in the African reserves rather than just his record of the objective conditions of poverty. By way of illustration, various propositions,

183

some of which are written almost as asides, will be isolated. These refer to economic and political issues of a rather diverse nature but, as will be suggested, they reveal some of Macmillan's working ideas about African society, and about the necessary attributes of progress. These were ideas that do not now seem surprising or much out of key with subsequent radical and liberal thought. They will, however, be placed in the context of some of the social and political changes in Herschel in the 1920s as a means of testing their adequacy.[50]

The following propositions have been selected somewhat at random:

1   'The district is peculiarly isolated'; 'except for native passengers by foot or on horseback, communication with the O.F.S. is negligible.'[51]
2   It was the 'home of scattered remnants, left over or fleeing from wars elsewhere' ... 'remnants still go to make its population, with no big chiefs and no cohesion, and indeed a sturdy spirit of resistance to the unity which might come of a District Council or "Bunga".'[52]
3   '... it has obviously received no tangible or visible benefit from public expenditure on its needs.'[53]
4   'It shared neither the benefits of efficient Native Administration such as that in the Transkei nor the system of Divisional Councils which served white agricultural districts.'[54]
5   'That Herschel in 1925 was seething with discontent was the quite inevitable result of two generations and more of almost total neglect.'[55]

All of these propositions contain important insights, and are in some senses valid. Many subsequent scholars would have agreed with their general drift, although they might not have shared Macmillan's optimism about the benefits of efficient native administration. The notions that reserve districts were isolated, neglected and underfunded, and that chieftaincy and pre-colonial cohesion had been shattered by conquest and colonization occur regularly in the literature. For Macmillan, the implication of such ideas was essentially developmentalist and incorporationist — that rural Africans should not be peripheralized in the national polity and economy and that their lot should be improved by education, development expenditure, and more land.

But let us look a little more closely at the propositions — first, the idea that districts like Herschel were increasingly isolated and peripheralized. From the vantage point of the central institutions of the society, this was undoubtedly true. But it glosses over the fact that Herschel was, in some senses, a hub of African political and cultural activity at the time. In an era of mass migrancy, the isolation of any rural district should not be exaggerated. Thousands of people moved from the district to centres of employment throughout the country. Admittedly these were only 'Natives on foot and horseback'; but in a sense this is the whole point. The migrant labour economy, while it peripheralized Africans as producers, incorporated them ever more as labourers into the national economy. In fact, as Macmillan knew, the hinterland of Herschel's migrants was probably wider than most. It was a largely Christianized district and mine labour was not very popular in such areas. Certainly there were a good number of Herschel men in Kimberley and on the Rand, but a significant proportion of the better educated tended to find a wide range of employment in the ports: Cape Town, where wages were often higher and conditions could be better, was a favoured centre. In addition, many men and women worked in Bloemfontein and, especially those from the poorer and more traditionalist sections of the community, on the farms of the Orange Free State and the northern Cape.

Furthermore, there were burgeoning connections through channels other than the labour market. The progressive élite was greatly involved in organizations such as the Teachers Association and the recently established branch of the 'Native Congress' which took their lead from their peers in the heartlands of the eastern Cape. The mission churches, particularly the Methodists and Anglicans, were well represented, and Herschel people had wide connections with church members in the eastern and northern Cape and Orange Free State, depending on the particular organization of circuits and dioceses in various denominations. African independent churches were spreading, especially from the Rand and Bloemfontein. At the same time, Herschel was the base of one of the earliest breakaways from the Methodist church: the African Native Church under Jonas Goduka, who sent missionaries far and wide from his base near Blikana. The well known educational institutions of Bensonvale and St Michael's drew students from many surrounding districts and, particularly in the 1920s, from Lesotho. Patterns of intermarriage, especially amongst the predominant Hlubi community, provided linkages with East Griqualand and the rural areas of Natal. All these

185

connections were reflected in the social and political thinking of the people of the district in the 1920s as they organized themselves in some remarkable political movements. Far from being an isolated district, it was — from the point of view of the African communities there — something of a crossroads for movements, ideas and networks. This point is of some importance. The marginalization of such reserve districts has often been stressed in the literature from Macmillan's time onwards. The experience of Africans in the reserves has been presented largely through an objective analysis of their underdevelopment and peripheralization in the national agrarian economy. This process was taking place, but such an analysis omits the enormous growth in mobility and its influence on subjective responses to domination.

This point becomes even more significant when it is put in the context of the nature of political responses in the district. In a sense, Macmillan was correct to say that Herschel's population was made up of 'remnants' with 'no big chiefs' — Bundy confirms this point in his brief history of the settlement of the district before its hey-day as an exporter of peasant-grown crops in the second half of the nineteenth century. Many immigrants and refugees moved into the district — from the Highveld, from Lesotho, from the eastern and north-eastern Cape — during the mid-nineteenth century, and no overarching chiefly political authority had been recognized by the state or people. The colonial administrative system had, to a greater extent in Herschel than many Transkeian districts, worked through government-appointed headmen who derived their authority from the state rather than through chiefs. But Macmillan's characterization was only very partially correct. In the first place, there was a considerable minority, if not a small majority, of Hlubi people in the district. Second, many of them, as well as others who may not have been 'Hlubi' in origin, were involved in a movement of cultural and political revival during the 1920s. This included widespread support for a popular claimant to a headmanship in one location of the district. But he was seen not only as an aspirant headman, but also as a prospective chief for the whole of the district who would represent popular opinion in opposition to the government-appointed headmen. The political responses of many people in Herschel would suggest that chieftaincy — of a certain kind — was more important and acceptable to them than Macmillan realized.

Macmillan clearly felt that unity and progress might come through the development of a district council, although he did not necessarily agree with the form and funding principles of the Transkeian 'Bunga'. This was a position strongly advocated both by local officials and the local African 'progressives'. The opposition, who seem to have carried the support of a significant majority of the district's diverse population — except perhaps of the Sotho-speaking minority — were adamantly opposed to councils. Their coherence as a political force under the leadership of the local *Iliso Lomzi* (Vigilance Association) arose not least because of this issue. The district did not lack political cohesion at all in the 1920s: it was divided into two well organized movements or groupings. The unity of the majority of the people was achieved precisely because of the 'sturdy spirit of resistance' to the 'Bunga'. Councils were seen to be directly inimical to any spirit of unity because they would be susceptible to domination by the 'progressive' element — the headmen and the state. A form of chieftaincy responsive to popular demands, and what were perceived as customary rights, was generally preferred.

These points may seem to indicate only a relatively minor misinterpretation of the district's politics by Macmillan, who had in any case little research interest in such questions. But the pattern of popular politics had important implications for the possibility of pursuing the kind of developmentalist approach which Macmillan had in mind. The problem in Herschel was not just that there had been limited 'public expenditure on its needs', but also that the popular movements had become deeply hostile to any state initiatives in the district. In part, this hostility stemmed from fears that the people themselves would be made responsible for funding all new public expenditure through the new tax which would accompany any implementation of the council system. The benefits that might result from such a tax — particularly expenditure on items such as roads, schools and agricultural development — were seen to be benefits largely for the 'progressive' minority. But the opposition to public expenditure in the district ran deeper, to include not only prospective council spending based on a new tax, but also centrally funded schemes such as anti-erosion works and land reorganization. The problem in Herschel district was that many of its inhabitants opposed all forms of public expenditure because they were seen to create unwanted costs, both financial and political: they would be the means whereby the remaining local control over resources would be undermined. Herschel was seething with discontent in the 1920s not so much because it was being neglected by the state, but because officials were beginning to try to implement a variety of measures on which they felt the district's future development depended.

Macmillan's insights and judgements on Herschel district thus accorded with those of officials and progressives. He also shared their disdain for 'reactionaries' who rejected the ideas of progress held up by this section of the population. Like the local officials, he tended to divide the African population into stark categories — of those who were for progress and those who were against it. Those against were the 'reactionary chiefs', the 'shrewd old fellows in blankets' and 'my lord, the greybeard of the kraal'. The popular movement in fact included educated men and women, many of them Christians belonging to either mission or, especially, independent churches. It was not so much that they were against progress, but that they conceived progress in a different way. While some of them were from families which had been improving peasant producers, they articulated a deep-seated suspicion of any improvement which implied accumulation of land, wealth or power by a minority: hence their support for communal land tenure and chieftaincy. They saw the local 'progressives' as political and economic accumulators whose activities threatened general access to resources in the district. Their battle was for a local autonomy, because further incorporation and further state intervention seemed likely only to result in the undermining of their remaining economic and political independ- ence. More widespread 'Africanist' ideas in the churches and political movements, relayed to and from Herschel along the diverse networks mentioned above, reinforced and affirmed the ideological coherence of the popular movement.

Macmillan was of course trapped by the common currency of discussion about African communities at the time, and he was dependent on local officials and the progressive African élite for much of his information. The alternative vision of 'progress' available amongst his intellectual peers at the time — not including the Left — was 'liberal-segregationist'. This was an approach — shared by academics such as Brookes and Loram, as well as some government officials — which has been associated with the decline of faith in the Victorian civilizing mission and the new imperatives created by an industrial economy.[56] White liberals had to come to terms with the dominant ideology of segregation if they were to retain influence on policy-making; a number of black leaders, grappling for concessions from an increasingly intransigent state also explored compromises which fell far short of incorporation into a common society but seemed to offer scope for local self-control. One of the major elements of the position, particularly evident from the time of the Natives Land Act (1913), was the notion of protective segregation: that Africans could not compete effectively in a common society and thus the remaining land which they held should be reserved or it would be lost. The older liberal optimism about the erosion of 'tribal' structures was dwindling and the value of 'traditional' institutions such as chieftaincy reassessed. Like Macmillan, liberal-segregationists were certainly committed to 'development', but they tended to argue, as in the *Report of the Native Economic Commission* (1932), that development should take place in segregated reserves, recognizing the 'differentness' of African culture, identity and capacity.

In the context of the 1920s, it can certainly be appreciated why Macmillan was hostile to such ideas, and the associated increase in sympathy for elements of what were seen as traditional African society and culture. In reprospect, the liberal-segregationism of this period seems a wayward deviation from the mainstream of liberal thought in South Africa; indeed, some of the intellectuals — as opposed to government officials — shifted away from this position by the 1930s. When he formulated the chapters in *Complex South Africa*, Macmillan did not have the benefit of the work of the more flexible and historically conscious anthropology which was to develop in the 1930s: a group of scholars who, for all the limitations of their work, could retain both deep respect for African society as it was, recognize some degree of change, and at the same time remain, for the most part, committed integrationists. (Macmillan would still have had difficulty with their approach and method.)

Macmillan's ideas about African societies seem therefore to have captured only one part of their reality. He apparently had little interest in their past and little understanding of the non-'progressive' forces operating within them.[57] Despite his ability to capture processes of agrarian change in an imaginative analysis and graphic language, he was not driven by the same social imagination about 'other' cultures which spurred anthropologists to their innovative and interesting research in the 1930s. He was prescient in his diagnosis of the extent of economic integration, and the extent of real impoverishment amongst rural Africans. But his assumptions led him to accept, often implicitly rather than explicitly, the ideas and aims of the articulate 'progressive' leaders who were so widely regarded as collaborators within their own communities. Although some of his arguments have been greatly extended and modified by subsequent research, the developmentalist and 'progressive' thread remained deeply embedded in the writing of liberals and radicals in the 1960s and 1970s. The approach adopted in the early phases of radical historiography laid great emphasis on the extent to which Africans had been incorporated into a common economy in the early decades of the twentieth century. The central capitalist economy was seen as the primary determinant of change. Much political analysis — geared particularly to a rediscovery of the roots of African nationalism and trade unions — took as its baseline Macmillan's views that the Africans were 'very nearly a proletariat' soon after the turn of the century.

But the conflict of approach between Macmillan and the anthropologists has by no means been completely resolved in more recent analyses of the South African political economy in the first few decades of the twentieth century. Overviews written in the early 1970s, which concentrated largely on the shaping influence of capitalist accumulation, subsequently came under some criticism. One such criticism was that changes in African society could not be analysed merely through a discussion of the dominant social forces in the country — nor could they be understood merely by using the kind of material of which Macmillan might have approved. A countervailing tendency took the changes within African communities as a far more central field of study and drew heavily, if critically, on the material collected by anthropologists. Fieldwork which involved lengthy interviews in rural districts again became an acceptable and essential method of research. 'Understanding the native mind', an exercise which Macmillan felt to be rather spurious, or at least not urgent, again became a central white academic preoccupation.

The two broad approaches pursued by radical historians in the 1970s were informed by not dissimilar theoretical perspectives, but they resulted in significantly different academic products: on the one hand, analyses of the forces which shaped the incorporation of Africans into the capitalist economy — particularly as a cheap labour supply; on the other, detailed monographs of the effects of incorporation on specific communities. Macmillan's insights which laid so much stress on the extent of economic incorporation influenced both strands of writing, but were perhaps more easily absorbed into the former than the latter. And it is perhaps out of the preoccupation with the minutiae of localized processes of change in African communities that a more rounded view of the balance of forces in the early twentieth century will emerge: a view that can explain the kinds of responses which Macmillan found difficult to understand in Herschel district in the 1920s; and an analysis which may help us to understand why liberal incorporationist ideology has proved so fragile a flower, amongst blacks as well as whites, in the harsh political ecology of twentieth-century South Africa.

9

W. M. MACMILLAN, SOUTH AFRICAN SEGREGATION AND COMMONWEALTH RACE RELATIONS, 1919–1938

PAUL RICH

IF the western liberal tradition was a delicate European plant that fared rather badly in the hot dry soil of southern Africa, it was one which still managed to sprout a number of separate shoots. In the wake of the political defeat of Union in 1910 and the failure to extend the Cape common franchise to the north, a reconsolidation of the liberal impulse took place on the Witwatersrand during and after the First World War where the Joint Council movement was founded in 1921 and was to become closely attached to the University of the Witwatersrand, established in the following year. The 'Johannesburg school of liberalism', as it was termed by Edgar Brookes, sought an empirical economic analysis which placed a 'greater reliance on economic facts in the place of sentiment and tradition'.[1] This reflected a growing professionalization of intellectual and academic knowledge in place of the previously amateur and informal charitable and philanthropic concern. In many respects, nevertheless, there were still, for a number of years, close links with the missionary tradition that sought to 'uplift' Africans into a common western civilization. These links were reflected especially in the figure of W. M. Macmillan.

Born in Scotland, Macmillan spent his childhood in the western Cape village of Stellenbosch, before returning to Britain and Germany for his university studies.[2] In 1910 he returned to South Africa to teach history at Rhodes University College in Grahamstown and was confronted by a British policy that was increasingly based upon accommodation with white settlers in the newly formed union. The implications of this were not immediately apparent as he became progressively involved in teaching and administrative duties but the ideology of territorial segregation began to erode the values of the surviving liberalism in the Cape. Despite the passage of the 1913 Natives Land Act and the debate surrounding the Native Administration Bill, by the time Macmillan joined the discussions on segregation in 1919, there was nevertheless still a feeling in some liberal circles that government policy was amenable to reason. They hoped it could be cajoled into a progressive direction. But, as one of the African liberals involved in this debate, S. M. Molema, pointed out, racial separation had to be 'equitable' and conducted on a 'proper constitutional basis' with 'cooperation' between black and white.[3] It was the hope of a number of English-speaking liberal intellectuals at this time that a form of political consensus could be established around a benevolent version of segregation which would both guarantee African land rights, preserve urban industrial jobs for 'poor whites' who had been thrust off the land, and ensure as far as possible the continuation of squatting by *bywoners* as part of a balanced and integrated economic system. It was with aims similar to these that Macmillan began his participation in the national debate, after moving to Johannesburg at what was to become the University of the Witwatersrand in 1917 as Professor of History.

The hope for a 'just' system of segregation

By 1919 Macmillan began to warn in *The South African Agrarian Problem and its Historical Development* of the forces which were reducing the *bywoners*, or white tenant farmers, to proletarian status. Comparing this process to the British Industrial Revolution in the eighteenth century, he perceived the growth of 'social caste, the landlord and the landless' which were in turn aggravating political feuds in the body politic. Race and colour were not really crucial to this process for 'the point on which to concentrate attention is not the colour of the man's skin, but his standard of life and his wage'. It was important, however, to establish 'safeguards' regarding the employment of blacks in industry while 'the superior skills and experience of the white will be the best security against the danger of undercutting white men by an inferior class of native'.[4]

Macmillan was acquainted with the phenomenon of poor-whiteism from the time he lectured at Rhodes University in Grahamstown. He thus supported the idea of establishing a political consensus in white opinion for a 'just' solution to African land demands in order to prevent competition in the towns between Africans and poor whites for jobs as far as possible. The publication of *The South African Agrarian Problem*, however, marked an important shift of emphasis from the study of 'poor whites' towards a recognition that there was a more general 'agrarian problem' in the Cape based not on race but economic forces impoverishing both white and black *bywoners*.[5] This became especially apparent from an historical perspective. As he began work on the John Philip papers, it appeared that the South African 'agrarian problem' was deep-rooted with 'many of the problems ... still essentially the same' — or perhaps aggravated by 'ignorance and neglect'. He also recognized that 'by learning all I can about the essentials of the modern problem, I do want to try to avoid obvious mistakes and pitfalls in interpreting its beginning in the last half century'.[6]

At this time Macmillan was not clear on the exact historical relationship of Philip's times to the contemporary land issue; but in his paper at the Conference of the Dutch Reformed Churches in 1923 he stressed the historical longevity of the 'native question' insofar as it was rooted in 'the land question'. Philip was upheld for realizing the saliency of land in white–black relations and advocating the demarcation of separate territorial areas for each group. He was also important for recognizing that whites should not overexpand in their settlement, though even before his death in 1851 he was a witness to the increasing expropriation of African land. While the 1913 Land Act in some degree returned to Philip's precepts it was, Macmillan considered, a measure 'born, not of a passion for justice to the weaker race, but too much as a defensive, if not a selfish, measure for the benefit of the dominant white race'.[7]

Macmillan's condemnation of segregation from the baseline of Philip's nineteenth-century liberalism struck a powerful chord amongst liberal critics of the South African segregationist model. In particular, it was buttressed by the arguments of the Eastern Transvaal Natives Land Committee under the chairmanship of Ernest Stubbs, who was later to become both a friend of Macmillan's and an ally in the Native Affairs Department. Stubbs' report opposed the opening up of the Transvaal lowveld to white settlement and argued that, from a long-term standpoint, it was better to lock up land for the sake of African agricultural prospects and so prevent the evictions that were starting to occur in some areas of the veld. Macmillan also opposed the overextension of white settlement, for it was still unclear in the 1920s what the long-term prospects of white agriculture were in the tropical and lowveld regions of the sub-continent.[8]

In a series of newspaper articles published as *The Land, The Native and Unemployment* in 1924 he expounded more fully the dilemmas confronting policy-makers for whom the central task had to be 'to lessen [the] fatal direct competition of black and white'. Unlike previous imperialists who had seen colonial terrains as wholesome pastoral outlets for the tensions of urban metropolitan societies, Macmillan viewed the industrialization of South African society as liable to result in some dangerous, if not pathological, social consequences. Far-reaching social reforms were needed since 'both for Europeans and for natives we are dealing with diseases rooted deep in the social system, and with habits of life heavily entrenched in the conservatism of human nature'.[9] It was a fallacy to imagine that the old idea of relieving poverty and distress through sub-tropical colonization could be continued for

It is a confession that we are to throw up the sponge before even trying the thing out, and turn our backs on the problem of making the temperate zone of South Africa a real national home. And what is much more, if the penetration by Europeans of the only obvious native areas remaining is to be carried to any serious lengths, it is going to be fatal to our hope of relieving the land starvation of the natives and of making real progress in the problems of sound native administration.[10]

Producing a map showing the increase of the African population between 1911 and 1921, Macmillan warned of the dangers of the growing congestion of the African reserves and the flight of white *bywoners* from the land. It was a fallacy to imagine that, through segregation, the issues of the reserves could be dealt with in isolation:

The moral is just this. The Transvaal cannot employ round about 200,000 male natives from the Union without being in some sense responsible for a vastly greater number of dependents, old men, women and children. To a very large extent the native territories are the homes of this great mass —our 'barracks'. We certainly could not, and for excellent reasons should not, even if we could, transplant these families to the towns. It is hard enough to secure decent sites for necessary locations. But with regard to these dependents it certainly is out of sight, out of mind.[11]

The issue thus hinged on the degree to which the South African state was willing to admit the legitimacy of African land demands in order for the system of benevolent segregationism, combined with the subsistence role performed by the reserves to work. Otherwise, the continuing employment of male African migrants in 'white' urban areas inevitably led to permanent African proletarianization, which was a phenomenon Macmillan hoped could be at least controlled and limited in South Africa. However, some economic analysts had by this time come to doubt the feasibility of establishing territorial segregation. R. A. Lehfeldt, for example, who was Professor of Economics at the University of the Witwatersrand, warned in 1920 that far from being a policy to maintain social cohesion in South Africa, segregation would act to 'revolutionise the country' given the degree to which Africans were 'so thoroughly incorporated' into its industries. It would, in short, 'be a heroic policy beyond the power of any statesman'. Nevertheless, Lehfeldt still suggested an east-west diagonal partition of the country into a 'colony of settlement' comprising the western Cape, Orange Free State and Transvaal, and a 'plantation colony' of the eastern Cape and Natal, so his argument had by no means freed itself of segregationist ideology.[12]

To a number of South African opinion-formers in the early 1920s, however, segregation appeared to contain the germ of a radical policy that would both restrict the activities of monopoly capitalists as well as ensure a degree of rational planning of the economy.[13] J. D. Rheinallt Jones, the editor of *The South African Quarterly*, looked to the possibility of the 'friends of the "poor white" and the friends of the native making common cause against the monopolistic landowner'.[14] Macmillan, however, considered this unlikely in the absence of effective black political pressure and urged the African members of the Joint Council in Johannesburg to demand more land at the next conference with the Native Affairs Commission and to resist as far as possible the pressures for white settlement in the Transvaal lowveld for growing cotton.[15]

In 1925, the Native Affairs Commission reported, after touring the eastern Transvaal in January, that at most white centres (except for Lydenburg) there were demands for a new Land Commission to be established.[16] These pressures for a stricter segregation policy intensified during the following year, though the Prime Minister, General J. B. M. Hertzog, proclaimed his commitment to an administrative policy based on the reports of the five land committees of 1918.[17] The objective of white liberal opinion on the Witwatersrand organized through the Joint Councils was to maintain the channels of communication to the centre of political decision-making as open as possible.

It was generally argued that the segregation policy on the land would be linked to a policy of political segregation leading to the establishment of what Rheinallt-Jones imagined would be an African 'parliament' not substantially different to the Union House of Assembly. This seemed feasible after Hertzog's speech at Smithfield in November 1925 outlining in detail the Pact Government's policy of consolidating the land demarcated for Africans into seven territories, each with its own elected white representative in the House of Assembly. Rheinallt Jones wrote to congratulate the Prime Minister on a 'very courageous' statement and to assure him of the continued support of the Joint Council in the unravelling of the proposals. These, he considered, served as 'a bold effort to frame a sound national policy on Native affairs'.[18] He continued to believe that Hertzog's Pact government could move beyond the simple policy of keeping African peasants on the land to a 'national' policy which would modernize agrarian social relations. Hopeful that the laws of supply and demand and economic efficiency would ultimately prevail, Rheinallt Jones appealed for a flexible system of land tenure. This he hoped would offer an avenue of escape to proletarianized farmworkers through either leaseholding or freeholding and would dismantle the old landed system which he saw as an anachronistic survival of 'patriarchal and slave owning days'.[19]

By 1925, Macmillan began to break away from the more con-ciliatory line of his Joint Council colleagues such as Rheinallt Jones. Turning to Patrick Duncan, a former minister in the Smuts government, he asked if anything could be done to 'check the [non-party] madness of the Govt's native policy' for the government seemed 'determined to carry out their one-eyed "white policy" at any cost'. It was possible that Hertzog himself cared more than his colleagues for 'justice and for the consequences', but he was unable to stand up to the die-hards such as Tielman Roos and Colonel Creswell. According to Macmillan, the policy's longer-term consequences would be catastrophic, for 'the placid and easily governed Bantu will presently become a grievance-bitten, ill-tempered proletariat and then we shall have constant squalls'.[20] This temporary resort to Duncan, a former member of the Milner Kindergarten and a prominent South African figure in the international Round Table network, perhaps indicated a change of political tack as Macmillan began to doubt the possibilities of influencing policy-making at the centre in any significant manner.

Macmillan had, in fact, been granted an interview with Hertzog shortly after the latter took office in October 1924 and a longer-term consequence of this was that, in late 1925, he was authorized to conduct a study of Herschel. While Hertzog may have seen this authorization as part of the government's policy for implementing a policy of territorial segregation, Macmillan hoped to use the study to demonstrate the inadequacy of the census data and to show the poverty of the reserves. The report was completed in January 1926 and despatched to Pretoria. Macmillan heard nothing of the government's response, however, so that by the time he began a series of articles in *The Cape Times*, it seemed as if the moment for a decisive impact on policy had passed. In the same month, he emphasized how the permanency of urbanization was creating a class of Africans who could not be sent back to the reserves. This class he saw as consisting of a small petite bourgeoisie that had emerged as a consequence of the industrial colour bar which denied Africans opportunities and forced them into 'bookish callings — as parsons (out of all proportion), teachers and clerks'. It was essential, he concluded, until the reserves became 'better developed', not to 'drive these people to recruit the ranks of a fourth class — the "agitators"'.[21]

The ideology of reserve 'development' began to appear increasingly as a chimera, however, since the fieldwork that he had conducted at Herschel indicated the general impossibility of reversing the trend towards proletarianization. Surveying the impact of the Glen Grey policy in the eastern Cape locations, Macmillan argued that, with many plots no larger than one morgen in extent, the income from labour was far more important in sustaining rural subsistence than the income from trade and peasant production. In Glen Grey itself there were some 8,000 allotments and a waiting list of 4,000; the growing density of population was resulting in soil erosion and the decline of cattle pasture. Ultimately, government policy was to be condemned for failing to inject into the 'Native Development Fund' money from general revenue which was raised from Africans when it was established under the Native Taxation and Development Act in 1925.[22]

On the one hand, Macmillan's general indictment of the

government put him at odds with the Joint Council strategy of building bridges with individual government departments. On the other hand, however, it accorded with growing doubts amongst some of the African members of the Council, such as Selby Msimang, as to the possibility of influencing government policy through the system of European–Bantu conferences.[23] The general style of government policy was towards ever-increasing bureaucratization. As the liberally-minded member of the Native Affairs Commission, Dr A. W. Roberts, conceded, this was forcing African leaders increasingly to distrust the older methods of personal consultation with officials of the Native Affairs Department.[24] The Joint Council had been able to establish some links with friendly officials in the NAD such as the controversial Ernest Stubbs, who unofficially helped in its memorandum on *General Hertzog's Solution to the Native Question*.[25] By 1926, however, there was strong pressure on the Joint Council liberals from the educationalist Charles T. Loram to establish closer consultative links with the senior echelons of the NAD under the Secretary of Native Affairs, Major Herbst. This was at a time when the department itself was seeking to expand its area of control and influence under the Native Administration Bill. The Joint Council significantly avoided debating this measure in public and established instead a sub-committee of five Africans, including Selby Msimang and Victor Selope Thema, to consider its provisions in detail.[26]

By the end of 1925, therefore, Macmillan was becoming known as a controversial figure whom Hertzog had attacked in a parliamentary debate as a 'comparative dabbler'. At this time he could still count on Smuts to intervene on his behalf, but the growing notoriety of his writings was leading to his progressive marginalization from the white liberal establishment on the Witwatersrand. The completed first volume of his research on Philip, *The Cape Colour Question*, was, he admitted to Pim, 'a tract on the present problem disguised as pure history'[27] and he used the holistic vision of Philip's conception of benevolent segregation to berate South African political leadership for its poverty of political imagination.

Macmillan's conception of South African history had always been influenced by his visits and his contact with a wider set of figures who perceived the logic of South Africa's segregationist policy in a more international setting, and whom he influenced in turn. Prominent among these was Sydney Olivier whom Macmillan had first met in 1920 but now visited whenever he came to England at his home at Ramsden in Oxfordshire. Olivier's book *The Anatomy of African Misery* in 1927 owed much to Macmillan's analysis of the destruction of African peasant communities by the migrant labour system, though his argument was significant for linking the internal dynamics of South African segregationism to a wider process of 'capitalist imperialism'. In contrast to Macmillan's rather oblique analogy in *The South African Agrarian Problem* between South African industrialization and the British Industrial Revolution in the eighteenth century, Olivier pointed out its historical uniqueness. He argued that 'the appropriation of the ownership of African land under the policy of capitalist development, of a character unprecedented in the history of mankind, is a very singular phenomenon'.[28]

Instead of dating the critical turning-point in white settlement policy as the mid-1850s, after the death of John Philip, as Macmillan had done, Olivier emphasized the critical decade of the 1890s. This, he maintained, was when the older school of Colonial Office administrators concerned with a *mission civilisatrice* lost out to a group of financiers and imperialist politicians who were abetted by the British High Commissioner in Southern Africa, Sir Henry Loch. The shift in emphasis reflected the importance of capitalist industrialization from the late 1870s and 1880. In the light of the Hobsonian analysis of capitalist imperialism, Olivier was concerned less with the factor of land in economic analysis than with land *and* capital, both of which, he argued, in neo-Ricardian fashion, could extract an unearned income in the form of either rent or profit.

More widely, Olivier's writings reflected an anxiety among some British officials in the late 1920s about the direction of South African segregation. They helped to shape a notion of 'counterpoise politics' that could offset 'Afrikaner' power to the south through the establishment of a British dominion in East and Central Africa.[29] In *The Cape Colour Question*, however, Macmillan still hoped for a continuation of the mid-nineteenth-century civilizing mission towards the Cape Coloureds and its extension to black Africans. Questioning the assertion of a number of observers, including Olivier, that South Africa's 'native problem' was unique, Macmillan argued that 'the problem thrashed out in the old Cape Colony is essentially a particular example of the World Race Problem' and thus one given to comparative analysis. He considered that the Cape Coloureds had failed to develop a national consciousness of their own, and remained suspended between white and black communities. They 'had no political grievance', were 'proud of their rights' and were 'definitely making upward progress'.[30] Despite its pretentions to being a 'political tract', however, Macmillan's book failed to investigate the contemporary political consciousness of the Cape Coloureds; its optimistic tone bespoke a similar faith in the value of a brown intermediary class which Olivier had manifested in the Jamaican context since the publication of the first edition of *White Capital and Coloured Labour* in 1906.[31]

In the year of the publication of *The Cape Colour Question*, Macmillan grew increasingly interested in the trajectory of black politics in South Africa as concern grew among the liberals on the Witwatersrand about the growing resistance amongst African political leaders to collaboration with the Joint Councils. At a meeting in August 1927 of the Johannesburg Joint Council, Macmillan called on the Council to gather more information on the ICU after Victor Selope Thema reported that efforts to get some of the officials of the Union to attend the Council's meetings had failed.[32] In an article for *The New Statesman* the following year he warned that 'Natives of any intelligence (and some without) are seething with suspicion and discontent' and there was a 'real danger of the ablest of the Natives pushing the uncivilised masses with them into this sharp hostility, instead of leading them up to civilisation'.[33] By the 1929 election and Hertzog's second defeat of Smuts' South African Party (SAP) he was clearly reaching a crossroads in his career and, in December of that year, Margery Perham described him as 'bitter' against the 'Dutch' whom he considered had replaced the former system of slavery with a new structure of legalised serfdom.[34]

A real break came in the middle of 1930 when Macmillan was able to take up an invitation to visit East Africa from Philip Mitchell, whom he had originally met when Mitchell visited South Africa on leave in 1924.[35] From 1925 until 1934 Mitchell was Secretary of Native Affairs in Tanganyika and in 1929 had been impressed by Macmillan's *Bantu, Boer, and Briton*. This book outlined in further detail the thesis on John Philip that he had propounded since 1923, with the special emphasis that it had been the withdrawal of British imperial power in the early 1850s which had led to 'the cementing of a defensive alliance of British and Boers against the natives'. This, he argued, laid the essential historical basis for the contemporary 'native problem'.[36] The argument confirmed for Mitchell the view that above all native land must be made secure. We have got much done in that we have a legal partition that is fairly satisfactory, but a protection in law has never yet been effective for ignorant people who do not know how to use it.[37]

Although a friend of Sir Hanns Vischer and member of the circle centred on the International Institute of African Languages and Cultures, which had been established in London in 1926, Mitchell was suspicious of the new school of professional anthropologists gathering around Bronislaw Malinowski at the London School of Economics. Macmillan voiced similar suspicions in the preface to *Complex South Africa* in 1930, arguing that 'excessive claims' had been made by the discipline for the 'government of native races'.[38] Macmillan's annual leave from mid-1930 to February 1931 thus turned out to be a critical turning-point in his relations with the South African liberal establishment as pressures to make Bantu Studies a focal point of research and political debate drew to a head.

New departures: anthropology and the problem of 'culture contact'

Although some anthropologists such as Isaac Schapera were still concerned in the 1920s to keep open links with historical research,[39] the general trend in the discipline was towards an assertion of a distinct 'science' of social processes. In part, this reflected a strong effort to obtain professional status and eliminate the still lingering Victorian image of anthropologists as amateur dabblers in the quaint customs of exotic peoples. Malinowski was the foremost spokesman for this strategy of professional closure and despite any nagging private fears, wrote with exuberant confidence that 'as soon as the study of man becomes "rationalised" it will proceed as ruthlessly to dehumanize human nature as science is even now obliterating the natural fact of the inanimate world'.[40] Mitchell tried as far as possible to resist the grandiose dimension of these claims for a functionalist scientism. Instead, he repeatedly urged a more empirical anthropological approach based on the application of results of scientific investigations to 'the solution of practical problems' at local level.[41]

Macmillan had been familiar with this debate since at least 1926 and during his East African visit in 1930 was probably able to discuss his ideas with Mitchell. The latter warned of relying too heavily on a 'small Europeanised group' of Africans who 'like the Nationalists in Egypt or India aspire merely to replace a white ruling caste by a coloured one'; the chief aim should be 'to guide and help the social and political forms common to all the peoples within the main stream of the 20th century instead of taking a very small number out of the life of their race and giving them your culture and social forms'.[42] Mitchell's message accorded to some degree with the contemporary British conception of liberalism as a doctrine that emphasized common citizenship. To this extent, he eschewed attempts to establish false barriers of 'culture' that both inhibited this process and created an obsession with preserving the past antiquities of African culture. This did not mean, however, that the reserve economies could not be made to assist in this basic 'civilizing' function:

Reserves, as understood in the union and Rhodesia, cannot be the only cradles of African civilisation, any more than the extreme and mountainous north of Scotland can be a cradle of Anglo-Saxon civilisation, but they may be the finest possible ground on which to train the raw material of your civilisation and in which to raise the hardy stocks which will in due course be drawn into your more progressive and advanced areas.[43]

This implied a continuing link between the 'scientific' investigation of African social and economic conditions and a political strategy of establishing an expanding African political class outside the narrow parameters of a tiny educated élite.

The model of economic development of the reserves propounded by Mitchell was one which Macmillan came to share to a considerable degree, both from his experience of the Herschel study and from his wider travels in Africa. The South African ideology of segregation had begun increasingly to define the terms of debate on 'native policy' in the Union itself, and Macmillan was seeking to move beyond a model of piecemeal socioeconomic reform. In the light of growing evidence indicating the decline of peasant agriculture, some liberals, such as Howard Pim, became attracted to the idea of encouraging African peasant enterprise in the reserves.[44] The approach emphasized that there was no insuperable barrier between 'European' and 'African' cultures. 'As ... both races are today in contact' Pim stated in an address at a European–Bantu conference in Lovedale in 1930, 'it is practically certain that the Bantu will gradually adopt individualism and develop as Europeans have done in conformity with certain laws.'[45]

The failure of the African reserve economies was thus to be explained through the ignorance and poor education of the African peasants themselves in the ways of 'European' market society rather than as a consequence of structural inhibitions on growth resulting from migrant labour and taxation. The 'problems' were thus conceived as being rooted in education and it was this issue which Winifred Hoernlé, who lectured in anthropology at the University of the Witwatersrand, moved into the forefront of the investigations of the new functionalist anthropology in the South African context. She argued that the anthropologist was to be compared to a physiologist 'analysing the way in which a living structure works', although there was the further need to maintain 'sympathy and understanding with the efforts of the Bantu people to maintain a culture' in order to bring them 'such enlightenment as we have ourselves attained'.[46]

This view not only reformulated the older missionary ideal in the terminology of an ostensibly 'neutral' anthropological social science; it also led to an abandonment of systematic historical investigation in favour of an 'inductive' study of the 'functioning of living societies and cultures'.[47] It accorded closely with the new climate of thought on South African 'native policy' epitomized by the Report of the Native Economic Commission in 1932 which argued for the 'adaptation' of African societies and their internal regeneration to 'European' norms rather than their 'assimilation' to, or complete 'separation' from, them.[48] The newly founded South African Institute of Race Relations shared this emphasis on anthropological research and Rheinallt Jones, its 'Adviser', lectured part-time in Native Law and Administration from 1927 onwards at the University of the Witwatersrand. During 1930 the Institute, under the aegis of Rheinallt-Jones and R. F. A. Hoernlé, agreed to a Bantu Studies programme that was to be funded by the Rockefeller Foundation and coordinated through the International Institute for African Languages and Cultures in London.[49]

Thus, after Macmillan returned from leave in February 1931, he became increasingly politically isolated as it became evident that his book *Complex South Africa*, published in 1930, was out of tune with the white liberal accommodation towards segregationism. The book's powerful plea for a reassessment of segregationism fell on deaf ears, and the Chief Native Commissioner in the Cape, Marmaduke

Apthorp, told the Native Economic Commission in June 1931 that Macmillan's Herschel survey exaggerated the level of poverty there as there was a 'tremendous reserve strength in that district' and 'given a good season these people in that area will all do well'.[50]

The Joint Councils, furthermore, came under growing political pressure in the early 1930s. The Minister of Justice, Oswald Pirow, for example, condemned their liberal white members as 'cranks, prigs, and notoriety seekers' who 'see between Europeans and Bantu only a difference in colour and not a distinction of 2000 years of civilisation'.[51] The emergence of a more coherent government 'native policy' on the basis of the Native Administration Act enabled the Department of Native Affairs to begin expanding its administrative apparatus after some crippling retrenchments in the early 1920s. The promulgation of a policy of land reclamation and the expansion of its staff of soil experts indicated that the bureaucracy was gaining in political and administrative self-confidence.[52] It appeared increasingly likely that the Joint Council liberals would have to moderate further their criticisms of government if they were to exercise any kind of influence on policy. Even before he had gone overseas in 1930 Macmillan had become aware of the growing rigidity of government attitudes when, in an interview with the Minister of Native Affairs, E. G. Jansen, he had been told there was 'one road for the white and another for the black and they never meet. Segregation'.[53]

This dilemma over relations with government, however, was compounded by a growing crisis in the Joint Council with complaints that the body was both paternalistic in its dealing with Africans and was attempting to control their political organizations. Accusations of this kind had been made from as early as 1928 by an anonymous correspondent, 'Enquirer', in the newspaper *Umteteli wa Bantu*, but they gained in poignancy after 1931 as the African National Congress declined in political influence.[54] For a number of the white liberals involved in the Joint Council's work, this growing mood of distrust appeared to undermine their hopes of making the Council a forum in which African political issues could be openly discussed. It also obstructed their recognition by government as a legitimate body concerned with the formulation of 'native policy'.[55] Despite efforts in the later 1920s to establish links with the black trade union movement, the Industrial and Commercial Workers' Union (ICU),[56] the Joint Council continued to be treated with suspicion by many African political activists. White liberal assistance in bringing out the

Scottish trade unionist William Ballinger in 1928 to assist in the organization of the ICU merely increased their suspicions. The splits in the union were blamed on white liberal interference and, by the early 1930s, African membership in the Joint Councils started to decline.[57] By 1934 only 12 of the 66 African members of the Johannesburg Joint Council were reported as having paid their subscriptions.[58] Reports from other Joint Councils such as those at Aliwal North, Ladybrand, and Kroonstad also indicated a decline of support.[59] The early 1930s marked a diminution in hopes for joint action by Africans and liberal whites in order to modify and reform state policy. It also became clear that African members were unwilling to cooperate in empirical investigations on living standards, such as those among the urban working class on the Rand, although work of this kind had been discussed while Macmillan was on leave in 1930.[60]

It thus appeared, by the time Macmillan returned to South Africa in late 1930 that, as Rheinallt Jones admitted, Africans were displaying a 'spirit of non cooperation' towards the Joint Councils, making political argument increasingly contentious[61]. Macmillan urged once more that the Joint Councils pay greater attention to African opinion outside its own tiny membership in order to 'educate and clarify that opinion' and 'make it known as widely as possible'.[62] But it was by no means evident that African political leaders were still interested in such tactics, given that the Joint Councils could not deliver on any serious political issues. In February 1931, for example, Rheinallt Jones admitted at a meeting of the Joint Councils that a forthcoming Native Conference at Pretoria with the Minister of Native Affairs would have no real status since the African members were to be there merely to express opinions.[63] This weakness in the Joint Councils' channels of political influence was compounded by the general lack of support from business interests, though Macmillan felt that funding from such sources was essential if the work of the Councils was to continue.

The comparative indifference of capitalists suggests that the assertion that the Joint Councils acted as 'agents of social control' in the management of class conflict is perhaps somewhat exaggerated.[64] 'Enquirer' in *Umteteli* attacked the Councils' work as a means of controlling African political leaders and organizations. Yet, as Macmillan replied in the same paper, it was '... the weakness and disharmony of purely African organisation and channels of self expression [that] often paralyses the African members and is one of the great obstacles to the success of the Joint Councils.' The Joint Councils' work was not to supersede but to 'interpret' African opinion and 'to help Africans, when their opinion is deliberately formed, to state it clearly and effectively'.[65] Macmillan's benign paternalism contrasted with the thinking developing in the Institute of Race Relations in the early 1930s, where a much more active policy for moulding African opinion through the press was being canvassed. This further distanced him from the liberals.

Rheinallt Jones, indeed, as the 'Adviser' of the new Institute of Race Relations expressed concern at the way that some of the Joint Councils developed into 'anti government organisations' and were apparently eager to rush to the press to attack the Minister of Native Affairs.[66] The less politically involved strategy of the Institute appeared to him a wiser course, and by early 1932 he began to establish links with business interests concerned to establish another African newspaper to complement *Umteteli*. This scheme eventually reached fruition in the form of *The Bantu World* under the editorship of the African Joint Council member Victor Selope Thema and with a working capital of a mere £500.[67] The general thrust of white liberal politics was moving in an increasingly conservative direction as the leadership of the African National Congress (ANC) passed from radical to conservative hands in 1930, and its radical paper *Abantu Batho* collapsed. By September 1934 Pixley ka Isaka Seme, the compliant president of the ANC, began to hope that a 'common programme' could be formulated by the ANC and the Joint Councils 'upon certain lines of cooperation'.[68]

By this time, however, Macmillan had abandoned internal South African politics for a wider international arena in order to develop his analysis and study of colonial rule. His decision to leave South Africa where he had spent so long both teaching and doing research was a painful one, but was prompted by a growing realization of his inability to influence, in any significant manner, the course of the government's segregation policy. The absence of any political base in African politics made his position different from that of other more radical critics of the cautious conservatism of the Johannesburg liberal school. The latter in turn had a focus in the Institute of Race Relations, and the development of the Wits department of 'Bantu Studies'.[69] Unlike William and Margaret Ballinger of the Friends of Africa, moreover, Macmillan was not by nature a very ardent political campaigner, preferring reasoned discussion and the presentation of a case through a book, article or seminar paper. It had been his hope that, through this quiet but rational Fabian approach, government policy-makers could be made to see reason and alter course. Now, with the doctrines of segregationism seemingly as entrenched as ever and the white liberals unwilling to make any major stand in opposition, it was time to move on to wider spheres and tackle the reasoning behind British colonial and Commonwealth policy.

A critique of the Commonwealth ideal:

In fact, as early as 1931, Macmillan had started broadening his ideas on African colonial development in a study then tentatively entitled *Whence and Whither Africa*.[70] The split with the Johannesburg liberals in 1931-32 enabled this project to be brought forward as Macmillan felt increasingly impelled to confront issues wider than those of South African domestic politics. His arrival in London coincided with growing criticism among liberals interested in African affairs on the direction of South African segregationism. Much of this, as in the case of Sydney Olivier, was somewhat second-hand or else, as in the case of the Rhodesian missionary Arthur Shearley Cripps, based on an intense moral loathing of white supremacy, with little detailed economic understanding of how white settler segregationism actually worked.[71] While some 'experts' such as Leonard Barnes and Norman Leys, author of *Kenya* had knowledge of segregationist societies, unlike Macmillan, none had carried out detailed fieldwork in a South African reserve. Barnes, however, had assisted the Ballingers in their investigations on the southern African protectorates and in *The New Boer War* (1932) urged that Britain develop the protectorates as part of a strategy of undermining 'Afrikaner' power to the south.[72]

While Macmillan did not emulate this campaign in quite the same terms, he was a welcome addition to the small *côterie* of critics of British colonial policy. It soon also became clear that, although he supported the overall ideals of the Commonwealth, he was not going to let this fall in with the Round Table view from the cloisters of All Souls. He urged Lionel Curtis to go and see developments more closely on the ground, for unless the Union government could be persuaded to accept the wider responsibilities entailed by its policy, the whole edifice of the Commonwealth was endangered: 'I beg you', he wrote to Curtis, 'in all kindness to consider how far the Union has really absorbed the higher ideals — or budged at all — and even if its cooperation, which we all want, can be bought at too heavy a cost.'[73]

These pleas were prompted by the apparently manipulated debate in the columns of *The Times*, edited by the former Kindergarten member and Round Table champion Geoffrey Dawson, over the question of the 'handover' of the protectorate territories to the Union. The participants in this debate, Lionel Curtis and Margery Perham, were only mildly in opposition to each other, with Curtis favouring an early transfer and Perham arguing for a stronger measure of trusteeship by the British government in the hope that delay might help prompt a liberalization of the Union's 'native policy'.[74] Neither party seemed aware of the economic dynamics at work in the protectorates integrating them into the Union's migrant labour system, and the issue was largely discussed at an élite level and sheltered from extensive publicity. For some of Macmillan's colleagues in Britain, such as Barnes, a 'handover' seemed more or less inevitable at some time, although it was hoped in some liberal circles, such as the London Group on African Affairs, that this could be delayed as long as possible.[75]

Macmillan felt that the protectorates issue reflected the same kind of blindness in British imperial circles to the dynamics of segregation as he had seen amongst the Johannesburg liberals. Lionel Curtis tried to maintain that white racial attitudes would slowly 'improve' in South Africa and opposed too hasty a condemnation of its 'native policy' by journals such as the *New Statesman*.[76] But, for Macmillan, such an outlook not only failed to take into account the opinions of protectorate Africans themselves but also represented a spurious form of imperial benevolence that was trying to blunt the edge of its liberal critics. He castigated Curtis's and the Round Table's assumption that accepting imperial limits might be more morally enlightened, although he also observed that:

... the moderation of their new imperialism makes it harder, though more necessary than ever with Liberalism waned and even Tory paternalists disturbed but dumb [for] ... well intentioned sentimentalists [to press that] ... the black man must have his place in any Commonwealth worthy of the name.[77]

Clearly, though, it was going to be hard to rouse British public opinion on southern African issues in the mid-1930s, when the Conservative-dominated National government had an overwhelming direction over political debate, and when there were competing issues concerning both domestic economic policy and the rising spectre of Hitlerism in central Europe.

Macmillan, therefore, spent the latter part of the 1930s largely in the political wilderness, although he was able to expand his range of expertise on colonial issues by writing a short critique of policy in the Caribbean in his timely *Warning from the West Indies* in 1936.[78] More particularly, he was able to develop a wider critique of the anthropological notion of 'culture contact' stemming from the Malinowski anthropology seminar at the LSE which he felt neutralized the political and economic dimensions of colonial 'contact' with less technologically advanced societies. He did not seek to develop this analysis into a sustained critique of all 'colonial' anthropology, but on occasions was able to put this more politicized view to good use. In March 1934, for example, he attacked a paper by Margery Perham entitled 'Some problems of indirect rule in Africa', read at a joint meeting of the Africa Society and the Royal Society of Arts, for failing to link anthropological study with a more historical approach. In some ways, this developed the earlier debate with Mitchell in East Africa into a wider attack on the 'worshipping' of static African institutions which, in a society like South Africa, led to 'indirect rule' being employed to the advantage of 'reactionaries'.[79]

This approach eventually culminated in his important study *Africa Emergent* (1938) in which the development of segregationism was outlined in the white settler states in east, central and southern Africa. Segregationist legislation was condemned as belonging not to the 'realm of sane everyday politics' but to be 'of the same genus as the racial decrees as Nazi Germany'.[80] The threat of the South African model of segregation extending further northwards was also considered a serious possibility as Olivier, Barnes and Leys had warned, though Macmillan doubted if two economic systems could co-exist in the same country on a horizontal basis as some segregationists imagined.[81] The work thus represented an interesting early critique of what would later, under the impact of the anthropological work of J. S. Furnivall, be termed a model of a 'plural society' in the colonial and post-colonial setting; it was also a plea for a return to more conventional Victorian concepts of extending the notion of 'civilization' to colonial peoples and widening citizenship rights to those dispossessed of them. Macmillan also wrote a memorandum on behalf of the London Group on African Affairs in 1937 which warned that South African legislation threatened the liberal tradition of imperial rule inherited from the last century and represented 'a positive danger to healthy relationships between the black and white races'.[82]

In South Africa itself, at this time, the liberal tradition took a new turn with the attempt by Alfred Hoernlé, Professor of Philosophy at the University of the Witwatersrand and President of the Institute of Race Relations, to accommodate liberal goals to the ideal of total racial separation. It is true that his Phelps-Stokes lectures of 1939, *South African Native Policy and the Liberal Spirit*, were not accepted by all South African liberals. Nevertheless, they provided an important sense of political direction in the wake of the 1936 legislation which deprived African voters in the Cape of the franchise on a common roll and further entrenched possessory segregation through the Native Trust and Land Act.[83] Furthermore, the lectures were partly intended as a reply to the international critique mounted by liberals such as Olivier and Macmillan, and Hoernlé hoped they would have a wide readership in Britain as the tenets of British colonial policy were debated.[84]

By the onset of the Second World War, therefore, Macmillan had begun to establish a new reputation for himself as an important expert and critic of British colonial policy. In one sense, his research path had followed, during the 1930s, the same pattern as his earlier intellectual development at Oxford, Aberdeen and Germany between 1903 and 1910 when he had moved out of the local and provincial world of the Cape into a wider academic setting. He had always tried to maintain a close intellectual affinity between the local and the general, seeing them as strengthening and reinforcing one another; so, also, in the 1920s and 1930s he sought to apply his understanding of the dynamics of segregation in South Africa to more general trends visible throughout the wider area of Africa under white settler rule. Beyond all this, too, loomed the spectre of the Nazi jackboot over Europe. Macmillan was thus of critical importance as a South African intellectual who warned and fought against the localization and isolation of South African issues from wider trends in world history. It is this dimension especially that makes his work of continuing importance and relevance in terms of contemporary South African political and economic debate.

211

10

MACMILLAN AS A CRITIC OF EMPIRE: THE IMPACT OF AN HISTORIAN ON COLONIAL POLICY

JOHN E. FLINT

DESPITE their claims to academic detachment and objectivity, historians are as much political animals as the rest of mankind. Perhaps deep in every historian lies a politician *manqué* with a wish to shape future events by conclusion from the meaning of the past. Yet few historians ever achieve specific influence upon current events or policies. Their influence, such as it may be, is normally indirect, upon former pupils who become legislators or office-holders, or more generally by affecting broad attitudes towards current questions of policy. W. M. Macmillan was an exception to this rule. He was an historian who extrapolated conclusions from his studies of South African history into a devastating critique of British colonial policy in tropical Africa and the Caribbean, out of which he elaborated proposals for colonial reform which had profound implications for the future, including that of ultimate decolonization. For once, history was on the side of the historian; Macmillan's most influential political books were published just as a number of colonial crises came to a head, against a background of deepening international tension in the two years before the outbreak of the Second World War. It is the purpose of this paper to attempt an assessment of Macmillan's impact on the remarkable changes which occurred in British colonial policy from 1938 to 1940, and which ushered in a colonial reform movement as significant for the black peoples of the British Empire as the reform movement exactly one hundred years earlier had been for the white colonists overseas.

Throughout the 1920s and for most of the 1930s the atmosphere in the colonial service, the Colonial Office, and among the Conservative Secretaries of State who defended their policies in Parliament was one of an intense and imperturbable complacency. Confident in the superiority of their race, the impeccable social origins of the officials, the financial rectitude of the policy of minimal government,[1] and the legitimacy of trusteeship principles for the government of 'the African', a stereotyped entity who might well lack the innate capacity ever to rule himself, the British colonies were regarded as enormously successful examples of the prudent practice of the art of the possible.

In the late 1930s this complacency suddenly cracked and then collapsed in the wake of serious riots in the West Indies. A new Colonial Secretary, Malcolm MacDonald, engineered a number of remarkable and sudden changes, which began the process which in the short span of about twenty years would revolutionize the history of Africa and lead to political decolonization. The entire set of attitudes which had characterized policy in the 1920s began to be turned upside down within the Colonial Office. The policy of minimal government was abandoned; colonies were now to be developed with imperial financial aid; indirect rule came under mounting attack; settlers came to be regarded with increasing suspicion as potentially obstructive or even disloyal. Above all the Colonial Office, perhaps for the first time in its long history, began to consider itself as the head and ruler of its empire, where policy would be formulated and imposed. Officials now began to attempt the definition of a consistent policy of positive trusteeship, designed not to protect Africans from change, but to 'develop' them economically, socially and politically. The colonial service was expected to carry out a new colonial policy determined in London, not in the colonies. Between 1938 and 1940, Malcolm MacDonald quickly stole the clothes of the critics of colonial policy in Africa. In this process, the ideas propounded by W. M. Macmillan provided a coherent programme of colonial reform which, more than that of any other writer, could lay the basis for a bipartisan colonial policy necessary for the wartime coalition government which was to come in 1940.

Macmillan, of course, was not the only critic of colonial policy, and his significance has to be assessed within the context of a number of people who articulated a sense of colonial malaise. In the 1920s none of these critics was an academic. Three groups can be discerned:[2] former colonial officials who had left the service in disgust, missionary writers often working in cooperation with the Anti-Slavery and Aborigines Protection Society of earlier fame; and a small knot of Labour Party members who specialized in colonial affairs. Increasingly the first two gravitated to the Labour Party, either by joining the Party, or by using it as a parliamentary lobby.

Significantly, the renegade[3] officials all emerged from experience in settler societies of East and Central Africa. The most outstanding of these was Dr Norman Leys, who, after working in the colonial medical service in Kenya and Nyasaland until 1918, devoted his life to the writing of sharply critical and incisive attacks on the racial discrimination underlying land and labour policies in East Africa, somehow finding time for this while working as a GP in economically depressed areas of England. Leys was one of the first to argue that land in Kenya was being alienated to settlers in such quantities as to force Africans into poorly paid labour for the whites, either as migrants or as quasi-feudal labour tenants on land which had once been theirs. He dramatized cases of land alienation by vivid writing shot through with a deep sense of the injustices which Africans had suffered.[4] This was not trusteeship but exploitation; the colonial state had become corrupted by the narrow-minded racism of settler capitalists. A true trusteeship would be positive, not rhetorical. It would not merely protect Africans against further losses of land, but ensure that their land and animals were sufficient for more than subsistence, provide agricultural research and advice to improve their standard of living, and promote social change with expanding educational opportunities. Leys had no sympathy with the social conservatism of the indirect rulers; the supposed evils of 'detribalisation' were mostly 'nonsense'.[5]

Other renegade colonial officials confirmed Leys' evidence and accusations from similar experiences. McGregor Ross, after twenty-three years as an engineer in Kenya, used his diaries to produce a damning indictment of injustice and exploitation in Kenya[6] and he, like Leys, continued to work for left-wing publications. Frank Melland, a former official of Rhodes' British South Africa Company in Northern Rhodesia, denounced Colonial Office complacency as a mask for dictatorship, and demanded that trusteeship be redefined to place the African at the centre of consideration so that eventually the trustee would be able to fulfil his duty by handing over to the ward.[7]

Missionary interests tended to take a more 'moderate' approach. In the 1920s the 'indirect rule' philosophy, even though it excluded their own converts from participation, had an impact on missionary thinking and came to be seen as a method of holding society together through a transition to a new 'Christian civilization'. Missionary leaders like Dr J. H. Oldham believed, with some reason, that by adopting moderate positions they could work to exert political influence with the Colonial Office, if necessary by mobilizing the support of church dignitaries at home.[8] Nevertheless, they were ready, on occasion, to denounce racial discrimination and injustice; Oldham even argued that white exploitation could lead to widespread rejection of Christianity by the oppressed.[9]

Another section of the missionary interest, however, was more openly political. The Anti-Slavery and Aborigines Protection Society was still actively representing the Christian humanitarian ideals of its earlier and more powerful days. Its parliamentary secretary, Sir John Harris, primed MPs with question-fodder and wrote regularly and extensively on political issues. The Society persistently highlighted cases of injustice and discrimination, complaining that colonial administrations regularly refused to control abuses by settlers, traders or mining interests. Harris picked up the theme that trusteeship needed to be implemented in a positive way, which meant state action for economic and educational development and ultimate self-government.[10]

Harris's friend and closest collaborator, Charles Roden Buxton, symbolized the drift of the old Christian anti-slavery activists into formal membership of the Labour Party. He was a great-grandson of Thomas Fowell Buxton, Wilberforce's successor who had led the anti-slavery movement through the triumphs of the abolition of slavery in 1834 and of apprenticeship in 1838. C. R. Buxton had become a Liberal MP in 1910, but his pacifism led him to join the Independent Labour Party in 1917. He later joined the official Labour Party and sat as a Labour MP in 1922–23 and again in 1929–31, serving as chairman of the Labour Party's Advisory Committee on International and Imperial Questions until 1939.[11] It was Buxton, with Leonard Woolf, secretary of this committee, who drew up *Labour and the Nation*, the Party's formal statement of policy in 1926.[12]

The partnership of Buxton, heir of the evangelical anti-slavery interests, and Leonard Woolf, another 'renegade' who had seen colonial service in Ceylon from 1904 to 1911, illustrates the way in which enthusiasts for colonial reform infiltrated the Labour Party and, in this case, actually wrote its policy. Colonial reform was the 'active concern chiefly of a small body of enthusiasts',[13] practically all of whom joined the Party because of their colonial and African interests and not from deeply felt concerns about British domestic politics. Almost all the renegade colonial officials joined the Labour Party and found in it a platform for their ideas. Norman Leys became an important member of the Party's Imperial Advisory Committee, on which McGregor Ross also served.[14]

Nevertheless the colonial critics, as an exotic small group of activists within the Labour Party, faced an uphill struggle. The Labour Party in the 1920s and 1930s was essentially a domestic movement, easily tempted into 'little Englandism'. Labour leaders had never much gloried in the Empire, and especially not in the tropical kind. Hobson's *Imperialism*[15] had convinced most of them to use the word as a term of abuse; imperialism was a device to delude the working classes, a policy which held down domestic standards of living by encouraging capital investment abroad rather than consumption at home, and it was a fundamental cause of war. Colonial critics, hitherto, seemed only to reinforce the negative image of empire. Though pleading for some kind of positive trusteeship which would 'develop' Africans towards self-government, in reality they offered as yet no concrete programme of how this might be achieved, and in particular shied away from the financial implications of such a course.

In the 1920s the 'internationalists' were a more powerful influence within the Labour Party than the colonial critics. Feelings of guilt at the mere possession of colonial territories was a tradition in the Party which went back to Hobson and had been developed by Brailsford[16] and others who became associated with opposition to the First World War in the Union of Democratic Control. For such people the causes of the 'great catastrophe' were to be found in the struggle for control of cheap raw materials and markets through imperialist territorial expansion, these naked appetites being concealed in secret diplomacy. Wars could be ended, and so could imperialism, by open diplomacy subject to democratic control.

But how could the end of imperialism be effected? Neither the pacifist–internationalists nor the enthusiasts for colonial reform could conceive of immediate self-government for Africans and other tropical peoples. To break up the colonial units which had resulted from partition, and to hand them back to the traditional monarchies and ruling classes would be reactionary, and open them up to aggression and acquisition by other colonial powers. Within the African colonies there were no new colony-wide nationalist movements capable of demanding sovereign independence, and no domestic institutions through which they could express themselves. The educated élites in West Africa were tiny and ineffective; in East and Central Africa they were non-existent.

The internationalists therefore looked to the creation of a world order, through the League of Nations, as a 'solution' to the problem. All colonies should be handed over to international administration by the world organization, to be run on principles of trusteeship and the open door (no possibility of conflict between these two principles was envisaged) by an international civil service drawn from all 'civilized' nations. The guilt of possessing colonies would be purged clean and the causes of war eradicated. How other colonial powers could be persuaded to hand over their colonies, or why an international administration operating 'open-door' economies would necessarily adopt a trusteeship policy, was never explained, nor was much attention given to the question of whether Africans would have any say in whether they wished to be transferred to an international regime. Nevertheless these impractical ideas died hard in the Labour Party and they obstructed the development of reformist ideas, which, of necessity, implied working through the existing imperial structure and acceptance of long-term responsibility for colonial administration.

The confusion of internationalist and colonial reform influences reveals itself clearly in the colonial policy section of the Labour Party's manifesto of 1928, *Labour and the Nation*. This began with a reference to 'the appalling evils produced by capitalist exploitation' in certain tropical and sub-tropical colonies. The welfare of 'indigenous races' must become the central consideration of colonial policy, 'to which all other interests must be rigorously subordinated'. The statement then doffed a cap at indirect rule, stressing that economic development must not be allowed 'by methods which undermine the independence, the social institutions and the *morale* of their inhabitants, and which thus are injurious both to them, and, ultimately, to the working classes of Europe'. A Labour government would watch over land alienation, labour recruitment and contracts, and encourage the development of health and educational services. Policy would be based 'upon the firm conviction that all the dependencies of the Crown ought, as soon as possible, to become self-governing States'. Gradual devolution of power would take place, with imperial responsibility maintained 'during the period preceding the establishment of democratic institutions....'. At the same time

217

Labour would make every effort to strengthen and extend the authority of the League of Nations Mandates Commission.[17]

While the 1928 manifesto shows that the Labour Party was already committed to a substantial base of colonial reform, it also reveals some important omissions and limitations. Talk of 'all the dependencies' eventually becoming 'self-governing States' with 'democratic institutions' was far more radical than any Conservative government of the time would have found acceptable. Yet the 1928 manifesto remained profoundly conservative on the question of social change in the colonies and failed to perceive any link between social policy and the evolution of self-government. Lugardian propaganda had evidently produced, even on the left, a considerable satisfaction with the idea of preserving traditional social structures and mores. This left the question of to whom power would eventually be transferred entirely vague and ill-defined. Likewise, though the stress on educational and health services implied a policy of 'colonial development', how the finances would be raised for this was not discussed. If it was to be left to colonial government, then the policy of minimal government had not in fact been breached. Nor were these gaps filled by Party pronouncements or by theoretical writings on the left during the early 1930s.[18] As one of the most important participants in what may be termed the academic lobby, W. M. Macmillan would play a key role in filling them, by providing, especially for the Labour Party, a coherent programme of colonial reform.

The inter-war period witnessed the rise of the academics, a curious phenomenon in which university scholars and researchers were listened to with increasing respect, then brought in as special advisors from the mid-1920s, and finally, rather indirectly, formulated the blueprints for colonial reform at the end of the 1930s. The academics responded eagerly and with increasing confidence, spurred on by a vested interest in seeking research funding. Their role was of great importance in shaping the new reformist attitudes for both the Labour and Conservative Parties. Their efforts to clothe the need for colonial reform with hard evidence culled from research happened to culminate exactly at the time when the Colonial Office was shaken from its complacency by the violent social upheaval in the West Indies. In this process the academics brought about two changes of the utmost significance. Within the Colonial Office they dethroned Lord Lugard as the grand panjandrum of colonial theory, undermined the sanctity of indirect rule, and crowned their own man, Lord Hailey, as the new king. Even more significantly, they smashed the vessel of minimal government in which colonial policy had hitherto been contained. This created the basis, in both the Labour and Conservative Parties, for a bipartisan colonial policy of economic, social and political development which accepted the need for the UK government to invest financial resources in such programmes.

The rise of the academics was itself a symptom of minimal government. Empire on the cheap implied experts on the cheap, and from the mid-1920s the Colonial Office began forming 'advisory committees', first for education in 1925, for medicine in 1926 and for agriculture in 1929. University teachers played a predominant role in these committees and, increasingly, it was historians who began to dominate the charmed circle of informal advisors on high policy.[19]

It was natural that Oxford University should play a key role in shaping this influence. Oxford, more than Cambridge, had traditionally been the recruiting ground for both the Indian and the colonial service, neither of which looked with favour on the graduates of London or the provincial universities. Oxford was also endowed for the study of British colonial history by Cecil Rhodes and Alfred Beit, Rhodes' closest associate on the diamond fields. The ethos of colonial studies in Oxford was one of reforming conservatism, committed to an almost mystical ideal of imperialism. This was exemplified by Reginald Coupland, who became Beit Professor in 1920. A deeply religious Anglican, Coupland saw the history of the British Empire as a vision of freedom's unfolding. In his inaugural lecture of 1921, he claimed that the 'answer of history' to the 'demon of an overweening nationalism' which had caused the First World War was to be found in the 'twofold idea of freedom and unity' which had already been realized in the British Commonwealth. The ideal would eventually embrace a self-governing India and ultimately the colonies of Africa and the Pacific. The Commonwealth ideal would solve 'the problem of race' and complete 'the longest and hardest stage ... toward the brotherhood of man'.[20] The same vision of freedom in unity was reiterated in the lectures he published in 1935, *The Empire in these Days*, in a specifically African context. 'A Dominion of Nigeria, for example? Why not?'[21]

Such a man was naturally attracted to imperial work where he might help shape the future which he prophesied. He served as a member of the Royal Commission on the Superior Civil Service in

India in 1923, on the Burma Round Table Conference of 1931, and on the Peel Commission in Palestine in 1936.[22] From 1926 the Colonial Office began sending its colonial service cadets to Oxford University's course on tropical African administration, known as the Devonshire course. Many cadets attended Coupland's lectures on British imperial history, which he devised with their interests in mind.

Coupland's visionary imperialism was not original and drew heavily on the enthusiasms of Lionel Curtis, his patron, whom he replaced as Beit Lecturer in 1913 and who engineered his rapid promotion to the Beit Chair. Curtis himself emerged from the high imperialist movement as a former member of Milner's Kindergarten in South Africa, and was a leading figure in the Round Table movement which advocated imperial federation of the dominions before the First World War. After 1919, from his base as a fellow of All Souls, Curtis began to preach the ideology of the new 'Commonwealth' which could reconcile freedom and unity and was soon preoccupied with how the dependent Empire could be fitted into these ideals.[23] From 1920 Curtis became interested in East Africa, joining Oldham in representations to the Colonial Office about the use of forced labour. As a result Curtis became convinced that Britain had no policy for African colonies and that it was almost impossible to devise one because so little was known about African conditions. In November 1920 he told Oldham that he felt that it was time for a comprehensive inquiry into the basic principles of how Colonial Office territories should be administered.[24] Later, after reading Norman Leys' book, he called it 'the most formidable indictment of British Colonial policy which has appeared for a century'. But how could the principle of native paramountcy be made into a practical policy when little or nothing was known about Africa? Curtis was beginning to formulate the idea of a comprehensive inquiry into policy and conditions in British Africa.

In 1929, in his Rhodes Memorial lectures at Oxford, Smuts called for a general survey of conditions throughout Africa, to include a review of the extent to which modern knowledge was being applied. Curtis and Coupland set out to respond to this challenge. Rhodes House had been completed that year, and they planned to establish a centre for African studies there, with four research professorships at All Souls. But the scheme collapsed. All Souls refused to sponsor the proposals and the Rockefeller Foundation would not provide funds.

The African research scheme was then reorganized under the auspices of the Royal Institute of International Affairs which agreed to attach the project to Chatham House. Curtis had by now secured powerful backing; Lord Lothian (Philip Kerr, secretary of the Rhodes Trust) agreed to serve as chairman of its management committee, on which Lord Lugard, Oldham and the biologist Julian Huxley also took their seats.[25] With this kind of support Curtis was now able to approach the Carnegie Corporation[26] with an eloquent plea which stressed the destructive results of imperial rule:

The continent is now exposed to the impact of European civilisation which will ruin the life of its ... people unless it is controlled. In order to control it we must study not only the ideas, institutions, customs and languages, but the effects which an economic revolution is having on them in all its aspects.... We must learn what administrative activities, education and physical science directed by government and private agencies can do to enable them to gain instead of lose by the changes which are being forced on them.[27]

The Carnegie Corporation agreed to provide funding. After consideration of more than thirty candidates (of whom Macmillan was one),[28] Curtis finally persuaded Sir Malcolm Hailey to direct the project, even though he could not begin work until 1935.

At first glance the choice of Hailey to direct the Survey seems quite bizarre. Hailey was in no way an academic or scholarly figure at the time, and he was innocent of knowledge or experience of Africa. He would be 63 years old when he began his duties and commencing retirement from a long and distinguished career in India.[29] However, it would appear that the choice of Hailey, rather than an established scholar of Africa, was a shrewd political move on the part of Curtis and his Oxford academic lobby. They were looking for a man of proven imperial experience, acceptable in Conservative political circles, who could gain access to contacts and informants in foreign as well as British colonial governments, and who could lead them to the promised land of government research grants and influence upon policy-making in a way that no professor could hope to do. If this was the motivation it was brilliantly successful. Hailey had a powerful, if cautious, intellect, enormous industry and the ability to accumulate encyclopaedic knowledge with great rapidity. He quickly surrounded himself with a galaxy of academic researchers, who fed him with information, advice and unpublished manuscripts, read his drafts and criticised. Hailey emerged as Lord Lugard's successor even before he published the *African Survey*, working on the book at the same time as he replaced Lord Lugard as Britain's representative on the Mandates Commission of the League of Nations from 1935 to 1939.

When the *African Survey* was published in 1938 it was recognized on all sides as the most important book yet to appear on the subject of African affairs, at once replacing Lugard's *Dual Mandate* as the standard work on African policy. The book carried 'authority' which no purely academic work could have hoped to attain and it was published exactly at the historical moment when the complacent self-confidence of the mid-war years had been shattered beyond repair. Even before its publication Colonial Office officials were extracting its key sections as blueprints for the future direction of colonial policy, and Hailey had become the chief political advisor of the Colonial Office in a way that Lord Lugard had never managed to be. Though highly conservative in tone and language, the *African Survey* began the process which would undermine the assumptions of minimal government. Its main themes were that 'development' was a British governmental responsibility requiring planning (and therefore research) and expenditure, that the colonies must be regarded as eventually self-governing territories, and that Lugardian concepts of indirect rule no longer had much to offer.

On the other hand, the *African Survey* was hardly likely to galvanize the British public conscience. Written in careful officialese, it was scarcely readable. Smuts, on receipt of the book, complained, 'I cannot stand that dull official language of a blue book. It is so different from the language of ordinary speech that it is almost another language.' As a result Smuts failed to see that Hailey had anything new to say; the book was merely 'an encyclopaedia of information' with 'little guidance or illumination.'[30]

This lacuna would be filled by W. M. Macmillan, at that time an academic on the outer fringe of Oxford life, but a man who could write with passion in a hard-hitting pungent style. If Oxford's academic entrepreneurial grantsmanship had provided, through Hailey, a new governmental colonial policy, Macmillan, much more in the tradition of the colonial critics like Ross, Leys and Melland, was the catalyst for providing the Labour Party with an articulate and consistent programme of colonial reform.

Readers of this book will find elsewhere the story of Macmillan's

222

early life and background in South Africa. Here it is the interaction between his writings and researches, his somewhat chequered academic career, and the advent of colonial reform in Britain, which need to be examined. As Professor of History in the University of the Witwatersrand, Macmillan began in the 1920s to publish works of historical research on South African themes which were decidedly iconoclastic and radical. One of his major documentary sources was the collection of papers of Dr John Philip, the early nineteenth century missionary and follower of Wilberforce, much hated by Afrikaner settlers as a 'kaffir lover' who, they alleged, had provoked the Great Trek by his reckless insistence upon equality of treatment of non-whites before the British courts.

In 1927 Macmillan published *The Cape Colour Question* followed two years later by *Bantu, Boer, and Briton*, both of which were powerful rehabilitations of the missionary factor in South African history, and which portrayed Afrikaner nationalism as narrow, illiberal, irrational and destructive. Throughout this time Macmillan was building on his Oxford contacts, particularly during a sabbatical leave in 1926–27 as an associate of All Souls. He became noticed by the Round Table circle, though he remained an outsider to it, being too radical for the tastes of Curtis and Coupland.[31] He received some financial support from the Rhodes Trust, but was also attracted to the Fabians, with whom he had been associated since 1911, as well as to the colonial critics of the left.

Throughout the 1930s Macmillan had also been publishing articles and pamphlets on current political and social conditions in South Africa. These he drew together in a book, *Complex South Africa*, published in 1930. His increasing activity in the politics of interracial cooperation ultimately proved to be his nemesis in South Africa. Macmillan attracted the ire of the pro-Nazi Oswald Pirow, Minister of Native Affairs in the Hertzog government, who in a bitter public dispute described Macmillan and his ilk as 'negrophilists', 'cranks' and 'prigs'. When Macmillan refused to be muzzled by threats from Pirow and published the correspondence between them, Pirow put pressure on the university authorities. Macmillan was asked to censor himself and keep quiet; he refused but offered to resign whereupon the Principal said that he would also resign with serious damage to the University as a result. Macmillan was due for another sabbatical leave at that time anyway, so he took it. He never returned to teach in South Africa.[32]

For the next eight years Macmillan was unable to secure any permanent salaried work, academic or other. As a result, he wrote extensively as a journalist, at the same time securing small travel grants for research, which enabled him to travel extensively throughout colonial Africa, where his interests had been shifting even before he left South Africa. These articles increasingly emphasized social change in Africa, the role of the educated African, racial questions and the need for reform.[33] They were in fact written to a plan, designed to culminate in a book which would survey the entire continent, stressing change, the emergence of new forces and the need for a rethinking of colonial policy. By 1933 he had accumulated sufficient material to write it and once again secured, through Lionel Curtis, an associate status at All Souls for two terms.[34] There he soon heard about the plans for an 'African Survey', which appeared to be exactly the kind of study for which he was well prepared. He was therefore bitterly disappointed when Curtis told him that Hailey had been asked and had accepted the directorship.[35] Macmillan then hoped to serve as Hailey's major assistant, but it was not to be. Instead he received a grant of £100 to complete the manuscript of what would become *Africa Emergent* so that Hailey could read it before leaving for Africa. Given the emphasis which Macmillan's draft laid on themes which became the major themes of Hailey's study — the need to end colonial self-sufficiency, to establish British funding for development and welfare schemes, to reconsider the indirect rule policy and plan for eventual self-government — it is odd that Macmillan's name was omitted from the list of contributors to the *African Survey*, a breach of academic etiquette about which he was driven to protest.[36]

Had it not been for a turn of fate Macmillan's *Africa Emergent* would have appeared in print long before Hailey's *African Survey*. In 1934 Macmillan received research travel grants from the Carnegie Corporation and the Phelps-Stokes Fund to make a short tour of the USA and a research trip to the British West Indies, where he wished to do some comparative studies relating those colonies to the African themes of his draft of *Africa Emergent*, whose publication was thereby delayed. But after visiting the islands in 1935, Macmillan was so appalled by the conditions he found there that he set down not a simple report for the Carnegie Foundation, but a powerful denunciation of British colonial policy, not just in the West Indies, but in the tropical African colonies as well. This appeared in

February 1936, with a title which would, sooner than Macmillan expected, become prophetic — *Warning from the West Indies*.

The British West Indies could be taken as a classic example of negative trusteeship and the working of *laissez-faire* colonial policy. The trusteeship had been strongly asserted in the abolition of slavery, the work of the British parliament in powerful opposition to the interests of the white slave-owning planters. The slaves had been made legally free, with the rights in law of British subjects, but the early Victorian state and its successors had not thought fit to consider that the ex-slave communities should be provided with any economic base or social services upon their emergence into legal freedom. The result, Macmillan argued, through page after page of detailed illustration, had been a human disaster. 'The British genius for colonization is an article of faith', Macmillan began. 'Here we would test its achievement by an examination of conditions in our oldest tropical possessions.'[37]

On every count Britain failed the test. The result of a century of *laissez-faire* government was steady economic and social destruction, malnutrition, grinding poverty, ignorance and needless disease. 'The landless proletariat of casual workers, left stranded by the long and gradual decline of the industry [sugar] which brought them there, is the distinctive West Indian "problem".'[38] Moreover it was useless to expect that some economic miracle would, in the future, allow the islands to pull themselves out of these depths by their own efforts, 'the economic state of the Islands has never yet been such as to enable any but a handful to maintain themselves at some decently adequate level of the civilization which all aspire to share more fully'.[39] The harsh truth of the situation was that the West Indies simply did not possess the resources, skills and potential for capital formation to create a decent society: 'the total output of these Islands is inadequate for the equipment and maintenance of a strong community of free men'.[40]

Development of the economy, society, and the quality of human life in the West Indies to any acceptable standard, Macmillan argued, could only be accomplished by an abandonment of the policy of minimal government. Britain must face up to its imperial responsibilities and pay to restore these slums of empire, these 'depressed areas', as if they were parts of the United Kingdom. The old principle that colonies should live off their own means must be abandoned. If a massive programme of 'Reconstruction' were not begun at once, he warned, there would be widespread 'riots and disturbances'.[41] Such reconstruction entailed land redistribution; experiments with collective and communal farming; greater emphasis on subsistence crops; the creation of industries to mop up urban and rural unemployed; large-scale public works for temporary relief of unemployment and as investment for the future; the creation of health services and a comprehensive educational system; the foundation of a local university to create skilled administrators, technicians and future leaders; and the establishment of a primary system of social welfare and health services.

But the purpose of all this was not merely to make a reality of trusteeship through paternalism. Ultimately, Macmillan insisted, the only true 'development' would be self-development through self-government. This entailed a reconstruction plan which was, in effect, a social and economic revolution directed ultimately to self-government. It was time to abandon the 'dual mandate': 'world interests, and ours, will best be served if we achieve at last complete singleness of purpose in directing development for the welfare of their own people.'[42] Self-government and development were inextricably intertwined; neither was possible without the other:

Undoubtedly the only ultimate remedy is to press on the preparation of the unrepresented majority; but the difficult and even dangerous corollary has rarely been faced. It is that in the first place the executive Government, the 'trustee', must show greater courage than has been at all usual in its exercise of authority on their behalf. The only rational way of preparing these colonies to stand by themselves is to strengthen the lower strata of society.... without second thoughts for British industry, for the precarious state of white colonists, or even for the interests of a black upper class....

It must not be as in South Africa, where Great Britain herself made 'the great refusal'.[43]

Warning from the West Indies was not simply a book about the West Indies; it was also 'A Tract for the Empire'. Throughout the book Macmillan emphasized that he had studied the West Indies 'to get new light on the study of the African colonies'.[44] He did not see the West Indies as some exotic neglected byway: 'the West Indies are in their weakness almost completely typical of the colonies at large.'[45] He saw the West Indies as foretelling the future of white settled colonies in Africa, the poverty of the people 'is really the crucial test — and measures the failure — of the white settlement in the West

Indies'.[46] The catastrophe of the West Indies would be repeated in Africa if present policies continued:

Several even of the newer African colonies are beginning their life almost as the West Indies did three centuries ago.... The crucial weakness is near the top, with the planter, farmer, settler, as the case may be, in West Indies, South Africa, or Kenya. Because his own position is insecure he is for cheap labour. The effect on the workers is disastrous. But criticism needs to be directed to its basic cause — the economic futility, even in the planters' own interest, of the planter-farmer system.... in Africa settlers lose the capital they sink in coffee, tobacco, maize or citrus estates; their own plaints are witness how precarious they feel their position to be. On drafts from Home — and bank overdrafts — they keep their standards high, while yet demanding more financial assistance; and in Kenya at least the British Government is expected to back the settler policy at the expense of the home taxpayer chiefly on the plea that the Government itself originally helped to launch it. The significance of West Indian experience is completely wasted and warnings go unheeded — with imminent risk to the well-being of both whites and blacks.[47]

Concluding the introduction to *Warning from the West Indies* in the first edition, Macmillan commented:

It is the besetting national sin to take credit for the benevolence of our intentions. This book will serve its purpose, if, by showing the state of our oldest colonies after centuries of British rule, it can at all shake this complacency and rouse at once a livelier sense of our responsibility to the old West Indies and an aspiration to do better in the New Africa.[48]

The reception given to *Warning from the West Indies* was something of a 'double-take'. The first edition published by Faber attracted little public notice. It was, however, read with interest in the Colonial Office. G. L. M. Clauson, the economic specialist, wanted it circulated to all colonial governments, who should be asked to consider why development had failed and 'on this basis to work out something like a "Five Year Plan"' for Colonial Development Fund grants to the West Indies.[49] But, within months of the book's first publication, Macmillan's warnings were dramatically justified. In 1937 major strikes, riots and disturbances broke out in Trinidad, Jamaica, Barbados and in the Bahamas. Thirty-nine people lost their lives, 175 were injured, and there were enormous losses of property.[50] For the first time revolutionary outbreaks were threatening in British tropical colonies — complacency was shattered. Macmillan's book was now launched in a second, paperback edition as a 'Penguin Special', to be bought for a few pence at railway bookstalls. He had become, almost overnight, a popular 'authority', with a corresponding increase in his influence on both government and opposition, although he had not been ignored by either before this time. From 1937 Macmillan began to attend meetings of the Labour Party Advisory Committee on a regular basis.[51] By early 1939 he was sufficiently well known at the Colonial Office to press them with detailed considerations of gubernatorial appointments.[52]

As a result of his West Indies visit, the draft of *Africa Emergent* which Macmillan had shown to Hailey was considerably recast before it was finally published in 1938.[53] Its emphasis was now on the same themes that permeated the West Indian book, but in an African context. Africa also needed 'reconstruction'; its settler colonies were potential slums unless African paramountcy could be converted to a positive policy of African development. African colonial governments had been 'supine', contributing little or nothing to the emergence of modern Africans. There had been important change, especially in education and the creation of an educated élite of potential future leaders, but this was almost wholly the work of missionaries, who had likewise provided the rudimentary framework of social services. Governments, and especially the Colonial Office at the centre, must now accept the responsibility for planning economic, social and educational development. As in the West Indies, this could not be financed from colonial revenues alone; the imperial government would have to bear the financial burden.[54]

Macmillan argued that such 'development' was intimately linked to 'emergent' groups among the educated Africans. These would necessarily form the cadres of the development process. He doubted the fitness of traditional 'indirect rule' methods — geared as they were to the preservation of tradition — to undertake a dynamic role in development. He saw development and self-government as intimately linked; development was 'a necessary part of the process of securing their independent status in the world'[55] but at the same time development in the transitional status could only be assured by increasing the participation of educated Africans in the process.

Africa Emergent appeared in the same year as Hailey's *African Survey*, the year in which Malcolm MacDonald came to office as

Colonial Secretary on 16 May 1938 in the midst of the crisis over the West Indian riots. On 14 June, after renewed rioting in Jamaica from 23–31 May, MacDonald reversed the stand of his predecessor Ormsby-Gore, who had been stonewalling opposition demands for a Royal Commission. But MacDonald went much further in announcing what became the Moyne Commission — in effect declaring that the government had now adopted a policy of colonial reform which incorporated all the demands made by Macmillan, and more obliquely, by Hailey. MacDonald blamed the riots on the Colonial Office's 'neglect and lack of foresight', described West Indian grievances as 'legitimate' and announced that the Colonial Office would now embark on a 'long term policy of recovery in the West Indies' which would expand the standard of living through programmes in housing, nutrition and medical care, revitalize the traditional staples of the islands, create new industries and encourage subsistence crops. All of this would be beyond the financial capabilities of the colonial budgets and would have to be financed by the UK government. MacDonald concluded by pleading with the Labour Party for cooperation, promising trade union reform, the establishment of colonial labour departments and new labour legislation.[56] The debate which followed revealed that, on all sides of the House, the cult of minimal government had collapsed and in particular that the Labour Party had now emerged with a coherent policy of colonial reform based almost precisely on Macmillan's *Warning from the West Indies*.[57]

In the next two years Malcolm MacDonald proceeded to transform colonial policy along the lines advocated by the colonial critics, not merely by enacting the Colonial Development and Welfare Act of 1940 — which for the first time established substantial funding for social welfare and education, as well as economic development — but also by galvanizing the Colonial Office into a rethink of all aspects of colonial government in tropical territories, including the future evolution of self-governing institutions. In the process the Labour Party was won over into general agreement on the lines to be followed, and this would form a basis for a bipartisan colonial policy to be operated by the coalition government formed in May 1940, when MacDonald left the Colonial Secretaryship.[58]

W. M. Macmillan had played a crucial role in this process. His line of reasoning in *Warning from the West Indies* was followed almost exactly in the report of the Moyne Commission which investigated the West Indian riots, a report which MacDonald used as ammunition to push through the 1940 Colonial Development and Welfare Act. True, it was Hailey who became the Colonial Office's chief advisor on African affairs and whose *African Survey* was mined for the blueprints of future African policy, but Macmillan's influence on Hailey has already been demonstrated, and Hailey was not a powerful or original thinker, especially in generalities. In his impact on public opinion and its acceptance of the new policy of imperial financial responsibility for tropical colonial development, and for imperial initiatives towards self-government, Macmillan was far more important and influential than the unreadable Hailey, and much more congenial to the left.

Macmillan himself was considerably mollified by the changes wrought by MacDonald; as policy shifted to colonial reform Macmillan used his influence in the Labour Party to try to shift opinion away from 'internationalism' and the early emphasis on mandates and the need for international administration, to undermine Marxist perspectives, and even to utter warnings of the risks inherent in political reform — warnings which show remarkable prescience in the light of events in Africa since the 1960s.

In 1941 Macmillan contributed an essay, 'Freedom for colonial peoples', to a collection of Fabian essays edited by Harold Laski.[59] Questioning the Marxist analysis, Macmillan insisted that colonies had been acquired mainly for strategic, even for humanitarian, purposes. The poverty of the tropics was 'absolute, not Marxist [induced] poverty; it is *natural* and the dominant fact is that there is and has been all too little to "exploit"'.[60] Poverty had 'always existed'[61] in Africa. It was rooted in the geographical and physical limitations of the continent; it was just as bad in areas where there had been no land alienation or white settlement as in the tropical colonies as it was in South Africa. The evil consequences of white intrusion, to which he had devoted so much attention in his writings, in a sense had diverted attention from Africa's fundamental problem — the poverty of land. But now Britain had embarked on a policy of colonial reform 'in a general forward movement for the colonies, backed by our determination to set them free...'.[62] Could Britain finance such a development and was the British taxpayer ready to shoulder the burden?[63]

This led Macmillan into an attack on the traditional internationalism of the Labour Party. It was no more just for a people to be ruled by a group of nations than by one colonial power, and no colonial people had expressed any desire for an international regime. The Mandate principle expressed a purely negative trusteeship but contained no positive programme of colonial development. He was ready to advocate International *Development* Boards, for regions of Africa, to recruit European and American experts and capital, but politically the colonies needed the link with British democratic traditions and parliamentary institutions, even to the extent, perhaps, of direct representation in the British Parliament.[64]

Macmillan remained faithful to the concept that ballot box representation must come to African colonies[65] but at the same time was fearful for the future of democratic institutions in Africa. In the Gold Coast, he found the educated élite preoccupied with constitutional theory, cocoa prices and chieftaincy disputes, and little concerned with social needs, although these were clear and desperate.[66] The war had demonstrated the loyalty of the colonial peoples against Nazism and had taught them to value justice, and abhor secret police and the concentration camp. But Macmillan was not so sure that Indians and Africans 'have so fully imbibed the highest ideals of freedom, tolerance and concern for the rights of others, as to be actively awake to the needs of their own backward masses...'.[67]

11

MACMILLAN, INDIRECT RULE AND
*AFRICA EMERGENT**

MONA MACMILLAN

MACMILLAN is best remembered for his major contribution to the historiography of South Africa and his broad approach to the study of the peoples of South Africa, not as separate groups but as forming a social whole. Though it became his principal preoccupation after he left South Africa in 1932, his work on other regions of the African continent is less well remembered, as indeed the spread of essays in this volume underlines. But this neglect is unfortunate, especially in respect of his pioneering work *Africa Emergent* which was largely in draft by 1934 but not published until 1938. This already envisaged a future which was then only dimly — if at all — perceived in the corridors of the European colonial offices — that of a free Africa. This book, along with his three Heath Clark lectures published in *Europe and West Africa* in 1940, are essential reading for any student of the high colonial period in tropical Africa and are amongst the first works to show an awareness of the need for the democratization and ultimate decolonization of the continent.

Before he left South Africa in 1932, Macmillan had already become familiar with East and Central Africa, but it was not until March 1933, when he had finished his first tour of West Africa, that he was ready to begin the book that was later to become *Africa Emergent*. The opportunity to begin it was provided by the granting of an Association Fellowship, for a second time, by All Souls College, Oxford, from January to June, 1933. This All Souls connection came through Lionel Curtis who had encouraged him and, as Macmillan has told in *My South African Years*, had led him to hope for an important role in the African survey which Curtis was planning, and which eventually materialized as the 'Hailey Survey'. As it happened, Macmillan's two terms at All Souls were almost entirely taken up with the writing of three chapters for *The Cambridge History of the*

British Empire — the invitation to contribute the gist of his research being a tribute to the value of his new estimate of South African history.

Although Macmillan finally broke with Curtis in 1935 over the latter's support of a proposal to hand over the British High Commission Territories of Basutoland, the Bechuanaland Protectorate and Swaziland to the Union, after All Souls, Curtis was friendly enough to make a room at Chatham House available for the writing of the book. A condition of the Chatham House hospitality was that a draft of the proposed book would be ready for Lord Hailey to use as a working paper for his coming tour of Africa. The book was intended to be, in Macmillan's words, 'an Adam Smith of Africa'. The idea had originated three years earlier when he first travelled beyond the Union visiting Central and East Africa on the suggestion of Philip (later Sir Philip) Mitchell. His talks with Mitchell and others had impressed on him how little was known in one quarter of Africa of the outlook and activities in another. Those were days when few of the civil servants who directed policy from Whitehall ever set foot in a colony. There was little machinery for coordinating ideas. A book might fill the gap, and it had to cover the whole ground and be comparative, helping to show what methods were being used to tackle the same problems in different areas; a complete statement of the conditions, the possibilities, and the influences at work on the continent. It had to correct the South African and imperial attitude which regarded Africa as a blank sheet — a wasted part of the world's resources — which, in the words of Lugard's *Dual Mandate*, must be made 'available for the world', almost in spite of the African peoples.

The 'blankness of Africa' was customarily attributed to a deficiency in the African peoples, and there was speculation as to whether they could keep pace with the rest of the world. It was because of such widespread discussion that the first chapter of the book has a title which seems curious today — 'The mission of civilisation'. It was directed to those who would relegate Africans to some sub-civilization; Macmillan's contention was that 'civilization' had many contributors and could not be confined to any section of the human race. In this chapter he also discussed the Marxist charge that 'all colonial empires are manifestations of economic imperialism'. He himself saw colonialism as the result of economics, but ascribed it more to uncontrolled individual greed than to government policy, and saw that the actual acquisition of territory by governments might be at times an attempt to control and regulate this greed.

The colonial status, condemned alike by Marxists and by hundred per cent Americans, is something inherent. A just system of human relationships is hard to establish just because of the natural weakness and incapacity of one of the parties. It solves no problem to eschew *de facto* annexation, and to recognise as independent natural dependents like the Republic of Liberia. Their development then falls inevitably to private enterprise which the infant state is powerless to control.[1]

Macmillan foresaw the neo-colonialism which has overtaken much of Africa in the wake of independence. When he spoke of 'natural weakness and dependence' he referred to economic weakness, and he believed that there must be internal economic development 'until Africa could act and speak on a level with the rest of the world'. There were no words at that time to express the idea he saw so clearly; neither 'underdevelopment' nor 'environment' had been coined in their modern significance. The weakness of the African peoples lay in their environment, and the book was ahead of its time in being strongly environmental in orientation, a plea both for conservation and enhancement of natural resources. His second chapter 'The roots of backwardness' began with a section entitled 'environment' and went on to discuss as 'backwardness' what has today become widely recognized and termed as underdevelopment. It is surprising that the condition of underdevelopment was so hard to impress on European public opinion until after the Second World War, when awareness seemed to spread to the media, the churches, and the charitably disposed public. Just how much a book like *Africa Emergent* contributed it is hard to tell, but certainly at the time it was written there was no such awareness, and the poverty and need of African countries was unknown and ignored even by colonial governments, let alone by colonizing nations. Within the British Commonwealth, in Macmillan's words, 'the Crown colonies were in a state of forgotten dependence'.[2]

As the last sentence implies, Macmillan had not ceased to be a critic of imperialism because of his interest in the British African colonies and his friendship with men like Philip Mitchell and Donald Cameron. He was delighted to find that such men were eager to talk of plans for future development — political as well as economic. It was a relief after the repression of South Africa to find all kinds of possibilities aired and discussed freely, and to find an enthusiasm for reform among some senior officials like Mitchell and Cameron, and a great many of the younger men. What the socialist in Macmillan looked for was a measure of state planning for development, and he thought this could be brought about through the British colonial system while it lasted — if Britain could be persuaded to give the funds and the expertise. He did not cease to uphold the rights of Africans to education and to better health — 'no one has yet seen what a really healthy African could do', was an often quoted remark of his — to full opportunities, and, finally, to independence. But the might and wealth of Britain, which was still considerable, could be used towards this.

Africa Emergent dealt with underdevelopment under the headings 'environment', 'health', and 'population'. The picture painted was a sober and by no means extravagant one; the facts uncovered by a later generation corroborate it all, and have in many respects proved worse than what was then thought a pessimistic picture. There was little research at the time, and he tapped what there was. His findings were based on interviews in the field over the length and breadth of Africa, visits to hospitals, much reading of reports on agriculture and health from the various colonies, and certain pioneer specialist papers. In South Africa Macmillan had focused on such questions as population density and land usage. On population he was in close touch with Dr R. Kuczynski, whose *Population Movements* was published in 1936 and with this man's backing, he contended that Africa had never been able to support a very dense population. He attacked South African assumptions about population based on Theal's view that 'before the coming of the Europeans the population was stagnant or declining because the tribes were "constantly killing each other", and that owing to a high natural rate of increase it had been "rapidly increasing" ever since', pointing out that population tended to be congregated in favourable areas and that there was no evidence that South Africa, or any other part of Africa, had been unoccupied as European settlers maintained. In Africa soils were light and infertile, and subject to erosion by water and overgrazing; cattle were either too numerous, or could not exist because of disease; rainfall was inadequate; and water conservation was beyond the people's means. 'In Africa nature continued to dominate man.'[3]

On agriculture, he used the work of O. T. Faulkner and J. R. Mackie, and the researches of Martin Leake. On the related subject of diet he was much impressed by the work of the Jamaican Dr William McCulloch, on the Hausa and Town Fulani of Nigeria;[4] and of J. L. Gilks and J. B Orr (Lord Boyd Orr) on the contrasted diets of the Kikuyu and the Masai in Kenya. To these he added what he already knew of experiments in diet being done on the Rand mines, and the findings of prison authorities from nearly every territory, who had noted that the physique of prisoners generally improved on prison diet. Much that was then loosely attributed by European employers to 'laziness', or backwardness, was, he was convinced, the result of early malnutrition, and the debilitating effects of malaria, parasites, or other disease.

The character of the people and their society, so much derided by the average European of the time, was dealt with in a chapter which was intended to be an answer both to those who condemned Africans as 'savages', and to those others, particularly anthropologists, who thought them so admirably adapted to their surroundings that no western ideas should be allowed to contaminate them. The Africans he knew best were those of the Ciskei and Transkei and more especially the emergent Africans of Johannesburg with whom he had many encounters through the Industrial and Commercial Workers' Union (ICU) and the Joint Council. Dame Lucy Sutherland, one of his early students, recalls that a group of these — mainly teachers and clergy — used to meet at his house with some of his senior white students. These were the product of Lovedale and Fort Hare, which he knew well. Later on he also knew the graduates of Achimota College, where his friend A. G. Fraser suggested the first version of the book's title — 'African renaissance'.

Macmillan's sense of history led him to see in these 'emergents' with their eagerness for learning and capacity to absorb, the men of the European renaissance. He sympathized with the dislike of such men for an education 'adapted' for them by Europeans, and was sure that in time they themselves would do the adaptation. He was at a disadvantage in not knowing any African language, or any African society in depth, but he was suspicious of anthropologists who, he thought, would like to tell Africans what was good for them. This suspicion was shared by his friend Norman Leys,[5] and by most educated Africans, who disliked seeing African societies studied as specimens, or as something apart from the mainstream of humanity.

236

Macmillan and Leys also had fears that Africa's rulers might find evidence from anthropology to back them in treating African subjects as inferior, or at best different; those who took anthropology most seriously were the educationalists, especially those of the missions such as J. H. Oldham, and of course they had a vital influence. Anxious to know more of the anthropologists' theory Macmillan persuaded his future wife to join Bronislav Malinowski's seminar at the London School of Economics. This was a brilliant group, containing such people as Audrey Richards, Meyer Fortes, Margaret Read, Margaret Wrong, and Jack Simons from South Africa. Malinowski was a stern theorist, who would allow no wandering from the 'functional' explanations of tribal custom, no historical or assimilationist influence. But he would begin by making his students describe the physical environment of the community they were studying, down to the distance and position of the water supply; this tied in well with Macmillan's awareness of the effects of environment. What was learnt from the seminar may have helped to keep the chapter on African society in step with the state of knowledge at the time.

Since then, a great deal has been learnt, and the growth of black studies and the decline of confidence in western capitalism has brought about a reaction in defence of African social values. Macmillan, however, maintained his criticism that African society gave too little opportunity to the individual, and made no place for the educated man. In land usage particularly, custom militated against a security of holding which would encourage improvement. Macmillan was far from being a devotee of private ownership, and in fact had a strong dislike of landlords which went back to the troubled history of the Scottish Highlands and in particular to his own grandfather's eviction from one farm to another at his landlord's whim. But he realized that small farmers, whether black or white, would be undercapitalized and short on expertise. He would probably have wished for a system of secure state tenancy.

The basis of the book which became *Africa Emergent* was the experience gained in two journeys, first in east and then in west Africa. In both, Macmillan was greatly helped by a young and enthusiastic administration, eager to show what it was doing to a sympathetic observer. Their respect for his observation must be measured by the freedom with which they always talked; other travellers did not always experience such a ready response. He brought with him from South Africa a practised observation of social situations, and a healthy scepticism of government intentions and methods, which prevented his losing a balanced judgement of what he saw. Although the two journeys were arranged for him by Donald Cameron and Philip Mitchell, the leading exponents of the then fashionable theory of 'indirect rule', he never became wholly enamoured of that theory or impressed by its results.

When he went to East Africa in 1930 Cameron was Governor of Tanganyika, and Mitchell his Colonial Secretary. Macmillan inevitably saw more of Tanganyika on this visit than of Kenya. The administration had a freer hand in Tanganyika which was not a colony, but a 'mandated' territory taken from the Germans after the First World War, and supervised to some extent by the then League of Nations. In Kenya he noted the strained relations between the settlers and the administration; and he showed some sympathy for the former, whom he looked upon as hard-pressed agriculturists.

The Uganda railway, which alone made settlement feasible, also saddled the colony with a burden of maintenance. The Government looked to the settlers to achieve the development of the country, and to increase its revenues, but was little inclined either to give them direct help, or failing this to give them a free hand to do things their own way.... Where native interests were concerned the Government was nervous, but had no clear policy of its own other than hoping and praying that settlement might disturb the native *status quo* as little as possible. When encroachments on native land began, inevitably, to cause friction, such administrative action as was taken aroused the distrust of both sides.[6]

These encroachments were soon to become his closer concern, and, in practice, he made as little excuse for the settlers as he did here for their government.

Macmillan saw East Africa for the first time during the Depression when the Europeans' lack of resources was having its effect on their political temper. Philip Mitchell, writing to him at the end of the tour, showed the ambivalent attitude of government towards white settlement, and quite correctly forecast its dangers, which he did not want to see increased in Tanganyika:

Fundamental mistakes must not be made; at the worst you can repair political mistakes or most of them — but if you plant in East Africa a large number of small white farmers, who must be destroyed economically by the black peasant farmers within a generation, or at most two, you will have created conditions which probably only bloodshed can solve.[7]

Various circumstances prevented the climax he foresaw occurring in East Africa, but not so in Zimbabwe.

Macmillan saw that white settlement was not only unjust but economically ineffective in the fight against poverty. Writing of Southern Rhodesia in *The Political Quarterly* of October 1932, he said:

The day of the middle-scale individual farmer is past ... it seems too late to rebuild the fortunes of a class in the wilds of Africa, with no place for the native inhabitants. If the old methods are persevered in, the settlers will clearly have to be content to sink to the humbler subsistence farming of the South African backveld. This in turn means the continuance of squalor, if not virtual serfdom, for at least a considerable proportion of the native Africans. If, however, there is to be any settled rural society of Europeans it may be that there are lessons to be learned from Zionist experiments in Palestine, or from more extensive communal schemes elsewhere. There may indeed be no practicable mean between the full-size plantation and the African peasant holding.[8]

This was a theme he was to return to in the West Indies but, although he was writing here in an objective manner which did not exclude a European contribution, the censure on small, independent white settlers was heresy to an influential class in Britain, and *The Political Quarterly* article (which *The Times* had refused) probably cost him the academic employment which he hoped for.

It was the existence of white settlers which forced the policy which Macmillan so strongly opposed, of carving a country up into white areas and 'native reserves'. He had seen and written of the deeply depressed condition of such 'reserves' in South Africa, and in Part II of *Africa Emergent* he analysed and criticized in detail the practice as it existed in South Africa, and as it was to be introduced into Kenya and Southern Rhodesia. He was appalled by the introduction and repetition, late in the day, of South African mistakes in the two colonies, where land commissions were then at work, apportioning the land between the races. He admitted the British government's concern to see that some land at least was reserved to Africans, and that the Rhodesians were priding themselves that, unlike the South Africans, they had allowed ample for future African needs. The now notorious Rhodesian Land Apportionment Act came into force in October 1931. Macmillan wanted *Africa Emergent* to include a map of the demarcation of land and the incredible patchwork of black and white, which was worse even than that of the South African reserves. However, the map was drawn, but dropped for lack of space.

To quote Macmillan in *The Political Quarterly*. 'Almost verbally this fundamental Rhodesian Act closely follows the model of the unhappy Union Act of 1913 ... six years from now white and black shall be separated into their own respective areas — saving always, necessary labourers'.[9] He spoke of 'the disastrous policy of penning all "superfluous" natives in crowded "Reserves"', and called for secure tenancy on white land for those who would not, or should not, be so penned. He pointed out that Africans had been allotted an unfair proportion of infertile or waterless soil, and that some of the areas already had a larger population than they could carry. As in South Africa, the African areas were inaccessible and lacked transport. There was only one agricultural officer to promote improved agricultural methods. Where there was white settlement everything was distorted, public health and education took a humble place, and the need for cheap labour on the farms was the overriding factor. The idea that Africans were quite capable of learning to do things by and for themselves could find little credence. Acute poverty was the lot of the reserves and yet they had to be the centre of any new African life. Applying his East African experience, Macmillan wrote that

Rhodesia is as far as the Union from appreciating the great lesson taught by Sir Donald Cameron in Tanganyika, that no African state can possibly afford to pay enough white officials for effective development or even for general administration. The only way is to teach and train the Africans themselves to do the work required. They must and can only learn by responsibility: advisory powers (why call these 'powers' I can never see) will never build up what is needed.[10]

Macmillan saw Kenya — then moving Africans off land in the highlands — as another example of settler injustice. At the end of 1930 a Joint Select Committee was appointed to consider closer union between the three East African territories, and he was urged by Norman Leys to help prevent the spread of the Kenya system. Leys wrote, 'I shall never forgive you if you don't come home in time to give evidence to the Select Committee'.[11] Mitchell also urged him likewise. The correspondence about this Select Committee is interesting evidence of the liaison role which Macmillan considered he should take, in a situation where little was known by one colony of another. His contemplated book would, he hoped, make vitally important comparisons possible. Mitchell encouraged him in this role, considering himself, for all his important position, isolated and helpless. He wrote, 'decisions of such vital importance are to be taken. . . . You will be there and be able to talk to people; I can only sit here and hope for the best.'[12]

Macmillan consulted J. H. Oldham of the International Missionary Council, and Lord Passfield (Sidney Webb) the Colonial Secretary, as to whether his evidence would be wanted. Neither of them had a positive answer, although Oldham thought it might be useful if he could talk privately with some of the members. It was said of Passfield that, as an ex-civil servant, he was capable of finding more objections to any proposal than his permanent advisers could. He answered that the Select Committee would not want to hear any more witnesses than was avoidable, and that they would have to hear some who 'would insist on being heard'.[13] However, Macmillan had his book *Complex South Africa* to see through the press, so he went to London and did meet members of the Select Committee.

In the field of administration and politics there was more serious debate over 'indirect rule'. Originating in Nigeria in Lugard's 'Instructions to Officers' of 1918, it had been refined by Cameron into something which might come nearer to democracy than the rule of the Muslim Emirs for which it had been designed. For their states in principle a British Political Officer was needed only to give advice; applied to other communities with less autocratic rulers, it had become a more subtle instrument, intended in theory to provide a basis of local government leading to self-rule in a modern world. Mitchell explained his version of the doctrine to Macmillan thus:

If you are going to do anything for the people as such and not merely to replace a white ruling caste by a coloured one, you must make the attempt to guide and help the social and political forms common to all the people into the main stream of the twentieth century. . . . I do not necessarily think that in due course democracy as we know it will be adopted by the Bantu. . . . But their system is now representative in any case ... it is no use making benevolent declarations unless you see to it that they take form in institutions — native courts, native administrations, native treasuries and so on; and such institutions must be native; if they are foreign they will collapse like a house of cards under the first serious strain, or even under the blight of neglect, but if they are native and have the spirit of the people in them ... they will go on of their own inward vital force, unless they are destroyed by deliberate violence.[14]

This was a hopeful outlook, and one borne out by succeeding events, the weakness being that it could not be put into effect by an alien power. Norman Leys expressed this very clearly:

The old world we ought clearly to protect and that is why 'indirect rule' is always right for a time. For a time I say — and here is where I part company with the Cameron school. For they think it is for them not only to determine the time, but to decide into what traditional tribal culture is to evolve. We are all familiar with such phrases as 'preserving all that is best in African traditional culture and helping it to evolve into' — well, words there are apt to fail because ideas get too undisguisably thin, — for the end these people always arrive at is, any evolution you like except ours. *Avaunt Europa* from Africa. Avaunt trousers and above all avaunt democracy.[15]

The amount of democracy that was to be encouraged formed the crux of the debate. Though Macmillan learned from Cameron and Mitchell, he was generally to be found in the same camp as Leys. His attitude to indirect rule was a constructive one: for him, the test of its sincerity was how far the Native Authority was allowed to collect and use its own funds. But such pragmatic endorsement was never sufficient for those dogmatically committed to the system.

An interview with the then Dominions' Secretary, J. H. Thomas, in November 1934 illuminates Macmillan's judgement of indirect rule. The interview was largely taken up by a discussion between him and the Minister on the application of what Thomas called 'The Tanganyikan system' to Bechuanaland. Macmillan made his point about the need to give full responsibility:

Having seen a pretty considerable variety it seemed to me the crux of the matter in all the colonies is the Treasury. In Northern Rhodesia, let alone in the Protectorates, the last thing they think of is of trusting a black with money, and they are missing the whole point. For example, the mineral arrangements lately made for the Protectorates; in case of royalties they are to be paid into a tribal fund that is not a Treasury in the Tanganyikan sense.

It means that anything that comes from mineral royalties will go into a Trust Fund which will be audited and controlled, but the blacks of Bechuanaland will not have any direct responsibility for that, whereas the very essence of the Tanganyikan plan is to teach them responsibility and make them do their own budgets.[16]

Sir Geoffrey Whiskard, assisting the Minister, broke in to describe new Proclamations which were being prepared with the object of diluting the autocratic power of the Chief, and compelling him to accept the existence of a tribal council. Macmillan added to this:

May I make what was rather my own suggestion. I had a long talk with Sir Herbert Stanley [High Commissioner for South Africa and responsible for the Territories], and I thoroughly agree with the way he put it, i.e. your object should be [to] make the Chief a sort of constitutional king with a council which is really doing the functioning. You have to start right away making the Treasury a real working thing, and get more good treasury work and budgeting, and so on, devolved.[17]

He suggested that the drafts of the new proclamations which were the subject of a tug-of-war between the Tshekedi Khama (Regent of the Bangwato) and the British Commissioner, might be submitted to Sir Donald Cameron as an impartial expert. As the minutes show, this suggestion was seriously considered by the Office but was dropped on the grounds that Sir Donald was too inaccessible. One of the most important considerations, in Macmillan's view, was to get educated men, who might not have hereditary claims, appointed to Councils. He ventured at this meeting to suggest that there was 'just a tendency that it [the new system] is leaning towards a new autocracy'.[18] Sir Geoffrey Whiskard took him up, and underlined the point, though with specific reference to the Tswana chiefs.

I understand you, Professor, to agree that ... in Bechuanaland and in all the territories from which large drafts of labour are drawn by the mines, the tribal system has undergone a very considerable change ... the change has been the Chief has tended to become an autocrat, much more than he would otherwise have done.

To this Macmillan replied: 'The shell is, I think there — and in some ways it is like Nigerian Mohammedanism, all the stronger for having been protected.'[19] What he meant was that the intervention of the overriding imperial power prevented any natural growth and adaptation, even when it tried to encourage and preserve 'traditional' forms.

This discussion came only after Macmillan had made his visit to the cradle of that system — West Africa — early in 1933. He began his tour as Cameron's guest at Government House, Lagos. Cameron refrained from talking specifically about Nigeria, wishing Macmillan to find out for himself; but speaking of Indirect Rule in general he said: 'You can't legislate for Native Administration — you can only give it legal power and make an authority which must *ex hypothesi* administer, by using some discretion; which is what "administer" means.'[20] To modern African nationalists, Cameron's Native Authorities were just another name for puppet rulers, but in fact the older dispensation of Emirs and great Chiefs may have lent itself more to that form of exploitation than Cameron's new model which, in theory at least, involved councils representing wider interests. Nevertheless, Macmillan's critical faculties were soon brought to bear and, at Abeokuta, his first stop after Lagos, he thought his official host 'quite reactionary' and added 'a lot of good officials are only benevolent despots really'.

In the huge and colourful town of Abeokuta he found that 'you can see the white man's case far better ... it needs millions spending to get the villages and rural towns clean ... and epidemics are the only things that get anything done'. He had hopes that the new councils and treasuries would become involved in providing some preventive medicine, as well as education and better agriculture, but he found that the relatively new 'technical' branches of the colonial service were not very welcome to the administrative establishment. Listening to district officers discussing between themselves he found them very jealous of medical or other rivals interfering, and 'quite reactionary about health'.

Abeokuta confirmed his belief that there was trouble ahead from 'the alliance of our political officers [Tories] with reactionary or conservative chiefs against the growing voluble class of intellectuals'. He was not reassured by a visit to a 'freak' school, where 'sporting public school boys are reproducing public school ideas in Africa, reinforced by Julian Huxley type biology and handwork'. (Julian Huxley had recently toured Africa and published a book, *Africa View* (1931), in which he advocated more scientific education.) Whether or not he was referring directly to Huxley, Macmillan thought the mistakes of the school in question were due to 'misinformed criticism, and inexpert public opinion'.

From the Yoruba towns of Ibadan, Oyo and Ife, Macmillan went by train north to Kaduna, the cradle of the original Lugardian indirect rule, but initially found it unfruitful. No one wanted to show him anything, and he was not expected to meet anyone but officials. He thought 'the set up over elaborate, — an absurd baby capital'. Zaria, another Emirate, was more hopeful, with prosperous farming but weak on health. The District Officers were only allowed to advise. He thought they were 'really keen and disinterested, but everything still to do and make'. The extraordinary mixture of advanced and primitive was 'the key to the whole complicated business, with officers in danger of expecting too much because of having found so much in some ways, and especially putting things on the Native Authorities before they are ready'.

At Kano he found the Resident none too pleased at having a visitor dumped on him, and too busy to listen to explanations; he often grew weary of explaining himself and trying to get his purposes across. On the other hand, there were those who saw the drift at once and helped by an instant sympathy; he felt he was making friends even in the proud North which felt it had all the answers and was not looking for change. But he was left to unravel a good deal for himself. There were puzzles such as the density of population in some places; and the complexity of land tenure. This he felt could not be satisfactorily dealt with by anthropology, since the need for a system only arose when land became a problem too great for tribal control. Above all, there was the problem of the North, that educated workers had to be imported from the South, since the domination of Islam had prevented Christian mission schools from being founded in the Emirates. Anyone reading his letters of that time can see where the later troubles of Nigeria sprang from. Already there were large numbers of Ibo occupying jobs for which northerners were unqualified, and kept in ghetto-like townships administered outside the jurisdiction of the local Native Authority.

In Jos, the centre of entirely different 'pagan' tribes (so-called because they were not Muslims), he found there were no emirs, and that indirect rule had to be built up from scratch. Here he had only two and a half days to absorb a totally new situation and he fretted through the first under the usual difficulty of explaining himself and

245

getting his host to break his routine. By the second day, as so often, he had broken down resistance and his hosts were ready to talk, and took him on an eight-hour drive from which he got a very full impression of the 'pagans'. He was impressed by their quite advanced agriculture, which he attributed to a readiness to learn which was not so evident among more sophisticated peoples. He was also amazed by the number of their tribes and languages, a happy hunting ground for anthropologists, and anthropology-minded missionaries. Some of these 'pagans' were ruled by Islamic emirs who had formerly raided them for slaves, but the whole area came under the Lieutenant Governor of the North who was somewhat out of touch with the anomalies of Islamic rule. His opposite number, the Lieutenant Governor of the South, was very ready to call the situation wrong, and went so far as to say that it would not have passed the test of the Mandates Commission.

The visit to Enugu, the capital of the South, had been especially asked for by a cable from the Lieutenant Governor, who was afraid that his province would be neglected. Macmillan had worked over the itinerary with Cameron and reduced the time allowed for the North to make room for the Enugu visit. This was symptomatic of the attention the North usually got over the South. British people were generally impressed by Islamic good manners and the feudal discipline of the North, and contrasted this unfavourably with the less well organized and more turbulent South. Enugu, capital of the South, had anomalous jurisdiction both over the very sophisticated Yoruba towns, and the Ibo and Ibibio peoples of the South-East who did not have the same political and social cohesion. For instance, whereas the North had a long tradition of paying 'tribute', the South was unused to any form of taxation.

Taxation was a subject much studied by Macmillan. It could be, as in South Africa, a source of injustice, but there was an obvious relationship between the raising of revenue and possibilities of development. In south-eastern Nigeria, villages were scattered through the forest, and even formal courts of justice were a novelty. South-eastern officers had grown up in the old tradition of direct rule, and were only clear that Lagos now wanted them to adopt a vague thing called 'indirect rule', as practised in the North, and adapt it to their many scattered peoples whose variations in language and custom might be accentuated by the application of anthropological criteria. Yet the south-east government, unlike that of the North, was conscious of the need to fit in the Christian educated element, which was extremely strong in an intelligent and go-ahead people who had received much attention from missionaries.

On returning to Lagos, Macmillan had his first introduction to the highly sophisticated black leaders of the so-called Colony, the nucleus of original foreign influence. Among these were the seventy-year-old Henry Carr, Sir Kitoni Ajasa, and others, with whom he dined one evening and toured the town the next day. He was deeply impressed by their old-fashioned English university education, and highly cultured talk; but he wrote a little sadly that they were 'rather a freak, and very little direct help to Nigeria'. However, he also toured the slums with a black Medical Officer of Health, something that could only have happened in Lagos Colony at that date. He spent several more days in Lagos seeing schools, medical services, and so forth, and ending with one and a half hours of hard talk with Cameron. He congratulated himself that, in four weeks, he had only wasted two days and felt that he had been able to absorb situations all the better for his previous experience in East Africa.

The Gold Coast, now Ghana, added considerably to that experience. There, Sir Shenton Thomas, the Governor, a pleasant, friendly man, was a different type from Cameron, and nearly in despair over his intelligent, prosperous and turbulent people. In a letter written to Macmillan after his departure, Thomas showed the preference common among British administrators for the more easily ruled Islamic peoples. He wrote enthusiastically of the people of the Northern Territories who provided the workers on the southern cocoa plantations:

... no politics, no petitions. Just a jolly, hard-working people, with real chiefs who look to our officers for help in all they do. There is real scope for native administrations there, and the work has already begun.... There native administration presents little difficulty, nor does it really I think in Ashanti, where the tribal spirit is still so strong ... but I confess that for the time I am defeated by the Colony, and I begin to fear that it is too late to do much.[21]

The Colony had numerous small chiefs, more or less democratically elected, and deposed or 'destooled' with alarming frequency by their constituents. The treasuries which Macmillan thought so important were hardly possible, as the people of the Gold Coast utterly refused any direct taxation. The Chiefs' or Stool

Treasuries were replenished by court fees, fees for allotting cocoa land, and other perquisites, and Macmillan remarked, 'God knows where the money goes'. The country on the whole was prosperous on the export of cocoa, but the ownership of cocoa land seemed endlessly complicated and indeterminate — it could neither be sold outright nor used to raise loans.

Out of the cocoa revenues the Government had built and staffed one of the best schools in Africa, Achimota College. Macmillan was the guest there of an old friend from his Oxford days, Kingsley Williams, a very radical missionary; A. G. Fraser, a man of lively ideas and a lively tongue, was Principal, and by strange coincidence Norman Leys was a visitor. It is disappointing that no one made a record of the conversation between the three radical friends, but it was probably at this meeting that Fraser suggested a title for the coming book, and it was certainly discussed. Macmillan thought the school rather too élitist, but that it had a useful place in raising yet further the level of education 'which is the highest yet anywhere, even Uganda'. Colonial schools in general were apt to be too afraid of a high level in education, as if they were producing too much, when, as Macmillan saw it, it was really too little. He was soon on the road again. From Kumasi he wrote:

The real work these days has been impression taking, endless forest and cocoa, very sticky, but with heavy rain. Indirect rule here is more like Basutoland than Nigeria, no control, and it will have to be imposed. It is quite a mad situation and almost more interesting than Nigeria, it's far more a problem in government, and they must learn the Tanganyikan lesson that what is needed is to evolve local government, while leaving no doubt that there is a central government in charge. The Colony near Accra is fairly out of hand — but to complete the picture here in Ashanti the new Prempeh[22] and his Chiefs are amenable to direction; the town is amazing, easily the best town I've seen, and yet quite African; made by a first rate doctor, whose orders have been cheerfully accepted, sanitary villages even out in the country, and a happy people and means of real Native Authority. But in the Colony they've a difficult time ahead. I'm not sure that the Gold Coast is not the warning of the dangers of the anthropologists — respect for custom has paralysed government, which seems afraid to govern, or to take responsibility for governing, and its respect for such custom has hardened bad ways.

Working over his notes, he came to the conclusion that in spite of a high level of education 'the familiar backwardness is the most obvious fact'.

He was troubled at meeting, in West Africa, with a class of materialistic, money-conscious Africans, such as he had not met elsewhere. They were the product of many generations of trade. He was to have further experience of this later and to become progressively disenchanted with the West African élites. But, at that time, they seemed to be only a comparatively small class and, although they and their countries had far greater prosperity than 'starving South Africa', they did not detract from the overall need for development. At Takoradi he wondered whether the late Governor Guggisberg had been 'far-sighted or merely rash' when he spent six million pounds on building a proper harbour to replace surf-ridden beaches, and even more on Achimota College; but concluded that he wished 'there were more rash venturers in Africa'.

On the voyage out, and later in Northern Nigeria, his path crossed that of J. R. Mackie, the agriculturist, who together with O. T. Faulkner had published the then standard work on tropical agriculture. With him he discussed 'the relative places of agriculture and mining'. Having lived so long in Johannesburg Macmillan realized how the South African government had profited from its tough agreements with the mining companies. Profits from the gold mines, on a sliding scale of taxation, had been used to sustain and improve white agriculture in South Africa, through subsidies and aid to research. He wanted to see the African colonies profit in the same way from their mineral wealth, and recommended that they should imitate this very successful practice. He said he had developed

... a prejudice in favour of working for something like strong public utility corporations to push mineral development by an alliance between Government and the big groups, to squeeze out the small weak shows that scratch the mere surface and over-work and under-staff, and don't first secure good conditions of labour to make life better for Africans and bearable for necessary Europeans.

His interest in the place of mining grew with visits to the tin mines of Nigeria, a number of Gold Coast mines, and finally the mines of Sierra Leone. In Northern Rhodesia (Zambia) and Katanga in the Congo (Zaire), he had been much impressed by the management of the copper mines, particularly by the housing and feeding of labourers, and by a more enlightened attitude than on the South African gold mines. In West Africa he found none of this organization. Mines were uncontrolled, contributing little to government finance, and nothing to social services. On his return voyage via Freetown, he fell in with three directors of the Selection Trust Group, which he felt was responsible for some of the best work he had seen in Northern Rhodesia, and was then embarking on diamond mining in Sierra Leone. These three, George Nicolaus, T. Doyle, and J. Parker, although on the board of their company, had been engineers and prospectors in the field and looked on mining as a profession rather than a financial speculation. Nicolaus was British, Doyle and Parker, American. They became Macmillan's firm friends.

Macmillan saw that the encouragement of strong international groups presupposed a governmental machine that could deal with them. This was conspicuously lacking in the Colonial Office and, on his return, he took up the matter, suggesting that government advisers on mining were often less qualified and less well-paid than the technocrats with whom they had to deal. He wanted a new draft Mining Ordinance to serve as a pattern for colonial governments, and tried to interest Lord Lugard in this, but Lugard was quite satisfied with the existing Ordinance which he had drafted himself in 1913. In the second edition of his book, Macmillan claimed that he had some influence in changing a system of taxation which bore heavily on the country of origin:

The first edition may have helped to call attention to a disability that is now on the way to being remedied. Since the capital engaged is necessarily imported, the product and the profits of African mining must normally leave their country of origin to pay its owners their rent. For convenience, tropical African mining companies are commonly registered in London, where income tax is deducted at what is not even by courtesy to be described as the source. Thus colonial governments, besides being in no position to discourage new capital ventures by adding to their burdens, could not even drive the best bargain by way of sliding-scale leases to companies which had this British tax to reckon with. Too heavy a share of the revenue from profitable enterprises, therefore, went to the country which was rich enough to supply the capital. Some effort is at last being made to establish a fairer equilibrium.[23]

Although much of the book dealt with physical underdevelopment, chapters on education and on 'politics and the educated classes', made it clear that development would have a political outcome. He made it quite clear that 'indirect rule' was not the final objective.

The problem remains that our rule does not fully secure African co-operation even when it is indirect, and where there is no complication due to the presence of Europeans. In proportion as Indirect Rule succeeds in the avowed aim of building up an effective system of local government, it should serve also to lay the foundations on which a system of central control healthier than the present, can best repose ... the greater the success in making the N.A. [Native Authority] narrowly African, the greater must be the risk of a disharmony arising from the consciousness in Africans of dependence on a superior, wholly European, central executive — when all is said and done, just such an alien authority as it is the purpose of Indirect Rule to do away with. This already expresses itself in a sense of grievance that there is little attempt to make room for qualified Africans, on equal terms, in the administrative and technical services.[24]

His fears that indirect rule would become a straitjacket for the emergent Africans was supported by the authority on education in the Sudan, Sir James Currie. Sir James summed up his own experience by saying:

Indirect administration as interpreted in the Sudan in recent years has been an unmitigated evil. If it means anything it should mean a stringent limitation of the number of British officials, particularly higher grade officials. This is emphatically what, in the Sudan, it has not meant.[25]

Currie's influence on Macmillan was a useful corrective to that of Mitchell and Cameron. In an article for the *Journal of the Royal African Society* in 1935, Sir James paid Macmillan the compliment of quoting one of his letters, and also of calling him 'one of the most acute critical minds devoted to the study of African problems'. In the letter Macmillan had written:

The educated Africans are the crux of the matter, and will be increasingly; political officers and others are inclined to write them down as a mere nuisance. There is, therefore, a definite danger of our good officers ... even seeming to side with tribal chiefs and old-fashioned blacks who are much less troublesome. But in the end the hopeful experiment of Indirect Rule will stand or fall — by its success in absorbing and carrying with it, the goodwill of these people of the near future.[26]

It can be seen from this quotation that Macmillan looked on indirect rule as a hopeful experiment, but one which needed constant monitoring and criticism. Cameron's and Mitchell's letters show that they were themselves by no means sure of acceptance, and that they felt the need to enlist Macmillan as a spokesman. But there were still some — whether in the Colonial Office, the universities, or the political parties — for whom a more rigid form of indirect rule had become an orthodoxy not to be criticized, and these were strong enough to exclude Macmillan from major conferences on colonial policy and the kind of academic position from which he could have had influence. His criticism, on the one hand, of indirect rule, and on the other of the South African situation, made him appear dangerous to both camps. The experience of South Africa is indeed latent throughout *Africa Emergent*, and constantly used as a touchstone. A whole section, forty-five pages, analysed South African policy and, when a paperback edition was published in 1949, an appendix was added giving a more explicit account of the history of that policy.

The journeys and personal encounters recorded in this essay were the raw material out of which *Africa Emergent* was made but the book could not be an account of them such as is given here; it had to be a treatise, a reasoned argument, a plea for a cause. Britain had responsibility for colonial peoples and had to be reminded where that responsibility lay.

A genius for the development of Africans themselves as exploiters of their country's resources has not been our forte, and now the democratic faith which was our only real strength itself grows dim and weak. The only warrant for our tenure of African colonies is that our presence is of service to Africa itself, and it must henceforth be based on something broader than selfish nationalist considerations, or mere self-assurance.[27]

Such work was difficult to write and took time. The resistance to new ideas, at least in the Colonial Office, was to be broken down by means of it, but not at once. The colonial field was so wide that material for another book intruded, and publication was delayed. The first draft of *Africa Emergent* was finished at the end of 1934 and, as had been agreed, was handed over to the African Survey Committee as a brief for Lord Hailey. Macmillan was never given any credit for this. He never tried to protect his ideas, but was only too happy to see them spread. During the previous ten years he had stood alone in giving concentrated thought to colonial policy and to African development.

It was perhaps a pity that he did not give the book to Faber as it stood in 1934, for by the time it appeared in 1938 it had lost some of its pioneer status. Its contents had already had an impact in the quarters that mattered through Hailey and through numerous interviews with the Colonial Office, political leaders and colonial officials, not to mention the British press. However, it had its acclaim. Julius Lewin, a critical friend, thought it

... free from those occasional obscurities which made some of your earlier writing hard reading. You need have no anxiety about it, this book will be read and cherished by all who, in your noble phrase, 'see the vision of Africa free'.[28]

At a meeting in 1966 of the African Studies Association of the United Kingdom, soon after its inauguration, a speaker looking around a room full of eminent Africanists dared to suggest that there was not one of them who had not cut his or her teeth on *Africa Emergent*.

12

PROFESSOR MACMILLAN GOES ON SAFARI: THE BRITISH GOVERNMENT OBSERVER TEAM AND THE CRISIS OVER THE SERETSE KHAMA MARRIAGE, 1951

MICHAEL CROWDER

ON 9 July 1951 Professor W. M. Macmillan, Director of Colonial Studies at St Andrews University, received a telephone call from the Commonwealth Relations Office: the Secretary of State would like him to join a three-man team of Observers that the government was sending out to the Bechuanaland Protectorate to determine whether the Bangwato Tribe* would agree to the return from exile of Tshekedi Khama, their former regent. Tshekedi had been banished from entering the Bamangwato Reserve fifteen months beforehand. At the same time his nephew, Seretse, for whom he had acted as regent from 1925 to 1950, was exiled from the Protectorate and excluded for a period of five years from the office of Chief of the Bangwato as a result of his marriage to an Englishwoman, Ruth Williams.

Tshekedi had conducted such a successful campaign against what he considered the injustice of his own exile that by 26 June 1951 the Labour government, with a slender majority of six, faced possible defeat in the House of Commons on an opposition motion calling for the rescindment of his banishment. To assuage those of their

---

*The term 'tribe' was used during the colonial period and is still used today, without the pejorative connotations associated with it elsewhere in Africa, to denote the individual pre-colonial Tswana states or *merafe* incorporated into the Bechuanaland protectorate by the British. The form 'Bamangwato' was used by the British rather than the more correct Bangwato. I have only used the form Bamangwato in specifically colonial contexts. In all other cases I have used the suffixes currently in use today.

supporters who had been convinced that Tshekedi had suffered real injustice at the hands of their own administration, and because they were genuinely concerned that Tshekedi's return would lead to major disturbances in the Reserve, the Labour cabinet agreed to sponsor a *kgotla*, or assembly, of the Bangwato tribe, at which two or three MPs would be present, to ascertain whether the tribe would agree to Tshekedi's return as a private citizen. The Conservatives and Liberals turned down the invitation. On account of its slender majority, the Labour government could not afford to send one of its own MPs if no opposition MPs were going, so the Commonwealth Relations Office (CRO) and its Secretary of State, Patrick Gordon-Walker, devised an alternative strategy — that of sending three men of public standing whose findings would be reported to Parliament.

Professor Macmillan was not the first choice as the 'academic' member of the team. The initial approach had been made to Professor K. C. Wheare, and then, when he had turned the invitation down, Professor Margaret Read of the Institute of Education at the University of London was invited. But, like Wheare, she had prior commitments. In the Commonwealth Relations Office there had been some debate about Macmillan's suitability for the task. W. A. W. Clark, former Deputy High Commissioner in South Africa and now in charge of the High Commission territories desk at the CRO, lunched with him on 4 July at the time when the relative merits of Macmillan and Margaret Read were being considered. Clark reported that Macmillan considered that 'the recognition of Seretse would have provoked and would still provoke an explosion in South Africa with serious consequences for the inhabitants of the three High Commission Territories ... only the irresponsible or ignorant could fail to see this...'.[1] Clark concluded that Macmillan's approach was 'therefore reasonable. But I am afraid he would not be content merely to observe.... He would do a lot of talking with Bamangwato leaders and other chiefs....' Another Dominions Office official, G. H. Baxter, commented that since

... it is *observers* [of the tribe's reactions and desires] that are wanted, I do not think that Professor Macmillan should be asked. He might well produce, in his report, an excursus on the merits of the matter (including things already done or undone) and — he being the expert — might even get the other 'observers' to subscribe to it. This wd. be all the more embarrassing since he — or them — wd. have been selected by H.M.G.[2]

Nevertheless Clark pushed Macmillan's case, trying to persuade Miss Emery, Gordon-Walker's Principal Private Secretary, that while Professor Read might be the more amenable, 'Professor Macmillan would readily confine comment and suggestion to a separate confidential report to the Secretary of State'. Furthermore, his name would 'carry more weight with the general public and press'.[3] Miss Emery was, however, not convinced and minuted to the Secretary of State that 'of the two, Professor Read is least likely to return determined to produce an embarrassing report'.[4]

In the event, the debate about their relative merits was of no consequence and, in ignorance of these reservations about him, Macmillan accepted with alacrity the invitation both to become an observer and to write a report on the Bechuanaland Protectorate for the Secretary of State. In accepting this apparently thankless assignment, Macmillan was probably influenced by the fact that it was for a Labour government and that it was the first time that he had ever been asked to serve on any kind of official commission.[5] However, in joining the observer team, he unwittingly took on a task that was to involve him in ridicule in the press, an unseemly falling out between his two colleagues on the team, and, worst of all, serious doubts as to the value of the report he produced. Whatever aspersions may have been cast at the time, today, with the advantage of hindsight on an African colonial crisis that probably occupied more cabinet time than any other except the Mau Mau emergency in Kenya, we can see that it provides a remarkably perceptive, if brief, account of the very critical situation that had developed in Gammangwato and which was later to explode into riots costing the lives of three policemen and to provide the Press Secretary at the High Commission, Nicholas Monsarrat, with the material for his novel, *The Tribe that Lost its Head*.

Background to the Bamangwato crisis

As Colin Legum, who followed the observers' progress more assiduously than any other journalist, wrote:

The observers have been placed in an awkward position. Their present terms of reference preclude them handling questions arising from the demand — which is unanimous — for the return of Seretse.... Yet it is clearly very difficult to deal with the case of Tshekedi as an isolated event unless the whole matter of the Banishment and the Administration's policies are inquired into.[6]

The exile of Tshekedi followed inexorably from the day when he received an airmail letter from his nephew in London. In it was a sentence that was to precipitate eight years of turmoil in Gammangwato: 'I realise that this matter will not please you because the tribe will not like it as the person I am marrying is a white woman.'[7] Seretse's prognostication was initially correct. At a *kgotla* meeting held, in Seretse's presence, from 15–19 November 1948 in Serowe, the vast majority of the tribe agreed with Tshekedi's view that Ruth Williams could not be accepted as their future chief's wife. Only seven gave any indication that she would be acceptable.[8] Tshekedi was already aware that he must not seem to be using the crisis to advance his own position,[9] and was making it clear that, if Ruth Williams were accepted, rather than live under a white queen he would leave Gammangwato for the neighbouring Kweneng,[10] the senior Tswana *morafe* or state from which the Bangwato had broken off in the eighteenth century.

From the British view point, the position taken by Tshekedi and the decision of the Bangwato was a welcome one since it avoided the problem of recognizing a mixed marriage in a Protectorate that was not only a neighbour of South Africa but had its capital within its borders at Mafeking. Since the victory of the National Party in May 1948, the prospect of a mixed marriage of a major chief in a Protectorate which the Union still aimed to incorporate under the terms of the South African Act of 1909 was unacceptable. For the time being the British government did not have to confront this problem. Over the succeeding months, however, support for Seretse grew, partly because factions traditionally opposed to Tshekedi saw this as a useful stick to beat him with, but more profoundly because the suspicion grew that Tshekedi was indeed trying to exploit the marriage to exclude Seretse permanently from the chieftaincy and that, if he were successful in this, he, as next in line of succession, would become their *kgosi* (ruler). At a *kgotla* attended by some 4,000 Bangwato in June 1949 the tables were turned on Tshekedi who made the grave mistake of calling upon his principal supporters, mostly headmen, to stand before Vivien Ellenberger, representative of the Resident Commissioner. Some forty came forward, mostly headmen. The next day, Seretse in a skilful counter-manoeuvre asked all those who still opposed his marriage to stand before Ellenberger. Not more than forty did so. He then called on those who now accepted his wife to stand. The whole assembly was brought to its feet with a great cheer of 'Pula'.[11] In pique, Tshekedi announced that he would carry out his earlier threat and leave the reserve with his followers and offer his allegiance to the ruler of the Bakwena. He accordingly went into voluntary exile, eventually establishing a village in the Kweneng, just on the borders of Gammangwato, at Rametsana.

The British administration were now faced with the problem of recognition of Seretse as Chief. While the tribe had almost unanimously voted to accept him as their ruler, white wife and mixed-blood heirs notwithstanding, Seretse could not exercise his functions as Native Authority without British recognition. Although the local administration were largely in favour of recognition and delighted to be rid of the overbearing Tshekedi,[12] Sir Evelyn Baring, the British High Commissioner in South Africa who had overall responsibility for the Protectorate, began to have serious reservations. In the context of hostile reactions in the Southern Rhodesian Legislative Assembly and representations by the South African Prime Minister, Dr Malan, against recognition of Seretse, Baring wrote to Sir Percival Liesching at the Commonwealth Relations Office that refusal to recognize would:

... open us up to accusations of having surrendered to representations made by the Union Government and of having flouted the views of the tribe. On the other hand to recognise Seretse ... would lead to a head-on collision with the Union at the worst possible time.[13]

He went on to emphasize that recognition would assist the fight for transfer, boost the National Party vis-à-vis the United Party, strengthen Strydom's position within the National Party, and reinforce demands for a Republic outside the Commonwealth. This view was accepted by the cabinet,[14] advised by a Commonwealth Relations Minister who was 'perhaps the most right-wing member of the entire administration'.[15] Indeed, as Kenneth Morgan has pointed out, anxiety not to offend the South Africans had been a major factor governing the exclusion of Seretse by a cabinet[16] under which, between 1945 and 1951, 'cultural, educational and sporting links with the Union remained undisturbed, while the naval base at Simonstown was prized as a strategic asset. More ominously, South African uranium was vital for the British nuclear weapons programme.'[17]

As a means of delaying taking a decision on the matter the British administration agreed to hold a judicial enquiry — a device recommended by both Tshekedi and Baring — as to whether the June *kgotla* had been properly convened, assembled and conducted and as to 'whether Seretse Khama was a fit and proper person to discharge the functions of chief'. The enquiry found that the *kgotla* at which Seretse had been designated as Chief had indeed been properly convened and assembled and that its proceedings had been conducted in accordance with native custom; but that, 'having regard to the interests and well-being of the Tribe, Seretse was not a fit and proper person to discharge the functions of Chief'.[18] The reasons they gave for their conclusion had nothing to do with Seretse's character but all hinged on the political situation in Southern Africa at a time when his marriage to a white woman would be unacceptable not only to South Africa but also to Southern Rhodesia. Since the headquarters of the Protectorate government were at Mafeking in South Africa, where Seretse was a prohibited immigrant, it would make it impossible for him to fulfil his functions as Chief.[19]

The enquiry's assessment of the political situation 'seriously complicated' the handling of the problem since a Labour government could hardly admit publicly that the reasons for non-recognition of Seretse were entirely extraneous ones rooted in racial prejudice. It was therefore decided to withdraw all copies of the report from circulation and, as a first step, to try and persuade Seretse voluntarily to relinquish the chieftaincy[20] on the grounds that his assumption of it would give stimulus to 'the disruptive tendencies inherent in the Tribe'.[21] Seretse was accordingly invited to Britain for discussions and, at the cabinet meeting of 3 March 1950, it was agreed that, if Seretse did not give up the chieftaincy, a decision on recognition should be postponed for five years. Meanwhile neither Seretse nor Tshekedi should be allowed to return to the reserve[22] which would be placed under direct administration, with Keaboka, a Seretse supporter and fourth in line of succession, acting as go-between between the Bangwato and the District Commissioner who now had assumed all the functions, as well as the title, of Native Authority. Seretse refused to give up his claim and the White Paper, which the government issued on 22 March, implemented these decisions with the exception that while Tshekedi was only banned from entering the Bamangwato Reserve — where his presence, according to the High Commissioner, would be a danger to peace — Seretse was to be exiled from the Bechuanaland protectorate.[23] According to the Territories Department of the Commonwealth Relations Office itself, the White Paper was 'at pains to make out that the Government was not influenced by any representations from the Government of the Union of South Africa or Southern Rhodesia on the matter'.[24]

Tshekedi's campaign for the restitution of his rights

Tshekedi was extremely bitter about his own banishment order. He had, after all, taken exactly the same line as the government had done, at least publicly, for he was as yet unaware that the real reason for Seretse's exclusion from the chieftaincy was pressure from South Africa and fear of its reactions.[25] He felt that he had been unjustly treated since he had neither committed any crime nor offended against native law and custom. As to the notion that he might present a threat to peace, he said that this was based on false allegations that he was a rival claimant to the throne and that these had been spread by a faction in the extended royal family, which he referred to as the Sekgomas, and were the result of a longstanding dynastic feud. The Sekgomas had exploited the rift over the marriage between himself and Seretse to gain the power from which they had been excluded by his father, Khama the Great. The rumour that he was trying to exploit the crisis to take the *bogosi** from Seretse had been exacerbated by Ellenberger's statement at the June *kgotla* that the Bangwato were assembled to decide the right of succession to the chieftainship. Ellenberger had argued that he was in error when he was taken to task about this statement by another visiting chief and had instructed that it should not be recorded. Nevertheless, this had fuelled the flames of Sekgoma propaganda against Tshekedi. The attacks on him and his supporters had been deliberately provoked by the Sekgomas who only represented a small fraction of the Bangwato

---

bogosi = kingship

ruling class. He insisted that he had much wider support than the June *kgotla* suggested, especially among the allied tribes under Bangwato administration. Furthermore, the local British officials were hostile to him and had done nothing to attempt to reconcile the opposing factions. The District Commissioner, as Native Authority, had pre-arranged the statements hostile to the return of Tshekedi that were made by each of the speakers at the *kgotla* the Secretary of State attended in February 1951. In addition, he had never been permitted to confront his accusers. Finally, he emphasized that though the 'Government asserts that Tshekedi's presence in the Bamanwato [sic] country would cause disturbances, yet for four months in the past year Tshekedi, having had permission to visit his cattle posts, moved freely through the Territory, even in populated areas like Serowe'.[26]

Tshekedi arrived in London in early April 1951 to put these arguments to the Secretary of State, the politicians of all three parties,[27] and, with very considerable effect, the British press.[28] His stance seemed most reasonable: he had publicly and on several occasions renounced his rights to the chieftaincy as next in line of succession to Seretse; if he were allowed back in the Bamangwato Reserve he undertook not to interfere in politics and to avoid populated areas as far as possible. All he was asking was for a partial freedom to enter the reserve and look after his extensive herds of cattle. The CRO had, however, been convinced by the Bechuanaland Protectorate administration that the Bangwato feared Tshekedi and 'did not want him back in any capacity'.[29]

In prolonged discussions and bargaining with the Secretary of State, Tshekedi was unable to arrange a deal satisfactory to him and began to exasperate both the CRO and, moreover, the High Commission which up until then still perceived Tshekedi as a possible long-term solution to the problem of administering the Bangwato.[30] The details of the points over which the negotiations stalled need not concern us here:[31] what is important is that Tshekedi orchestrated so successful a campaign against the injustice of his banishment and the reasons given for its continuation among some Labour MPs that the government became fearful about the prospects of surviving the forthcoming debate on Tshekedi's continued exile in the House of Commons.[32] It was only the government's decision to sponsor a *kgotla* at which Tshekedi could put his case to the Bangwato in the presence of official observers that persuaded Labour

MPs who were planning to abstain or vote for the motion to support the government.[33]

Getting the government off the hook

Professor Macmillan and his two colleagues, H. L. Bullock, former President of the Trade Union Congress, and D. L. Lipson, one-time Independent MP for Cheltenham, arrived in the Bechuanaland Protectorate on 27 July in their capacity as 'observers'. Already the situation in the Bamangwato Reserve had deteriorated in such a way as to make the task of what eventually proved to be an ill-assorted team even more difficult than it had seemed at the time of its original suggestion. Although Baring had welcomed the idea of the joint *kgotla* of Seretse's and Tshekedi's supporters, he had warned that the observer team should be told that 'right up to the day there is a possibility that it will be a fiasco'.[34] While Tshekedi, too, welcomed the *kgotla* as an opportunity to put his own case before the tribe, his lawyers had raised awkward questions about its constitution and conduct.[35] In Serowe, the District Commissioner was unable to get the Bangwato leaders to agree to a *kgotla* with Tshekedi unless Seretse himself were present — a measure that Gordon-Walker was not prepared to countenance. Opponents of Tshekedi spread rumours that he was coming to the *kgotla* to claim the chieftaincy. The Bangwato leaders also argued that Tshekedi and his followers, having given their allegiance to the ruler of the Bakwena, had no business in their *kgotla*.[36]

The resentment against the Bo Rametsana — as Tshekedi's supporters were known — still living in Serowe, had flared up on 7 July into an attempt to round up a group of them and evict them from the reserve. Among them was Rasebolai Kgamane, Tshekedi's cousin and Seretse's uncle and third in succession to the throne. So tense was the situation in Serowe that, on 11 July, a contingent of police from Southern Rhodesia was called in to arrest those responsible for the attack on the Bo Rametsana.[37] Worse still, reports were coming in to the CRO that, if Tshekedi were to enter the reserve for the promised *kgotla*, attempts would be made on his life.[38] Then Seretse further complicated matters by offering to mediate as 'Chief of the Bamangwato': 'the overwhelming and devoted support of the tribe, enables me alone to solve the present issues without the use of force, and events will prove that I am right.'[39] His services were, of course, rejected. Meanwhile the South African government had again intimated that, if the British allowed Seretse to return, 'the consequences would be deplorable'. Dr Malan had made it privately known that he would have recourse to economic measures and that, if he 'put the screw on hard' to force transfer, he would have the whole of South Africa behind him.[40]

On arrival in Palapye, where they were accommodated in a railway coach, the observers were met by Baring, who made available to them much of the correspondence that had passed between him and the CRO, though with some of the more overt references to South African pressure omitted.[41] Meanwhile, Tshekedi had still not indicated when or if he would be returning for the *kgotla*. For a time, it seemed as though *Hamlet* might have to be played without the Prince.

The observers go on safari

By the time Tshekedi did eventually return to the Protectorate on 5 August, the observers had set off on safari, with the aim of sounding out opinion in the outlying districts. This course of action had been suggested by the Bangwato representatives, who, while they would not countenance Tshekedi's presence in the main *kgotla* at Serowe except under the presidency of Seretse, avowed they had no objection to the participation of his supporters in local *kgotlas*.[42] Professor Macmillan quickly chose the longest and most arduous of the itineraries offered to the three observers who were designated alphabetically: he was Observer B. His journey was to take him nearly 1,000 kilometres round the reserve to Gweta, Rakops and Sebina (Figure 1). As he told the correspondent of *The Scottish Daily Express*, 'I have not come all this way from Scotland just to sit around in a railway siding.'[43]

Even before Tshekedi's arrival it had become clear to the observers that the prospects of organizing a joint *kgotla* were remote. At the one *kgotla* all three observers attended in Mahalapye before they left on tour, five Bo Rametsama were driven away by the pro-Seretse participants and were apparently lucky not to have been physically molested owing to the presence of police.[44] All speakers at the *kgotla* made it clear they were opposed to Tshekedi's return.[45] At the

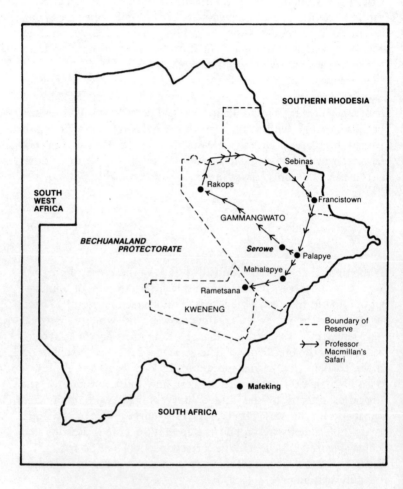

Figure 1   Macmillan's safari round the Bamangwato Reserve

meeting with the Bangwato leaders and the High Commissioner at Palapye on 29 July to discuss the organization of a joint *kgotla* Macmillan had already seen just how adamantly they were set against it.[46] But Lipson, 'who likes to walk alone', as Macmillan wrote to his wife,[47] nevertheless was sticking stubbornly to the idea of one *kgotla*, and 'might bring it off which would be an achievement'.[48]

On a safari that took him a week and on which it was reported by the British national press that he was lost, Macmillan only managed to attend one *kgotla* in Rakops on the very fringes of the Kalahari Desert. Here, apart from the headman, there were few Bangwato as such, the bulk of the population being made up of groups incorporated by them at time of the expansion of the Ngwato polity in the mid-nineteenth century. Even so every speaker at the *kgotla* made it clear that he was against the return of Tshekedi: the most any would concede was that, once Seretse had been allowed to take up the chieftaincy, Tshekedi could come back. Sumae of Rakops, a Mokgalagadi headman, summarized the general feeling: 'If a Regent has caused as much trouble as Tshekedi Khama has, he can say nothing. The Regent ate Seretse.... We don't want Tshekedi or his property....'[49] However, privately Macmillan had been told by a local trader and a veterinary inspector that the two sides were about equal 'but the speakers all spoke for Seretse (become a local hero in his absence) not one for Tshekedi — as no one dared against the prevailing local Headman'.[50] Cardross-Grant, the official who accompanied Macmillan, reported to the District Commissioner on the Rakops meeting:

Professor Macmillan's sympathies are with the under-dog largely because of the small number of Tshekedi's followers and because they appear to be fighting a losing battle, he would like to see Tshekedi and his band given every opportunity to fight back. He thinks many English men take up the same attitude, but at the same time his knowledge with the African people has enabled him to grasp quickly that there is a likelihood of disorders if Tshekedi is allowed to return. He believes that public opinion in the tribe is ruled by Keaboka and his senior advisers and that some of the speakers at Rakops conceal their true feeling out of fear of the majority. I do not think that he doubts that, as things are at present, the majority of the people are strongly against Tshekedi Khama's returning.[51]

In Sebinas, Macmillan informed Kalanga headmen that he thought it was 'high time that the Bamangwato stopped quarrelling about Tshekedi and Seretse and begin to take measures to improve their country',[52] a theme to which he returned in his private report to the Secretary of State.

Back in the railway coach at Palapye, Macmillan found not only that his colleagues were not on speaking terms but that the British press, in particular the *Observer* and its correspondent Colin Legum, had placed a question mark on the value of their mission. In a despatch from Palapye on 4 August, the day after Macmillan left for Rakops, Legum wrote that an unnamed but 'experienced local observer' had remarked somewhat wryly: "They'll hear what the people are told to tell them."' This remark was prompted by 'what is common knowledge here of a long campaign of intimidation, victimisation and calumny against Tshekedi and his supporters'.[53] Legum was himself not altogether an impartial 'observer', having arrived armed by Tshekedi with a series of introductions to friends[54] and, after Tshekedi's own return, acting as a go-between between Tshekedi and Lipson[55] who seemed to be the only observer sympathetic to Tshekedi's cause.

Legum was very much a campaigning journalist who, though he supported the return of Seretse for whom he recognized 'support is almost unanimous'[56] was primarily concerned, as was his editor, David Astor, in securing a fair deal for Tshekedi.[57] He was convinced, like Lipson, that the priority was to persuade the Bangwato that, if they agreed to Tshekedi coming back, it would be a first step towards the return of Seretse. Before Tshekedi's arrival in the Protectorate he consulted with Rasebolai and others among his supporters who did not have 'the political savvy of the "wonder boy"' and 'badly need guidance' and helped them work out their address to the observers.[58] He repeated Tshekedi's own arguments almost verbatim and, at one stage, even wrote to Tshekedi and asked him to let him have a story to keep his situation in the news.[59] He was distrusted by the administration, who referred to him as 'the abominable vegetable', and did much to raise doubts about the observers and consequently their reports.[60]

As it was, the observers themselves — or rather Lipson and Bullock — gave the press ample ammunition to do just that: their mutual antipathy had been manifest at the *kgotla* organized in Rametsana to listen to Tshekedi and his supporters. There Bullock had informed the assembly that Lipson 'told you he was an Independent Member of Parliament from Cheltenham but he did not say that the British people, in their wisdom, flung him out at the last election'[61] — at which, Tshekedi grinned hugely.[62] At this meeting, which was rightly criticized by the press as being the only one at which Tshekedi and his supporters were able to give the three observers their views, no one said anything new except that Tshekedi now seemed prepared to accept Ruth Williams as 'Queen'. The stumbling block was, however, the children of the marriage and their succession rights.[63]

It was at Palapye two days later that Bullock and Lipson could no longer contain their differences. The local headman, Nwako Kediretse, refused to allow five Bo Rametsana to remain at the *kgotla* called for the observers. Lipson told him: 'I refuse as a matter of principle to agree to their being driven away.' Macmillan tried to intervene by telling Lipson that 'The Headmen will bust up the meeting if you insist on the Tshekedists staying'. With foresight Lipson retorted: 'He can break up the meeting if he likes. People in England will blame us if we allow the Tshekedists to be driven away.' At this point Bullock and Macmillan overruled Lipson and agreed that the five Bo Rametsana should be seen in the afternoon. Bullock did not even bother to attend while Macmillan only stayed a few minutes because of another engagement at Serowe. Lipson had the last word saying: 'I am satisfied Tshekedi has not had a square deal. His followers are being intimidated.'[64]

This unseemly quarrel, carried on in public, gave journalists a field day and ensured that little credence would be given in the press to the report submitted by the observers especially as, despite valiant efforts, they were quite unable to organize the joint *kgotla* which the Secretary of State had promised parliament.[65] As it was, only once had an observer — in this instance Lipson — managed to hold a joint *kgotla*, at Sefhare where some Bo Rametsana were able to speak, although this did not alter the outcome of the meeting where the vast majority were either against the return of Tshekedi altogether or would only accept it if Seretse too returned as chief.[66] The final *kgotla* at Serowe was as predictable as the one at Rametsana had been,[67] and was distinguished only by a separate meeting in the afternoon with a thousand or so women who were, if anything, more vehemently opposed to Tshekedi's return than their menfolk.[68]

The British press may have tried to paint a picture of the observers as the Marx Brothers on safari, but the Bangwato made a shrewder assessment of them. As K. T. Motsete, a highly educated opponent of Tshekedi, wrote to Marjorie Nicholson, the Secretary of the Fabian Colonial Bureau:

... we soon discovered that the 3 observers are different. Mr Lipson impressed us as being too dictatorial, rather too pro-Tshekedi, so much so that he was soon nicknamed 'Rametsana' = Tshekedi's adherent. Mr Bullock has earned for himself memories of love and respect. He was typical English with a fine Christian spirit. And he won the confidence of the Kgotla to such an extent that although most of my people were sullen and determined throughout the meeting he made the [sic] smile and laugh.... This is the type of Englishman you should send to Africa or to any of the coloured races; a true Briton! enthusing his audience with the true British spirit of fairplay and kindness and justice. We call him here 'the Peacemaker'. The Professor is the only one who has left us without some characteristic sobriquet, for his speeches were erudite, and knowing the African from his stay in Johannesburg he knew better than the other two how to address us without treading on any corns.[69]

Producing the report

Even though it had proved impossible to arrange a joint *kgotla* the CRO was anxious that the observers should at least produce a joint report.[70] But in view of the antipathy between Bullock and Lipson, and Macmillan's own view that Lipson was 'intolerable',[71] it was unlikely that this would be forthcoming. Indeed, Macmillan avoided the other two observers and was dismayed when Turnbull, the acting High Commissioner, told him that, in view of the strained relations between Bullock and Lipson, the success of the joint mission would now depend on his efforts to influence the latter.[72] The concerned officials just had to hope that whatever the observers wrote separately or jointly would confirm their conviction that Tshekedi's return to the reserve would bring trouble and would be deeply resented by the Bangwato. They made a start by getting Macmillan and Bullock to agree to collaborate on a report for which Turnbull produced a first draft. This draft was welcomed by Macmillan who promised to put something along its lines to Lipson while all three were in Swaziland discussing Tshekedi's case with Sobhuza, the Paramount Chief of Swaziland.[73] However, Turnbull was horrified when Macmillan subsequently produced two documents for incorporation into the draft. One from Bullock was 'unexceptionable'; the other from Macmillan included 'damaging qualifications without apparently appreciating how they might be

used'. 'He was tired', Turnbull wrote, 'and I think confused. ...' While
Macmillan was convinced that the Bangwato did not want Tshekedi
back in any guise he did believe that:

(1) the active supporters of Tshekedi include a high proportion of the ablest
and administratively most experienced members of the Bamangwato people,
and we feel strongly that there should be no question of yielding to the
factious spirit which threatens the impoverishment of the tribe by
demanding their expulsion or even their permanent exclusion from the
Bamangwato Reserve.

(2) it ... almost must be that the opposition to Tshekedi's return is ... being
stirred up by men afraid of losing the sweets of the offices in which they
have superseded various of Tshekedi's followers.

(3) we sympathise with Tshekedi's contention that the Bamangwato
country needs to import settlers rather than expel anyone and we express
the hope that the tribe may speedily come to this way of thinking.

Turnbull was nevertheless confident that he would be able to
persuade Macmillan to amend or delete these statements.[74]
Not only were the administration anxious to get a joint report
from the observers, they were concerned to have it published as soon
as possible, since speculation about its contents was adding to tension
in the reserve.[75] Tshekedi, who was convinced that it would be
hostile to him, threw a spanner in the works by getting his friend,
Chief Bathoen of the Bangwaketse, to call a meeting of chiefs and
other notables in Mafeking which passed resolutions deeply critical
of the Bechuanaland Protectorate administration and called for the
return of both Seretse and Tshekedi to the reserve, declaring that
'The traditional faith of the Bechuanas in the British Government in
respect of human rights has received a tremendous shock'.[76]
The deliberations of the meeting, of which the local
administration was itself ignorant, were given major coverage by
Legum in the *Observer* on 2 September, who informed readers that
the three observers' visit created the impression that Tshekedi was
most unpopular. 'This is far from the truth. Nothing more clearly
shows the high esteem in which Tshekedi is held than widespread
support for his case among Africans throughout the Protectorates
and farther afield in Central and Southern Africa.'[77] The CRO were
taken aback by the article and G. H. Baxter dismissed it as 'a
thoroughly dishonest as well as mischievous piece of journalism'.[78]

But Legum's report was confirmed as substantially accurate both by Reuter's and the local administration which set about bringing the chiefs to heel — with some success.[79] But the damage had been done. Further doubt had been cast on the observers' integrity. The rumours to the effect that the British government was planning to partition the northern and southern Protectorate between South Africa and the proposed Central African Federation — which the administration believed to have been floated by Tshekedi — gave rise to further suspicions as to the intentions of a British government which, in this case, was innocent.[80]

As it was, the long delay in publishing the reports resulted neither from obstructionist tactics by Tshekedi nor divisions among the observers, but from British domestic considerations. Macmillan and Bullock submitted their joint report[81] in good time for it to be published as soon as Gordon-Walker returned from his tour of Central Africa — as did Lipson with his shorter report.[82] Although both reports basically supported the government's contention that Tshekedi's return would be unacceptable to the Bangwato and would possibly provoke disorders, the Labour cabinet felt it best not to publish them during the run-up to the general election, as they did not wish to trammel their election campaign with further criticism for continuing to exclude Tshekedi from the reserve.[83] The local administration, which had earlier been assured that the report would not be delayed by electoral considerations,[84] still had to assuage local Bangwato opinion which was becoming concerned at the delay in publication and the possibility of the return of a Conservative government committed to Tshekedi,[85] who had done nothing to increase his popularity by applying to the High Court for an order restricting Keaboka from acting in opposition to his interests and from exercising any of the powers of the tribal administration.[86]

In the cabinet, when the observers' reports were discussed in detail, it was emphasized by the Secretary of State that 'it would be difficult for us to sustain the case for keeping out Seretse if we let Tshekedi back, unless we were prepared to confess that we were yielding to fear of South African reactions'.[87] These he detailed as a possible refusal to cooperate in defence, an economic blockade on the High Commission Territories and the grave risk of their loss. So it was decided that, after the election had been won, the government would reaffirm its policy to exclude both for a period of not less than five years.

In the event, the Labour Party lost the election and Winston Churchill, anxious to get the Bangwato problem off his hands, instructed his newly appointed Commonwealth Relations Secretary to settle it once and for all.[88] The Conservatives were just as aware of the political implications of offending South Africa: Smuts had spelt them out to Churchill quite clearly when he was in opposition.[89] Knowing that they could not be charged by the Labour opposition with acceding to South African pressure for fear that its own devious dealings in this respect might be revealed, they decided to exclude Seretse from the chieftaincy on a permanent basis. To rid themselves of the very powerful protest in press and Parliament that he had marshalled against their predecessors, they decided to let Tshekedi return to the reserve as a private citizen. But this was to be on a timetable to be set by the local administration and on the strict understanding that he would not take any part in the tribe's political life.[90] Tshekedi accepted these conditions and his return was not marked by the violence feared by the local administration. But the Conservative government had not in fact disposed of the Tshekedi problem for, over the next four years, he continued to campaign for the restoration of his political rights.

The Bullock–Macmillan report in retrospect

Critics of the Bullock–Macmillan report have dismissed it as of little value since Tshekedi was eventually able to return to the reserve and live there without further violence to his person or property.[91] Nevertheless, the burden of the report on the attitude of the mass of the Bangwato to Tshekedi and the reasons for them, albeit based on a first draft supplied by the administration, were surprisingly accurate given the short time that they were there and the difficulties they encountered in obtaining evidence. And we must remember that they were asked to answer a single question about 'the attitude of the tribe to Tshekedi Khama's return to the Reserve as a private individual'.

The principal conclusion of the observers was that the Bangwato feared that, if Tshekedi returned and were allowed to attend a *kgotla* without Seretse as president, he would automatically take precedence by virtue of his seniority and that they would once more be saddled with him as ruler. There is no doubt that Macmillan and Bullock correctly assessed the importance that the Bangwato, and indeed

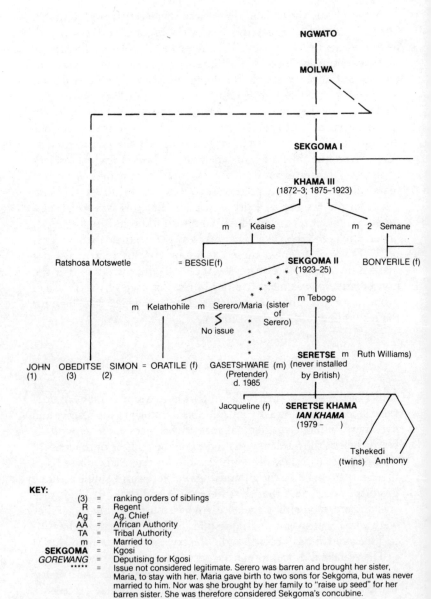

KEY:

(3)	=	ranking orders of siblings
R	=	Regent
Ag	=	Ag. Chief
AA	=	African Authority
TA	=	Tribal Authority
m	=	Married to
SEKGOMA	=	Kgosi
GOREWANG	=	Deputising for Kgosi
*****	=	Issue not considered legitimate. Serero was barren and brought her sister, Maria, to stay with her. Maria gave birth to two sons for Sekgoma, but was never married to him. Nor was she brought by her family to "raise up seed" for her barren sister. She was therefore considered Sekgoma's concubine.

Figure 2 Rulers of the Bangwato tribe, 1875 to date

272

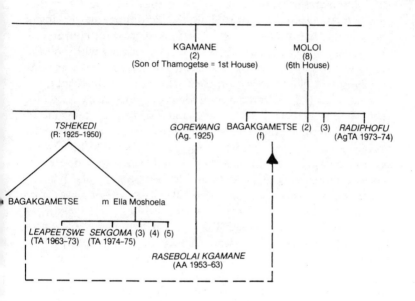

NOTES:
1949–1953   The District Commissioner, Serowe, was designated Native Authority.

1975–to date   *Mokgacha Mokgadi* served as Tribal Authority, deputising for Kgosi SERETSE
KHAMA IAN KHAMA, who has a full-time career in the BDF.

other Tswana groups, attach to genealogical precedence in determining the right to office. Keaboka himself had complained that his authority was undermined by the presence of Rasebolai who was his immediate genealogical senior[92] (Figure 2). Similarly, when Rasebolai took over as African Authority heading the Bamangwato tribal administration, he consulted and deferred to Tshekedi who thus, as a private citizen excluded from politics, had considerable indirect influence on the course of Bangwato affairs.[93] Later, when the administration wanted to persuade the Bangwato to permit mining in their reserve, it proved impossible without the blessing of the 'sons of Khama', and one of the reasons for allowing both Seretse and Tshekedi to return in 1956 as private citizens with political rights was to ensure the tribe's support for mining.[94] Furthermore, the Bangwato did not allow, in their own view of chieftaincy, the concept of a royal becoming a commoner or a 'private citizen':[95] for them Seretse remained their *kgosi* and Tshekedi next in line of succession until the birth of Seretse's son. The British were quite unable to persuade the Bangwato to accept Rasebolai as Chief, which became their plan after their disillusionment with Tshekedi. He was merely accepted as head of the tribal administration.

The overall conclusion of Macmillan and Bullock was that Tshekedi's return would be contrary to the wishes of the majority of the tribe and bitterly resented. The fact that a number would accept him back, provided Seretse were allowed to return as Chief, was noted by them in many speeches made in the *kgotlas* they attended, but was outside the terms of reference for their report. They accurately diagnosed the reasons for the bitter resentment of Tshekedi. The first was the series of personal grievances and grudges which 'after 26* years of personal rule' were perhaps to be expected. These were not spelt out in the report but allusion was made to the fact that Tshekedi's 'personal exercise of power paid little regard to the individual or his rights'.[96]

In the course of his long regency Tshekedi had exiled many royal relatives who opposed him, used regimental labour freely for public projects which he considered to be in the tribal interest and made it clear that he would brook no opposition, whencever it came. He had a reputation as a man 'who never forgets or forgives'. And it is

*Actually 24 years

significant that the crisis over Seretse's marriage came at a time when Tshekedi was engaged in his greatest enterprise yet — the building of Bamangwato National College at Moeng, for which a levy of one oxen per every two hut taxpayers was imposed, and for which regimental labour was used on a monumental scale.[97] This caused considerable resentment throughout Gammangwato and in particular, as the observers noted, among so-called 'allied tribes' who, Tshekedi in fact contended, supported him.[98] Indeed, one of these groups — the Mswaswis, who had had earlier confrontations with Tshekedi — refused to pay the levy and consequently had their property seized by Tshekedi's regiments and were forced into exile in Southern Rhodesia whose officials, although not noted for the benign nature of their native policy, were shocked that, in a British territory, a chief could behave as he had done.[99] Macmillan himself at Rakops was satisfied that opposition to Tshekedi was not just confined to a faction among Bangwato proper but was deep-rooted in the 'allied tribes in the "back blocks"'.[100] Perhaps more surprising was their encounter with more than 1,000 women 'a succession of whom passionately and even threateningly elaborated the theme "we do not want Tshekedi back"'.[101] The reason for this opposition has yet to be successfully explained, but it marked a turning-point in Bangwato politics with women, for the first time, actively participating in them.[102]

Neil Parsons has recently made a searching analysis of the reasons for the dramatic change in the attitude of the Bangwato to Seretse's marriage.[103] With the advantage of hindsight and access to the administrative records, he makes an understandably more elaborate analysis than did the observers laying emphasis on the Bangwato's belief that Tshekedi's real aim was to seize the *bogosi* from Seretse, resentment at the removal by Tshekedi and his followers of so much wealth from the reserve — some of which they considered was really Seretse's by virtue of his position as their chief — and bitterness, almost certainly misdirected, against Tshekedi over delays in the payment of war benefits to veterans. But, in essence, his conclusions are identical to those of Macmillan and Bullock: that the vast majority of the Bangwato did not, at that time, want the return of Tshekedi in any capacity.

Even so, given that the Macmillan–Bullock report was basically the one that was wanted by the administration, which had anyway had a hand in its drafting, it might still be easy to dismiss it as one that emanated from men who had already made up their minds and were basically prejudiced against Tshekedi. In fact, this was far from the case. Bullock, in a private note to Gordon-Walker, wrote of Tshekedi as a 'great man' and argued that the tribe needed a strong man. 'We should not be averse to seeing Tshekedi back with a regiment to ensure the peace for a short time ... if only the Government would ease up on his despotic ruling.' Nevertheless he informed Gordon-Walker in a later note: 'I would say that the opinion against Tshekedi is more than 90% of the tribe.'[104]

Macmillan likewise thought highly of Tshekedi after meeting him at Rametsana — 'very remarkable indeed'. But he was perhaps more shrewd in his judgement that his 'troubles have come from his brain and his ideas being so much his own that he never either devolves or takes professional advice and gets the work bungled. His (uncontrolled) NA got too ambitious for its poor staff. ...'[105] In the final version of the joint report with Bullock he insisted on the retention of his statement about Tshekedi's active supporters including 'a high proportion of the ablest and administratively most experienced members of the Bamangwato and that their permanent exclusion from the Reserve would represent an impoverishment of the tribe'.[106]

The Bamangwato 'were pleased with your report and cheered up a bit when they got it on 6 Dec.', Cardross-Grant, who had accompanied Macmillan on his safari, wrote to Macmillan. 'But their hopes were dashed down again a fortnight later when the HC said TK would be allowed in for a trial period.'[107] Although the Conservative government had chosen to act against the advice of the Bullock–Macmillan report and although the violence predicted by the administration on Tshekedi's return never materialized, the Bangwato crisis was not resolved. Hamlet was allowed to return, but the King was not. And the reserve remained in an agitated state, culminating in the Serowe *kgotla* riot of Sunday 1 June 1952. Neil Parsons has suggested that this riot was the result of the Bangwato being 'baited by continuous British breaches of faith to beyond breaking point'.[108] From their point of view, one example of this was the observers' report. They had been told that the observers had been sent out to ascertain whether the Bangwato would accept Tshekedi's return, and they believed that they had convinced them — as indeed they had — of their bitter resentment of his re-entry in any capacity into the reserve, which after all he had voluntarily left. Yet here he was permitted by the government to return.

For Macmillan, the report he wrote with Bullock was wasted effort since its burden was effectively ignored. But his trip was not, neither from his point of view nor that of the peoples of the Bechuanaland Protectorate. He did produce the frank and perceptive critique of British administration of the Protectorate that he had promised the Secretary of State. Entitled 'Notes on the Bechuanaland Protectorate suggested by Tour in July–August 1951', it made four major recommendations. The first was that the European staff of the Protectorate should be strengthened, if only temporarily, to meet the present situation. The second was that the Bechuanaland Protectorate should be taught to think and act as a unit and this suggested, 'following the current fashion to the extent of associating the Administration with some form of representative Council', a measure Tshekedi himself was advocating. Third, relations with the Union of South Africa had to be better defined sooner or later. However, the Union had to understand that the Territories were not 'ours' to dispose of. Finally, as a footnote by a man who had already been involved in advice on the democratization of indirect rule elsewhere, 'the British public must be taught why the straight return of any of the possible chiefs is impossible except on terms implying a much tighter control than of old'.[109] He concluded:

The Bamangwato troubles are ultimately due to a weak and distant Central administration having so long followed the line of least resistance and left the Chiefs to run the country, or as the Union critics inconveniently allege, *not* run it.

Here, he echoed his criticisms of twenty years earlier, when he first visited the Bechuanaland Protectorate. After meeting Tshekedi — whom he found 'rather royal and suspicious' — and other chiefs he had concluded: 'There is no doubt about the mischief of these autocratic chiefs — they have done as they pleased, progressed or not, chiefly not....'[110]

It is difficult to judge how far policy was influenced directly or indirectly by Macmillan's private report. A minute on the report passed to Mr Baxter agreed with Macmillan's comments on the weakness of the administration and recommended the appointment of two senior District Commissioners, one at Francistown for the north and one at Gaberones or Lobatsi for the south.[111] This measure was in fact implemented, and policy in the Protectorate developed over the next decade much as Macmillan had envisaged.

W. M. MACMILLAN

Conclusion

In the last analysis, Macmillan and his fellow observers had been set an impossible task, for the real issue at stake was not, as Macmillan himself observed, Tshekedi's return but the reinstatement of Seretse. The observers were much criticized by press, parliament and the small public interested in colonial affairs for apparently lending support to the restriction of the rights and liberties of a man who himself had been none too careful in this respect with those of his own subjects. What still continues to surprise is that so many of those 'liberals' did not devote equal energy to righting the real injustice. And that was the exile of a young chief — so groomed by his devoted uncle that no other chief in British Africa was better prepared for his task — because he married the woman he loved, who also happened to be white.

NOTES

INTRODUCTION

1 W. M. Macmillan to J. X. Merriman, 20 May 1920, Merriman papers, Cape Town; W. M. Macmillan, *The Cape Colour Question* (London, 1927), pp. 10, 171. W. M. Macmillan, *Bantu, Boer, and Briton* (London, 1929), p. 140.
2 Macmillan, *Bantu, Boer, and Briton*, p. 58.
3 Ibid., p. 318.
4 For Macmillan's earlier views on 'parallel institutions', the industrial colour bar etc., see 'Draft Memorandum on South African Affairs' prepared for British Labour Party, Advisory Committee on International Questions, and MS lecture on South Africa probably given to the Fabian Society, both December 1920, in Macmillan papers, Long Wittenham, Oxford, England. For the views of early radical socialists such as Sidney Bunting and W. H. Andrews, see H. J. and R. E. Simons, *Class and Colour in South Africa* (Harmondsworth, 1969).
5 N. Majeke (D. Taylor), *The Role of the Missionaries in Conquest* (Cape Town, 1952), pp. 44, 120.
6 Ibid., p. 139.
7 Macmillan, *Bantu, Boer, and Briton*, p. 289.
8 Majeke, op. cit., p. 120.
9 J. S. Galbraith, *Reluctant Empire* (Berkeley, 1963), pp. 1, 81.
10 The omission of any reference to the death of Hintŝa in the *Oxford History* was a reflection of its late liberal emphasis on cooperation rather than conflict. See below.
11 J. B. Peires, *The House of Phalo* (Johannesburg, 1981), pp. 180, 289.
12 Cf. for example, 'Ideological confusion went hand in hand with economic erosion and political disruption. Secure in the wisdom of his diviners and the mastery of his destiny, the Xhosa had looked forward to the future with confidence. Traditional usages were tested and established, some were quietly added and others were quietly dropped, and there was every reason to expect that what had worked in the past would work in the future. Good management would lead to good fortune and if all dangers could not be warded off they could at least be explained. But the pale animals from across the sea disordered a universe in which they had no place and the Xhosa had to think again.' Ibid., p. 164.
13 Ibid., p. 66.
14 Ibid., pp. 68, 95-7.
15 Cf. for example 'For the Xhosa British Kaffraria was a monster which swallowed them up, tore them from their children, and squeezed them off

279

their land on to the labour market. Weary and despondent they prepared to make a final stand.' Ibid., p. 169.

16 Ibid., pp. 119, 238–9.

17 M. Legassick, 'The frontier tradition in South African historiography' in S. Marks and A. Atmore *Economy and Society in Pre-industrial South Africa* (London, 1980), p. 51.

18 M. Legassick, 'The northern frontier to 1820: the emergence of the Griqua people' in R. Elphick and H. Giliomee, *The Shaping of South African Society, 1652–1820* (Cape Town, 1979), p. 244.

19 Macmillan's contribution to the formulation of this aspect of the frontier tradition is noticed in William Beinart's essay in this collection. See below. Beinart notices Macmillan's earlier readiness to deal in cultural explanations.

20 Legassick, 'The frontier tradition', p. 65.

21 Macmillan, *Bantu, Boer, and Briton*, p. 168; see also Legassick, 'The frontier tradition', pp. 66–7.

22 Macmillan, *The Cape Colour Question*, pp. 23–4, 174, 240, 266.

23 This point is made in the first paragraph of H. M. Robertson, '150 years of contact between black and white', *The South African Journal of Economics*, ii, 4 (1934), p. 402, but the emphasis of the article is almost entirely on trade and cooperation.

24 For example, Macmillan, *Bantu, Boer, and Briton*, p. 31: 'There was very little difference between peace and war in those parts.'

25 Macmillan, *My South African Years* (Cape Town, 1975), p. 24. But see also Macmillan, *The South African Agrarian Problem and its Historical Development* (Johannesburg, 1919), p. 87, where he quotes Hegel. 'Theoretical work brings more to pass in this world than practical; reality can make no stand against a revolution in the world of ideas.'

26 P. Honigsheim, 'The sociological doctrines of Oppenheimer', in H. E. Barnes (ed.) *An Introduction to the History of Society* (Chicago, 1948), pp. 332–52.

27 Macmillan, *My South African Years*, pp. 100–4; C. E. Schorske, *German Social Democracy, 1905–17: the development of the great schism* (New York, 1965, 1st edn., 1955); J. P. Nettl, *Rosa Luxemburg*, i (London, 1966), pp. 414–50.

28 R. Luxemburg, *The Accumulation of Capital* (London, 1951), pp. 295–6. Luxemburg's main quarrel with Schmoller and the other 'socialists of the chair', Wagner and Schaeffle, was on the question of autarky and the possibility of capitalist development in isolation from the world market. On Macmillan's attitude to the war see *My South African Years*, pp. 126–7. On the 1922 Strike see article by 'Z' (Macmillan), 'War on the Witwatersrand' in *The South African Quarterly* (March 1922), and Krikler, below.

29 Legassick, *The Frontier Tradition*, pp. 51–2.

30 Macmillan, *Bantu, Boer, and Briton*, pp. 313–14.

31 Ibid., p. 312; Macmillan, *Complex South Africa* (London, 1930), p. 258.

32 Ibid., p. 274.

33 The assistance of C.F. Andrews was acknowledged in the preface to *The Cape Colour Question*. There are references to Tagore in the card index

notes for *Africa Emergent*, Macmillan papers.

34 Macmillan, *Bantu, Boer, and Briton*, viii, p. 314; *Complex South Africa*, p. 265.
35 The view of Boas and the history of the concept of culture given here is largely derived from G. Stocking, *Race Culture and Evolution* (Chicago, 1982, 1st ed., 1968).
36 Macmillan, *Complex South Africa*, p. 279. The phrase 'on the upgrade' appears first in Macmillan, *Economic Conditions in a Non-industrial South African Town* (Grahamstown, 1915), p. 6.
37 Macmillan, *Complex South Africa*, p. 254.
38 Macmillan papers, notes for 'Whence and Whither in Africa', nd, 1931.
39 Macmillan to S. H. Frankel, 16 January 1934, letter in the possession of Professor S. H. Frankel, Oxford.
40 Chapters III, IV, and V, pp. 41–115, in C. K. Meek, W. M. Macmillan, and E. R. J. Hussey, *Europe and West Africa, some Problems and Adjustments* (London, 1940); W. M. Macmillan, 'Freedom for Colonial Peoples' in Fabian Society, *Programme for Victory* (London, 1941); W. M. Macmillan, *Democratise the Empire* (London, 1941).
41 Macmillan, 'Freedom for colonial peoples', p. 91.
42 Macmillan, *Europe and West Africa*, p. 94; Polly Hill, *The Migrant Cocoa-farmers of Southern Ghana: a study of rural capitalism* (Cambridge, 1963), p. 23. The same point on Macmillan's recognition of African initiative is made in Cyril Ehrlich, 'Building and caretaking: economic policy in British tropical Africa, 1890–1960', *Economic History Review*, 2nd series, xxvi, 4 (1973), p. 648–67.
43 Macmillan, *Africa Emergent*, (London, 1938), pp. 23–6; 'Freedom for colonial peoples', pp. 95–6.
44 Macmillan *My South African Years* (Cape Town, 1975), p. 195.
45 R. Hinden, *Empire and After, a study of British imperial attitudes* (London, 1949), pp. 122–3.
46 A. Creech Jones in introduction to R. Hinden (ed.), *Fabian Colonial Essays* (London, 1945), p. 14.
47 Macmillan, 'Freedom for colonial peoples', pp. 91, 114–15.
48 Macmillan, *Africa Emergent* (1938), pp. 222–40, 385.
49 Ibid., p. 385.
50 Mona Macmillan, *Champion of Africa. W. M. Macmillan, the second phase* (Long Wittenham, 1985), pp. 128–87.
51 Macmillan, *Europe and West Africa*, pp. 108–12; 'Freedom for colonial peoples', pp. 95–6.
52 Macmillan, *Africa Emergent* (Revised Penguin edn., Harmondsworth, 1949), pp. 284, 290.
53 L. Barnes, *Empire or Democracy?* (London, 1939), pp. 276–7, quoted in R. Hinden, *Empire and After*, p. 111.
54 Macmillan, *Africa Emergent* (1949), pp. 283–4.
55 Ibid., pp. 288, 290.
56 Macmillan, 'Freedom for colonial peoples', p. 91.
57 Macmillan, *Europe and West Africa*, p. 111.

58 Macmillan, *The Road to Self-rule: a study in colonial evolution* (London, 1959), p. 275.
59 Personal information; Mona Macmillan, *op. cit.,* p. 45.
60 Lord Olivier, *International Review of Mission,* xxviii (1939), p. 109; Norman Leys, *Time and Tide,* 30 July 1939. Leys commented: 'Alas that the Colonial Office prefers to have its recruits fed upon the barren fantasies of the "functional anthropologists" herein so devastatingly refuted.'
61 J. Iliffe, *The Emergence of African Capitalism* (London, 1983), p. 24. Iliffe notes that the study of African rural capitalism begins with the publication of Polly Hill's first book in 1956.
62 Dame Lucy Sutherland, 'Address delivered … at the funeral of W. M. Macmillan, 28 October 1974'; Macmillan, *My South African Years,* viii.

1. WILLIAM MACMILLAN AND THE WORKING CLASS

*I am grateful to Colin Bundy for his criticisms of an earlier draft of this article. Mona Macmillan provided important biographical data — not available in written sources of any kind — in stimulating discussions held while I was working on the Macmillan Papers which are held in her house in Oxfordshire: her kindness and hospitality will not be forgotten. The editors of this volume also provided helpful criticisms and information.

1 The backwardness and manifold prejudices of 'pre-Macmillanite' historical studies in South Africa has recently been explored by Jayaraman Naidoo in 'W. M. Macmillan: South African historian' (unpublished MA thesis, University of South Africa, 1983), pp. 1–31.
2 See Bruce Murray, *WITS, The Early Years: A History of the University of the Witwatersrand Johannesburg and its Precursors 1896–1939* (Johannesburg, 1982), p. 129.
3 W. M. Macmillan *The South African Agrarian Problem and its Historical Development* (Johannesburg, 1919), p. 23.
4 See, for example, Saul Dubow, *Land, Labour and Merchant Capital in the Pre-Industrial Rural Economy of the Cape: The Experience of the Graaf-Reinet District, 1852–72* (Cape Town, 1982), p. i. Perhaps the most well known use of Macmillan's insight and data in a recent study is Colin Bundy's in his chapter on the peasants of Herschel in his *The Rise and Fall of the South African Peasantry* (London, 1979).
5 See the first four chapters of Macmillan's autobiography *My South African Years* (Cape Town, 1975); quotations from pp. 7, 57, 58 and 64.
6 See ibid., pp. 48–9. On these pages of his autobiography, Macmillan details 'the favourite national stories' at which he 'chafed' whilst at school. Two of these — 'the tale of the Black Circuit' and 'the sorrowful tale of Slagter's Nek' — he was to 'demythologize' in his first major historical work: see *The Cape Colour Question: a historical survey* (Cape Town, 1968 edn.), pp. 88–91.
7 Macmillan, *My South African Years,* p. 52.
8 For the information on which this paragraph is based, see ibid. Chapters

1–4; quotations from p. 24.

9 Ibid., pp. 21–2, 52 and 60.

10 For the information on which this paragraph is based, see ibid., pp. 66–8 and 79; quotations from pp. 66 and 67 (my brackets).

11 Ibid., pp. 62, 68, 74–6.

12 Perry Anderson, *Arguments Within English Marxism* (London, 1980), pp. 45.

13 The distinction is, of course, Marx's. Its explicit formulation is to be found in 'Results of the immediate process of production', an appendix to the Pelican edition of *Capital*, Vol. 1. Formal subsumption refers to the mere subordination of an existing (let us say, artisanal) labour process to capital; the real subsumption of labour under capital takes place when a labour process, subordinated to capital, is transformed by it as well. The displacement of manu- by machinofacture is an example of the latter; historically this was associated with the destruction of artisanal forms of production and their replacement by the capitalist mode proper. See K. Marx, *Capital*, i (Harmondsworth, 1982), pp. 1019–38.

14 For these statistics, see Eric Hobsbawm, *Industry and Empire* (Harmondsworth, 1972), p. 165 and David Thomson, *England in the Nineteenth Century* (Harmondsworth, 1973), p. 187.

15 Hobsbawm, *op. cit.*, pp. 125–6.

16 See, for example, the comments of the conservative Lewis Namier in *The Revolution of the Intellectuals* (Oxford, 1971), p. 3; the argument on p. 375 of that classic radical work, *The Common People 1746–1938* (London, 1938) by G. D. H. Cole and Raymond Postgate; and, finally, from the Marxist tradition, see the quotations from Perry Anderson, 'Origins of the present crisis', *New Left Review*, 23, cited by E. P. Thompson in 'The peculiarities of the English' in *The Poverty of Theory and Other Essays* (London, 1980), p. 70. On pp. 70–1, Thompson also supports the contention that the working class's passage to reformism followed the defeat of Chartism. (I have had to cite a secondary source for Anderson's views because *NLR* 23 appears not to be available in South Africa, where this article was written.) We should also note that the decline of a revolutionary class-consciousness amongst English working people that followed the defeat of Chartism is *implicitly* argued by Namier and Cole and Postgate.

17 Quotations from (respectively) Hobsbawm, *op. cit.*, p. 126 and Leon Trotsky (quoting Lenin) in *The Revolution Betrayed: What is the Soviet Union and Where is it Going?* (New York, 1980), p. 303.

18 The classic study of this process is John Foster's *Class Struggle and Industrial Revolution: early industrial capitalism in three English towns* (London, 1974).

19 See Eric Hobsbawm, *Labouring Men* (London, 1964), p. 260. Hobsbawm, however, does not mention the trade unions in this connection.

20 Ibid., pp. 267–8.

21 The political milieu described in this paragraph is perhaps best known as Fabianism. I have drawn its essential features from sources too numerous

to mention — Trotsky's polemics and Cole and Postgate's knockabout, though not inaccurate, portrait amongst them. A fine compressed description of Fabianism may be found in Leslie Derfler, *Socialism Since Marx: A Century of the European Left* (London, 1973), pp. 29–31; and Eric Hobsbawm's essay 'The Fabians reconsidered' in *Labouring Men*, pp. 250–71, is indispensable.

22 For Thorold Rogers and the context in which he wrote, see Raphael Samuel (ed.), *People's History and Socialist Theory* (London, 1981), pp. xxiv–xxvii and Raphael Samuel, 'British Marxist historians, 1880–1980: Part One', *New Left Review*, 120 (March–April, 1980), pp. 38 and 40.

23 See Cole and Postgate *The Common People*, p. 470.

24 Macmillan, *My South African Years*, pp. 76 and 78.

25 Ibid., pp. 79–80.

26 For Macmillan's visits to his Scottish cousins, see ibid., pp. 83–5. The removal of Macmillan's family from its ancestral plot and its placement upon inferior ground is information provided by Macmillan's wife, Mona, in a conversation with the writer in February 1984. According to Hugh Macmillan Duncan Macmillan was a fairly substantial tenant farmer, not a traditional crofter. In his essay, 'Highland Deer Forest' (see note 27), Macmillan noted that his paper was based upon his summer travels to the Scottish Highlands: see p. 1 of 'Highland Deer Forest'.

27 Macmillan papers (in the custody of Mona Macmillan of Long Wittenham, Oxfordshire), writings, pamphlets etc., folder entitled '1907–1910, Oxford and Glasgow', unpublished paper entitled 'Highland Deer Forest' presented to the Broderick Club at Oxford University: manuscript dd. 8 March 1906, 7 pp.

28 Ibid., pp. 1–2.

29 Macmillan, *The South African Agrarian Problem and its Historical Development*.

30 It can be argued that Macmillan engaged in field research for this slim undergraduate study. As noted (and referenced) in note 26, his paper was partly based upon his summer travels in Scotland.

31 This statement needs qualification: it only applies to Macmillan's later *sociohistorical* studies.

32 Macmillan, *My South African Years*, p. 88.

33 Hobsbawm, for example, notes that 'the bulk of the politically conscious working class' voted for the Liberal Party in the latter half of the nineteenth century. See *Industry and Empire*, p. 132. As Raphael Samuel has noted, on p. xxiv of *People's History and Socialist Theory*, people's history first emerged in Britain as 'a self-conscious literary and intellectual practice', politically linked to the radical wing of the Liberal Party which, in the 1860s and 1870s, was making its 'first hesitant alliance' with the trade unions. When such facts are recalled, Macmillan's 'Liberal' (with a capital 'l') opinions are explicable.

34 Macmillan, *My South African Years*, pp. 90, 99–104.

35 Ibid., pp. 101–2, 104–5.

36 Ibid., p. 106.

37 See W. M. Macmillan, *Economic Conditions in a Non-Industrial South African Town: A Preliminary Study* (Grahamstown, 1915), pp. 1, 9 and 16.
38 See ibid., pp. 2–3 and Macmillan, *My South African Years*, pp. 120–1.
39 Macmillan, *Economic Conditions in a Non-Industrial ... Town*, p. 4.
40 Ibid., pp. 1–2, 16.
41 For Macmillan's proposals for local action, see ibid., pp. 12–13 and 15–16; Macmillan's advice to women workers and his belief in the necessity for combination can be found on pp. 12–13.
42 See W. M. Macmillan, *The Place of Local Government in the Union of South Africa* (Johannesburg, 1917).
43 See Macmillan, *My South African Years*, pp. 124–5.
44 See *Economic Conditions in a Non-Industrial ... Town*, pp. 6 and 11.
45 Ibid., pp. 6 and 12.
46 See Macmillan, *My South African Years*, pp. 124–5 and 195. For evidence of Macmillan's contact with the Fabians in his private papers, see Macmillan papers, Letters; 1917–18 File: Peace (hon. sec. of the Fabian Society) to Macmillan dd. 26 April 1917, 17 October 1917, 14 May 1918; and Galton (general secretary of the Fabian Society) to Macmillan dd. 18 July 1923 in the 1922–25 File. Quotations from the autobiography.
47 See Macmillan, *My South African Years*, pp. 119, 121 and 127.
48 Macmillan, *Poverty and Post-War Problems* (Grahamstown, 1916).
49 Macmillan, *My South African Years*, pp. 129–30.
50 For this research and investigation, see ibid., pp. 130–46.
51 See W. Beinart, P. Delius, S. Trapido, (eds) 'Introduction', *Putting a Plough to the Ground: accumulation and dispossession in rural South Africa 1850–1930* (Johannesburg, 1986), pp. 2–6.
52 Macmillan, *Agrarian Problem*, pp. 24–33, 35, 38–9, 41, 45, 48–51, 58–9, 72–5 and 98.
53 Ibid., pp. 36 and 41.
54 Ibid., p. 63.
55 Ibid., pp. 63, 69 and 81.
56 Ibid., pp. 63, 78–9 and 81.
57 Ibid., p. 2.
58 Macmillan, *My South African Years*, p. 146.
59 He made this latter point in his autobiography: see ibid., p. 146.
60 Macmillan, *Complex South Africa* (London, 1930), p. 120.
61 Macmillan's studies of farmworkers and reserve dwellers are to be found in *Complex South Africa* and *The Land, the Native and Unemployment* (Johannesburg, 1924). Quotation from p. 10 of the latter.
62 See, for example, *The Land, the Native and Unemployment*, pp. 6, 9 and 10.
63 In one of the last letters that he wrote to Marx, Engels argued that 'it is certain that serfdom and bondage are not a peculiarly medieval–feudal form, we find them everywhere or nearly everywhere where conquerors have the land cultivated for them by the old inhabitants'. Quoted on p. 33 of Rodney Hilton *et al.*, *The Transition from Feudalism to Capitalism* (London, 1982).

64 Macmillan *The Land, the Native and Unemployment*, pp. 5–6.

65 For such prescriptions, see ibid., pp. 3, 9, 10, 12–13; and Macmillan, *Complex South Africa*, pp. 102 and 261; also Macmillan, *Agrarian Problem*, pp. 66, 94–5.

66 For this reiteration, see Macmillan, *Complex South Africa*, pp. 102, 253 and 263 and Macmillan, *The Land, the Native and Unemployment*, p. 13.

67 See Macmillan, *Complex South Africa*, pp. 102 and 253.

68 Macmillan, *My South African Years*, pp. 133–4.

69 Macmillan called for an improved share for the sharecroppers in *Agrarian Problem*: see pp. 82–3.

70 Macmillan, *The Land, the Native and Unemployment*, p. 13. In his *Complex South Africa*, Macmillan wrote: 'There is no reason why … some natives should not — like some European bijwoners — have their chance as peasant-holders: so long as they pay reasonably fixed dues, and at least the best of them be given secure tenure and full inducement to improve both their land and themselves' (p. 253).

71 Macmillan, *Agrarian Problem*, p. 103.

72 Ibid., p. 6.

73 Ibid., p. 16.

74 Ibid., p. 85.

75 See Macmillan, *My South African Years*, pp. 152–3. Hugh Macmillan provided the information regarding the connection between the titles of Tawney and Macmillan's books on the agrarian problem.

76 See Raymond Williams, *Culture and Society, 1780–1850* (Harmondsworth, 1961), pp. 214–23.

77 Macmillan, *Agrarian Problem*, p. 19.

78 Macmillan, *My South African Years*, pp. 147 and 154–5.

79 Ibid., pp. 152, 159 and 161.

80 Macmillan papers, writings, pamphlets etc., File: 'SA 1913–24', papers labelled 'Tr. Unions & WEA 1922 < +', lecture entitled: 'Typo Union 19 May 1924'.

81 These quotations are drawn from the second of two lectures which Macmillan delivered to the Amalgamated Engineering Union after the Rand Revolt. So that researchers might locate this untitled document more easily, I have entitled the first of these lectures: 'The Trades Hall etc. —Elston. The AEU' The lectures are to be located in ibid.

82 The sources of these quotations will be found in notes 79 and 80; the text makes clear, at various points, from which of the lectures the various quotations are drawn.

83 Macmillan, *My South African Years*, p. 158. For the letter inviting Macmillan to Mann's address, see Macmillan papers, letters etc., 1922–1925 file, Johannesburg No. 1 Branch of the Amalgamated Engineering Union to Macmillan dd. 10 October 1922.

84 Again, see the sources in notes 79 and 80 for these quotations.

85 See for example, the 14 May 1926 entry to Beatrice Webb's diary in Margaret Cole (ed.), *Beatrice Webb's Diaries 1924–1932* (London, 1956), p. 97. With reference to certain middle-class intellectuals who militantly

supported the 1926 General Strike: 'What is the good of having professional brain-workers to represent you [i.e. workers], if they refuse to give you the honest message of intelligence...?'

86 The quotations come from Macmillan papers, writings, pamphlets etc., File: 'SA 1913–1924', papers labelled: 'Tr. Unions & WEA 1922 < +', lecture entitled: 'Typo Union 19 May 1924'.

87 R. M. Brown to Macmillan, nd, quoted in Macmillan, *My South African Years*, p. 159. I could not locate this letter in the Macmillan papers; it may have strayed into an incorrect file.

88 See Macmillan papers, writings, pamphlets etc., File: 'SA 1913–1924', papers labelled: 'Tr. Unions & WEA 1922 < +', lecture entitled: 'The Trades Hall etc. — Elston. The *AEU*' (given after the Rand Revolt). Macmillan appears to have inclined to craft unionism: for example, in 1919, he called 'the attention of the leader of the parliamentary Labour Party, Colonel F. H. P. Creswell, to the point of view of "craft" as against "industrial" unionists'. See Macmillan, *My South African Years*, p. 155.

89 Macmillan papers, writings, pamphlets etc., File: 'SA 1913–24', papers labelled: 'Tr. Unions & WEA 1922 < +', lecture entitled: 'Typo Union 19 May 1924.'

90 See ibid., second lecture (no title, nd) to the Amalgamated Engineering Union.

91 See Macmillan, *My South African Years*, p. 212.

92 See Macmillan, *Complex South Africa*, pp. 63–4.

93 Ibid., p. 16.

94 Ibid., p. 42.

95 The information in this paragraph is drawn from the numerous articles on the municipal strike in the editions of the *Rand Daily Mail* of March and April 1919. The quotations are from, respectively, the *Rand Daily Mail*, 1 April 1919, p. 5, 'Town council and the strike' and *Rand Daily Mail*, 19 April 1919, p. 6, 'The strike and unrest' — the latter was an unsigned article by Macmillan.

96 Paragraph constructed from *Rand Daily Mail*, 10, 27, 29 March and 1, 2 and 3 April 1919.

97 *Rand Daily Mail*, 19 April 1919: 'The strike and unrest: some thoughts on present discontent'. This article was not signed by Macmillan but there can be no doubt that he was its author. Not only is there a copy of it in the Macmillan papers (see writings, pamphlets etc., File: 'SA 1913–1924') it is replete with the telltale signs of his idiom. It refers, for example, to 'brain workers', 'the new social order' etc.

98 Ibid.

99 See Macmillan, *My South African Years*, pp. 156–7 and 'War on the Witwatersrand' by 'Z' (actually Macmillan himself, as confirmed by Hugh) in *The South African Quarterly*, iv, 1 (March 1922), p. 8.

100 The full title of the article was 'War on the Witwatersrand, March 1922'.

101 'War on the Witwatersrand', pp. 6, 7 and 8.

102 The quotations to which this note refers are from ibid., pp. 7 and 8.

103 Frederick Johnstone, *Class, Race and Gold* (London, 1976), pp. 49–50.

104 Ibid., pp. 133-4.
105 See Macmillan, 'The truth about the strike on the Rand', *The New Statesman*, xix, 474 (13 May 1922), pp. 145-6. The article was unsigned: for proof that it was Macmillan who wrote it, see his autobiography (p. 158).
106 Johnstone, *Class, Race and Gold*, p. 136.
107 Macmillan, 'The truth about the strike on the Rand'.
108 The young schoolboy was Eddie Roux: see Eddie and Win Roux, *Rebel Pity: the life of Eddie Roux* (London, 1970), p. 10.
109 Macmillan, 'The truth about the strike on the Rand'.
110 In 'War on the Witwatersrand' (p. 7), Macmillan referred to the racism of the white workers, their attacks upon black people 'which preceded the crisis' and the hypocrisy of the mine-owners who were 'not in general "negrophilists"' even as they attempted to destroy certain racial privileges enjoyed by white workers. 'Admitted also, the natives do not get full justice', wrote Macmillan. His analysis of the importance of racism in this insurrection went no further than this.
111 Macmillan, 'The truth about the strike on the Rand'.
112 Tawney's influence upon Macmillan has already been made manifest in this paper. In *The Cape Colour Question*, in fact, Macmillan made specific reference to Tawney's *Acquisitive Society*: see pp. 30 and 278 of the 1968 re-issue of *The Cape Colour Question: A Historical Survey* (Balkema, Cape Town). In *My South African Years*, Macmillan was to write: '... I was eager to throw what light I could on my particular branch of social history from others working in parallel fields and this time [i.e. a visit to London in the 1920s] I found not only R. H. Tawney but J. L. Hammond, whose work I found highly relevant and who passed me on to others in his field' (p. 194 of the autobiography). See also Naidoo's thesis, 'Macmillan: South African historian', pp. 49 and 55 for the influence of these historians upon Macmillan. Whilst I was researching this paper Mona Macmillan confirmed the importance of the Hammond's social histories for Macmillan.
113 This is the implication of comments of his on p. 100 of *Complex South Africa*, from which the quotation is drawn.
114 See Raymond Williams, *Culture and Society*, p. 219. I should state here that my insertion within the final set of brackets renders the tone of Williams's judgement more strident than it is. But it has been included with particular reference to Macmillan to suggest the antithesis of his own political programme. It would most probably apply to Tawney as well.
115 Ibid., p. 220.
116 See Macmillan, *My South African Years*, p. 186.
117 Macmillan, *Complex South Africa*, p. 278.
118 Macmillan, *My South African Years*, pp. 210-11; quotations from p. 211.
119 Ibid., p. 146.
120 Ibid., pp. 196-7.
121 See the comments of one leading Marxist historian, John Foster in 'The declassing of language', *New Left Review*, 150 (March-April 1985), p. 37.
122 Macmillan, *Complex South Africa*, pp. 13, 277-8; quotations from pp. 13 and 277.

2 'PARALYZED CONSERVATIVES': W. M. MACMILLAN, THE SOCIAL SCIENTISTS
AND THE 'COMMON SOCIETY' 1923–48

1 W. M. Macmillan, *My South African Years* (Cape Town, 1975), p. 219.
2 W. M. Macmillan, *Complex South Africa* (London, 1930), p. 42.
3 W. M. Macmillan, *Bantu, Boer, and Briton* (London, 1929), p. vii.
4 W. M. Macmillan, 'Black and white in South Africa' in E. Smith, *The Christian Mission in Africa: a study based on the proceedings of the international conference at Le Zoute, September 14th to 21st, 1926* (London, 1926), p. 156.
5 Foreword by C. W. de Kiewiet in W. M. Macmillan, *The Cape Colour Question* (Cape Town, 1968), pp. vi–vii.
6 'The Freedom Charter' in N. Mandela, *The Struggle is my Life* (London, 1978), p. 50.
7 Macmillan, *Complex South Africa*, p. 280.
8 Macmillan *My South African Years*, p. 215.
9 Ibid., p. 214.
10 W. Fischer, 'Gustav Schmoller' in D. Sills, (ed.) *International Encyclopaedia of the Social Sciences* (New York, 1972), xiv, pp. 60–3; J. A. Schumpeter, *History of Economic Analysis* (New York, 1954), pp. 809–24; W. E. B. DuBois, *The Autobiography of W. E. B. DuBois, a soliloquy on viewing my life from the last decade of its first century* (USA, 1968), pp. 162–6.
11 W. M. Macmillan, *The South African Agrarian Problem and its Historical Development* (Johannesburg, 1919), p. 6.
12 Macmillan, *Complex South Africa*, p. 279.
13 W. M. Macmillan, *The Cape Colour Question* (London, 1927), p. 29.
14 Ibid., p. 54.
15 Ibid., p. 236; W. M. Macmillan, *Africa Emergent* (London, 1938), p. 315.
16 Macmillan, *Complex South Africa*, p. 142.
17 Macmillan, *The Cape Colour Question*, p. 175.
18 Macmillan, *Africa Emergent*, p. 13.
19 Ibid., p. 374.
20 Ibid., p. 375.
21 Ibid., pp. 88, 93–4, 374–5.
22 Macmillan, *The Cape Colour Question*, p. 288.
23 Macmillan, *My South African Years*, p. 182.
24 A. Kuper, *Anthropologists and Anthropology, the British School, 1922–72* (London, 1973); see also P. Rich, *White Power and the Liberal Conscience: racial segregation and South African liberalism* (Johannesburg, 1984), pp. 54–76.
25 A. R. Radcliffe-Brown, 'The methods of ethnology and social anthropology', *South African Journal of Science*, xx (1923), pp. 12, 4–56.
26 Ibid., p. 141.
27 Ibid., p. 142.
28 E. Krige, 'A. W. Hoernlé', *African Studies*, xix (1960), pp. 138–44.
29 A. W. Hoernlé, 'New aims and methods in social anthropology', *South African Journal of Science*, xxx (1933), pp. 74–92.

289

30 A. R. Radcliffe-Brown, 'The present position of anthropological studies' (1931) in M. N. Srinivas, ed., *Method in Social Anthropology* (Chicago, 1958), p. 84.
31 A. W. Hoernlé, 'New aims and methods', p. 82.
32 Ibid., pp. 85–92.
33 A. R. Radcliffe-Brown, 'The present position', p. 42.
34 A. W. Hoernlé, 'New aims and methods', p. 74.
35 J. D. Rheinallt Jones, 'The need of a scientific basis for South African Native policy', *South African Journal of Science*, xxiii (1926), p. 80.
36 Ibid.
37 E. Brookes, *The Colour Problems of South Africa* (Lovedale, 1934), pp. 109–29.
38 Ibid., p. 128.
39 Macmillan, *My South African Years*, p. 212.
40 Ibid., p. 228.
41 Macmillan, *Complex South Africa*, p. 275–80.
42 'Programme of the Communist Party of South Africa adopted 1st January, 1929', *South African Communists Speak. Documents from the history of the South African Communist Party, 1915–80* (London, 1981), pp. 100–6.
43 *The South African Worker*, 30 March 1929, quoted in H. J. and R. E. Simons, *Class and Colour in South Africa, 1850–1950* (Harmondsworth, 1969), p. 376.
44 Macmillan, *Complex South Africa*, p. 8.
45 Macmillan, *Africa Emergent*, pp. 31, 373–9.
46 Ibid., p. 183.
47 Ibid., p. 376–7.
48 B. Malinowski, 'Native education and culture contact', *International Review of Mission*, xxv (1936), p. 480.
49 Ibid., p. 494.
50 Ibid., p. 502.
51 Ibid., pp. 503–4, 513.
52 B. Malinowski, 'The Pan-African problem of culture contact', *American Journal of Sociology*, xlix (1943), p. 661. (pp. 649–65).
53 R. F. A. Hoernlé, *South African Native Policy and the Liberal Spirit*, viii, (Cape Town, 1939), pp. 63–5.
54 Ibid., p. 158; see also M. Legassick, 'Race, industrialization and social change in South Africa: the case of R. F. A. Hoernlé', *African Affairs*, xxv (1976), pp. 224–39.
55 Hoernlé, *South African Native Policy*, p. 72.
56 Eiselen and Verwoerd both delivered papers at the meetings of the South African Association for the Advancement of Science in 1928 and 1929. Verwoerd was elected a council member for the Cape in 1929. Macmillan was a committee member of Section F (Education, History etc.) in 1924 and 1925, and was a Vice-President of the section in 1926 and 1928.
57 W. M. Eiselen, 'Christianity and the religious life of the Bantu' in I. Schapera, 'Religious beliefs and practices' in I. Schapera (ed.), *Western Civilization and the Native* (London, 1934), p. 65; and W. M. Eiselen and I. Schapera (ed.),

The Bantu-speaking Tribes of South Africa (London, 1937), p. 247.

58 W. M. Eiselen, *Die Naturellevragstuk* (Cape Town, 1929). Reference in I. Schapera, *Select Bibliography on South African Native Life and Problems* (Oxford, 1941), p. 125.

59 W. M. Eiselen, 'The meaning of *Apartheid*', *Race Relations*, xv (1948), pp. 77-8; see also 'The Eiselen line', *South African Outlook* (March 1949) in F. Wilson and D. Perrot (eds.), *Outlook on a Century* (Lovedale, 1972), pp. 616-19.

60 W. M. Eiselen, 'The meaning of *Apartheid*', p. 86; see also W. M. Eiselen, 'Harmonious multi-community development', *Optima* (March 1959), pp. 1-15.

61 A. W. Hoernlé, 'Alternatives to *Apartheid*', *Race Relations*, xv (1948), pp. 90-1.

62 Ibid., pp. 95-9.

63 A. Kuper, *Anthropologists and Anthropology*, pp. 162-3.

64 I. Schapera, review of *Bantu, Boer, and Briton* and other books, *Africa*, ii (1929), p. 426.

65 E. Smith, review of *Complex South Africa*, in *Africa*, iv (1931), p. 370.

66 B. Malinowski, *Coral Gardens and their Magic*, ii (London, 1935), p. 480.

67 B. Malinowski, 'Introductory essay: the anthropology of changing African cultures', in L. Mair (ed.), *Materials for the Study of Culture Contact*, xxvi-xxxi. (London, 1938).

68 M. Fortes, 'Culture Contact as a dynamic process. An investigation in the northern territories of the Gold Coast' in Mair, (ed.), *Materials for the Study of Culture Contact*, p. 62; and I. Schapera, 'Contact between European and Native in South Africa. Part II.', p. 26.

69 B. Malinowski, 'Introductory essay', pp. viii-xiv.

70 M. Gluckman, *Analysis of a Social Situation in Modern Zululand* (Manchester, 1958), p. 9. The articles were first published in *Bantu/African Studies* (1940-42).

71 Ibid., *passim*.

72 M. Gluckman, 'The Tribal Area in South and Central Africa' in L. Kuper and M. G. Smith (eds.), *Pluralism in Africa* (Berkeley, 1971), pp. 375-6, 405; see also M. Gluckman, 'Anthropology and apartheid' in M. Fortes and S. Patterson (eds), *Studies in African Social Anthropology* (London, 1975).

73 Ibid.

74 For example, Macmillan, *Complex South Africa*, p. 33.

75 M. Gluckman, *Analysis of a Social Situation*, pp. 43-4.

76 M. Gluckman, *Malinowski's Sociological Theories* (Manchester, 1968), pp. 1-21. The two articles in this pamphlet first appeared in *African Studies* in 1947. The first of them was an extended review of B. Malinowski, *The Dynamics of Culture Change; An inquiry into race relations in Africa*, edited with an introduction by P. Kaberry (New Haven, 1945).

77 W. M. Macmillan, *Africa Emergent* (Harmondsworth, 1949), preface to Penguin edition, p. 8.

78 For an early anthropological defence of history see G. Wilson and M. Wilson, *An Analysis of Social Change* (Cambridge, 1945), pp. 167-8.

79 A. Paton, *Hofmeyr* (Cape Town, 1964), pp. 167, 243–4, 263–4, 271–2, 297.
80 P. Walshe, *The Rise of African Nationalism in South Africa* (London, 1970), pp. 346, 379. Walshe refers to a letter in the Xuma papers, University of the Witwatersrand Library, from Macmillan to Xuma, 17 December 1942. I have seen this letter and it is not from Macmillan. However, Mrs W. M. Macmillan recalls that he was consulted on the constitution. See also, H. J. Simons, 'Our Freedom Charter', *Sechaba* (June 1985), p. 9.
81 Z. K. Matthews, 'An African Policy for South Africa', *Race Relations*, xvi (1949), pp. 71–82; Z. K. Matthews, 'Social relations in a common South African society', supplement to *Optima* (March 1961).
82 Macmillan, 'Black and white in South Africa', p. 154.
83 Macmillan, *Bantu, Boer, and Briton*, p. 11; R. V. Selope Thema, 'The race problem', *The Guardian*, September 1922, reprinted in T. Karis and G. M. Carter (eds), *From Protest to Challenge*, i (Stanford, 1972), p. 213; W. M. Macmillan, *The Road to Self-Rule* (London, 1959), p. 231.
84 Thema used the phrase in his evidence to the Select Committee on Hertzog's Bills in 1927. Macmillan, *My South African Years*, p. 215.
85 Winifred Holtby Papers, Hull Local Studies Library, W. M. Macmillan to Winifred Holtby, 27 April 1932.
86 Macmillan, *Africa Emergent* (London, 1938), p. 179.

3. A LIBERAL DESCENT? W. M. MACMILLAN, C. W. DE. KIEWIET AND THE HISTORY OF SOUTH AFRICA

* I acknowledge the assistance of the Human Sciences Research Council, which bears no responsibility for my text.

1 The fullest recent discussion is F. A. van Jaarsveld, *Omstrede Suid-Afrikaanse Verlede* (Johannesburg, 1984), pp. 38–51. While van Jaarsveld showed respect for Macmillan's work in his introduction to the new edition of *The South African Agrarian Problem* (Pretoria, 1974), concerned as it was with white poverty, in other writing he has been much more positive about de Kiewiet than about Macmillan. Cf. his *The Afrikaner's Interpretation of South African History* (Cape Town, 1964), pp. 139–43 and *Wie en Wat is die Afrikaner?* (Cape Town, 1981), pp. 82–7.
2 B. Murray, *Wits: the early years* (Johannesburg, 1982). Note the photograph of de Kiewiet as member of the 1922 Students' Representative Council, p. 347.
3 Letter by de Kiewiet to J. Naidoo, 17 August 1980, one of a series of seven such letters written between July and November 1980 (hereafter called the Naidoo Letters). I thank J. Naidoo of Niort, France, for his kind permission to quote from these letters.
4 Some of his notes on the Philip Papers are preserved in the collection of Philip notes presented to Rhodes House Library, Oxford, by W. M. Macmillan.
5 Interview with C. W. de Kiewiet, Washington, 1983 (hereafter Interview); Naidoo Letters.

6 Macmillan to de Kiewiet, 21 September 1924: Cornell University Library, de Kiewiet Papers.

7 Walker to Macmillan, 28 August 1925: Long Wittenham, Oxfordshire, W. M. Macmillan papers (hereafter Macmillan papers); Interview.

8 Naidoo Letters.

9 De Kiewiet to Herbert and Boet, 22 August 1924: De Kiewiet papers.

10 It was only after *The Agrarian Problem* (1919) that Macmillan switched his attention to blacks. On Johannesburg influences, see his *My South African Years* (Cape Town, 1975), p. 129ff; Murray, *Wits*; ch. 5 (e.g. p. 142 on the economist R. A. Lehfeldt); P. B. Rich, *White Power and the Liberal Conscience* (Manchester, 1983).

11 De Kiewiet to Frankel and Harvey, nd: de Kiewiet papers; the report of the commission is Southern Rhodesia paper 20 of 1925.

12 Macmillan to de Kiewiet, 14 March 1925: de Kiewiet papers. The 'tract' by Brookes was his *History of Native Policy in South Africa* (Pretoria, 1924). A. F. Pollard was Director of the Institute of Historical Studies, University of London.

13 Published as J. A. I. Agar-Hamilton, *The Native Policy of the Voortrekkers 1836–1858* (Cape Town, nd [1928]).

14 De Kiewiet to Macmillan, 19 July 1926: Macmillan papers.

15 Cf. Macmillan, *My South African Years*, pp. 100–4.

16 De Kiewiet to Macmillan, 19 July 1926: Macmillan papers.

17 Interview.

18 Macmillan to de Kiewiet, 10 September 1929: de Kiewiet papers.

19 De Kiewiet to Macmillan, 1 March 1931: Macmillan papers.

20 Cf. Macmillan to Frankel, January 1934, copy in possession of Mrs Mona Macmillan; Murray, *Wits*, p. 269; Mona Macmillan, *Champion of Africa. W. M. Macmillan: the second phase* (Long Wittenham, 1985), p. 56.

21 De Kiewiet to Macmillan, nd [1936]: Macmillan papers; file on the King George V chair of History, University of Cape Town Archives.

22 De Kiewiet file: Carnegie Corporation of New York Archives; M. Macmillan, *Champion of Africa*, p. 198.

23 *American Historical Review* (October 1938); *New Statesman*, 29 January 1938.

24 J. Mulgan to de Kiewiet, 25 October 1937: Oxford University Press Archives.

25 De Kiewiet to Macmillan, 14 March 1938: Macmillan papers; de Kiewiet to Clarendon Press, 10 March 1938: de Kiewiet papers.

26 De Kiewiet, 'Foreword' in W. M. Macmillan, *The Cape Colour Question* (re-issue, Cape Town, 1968).

27 Macmillan, *My South African Years*, pp. 1, 2, 9.

28 Interview.

29 Macmillan, *My South African Years*, p. 61; Naidoo Letters.

30 Macmillan, *My South African Years*, pp. 76, 104–5; 119, 121, 127 — for references to his earlier writings; and *passim*.

31 Naidoo Letters.

32 Interview; Naidoo Letters.

33 *British Colonial Policy and the South African Republics* (London, 1929).

34 Naidoo Letters.

35 C. W. de Kiewiet, 'Social and economic developments in native tribal life' in *Cambridge History of the British Empire*, viii (1936).

36 Cf. R. Winks (ed.), *Historiography of the British Empire-Commonwealth* (Durham, NC, 1966).

37 C. W. de Kiewiet, *The Imperial Factor* (Cambridge, 1937), p. 5.

38 *New Statesman* (29 January 1938) p. 176.

39 Ibid.

40 Macmillan, *The Cape Colour Question*, p. 11.

41 R. Elphick and H. Giliomee (eds), *The Shaping of South African Society* (Cape Town, 1979), p. 244.

42 C. W. de Kiewiet, *A History of South Africa, Social and Economic* (Oxford, 1941), p. 19.

43 Macmillan to de Kiewiet, 21 September 1924: de Kiewiet papers.

44 For more detail see my article on the writing of his *History* in *History in Africa*, xiii (1986).

45 C. W. de Kiewiet, *The Anatomy of South African Misery* (London, 1956); W. M. Macmillan, *Bantu, Boer, and Briton* (2nd rev. edn., Oxford, 1963).

46 For example, 'Among savages with no government save the intermittent one of councils, the party of action and violence must always prevail' de Kiewiet, *The Imperial Factor*, p. 231.

47 I elaborate on this in a longer work now under way.

48 Cf. S. Marks, 'Khoisan resistance to the Dutch', *Journal of African History* (1972); Colin Bundy, *The Rise and Fall of the South African Peasantry* (London, 1979); the phrase is from de Kiewiet, 'Social and economic developments'.

49 A. T. Bryant's *Olden Times in Zululand and Natal* (London, 1929) was based in part on a series of lectures given while Bryant was lecturer and research fellow at Wits in 1923. : *Olden Times*, p. 70 note. For Macmillan's criticisms of anthropologists and his fight with 'Bantu Studies' see *My South African Years*, pp. 214–6. and Rich, *White Power*, ch. 3. De Kiewiet did attend Malinowski's famous anthropology seminar at the University of London for a time: Interview.

50 The most incisive critique is A. Atmore and S. Marks, 'The imperial factor in South Africa in the nineteenth century: towards a reassessment', *Journal of Imperial and Commonwealth History*, 1 (1974).

51 Perhaps above all R. H. Tawney — whom Macmillan met in 1920 — and J. L. and Barbara Hammond, whose work both Macmillan and de Kiewiet often cited. In Berlin Macmillan had been much influenced by Gustav Schmoller, and de Kiewiet by Hermann Oncken: Macmillan, *My South African Years*, p. 101; Naidoo Letters; Interview.

52 For example, '...the most distinctive feature of the history of whites and natives is not race or colour, but a close economic association': de Kiewiet, *The Imperial Factor*, p. 1, or Macmillan's remarks about 'thinking ... in terms of colour' in *My South African Years*, pp. 160–1. Cf. J. Lonsdale, 'From colony to industrial state: South African historiography as seen from

England', *Social Dynamics*, ix, 1 (1983), p. 72; de Kiewiet, *History*, ch. 8 'Poor whites and poor blacks'.

53 de Kiewiet, *The Imperial Factor*, p. 1.

54 de Kiewiet, *The Anatomy of South African Misery*, pp. 47, 65. In his *History* de Kiewiet described segregation as 'a myth, a fancy, anything but a fact' (p. 242). He meant that it could not work, but segregation was, of course, very much a fact by the late 1930s.

55 Both men often thought of segregation in terms of the colour bar, or the removal of Africans from the common voters' roll, but rarely of the established migrant labour system.

56 Cf. J. W. Burrow, *A Liberal Descent* (London, 1982).

57 Inscription in book in Macmillan's study, Long Wittenham.

58 This dependence extended to direct borrowing: for example, de Kiewiet's phrase about people going to towns 'for the same reason that water flows uphill when driven by machinery' (*History*, p. 196) is taken from Macmillan's *Agrarian Problem*, pp. 2 and 7.

59 The initial print-run was 1,000 copies; a new printing of an additional 1,000 copies was ordered in December 1941 and the book was regularly reprinted in hardback until 1968: a paperback appeared in 1966 and is still in print (information from Oxford University Press).

60 J. Naidoo, 'W. M. Macmillan: South African historian', University of South Africa MA thesis, 1983, p. 240. De Kiewiet flirted with socialism while in Rhodesia: see his letters from there in his papers at Cornell University. Macmillan's adherence to socialism weakened over the years.

4. W. M. MACMILLAN: POVERTY, SMALL TOWNS AND THE KAROO

* This paper was discussed at the London conference in October, 1985, and at the research seminar at the Southern African Research Program in New Haven. I thank all those who contributed but especially Shula Marks and Hugh Macmillan.

1 See the admiring preface by F. A. van Jaarsveld to a State Library, Pretoria, reprint in 1974 to Macmillan's *The South African Agrarian Problem and its Historical Development* (Johannesburg, 1919). This admiration by Afrikaners is confined to Macmillan's work on poor whites.

2 J. Naidoo, 'W. M. Macmillan: South African historian', MA thesis, University of South Africa, v (Pretoria, 1983), pp. 217–40.

3 W. M. Macmillan, *My South African Years* (Cape Town, 1975), pp. 146, 164. See Alan Paton, *Towards the Mountain* (Cape Town, 1980), pp. 268–74 for his account of his decision to write *Cry, the Beloved Country*.

4 See note 1 above.

5 Macmillan, *My South African Years*, p. 7.

6 Ibid., pp. 38, 57–58.

7 Ibid., pp. 33, 51.

8 Macmillan senior wrote of the 'disloyalty of South Africa' in 1906. Ibid., p. 58.

9 '... men like Geyer were able to develop Nationalist theories which they
   would never have been able to maintain against their friendly contemporary
   critics' ibid., p. 115. Macmillan edited a memoir of the student: *A South
   African Student and Soldier: Harold Edward Howse* (Johannesburg, 1919).
10 Macmillan, *My South African Years*, pp. 80, 87, 94. As late as September
   1910, he was still taking a divinity course at Glasgow University, ibid.,
   p. 104.
11 Ibid., p. 122.
12 For the 1923 conference see Naidoo, 'W. M. Macmillan', pp. 50-1; for Geyer
   see Macmillan, *My South African Years*, p. 183. He described his Afrikaans
   as idiomatic, and wrote at least one letter to *Die Burger* in November, 1927.
   Information supplied by Hugh Macmillan, 16 April 1986.
13 Ibid., pp. 184-7, 188-91; for Hertzog pp. 213, 223-30; for Pirow pp. 223-30.
   See Bruce K. Murray, *Wits: the Early Years: a history of the University of
   the Witwatersrand, Johannesburg and its precursors 1896-1939* (Johannesburg, 1982), pp. 129-31.
14 Naidoo, 'W. M. Macmillan', pp. 56-7. However, Macmillan could hardly be
   accused of being generally 'anti-Afrikaner'.
15 Macmillan, *My South African Years*, p. 65; Naidoo, 'W. M. Macmillan', p. 37.
   Macmillan later described Toby Muller as 'one of the finest spirits of young
   South Africa', *Rand Daily Mail*, 15 October 1929.
16 Macmillan, *My South African Years*, pp. 76, 78.
17 E. T. Williams (ed.), *A Register of Rhodes Scholars 1903-1981*, p. 2;
   (Oxford, 1981) p. 2; Macmillan, *My South African Years*, pp. 124-5.
18 Ibid., pp. 100-2.
19 Ibid., pp. 104, 106; Patricia Pugh, *Educate, Agitate, Organize: 100 years of
   Fabian socialism* (London, 1984), p. 324.
20 Macmillan, *My South African Years*, pp. 119, 121, 146, 162.
21 Ibid., p. 121.
22 For his remark about parliament, see ibid., p. 247; according to Naidoo in
   'W. M. Macmillan', p. 62, Mrs Mona Macmillan believes that Macmillan left
   South Africa 'with the definite aim of preventing the spread of South
   African policy to the rest of the Commonwealth'. For his letter of November
   1931, see his *My South African Years*, p. 239.
23 Ibid., pp. 118-20.
24 W. M. Macmillan, *Economic Conditions in a Non-Industrial South African
   Town: A preliminary survey* (Grahamstown, 1915), pp. 5-6. This paper was
   delivered on 12 September 1915 to the ECMS (English Church Mens
   Society?). Macmillan, in *My South African Years*, p. 11, remembered it as
   'the Bishop's Men's Society'.
25 Macmillan, *Economic Conditions*, p. 6.
26 Ibid., p. 5.
27 Ibid., p. 6.
28 Ibid.
29 Ibid., pp. 11, 12.
30 Ibid., p. 12.
31 Ibid.

32 Ibid., p. 14, footnote.
33 Ibid., p. 14.
34 Ibid., p. 7.
35 Ibid., p. 8.
36 Ibid., pp. 9, 16.
37 Ibid., p. 1.
38 Ibid., p. 6.
39 Macmillan, *My South African Years*, p. 162.
40 See above. This piece was not ignored by contemporaries: it was noted by John X. Merriman, Sidney Webb, and presumably by the DRC members who invited him to talk at Cradock in 1916. See his *My South African Years*, pp. 121–2, 124–5.
41 Macmillan, *Economic Conditions*,: on incomes see pp. 4–5; on house ownership see pp. 7–8.
42 Ibid., pp. 8–9, 14: 'The present and actual result of this evil is a terribly serious moral danger to the race.'
43 Ibid., pp. 14–15.
44 *The Midland News* (Cradock, 22–25 and 27–28 November 1916).
45 Macmillan, *Economic Conditions*, p. 1. The official report is *Het Arme Blanken Vraagstuk: Verslag van Het Kerkelik Kongres Behouden Te Cradock, op 22 on 23 November, 1916* (Cape Town, 1917). There is a puzzle here: in the twentieth century, 'Eerwaarde' came to be a title for ministers working in the Zendingkerk (mission church) which became an entirely coloured body in its laity. The white conference was, as we have seen, organized by the Inwendige Zending Kommissie. Was white poverty regarded as a Zending responsibility, and was M. C. Theron sent to Grahamstown primarily to care for the Afrikaner poor? And did he, therefore, meet Macmillan as a man interested in the poor rather than as someone who also found Afrikaners congenial on religious and perhaps social grounds?
46 Macmillan, *My South African Years*, pp. 122–3.
47 It may be that Macmillan was reported at greater length in *Grocotts Penny Mail* or *The Grahamstown Journal*.
48 *Midland News* (28 November, 1916).
49 *Verslag*, pp. 59–60.
50 Ibid., p. 10–12.
51 Ibid., pp. 53–5. Searle, an English-speaker, made a point of addressing the conference in Afrikaans.
52 Macmillan, *Economic Conditions*, p. 16.
53 Naidoo, 'W. M. Macmillan', p. 244.
54 Ibid., pp. 46–7. In *My South African Years*, pp. 127–8 Macmillan says very little about how he decided to remain a civilian; he advanced no pacifist reasons.
55 Macmillan, *Economic Conditions*, p. 15: '...Our power of local government... is a serious and little recognized moral responsibility for the health and welfare of all classes.'
56 Macmillan, *My South African Years*, p. 146.

57 Ibid., pp. 162–9; Naidoo, 'W. M. Macmillan', p. 50.
58 Macmillan, *My South African Years*, p. 122.
59 Macmillan, *Agrarian Problem*, p. 2: on p. 7 he identified the quote as from *Tess of the D'Urbervilles*.
60 Macmillan, *Agrarian Problem*, pp. 12, 43–54.
61 Ibid., p. 46.
62 Ibid., p. 13.
63 Ibid., p. 7.
64 Ibid., p. 15.
65 Ibid., p. 13.
66 Ibid., p. 18.
67 Ibid., p. 95.
68 Ibid., p. 100.
69 Ibid., p. 101.
70 Ibid.
71 Ibid., p. 67. He may have been referring to G. H. Stanley, 'A South African Iron industry', *South African Journal of Science* (1917) pp. 116–22.
72 Macmillan, *Economic Conditions*, pp. 1, 4, 14–15.
73 Ibid., pp. 8, 13–14.
74 Macmillan, *Agrarian Problem*, p. 60.
75 Ibid., p. 19.
76 For the above three quotations, see ibid., p. 40. For this paragraph, see ibid., p. 83.
77 Ibid., p. 83.
78 Ibid., p. 19.
79 Ibid., p. 54.
80 Ibid., p. 59.
81 Ibid., p. 60.
82 Ibid.
83 Ibid.
84 Ibid., p. 63.
85 Ibid., p. 65.
86 Ibid., p. 66.
87 Macmillan, *My South African Years*, p. 182.
88 There is no space here for historiographical debate, but Macmillan deserves to be recognized for the interventionist he was. See Naidoo, 'W. M. Macmillan', pp. 170–8, and 211–16, for discussions of Legassick's and Bundy's work on Macmillan.
89 Macmillan, *Agrarian Problem*, p. 99. Macmillan quoted John Morley in this context.
90 Jeffrey Butler, 'Housing in a Karoo *Dorp*: a survey of sources and an examination of developing segregation before the Group Areas Act, 1950 (forthcoming), p. 15.
91 Ibid., pp. 30–3.
92 This material will be made available in a later paper.

5. JOHN PHILIP: TOWARDS A REASSESSMENT

1   Andrew Nash, 'Dr Philip, the spread of civilisation and liberalism in South Africa', *Proceedings of the Conference on Opposition in South Africa* (Johannesburg, 1978).

2   Anyone who writes history seriously cannot cut themselves off from their present, nor should they — perhaps particularly in the case of South Africa. John Philip has suffered, however, from studies where historical analysis of his life and work were secondary to the author's concern about his own day. This is something quite different from Shula Marks' valid insistence in a communication to me that it is 'the legitimate function of history to give us a critical vantage point from which to understand the complexities of the present'.

3   Julius Lewin, 'Dr Philip and liberalism', *Race Relations*, xxvii (1960), pp. 82–90.

4   This was the popular form of the more fully developed study, 'James Read: towards a re-assessment', Institute of Commonwealth Studies, London, *Collected Seminar Papers, Societies of Southern Africa in the 19th–20th centuries* (henceforth CSP), vii (1977), pp. 19–25.

5   W. M. Macmillan, *The Cape Colour Question* (London, 1927), p. 139.

6   Hugh Macmillan has drawn my attention to the hint on page 172 of his father's volume of reminiscences, *My South African Years* (Cape Town, 1975) that W. M. Macmillan was aware of a tradition, still alive in the Eastern Province, that the Reads were involved in the socalled 'Kat River Rebellion'. In his father's papers, Hugh has informed me, it appears that Macmillan made contact with a granddaughter of James Read who referred to the existence of a Read diary and thanked him for his interest in Philip and Read — those 'pioneers of truth and righteousness'.

   This seems to confirm that Macmillan was well aware of the closeness of Philip and the Read family and that he played down the role of Read and his sons for the reasons I have suggested. It was difficult enough to extricate the memory of Philip from the tradition enshrined in Theal's work without embarking on the same task for James Read.

7   Philip sent to the Directors thirteen of the principal letters dealing with the affair enclosed in his letter to the Directors, 31 March 1846 (Incoming Letters, Box 22, Folder 1). These letters are in the LMS archives now housed in the library of the School of Oriental and African Studies, London. They are referred to hereafter as 'Incoming Letters'.

8   Ibid.

9   Macmillan, *The Cape Colour Question*, pp. 173–4.

10   Incoming Letters, Box 1, Folder 2, Philip to Directors, March 1821.

11   *The Missionary Herald*, xxix (November, 1983), pp. 415–20.

12   Hugh Macmillan states in a communication 'For all that WMM played down the race issue it may be significant that W. M. Eiselen in his review of *The Cape Colour Question* in *Die Burger* (19 November 1927) spent a great deal of space dealing with the suggestion that some Blacks and Coloureds may be superior to some whites. He granted that this might be true but said that it

was necessary to look at group norms rather than at individuals. In a pamphlet in 1929 he apparently accepted that there was no proof of white mental superiority but in 1948 he used precisely the same argument as the main justification for apartheid. Each cultural group must have its own "area of freedom". The point is that even if WMM pulled his punches on the race issue, they still hit the target, possibly influencing a major ideologist of apartheid away from racial and towards cultural explanations.'

13 Miss Gertrude Edwards was formerly headmistress of the Godolphin School, Salisbury, England, and latterly Lady Warden, Oriel House, Rhodes University, Grahamstown, CP.

14 G. Edwards to W. M. Macmillan, 3 August 1925. This reference to a letter in Macmillan's private papers was kindly given me by Hugh Macmillan.

15 T. C. Smout, *A History of the Scottish People, 1560–1830* (Glasgow, 1972), p. 282.

16 My many friends among the 'so-called Cape Coloureds' as they refer to themselves on public occasions dislike this nomenclature. In their mother tongue, Afrikaans, they refer to themselves as 'die Kaapse Volk' — the Cape Folk or People. It is very difficult to find an acceptable English alternative. In my recently published *John Philip: Missions, Race and Politics in South Africa* (Aberdeen, 1986) I have used the form Cape Folk, a form that is acceptable to those used to the Scottish form of the English language but somewhat odd to others. As a result in this essay I have used 'Kaapse Volk' throughout to refer to this people who were beginning to emerge from their Khoi, mixed race and freed slave roots.

17 C. W. de Kiewiet, *A History of South Africa* (London, 1957), 2, *passim*.

18 G. Sorin, *The New York Abolitionists* (Westport, 1971); T. L. Smith, *Revivalism and Social Reform in Mid-nineteenth Century America* (Baltimore, 1980); A. Duberman (ed.), *The Anti-Slavery Vanguard* (Princeton, 1965); R. H. Abzug, *The Passionate Liberator: Theodore Weld and the dilemma of reform* (New York, 1980).

19 Radical evangelicalism was a movement among Protestant evangelicals made up of those who believed passionately in the demand of the Christian faith upon them for the reshaping of society. In their perception of the nature of the necessary reforms they all agreed on the need to abolish slavery, but ranged from John Brown who tried to arm the slaves of Virginia for a righteous rebellion to William Wilberforce with his desire for 'the reform of manners'. It is vital to distinguish them from their fellow evangelicals of the quietist tradition who saw Christianity entirely in terms of personal morality and the separation of Christianity from politics, and who were to come close to obliterating the radical tradition in the second half of the nineteenth century.

20 J. C. Brauer, *Protestantism in America* (Chicago, 1968), p. 176.

21 Abzug, *The Passionate Liberator*, p. 92–3.

22 As with most of those who stayed loyal to the Congregationalist churches associated with the initial work of the Haldanes, Philip was very critical of them in later life. The Haldanes, at the height of their influence, had broken with the Congregationalist tradition and had adopted Baptist principles,

splitting the newly created Scottish evangelical groups with great bitterness. This attitude is reflected in the passages in Philip's writing referred to in Macmillan, *The Cape Colour Question*, p. 98.

23 Robert Haldane, *Address to the Public concerning Political opinions* (London, 1800), pp. 4–6.

24 Philip Curtin, *The Image of Africa* (Madison, 1964), pp. 414–16, 424–8, 473–6.

25 See the views expressed by Miss Edwards to Macmillan above.

26 During this same period, the CMS missionary, Henry Williams, was waging a campaign in New Zealand to protect the Maori from the encroachment of white settlers upon their land. See his biography, L. M. Rogers, *Te Wiremu. A biography of Henry Williams* (Christchurch, 1973).

27 Quoted in D. Eltis and J. Walvin (eds), *The Abolition of the Atlantic Slave Trade* (Madison, 1981), p. 42.

28 See Martin Legassick's seminal essay 'The frontier tradition in South African historiography' in S. Marks and A. Atmore, *Economy and Society in Pre-industrial South Africa* (London, 1980), pp. 44–79.

29 J. B. Peires, *The House of Phalo* (Johannesburg, 1981), p. 118.

30 The whole speech is contained in J. M. Bowker, *Speeches, Letters and Selections* (1st edn, Grahamstown, 1864, reprint, Cape Town, 1962), pp. 116–25.

31 That this new form of systematic racism arrived in South Africa through the British is implicit in Legassick, *The Frontier Tradition*; see also S. Marks and S. Trapido, 'Lord Milner and the South African State.' *History Workshop*, viii (1979), pp. 50–80. The issue is also dealt with by Saul Dubow in S. Marks and L. Trapido (eds), *The Politics of Race, Class and Nationalism* (London, 1987) and in the introduction to that work.

This work has suggested that British channels were the vehicle for the introduction of modern racist philosophy into South Africa. My own work has suggested that this happened a little earlier and that the kind of racist philosophy being articulated in Britain and the United States in the 1840s was being taken up in that same decade by the leaders of the 'English' settlers in Grahamstown. This philosophy was, at that period, also the intellectual faith of a number of senior figures in colonial affairs. A fuller discussion of this can be found in A. Ross, *John Philip: missions, race and politics in South Africa* (Aberdeen, 1986), pp. 185–215.

32 Quoted in J. J. Freeman, *A Tour of South Africa* (London, 1851), pp. 212–13.

33 Quoted from a letter to Grey in J. S. Galbraith, *Reluctant Empire* (Berkeley, 1963), pp. 257–8.

34 The radical evangelical tradition that saw the Christian gospel as having direct relevance to politics and society was now totally obscured by the domination of the quietist tradition with which it had competed in the ante-bellum period. This quietist tradition triumphed in the United Kingdom also at the same time. The terrible bloodshed of the Civil War, often blamed on the fanaticism of the abolitionists, goes a long way to explain this change in American evangelicalism; the change in Britain is more difficult to explain satisfactorily.

6. JAMES CROPPER, JOHN PHILIP AND THE *RESEARCHES IN SOUTH AFRICA*

1 W. M. Macmillan, *The Cape Colour Question: a historical survey* (London, 1927), p. 226.

2 It will be remembered that the slaves of the British Empire were emancipated in 1834, but until 1838 they were considered to be 'apprentices' and forced to serve their masters as before.

3 Cropper had indeed contributed £45 to the fund set up in Britain to cover Philip's costs. He was apparently the most generous single donor, in a list which contains many of the leading figures of the abolitionist movements, including Wilberforce and Hannah More, and many lesser lights. In total more than £1,100 was subscribed. See *The Evangelical Magazine and Missionary Chronicle*, New Series IX (1831), p. 87.

The volume also contains, on p. 135, a poem of praise for Dr Philip which is one of the worst conceivable examples of pious verse.

4 On these, see above all W. M. Macmillan, *Bantu, Boer, and Briton, the making of the South African native problem* (2nd edn., Oxford, 1963), especially chs 6–10.

5 Macmillan, *The Cape Colour Question*, p. 96, emphasis in original.

6 See, for instance, Sir George Cory, *The Rise of South Africa*, 6 vols, ii (London, 1910–1930), pp. 403–440.

7 John Philip, *Researches in South Africa: illustrating the civil, moral and religious condition of the native tribes including journals of the author's travels in the interior; together with detailed accounts of the progress of the Christian missions, exhibiting the influence of Christianity in promoting civilization*, 2 vols, ii (London, 1828), p. 365.

8 Ibid., ii, p. 370.

9 Macmillan, *The Cape Colour Question*, p. 98. It may of course have been a purely tactical decision, and later in his life he would stress the religious function of the missionary institutions, when arguing with those who, in the interests of a yet more all-inclusive economic liberalism, wished to provide their inhabitants with individual title to their land, and thus open them to purchase by Europeans. Ibid., p. 276.

10 On this conflict, see Martin Legassick 'The Griqua, The Sotho-Tswansa and the missionaries, 1780–1840: the politics of a frontier zone', (UCLA, 1969) ch. 9, although Legassick stresses the political content of the conflict more than the more strictly missiological.

11 Philip, *Researches*, i, p. xxviii.

12 Ibid., i, p. 216.

13 See above and ibid., p. 356f.

14 Ibid., i, pp. 218–19.

15 Ibid., i, p. 218.

16 John Philip, 'A narrative written for Buxton', (hereafter 'Narrative') in LMS archives, Africa Odds, Philip papers, Box 3, folder 5. Such matters were indeed taken seriously: Before Andries Waterboer dined with Governor Benjamin D'Urban in 1834 he was put through a course in table manners by Mrs Philip: Macmillan, *The Cape Colour Question*, p. 174.

17 Philip, *Researches*, i, p. 219.
18 C. Duncan Rice, 'Controversies over slavery in eighteenth and nineteenth century Scotland' in Lewis Perry and Michael Fellman (eds.), *Antislavery Reconsidered: new Perspectives on the abolitionists* (Baton Rouge, 1979), pp. 24-48.
19 Macmillan, *The Cape Colour Question*, p. 278. In his book, *John Philip (1775-1851): missions, race and politics in South Africa* (Aberdeen, 1986), pp. 65-6, which I only saw after this paper was largely completed, Andrew Ross points out that this comment by Philip does not mean that he had himself become a factory owner, but rather an independent artisan. This strengthens the case for Philip seeing his own career as a role model for the Khoi.
20 Philip, *Researches*, i, p. 218.
21 Cited in Philip, 'Narrative'.
22 Macmillan, *The Cape Colour Question*, p. 109f.
23 Philip, 'Narrative'; Harry A. Gailey jr., 'John Philip's role in Hottentot emancipation', *Journal of African History*, iii (1962), p. 426.
24 On brutality, see Henry C. Bredekamp and Susan Newton-King, 'The Subjugation of the Khoisan during the 17th and 18th Centuries', Conference on Economic Development and Racial Domination, University of the Western Cape, Bellville (1984), pp. 28-35, and Susan Newton-King's forthcoming thesis for the University of London; on the code, Hermann Giliomee, 'Die Administrasie-tydperk van Lord Caledon, 1807-1811', *Archives Year-Book for South African History*, xxix (1966), pp. 274-9; on the problem in general, D. van Arkel, G. C. Quispel and R. J. Ross, *'De Wijngaard des Heeren?': Een onderzoek naar de wortels van 'die blanke baasskap' in Zuid-Afrika* (Leiden, 1983), ch. 4.
25 Philip, *Researches*, i, pp. 142-174.
26 Ibid., pp. 175-89.
27 Ibid., pp. 384-6.
28 Ibid., i, p. 366.
29 For example, ibid., i, pp. 369-70. He also quotes from David Hume, a more unlikely source for a Christian minister, given Hume's notorious irreligion
30 Ibid., i, p. 378.
31 Macmillan, *The Cape Coloured Question*, p. 217.
32 Ibid., p. 218.
33 Philip 'Narrative', section entitled 'Beneficial effects of the labours of the missionaries in South Africa'.
34 Gailey, 'John Philip's role', pp. 431-2.
35 Philip, 'Narrative'.
36 Keith S. Hunt, *Sir Lowry Cole: Governor of Mauritius 1823-1828, Governor of the Cape of Good Hope 1828-1833; a study in colonial administration* (Durban, 1974), pp. 87, 94.
37 See, for example, William Green, *British Slave Emancipation: the sugar colonies and the grest experiment, 1830-1865* (Oxford, 1976).
38 This seemingly negative description of Buxton's activities would probably not have been disavowed by the man himself certainly not by the modern

historian most sympathetic in outlook to the abolitionists. See David Brion Davis' 'Commentary' on Roger Anstey, 'Slavery and the Protestant Ethic' in Michael Craton (ed.) *Roots and Branches; current directions in slave studies* (Waterloo, 1979), p. 180.

39 See, for example, Howard Temperley, 'Capitalism, slavery and ideology', *Past and Present*, lxv (1977), pp. 97–8, commenting on Reginald Coupland, *The British Anti-Slavery Movement* (London, 1933).

40 Eric Williams, *Capitalism and Slavery* (Chapel Hill, NC, 1944); Seymour Drescher, *Econocide: British Slavery in the Era of Abolition* (Pittsburgh, 1977).

41 David Brion Davis, *Slavery and Human Progress* (New York and Oxford, 1984), p. 119; see also *idem, The Problem of Slavery in the Age of Revolution, 1770–1823* (Ithaca and London, 1975); Temperley, 'Capitalism, slavery and ideology'; and the various essays in Christine Bolt and Seymour Drescher (eds), *Anti-Slavery, Religion and Reform: essays in memory of Roger Anstey* (Folkestone, 1980) and in James Walvin (ed.), *Slavery and British Society, 1776–1846* (London, 1982), especially David Eltis, 'Abolitionist perceptions of society after slavery'.

42 Istvan Hont and Michael Ignatieff, 'Needs and justice in *The Wealth of Nations*: an introductory essay', in *idem*. (eds), *Wealth and Virtue: The Shaping of Political Economy in the Scottish Enlightenment*.

43 Seymour Drescher, 'Public opinion and the destruction of British colonial slavery' and James Walvin, 'The propaganda of anti-slavery', both in Walvin (ed.), *Slavery and British Society*.

44 Davis, *Slavery and Human Progress*, pp. 180–91.

45 Whether or not Philip's recollections of his motives half a century earlier are accurate is beside the point. If they were, he was well ahead of his time in condemning child labour. Further, the relationship between early liberalism and the evangelical remodelling of the family, which determined its age- and sex-specificity, has not been fully discussed, so far as I am aware, but see for example Catharine Hall, 'The early formation of Victorian domestic ideology' in Sandra Burman (ed.), *Fit Work for Women* (London, 1979).

46 Macmillan, *The Cape Colour Question*, pp. 97–8.

47 Susan Newton-King, 'The labour market of the Cape colony, 1807–1828', in Shula Marks and Anthony Atmore (eds), *Economy and Society in pre-industrial South Africa* (London, 1980), pp. 171–208. The quotation is from p. 197.

48 *South African Commercial Advertiser*, 21 November 1838 (emphasis in original), cited in Nigel Worden, 'Cape slave emancipation and rural labour in a comparative context', unpublished paper, 1983.

49 Macmillan, *The Cape Colour Question*, pp. 249–59. An attempt to introduce a Squatters Act in 1851, of much the same tenor as the Vagrancy Act, was to be torpedoed by the resistance of the western Cape agricultural proletariat, or at least by fears of this among the white élite. See John Marincowitz, 'From "Colour Question" to "Agrarian Problem" at the Cape: reflections on the interim', below Chapter 7.

50 Cited in Macmillan, *The Cape Colour Question*, p. 227.

51 L. C. Duly, 'A revisit with the Cape's Hottentot Ordinance of 1828' in
    Marcelle Kooy (ed.), *Studies in Economics and Economic History: essays in
    honour of Professor H. M. Robertson* (London, 1972); J. S. Marais, *The
    Cape Coloured People, 1652–1937* (London, 1939), pp. 179–86.
52 Macmillan, *The Cape Colour Question*, p. 287.
53 It is not just the disenfranchisement of the so-called 'Cape Coloureds' in the
    1950s and 1960s which is of importance here, but also the workings of the
    Industrial Councils and Apprenticeship Boards from the late 1920s on,
    which greatly restricted 'coloured' entry into the skilled trades. On this, see
    the forthcoming Leiden PhD thesis by Pieter Van Duin on the Cape Town
    artisanate and, in the meantime, S. T. van der Horst, *Native Labour in South
    Africa* (Oxford, 1942), pp. 24–45.

7. FROM 'COLOUR QUESTION' TO 'AGRARIAN PROBLEM' AT THE CAPE:
REFLECTIONS ON THE INTERIM

1 'The Cape Colony ceased to know any legal distinction between white and
   coloured....' W. M. Macmillan, *The Cape Colour Question. A historical
   survey* (London, 1927), p. 257.
2 W. M. Macmillan, 'The problem of the Coloured people 1792–1842' in E. A.
   Walker (ed), *Cambridge History of the British Empire*, viii (London, 1963),
   p. 299.
3 Macmillan, *The Cape Colour Question*, p. 265.
4 For example, P. L. Scholtz, 'The Cape Colony, 1853–1902' in C. F. J. Muller
   (ed), *Five Hundred Years. A History of South Africa* (Pretoria, 1969); T. R.
   H. Davenport, 'The consolidation of a new society. The Cape Colony' in M.
   Wilson and L. Thompson (eds), *Oxford History of South Africa* (Oxford,
   1969).
5 These views are outlined in B. J. Liebenberg, 'Die vrystelling van die slawe in
   die Kaapkolonie en die implikasies daarvan', MA thesis, (Univ. of the
   Orange Free State, 1960), pp. 183–99.
6 For example in his article, 'The abolition of the Masters and Servants Act',
   South African Labour Bulletin, ii, (1979), Colin Bundy is quite correct to
   emphasize the continuities in the conditions of farm work and the
   composition of the farm labour force during and after slavery. However, his
   assertions that the 1841 and 1856 Masters and Servants Acts entrenched
   racial domination at the same time as it did class domination because all
   servants were 'browns' and all masters were 'whites', and that the 1873 Act
   was merely a quantitative step towards increased coercion, both fail in their
   blandness to grasp the complexities, struggles and sense of process involved
   in constituting the western-Cape's labouring classes. Macmillan stated:
   '... the study of events in the second half of the nineteenth century makes it
   clear that those have done a disservice to historical understanding who have
   deprecated the fundamental importance of the abolition of slavery.'
   Macmillan, *The Cape Colour Question*, p. 6.
7 Macmillan, *The Cape Colour Question*, pp. 267, 271.
8 Ibid., p. 267 *et seq.*

9 'Public land' includes: 'crown', 'waste', 'unappropriated' and 'government' land.
10 From 9d to 12d in 1839 to 1s 6d to 3s in the late 1840s. Church of the World Mission (CWM), London Archives, Box 17, Folder 1, Jacket C, Cape Town, Report on Salaries, March 1840; *South African Commercial Advertiser* 27 November 1839.
11 *Zuid Afrikaan* 28 September 1848.
12 CO.48.327., Desp. 27, Correspondence from the Governor re Alarm in the Western Districts, 12 February 1852.
13 For further details see J. Marincowitz, 'Proletarians, privatisers and public property rights: mission land regulations in the Western Cape between emancipation and industrialisation', unpublished paper presented at the African History Seminar, School of Oriental and African Studies (January 1985).
14 Namely, the missions at Mamre (Groenekloof), Zuurbraak, Genadendal, Elim, Pacaltsdorp, Lily Fountain and Ebenezer.
15 L. Marquard, *The Story of South Africa* (London, 1954), p. 164.
16 *A Handbook to South Africa* (London, 1891), pp. 57-9.
17 As one report from the eastern Cape put it: 'Perhaps they [the rebels] believed the lying prophet Umlangeni, that the time was arriving for chasing the whites into the sea; or possibly, ... that the British designed, by the Vagrant law, to enslave them once again.... Such rumours were spread before the outbreak of the war by some evil-disposed persons ....' Moravian Periodical Accounts (MPA), letter from Shiloh, 21 August 1851.
18 *Cape Parliamentary Papers* (CPP), memo from Genadendal, 5 November 1850.
19 *Cape Town Mail* 24 March 1849.
20 *Cape Town Mail* 14 December 1850.
21 MPA xxx, Report on Shiloh.
22 MPA, 'Shiloh's destruction', January 1851.
23 T. Kirk, 'The Cape economy and the expropriation of the Kat River settlement, 1846-1853' in S. Marks and A. Atmore, (eds) *Economy and Society in Pre-industrial South Africa* (London, 1980), pp. 226-42; MPA, Genadendal, letters of 1851, *passim*, 22 January, 23 February 1852.
24 MPA, Genadendal, letter of February 1851.
25 MPA, Genadendal, Diary for 1846, *passim*, letter, 28 February 1847, letters, March and April 1847, *passim*, May 1848, *passim*.
26 MPA, Genadendal, Letters, February-September 1851.
27 CO.48.324., Desp. 27, Gov. H. Smith's confidential report on the alarm in the Western Districts, 12 February 1852, Append. IX, 37/8 and *passim*.
28 CWM, Box 28, Folder 2, Jack. A., Zuurbraak, 1 March 1853.
29 CO.48.320., Unno., Appendix to Owen's report on Genadendal and Elim, 29 July 1851; MPA, Groenekloof, November 1851.
30 CO.48.324., Desp. 27, Governor H. Smith's confidential report on the alarm in the Western Districts, to the Secretary of State, 12 February 1852.
31 Ibid., App. XXX, pp. 82-3.
32 Ibid., App. IV, pp. 30-1. 'Kafirs' probably refers to Cape Nguni.

33 Ibid., App. IX, pp. 32-3, and *passim*.
34 Ibid., App. XVI, p. 46.
35 Ibid., App. XVIII, pp. 47-9.
36 Ibid., attached evid. of B. R. Daneel.
37 Ibid., App. XIII, p. 43; App. XVII, p. 47.
38 Ibid., App. XV, pp. 45-6; App. XII, p. 44,; CWM, Box 26, Folder 3, Jack. A, Paarl, 14 October 1851.
39 Ibid., App. V, p. 34.
40 Ibid., App. XXXI, pp. 83-5.
41 Ibid., App. XVII, p. 47.
42 Ibid.
43 T. Strauss, *War along the Orange: The Koranna and the Northern Border Wars of 1868-1869 and 1878-1879* (Cape Town, 1977).
44 C. 48.320., Unno. Desp., of Governor to Secretary of State, on panic in the Western Districts, 27 December 1851.
45 Ibid.
46 CWM, Box 26, Folder 3, Jack. B, 25 December 1851.
47 Figures derived from, A. Wilmot and J. C. C. Chase, *History of the Colony of the Cape of Good Hope* (Cape Town, 1869), p. 454; *Handbook to South Africa* (London, 1891), pp. 57-9.
48 See for example, M. Simons, 'Organised political movements' in H. W. van der Merwe and C. J. Groenewald (eds), *Occupational and Social Change among the Coloured People in South Africa* (Cape Town, 1976), p. 206.
49 D. C. Joubert, 'Die Slawe-opstand van 1808 in die Koe-, Tygerberg, en Swartland distrikte', MA thesis (Univ. of South Africa, 1946); CWM, Box 28, Folder 4, Jack. A, Paarl, 1854.
50 See for example, Macmillan, *The Cape Colour Question*, pp. 24-5.
51 For a fuller account see J. Marincowitz, 'Rural production and labour in the Western Cape, 1838 to 1888, with special reference to the wheat growing districts', PhD thesis (School of Oriental and African Studies, University of London, 1985) pp. 159-69 *et seq.*
52 G39-93., Report of the Select Committee (RSC) on labour, Evid. J. X. Merriman, pp. 146-7.
53 Some even agitated for a flogging provision to be applicable to all workers irrespective of race.
54 G3-94., RSC, Labour, 1894, pp. 6-9; see also, G39-93., evidence of S. D. Fick, pp. 340-4.
55 G39-94., RSC, Labour, evidence of J. D. van der Westhuizen, pp. 115-17, Evidence of J. P. Fourie, p. 114.
56 Ibid., Evidence of J. J. J. Fourie, casual labourer and sharecropper, pp. 95-6.
57 G39-93., RSC, Labour, evidence of P. Klopper, p. 436.
58 Ibid., evidence of C. F. J. Muller, p. 123 and *passim*.
59 C. Bundy, 'Vagabond Hollanders and runaway Englishmen. White poverty in the Cape before poor whiteism', in W. Beinart, P. Delius and S. Trapido (eds), *Putting a Plough to the Ground: accumulation and dispossession in rural South Africa 1850-1930* (Johannesburg, 1986).
60 G3-94., RSC, Labour, evidence of J. M. Heynes, pp. 39-40.

61 W. M. Macmillan, *The South African Agrarian Problem and its Historical Development* (Johannesburg, 1919) pp. 33–4.

8. W. M. MACMILLAN'S ANALYSIS ON AGRARIAN CHANGE AND AFRICAN RURAL COMMUNITIES

* Discussions with Peter Delius, Saul Dubow and Jeremy Krikler on various aspects of Macmillan's work have been very helpful, as have comments by the editors.

1 W. M. Macmillan, *The South African Agrarian Problem and Its Historical Development* (Johannesburg, 1919). The 1974 reprint, introduced by F. A. van Jaarsveld (see comment below), has been used.

2 Ibid., and W. M. Macmillan, *Complex South Africa: an economic footnote to history* (London, 1930).

3 C. Bundy, *The Rise and Fall of the South African Peasantry* (London, 1979), ch. 5; and C. Bundy, 'Peasants in Herschel: a case study of a South African frontier district' in S. Marks and A. Atmore (eds), *Economy and Society in Pre-industrial South Africa* (London, 1980).

4 Macmillan, *Complex South Africa*, p. 121.

5 See especially chapters 2 and 4 in this collection by H. Macmillan and J. Butler respectively, and W. M. Macmillan, *My South African Years* (Cape Town, 1975).

6 During the 1920s, the academics working in this field seem to have been quite closely involved with the growing research branches of the Department of Agriculture. For example, H. D. Leppan and G. J. Bosman, *Field Crops in South Africa* (Johannesburg, 1923); S. H. Frankel, *Co-operation and Competition in the Marketing of Maize in South Africa* (London, 1926); A. R. Saunders, *Maize in South Africa* (Johannesburg, 1930). R. Lehfeldt, *The Natural Resources of South Africa* (Johannesburg, 1922), was an early attempt at a more overarching approach, which does include figures for production in the African reserves, but which is largely descriptive and statistical.

7 The 1920s also saw the beginnings of an interest in agrarian issues by the Left and the Communist Party in South Africa, culminating in the emphasis laid on agrarian transformation in the 'native republic' programme. Those on the left would clearly have shared Macmillan's general approach to agrarian analysis. Discussion at the conference did not reveal much about the relationship between Macmillan and the left-wing intellectuals but contributions suggested that his work influenced members of the ISL and CP rather than vice versa.

8 Macmillan, *Complex South Africa*, p. 8

9 Macmillan, *Agrarian Problem*, p. 6.

10 Ibid., p. 84. While Macmillan drew on such key government commissions which assembled and analysed large quantities of contemporary evidence, his sections in the *Agrarian Problem* on poor whiteism and agricultural change in the sheep-farming areas of the Karoo and Eastern Cape may have

influenced the very significant *Final Report of the Drought Investigation Commission, October 1923*, UG 49-1923. This report, however, makes far more of ecological decay (its major concern) as a cause of poor whiteism than Macmillan, and attributes less significance to the concentration of farm ownership.

11 Newspaper cuttings in Macmillan's papers, in the possession of Mrs M. Macmillan, indicate that many of his general propositions had been formulated in the early 1920s — see *Rand Daily Mail*, May 1921 and *The Star*, 25, 26, 27 and 28 August 1924; 25 September 1924. Macmillan uses the term 'Native', or occasionally 'Bantu', in *Complex South Africa*.

12 Macmillan, *Complex South Africa*, p. 16. It is significant that Macmillan uses the term 'reservoir' in this sense, and he also applies it to African reserves. Whether or not he was the first to do so is unclear, but the usage did become a central feature of later analyses of the reserves.

13 Ibid., p. 16.

14 Ibid., p. 18.

15 Ibid.

16 See especially, ibid., ch. 16 'The South African whole'.

17 Ibid., pp. 171 and 260.

18 Macmillan, *Agrarian Problem*, p. 21. Some of the points in the following section have been taken from 'Introduction', W. Beinart and P. Delius, *Putting a Plough to the Ground* (Johannesburg, 1986).

19 Macmillan, *Agrarian Problem*, p. 24ff.

20 Ibid., pp. 63, 64.

21 Ibid.

22 Ibid., p. 85.

23 Macmillan, *Complex South Africa*, p. 71.

24 Ibid., p. 15: 'The Natives today are a conquered and economically dependent mass, very nearly a proletariat.'

25 Ibid., pp. 195, 196.

26 Ibid., p. 196.

27 Ibid., pp. 197, 199, 213. Macmillan is, however, quite approving of communal tenure, as opposed to individual tenure, given the difficult conditions facing reserve districts, because of its greater flexibility. See ibid., p. 189ff.

28 Ibid., p. 196.

29 Ibid.

30 See Chapter 2 in this collection by Hugh Macmillan. For discussions of the liberal ideas and anthropological work see Paul Rich, *White Power and the Liberal Conscience* (Manchester, 1984), especially ch. 3; Saul Dubow, 'Race, civilisation and culture: the elaboration of segregationist discourse in the inter-war years' in S. Marks and S. Trapido (eds), *The Politics of Race, Class and Nationalism in Twentieth Century South Africa* (London, 1987); S. Dubow, '"Understanding the native mind": anthropology, cultural adaption and the elaboration of a segregationist discourse in South Africa, c. 1920-36', unpublished paper, (History Workshop, Johannesburg, 1984).

31 C. W. de Kiewiet, *A History of South Africa, Social and Economic* (London,

1941); E. Walker, *The Frontier Tradition in South Africa* (Oxford, 1930) and *The Great Trek* (London, 1934); W. K. Hancock, *Survey of British Commonwealth Affairs*, ii (London, 1940, 1942); P. J. van der Merwe, *Die Trekboer in die Geskiedenis van die Kaapkolonie (1652-1842)* (Cape Town, 1938).

32 H. Robertson, '150 years of economic contact between white and black', *South African Journal of Economics*, ii (1934).

33 Martin Legassick, 'The frontier tradition in South African historiography' in Marks and Atmore, *Economy and Society*. Legassick refers to Macmillan as one of those who helped to define the frontier tradition although he does not suggest that Macmillan was the earliest liberal protagonist of this view, nor does he explore those elements in Macmillan's analysis which qualified his view of the primacy of the frontier. The alternative view of agrarian history was explored particularly in Trapido's work.

34 M. Morris, 'The development of capitalism in South African agriculture: class struggles in the countryside', *Economy and Society*, v (1976).

35 The Macmillan papers contain a little correspondence with government officials about the Herschel research. The quote is from a letter by Munscheid, the magistrate in Herschel, to the Chief Native Commissioner Ciskei (10 August 1927) asking for permission to forward his comments on the survey to Macmillan, in the Cape Archives, Magistrate and Bantu Commissioner Herschel papers, 2/SPT 18 file 1/12/6. Ironically this file is entitled 'ethnology and customs' — a description of which Macmillan would not have approved.

36 Macmillan, *Complex South Africa*, p. 185.

37 Ibid., p. 186.

38 E. Hellman, *Rooiyard; a sociological survey of an urban native slumyard* (Manchester, 1948). Hellmann's research was done in 1934 but published much later by the Rhodes-Livingstone Institute. She suggests in her preface that she would have liked, in retrospect, to place her findings in the context of a more detailed analysis of the economic conditions which gave rise to the slumyard, but in fact there are many pointers in the survey to this larger context.

39 M. Hunter, *Reaction to Conquest* (London, 1936).

40 Ibid., p. 546 and see also her quote from the Native Economic Commission at p. 105. For rich and poor in African society see especially p. 135ff. There is of course a large amount of detailed information about the economic position in the reserves in this book and Hunter may not be wrong to see a considerable degree of autonomy still operating.)

41 My own as yet unpublished re-evaluation of the quantity of production suggests that this might have been the case. C. Simpkins, 'Agricultural production in the African reserves of South Africa, 1918-1969', *Journal of Southern African Studies*, viii (1981) argues that there was at least no significant fall in the value of production in the reserves at this time — although the agricultural census statistics he uses are, as suggested below, rather dubious.

42 Cape Archives, 2/SPT 18 1/12/6, Munscheid to Macmillan, 10 August 1927;

Macmillan papers, H. A. Key to Macmillan, 11 January 1930.
43 Macmillan papers, Munscheid to Macmillan, 23 October 1927.
44 Cape Archives, 2/SPT 18 1/12/6, Munscheid to Macmillan, 10 August 1927.
45 Macmillan papers, Key to Macmillan, 11 January 1930. Key asked Macmillan not to mention his name at all as a source: 'Don't make any allusion to me please — "Mum" is the word.'
46 See note 41 above.
47 Macmillan papers, Key to Macmillan, 11 January 1930.
48 Macmillan, *Complex South Africa*, pp. 177-81.
49 Ibid., p. 155. It is worth noting that, partly because of this very high value assigned to milk production, Macmillan's figures suggest that only ca. 8.4 per cent of the total value of income from agriculture (£163,086) and wages (ca. £15,000) came from wages returned to the district. Even if the whole 'deficit' between value of imports and value of exports calculated by Macmillan (£35,000 to £50,000) is taken to represent wage income, then wages would make up at most 23.5 per cent of total income from all sources. This is much lower than in Simpkins' values for the same period. However, the high value for milk production does not affect Macmillan's calculations of the deficit between imports and agricultural exports as milk is not an exported item.
50 See W. Beinart, '*Amafelandawonye* (The Diehards): Popular protest and women's movements in Herschel district in the 1920s' in W. Beinart and C. Bundy, *Hidden Struggles in Rural South Africa* (London, 1986).
51 Macmillan, *Complex South Africa*, pp. 145, 146.
52 Ibid., p. 147.
53 Ibid., p. 147.
54 Ibid., p. 150.
55 Ibid., p. 150.
56 See note 30; also M. Legassick, 'The making of South African "Native Policy", 1903-1923: the origins of segregation', unpublished seminar paper, Institute of Commonwealth Studies, (University of London, 1971); and M. Legassick, 'Race, industrialisation and social change in South Africa: the case of R. F. A. Hoernlé', *African Affairs*, 75 (1975). Marks and Atmore in *Economy and Society*, 64 use the term 'liberal-segregationism' to refer also to Smuts' position (or at least this rhetoric in speeches in Britain) in the late 1920s when he was in opposition to Hertzog, Rich and Dubow seem to be more restrictive in their references primarily to intellectuals and academics such as Hoernlé, Brookes and Loram. All would seem to agree that, as Hertzog appropriated the ideology of segregation in the late 1920s, liberals shifted away from this position. Peter Walshe, *The Rise of African Nationalism in South Africa* (London, 1970), pp. 100-6 illustrates the extent to which Mahabane, ANC President in the mid-1920s, was prepared to accommodate to segregationist policy: accepting with the Cape Congress that a separate voters' roll may be necessary; accepting separate urban residential areas for blacks; and accepting a degree of segregation on the land, although not on the terms then offered. See also Paul Rich, *White Power*, p. 26; Shula Marks, 'Natal, the Zulu Royal Family and the ideology of segregation', *Journal of Southern African Studies*, iv (1978) for Dube; W.

311

Beinart, *The Political Economy of Pondoland* (Cambridge, 1982), pp. 123, 154ff, for Cingo; Beinart and Bundy, *Hidden Struggles* for radical Transkeian movements in favour of chieftaincy.

57 A few notes in Macmillan's diary indicate that he was aware that many Herschel African voters had supported the 'Bond'. (J. W. Sauer who moved the Natives Land Act was their MP up to his death in 1913.) By the 1920s, however, some seemed to vote for Hertzog against Smuts' South African Party which had incorporated the Cape Afrikaner Bond. Radical Cape nationalist spokesmen such as the Garveyite Thaele, who was active in Herschel in the late 1920s, advocated a vote for Hertzog as they mistrusted Smuts' links with mining capital and hoped for gains from segregationist policy. Macmillan also indicated that he was aware of the deep divisions between 'Witvoets (Govt. party)' and die-hards who opposed them and suggested that the die-hards, whose position has been described above, had a case as they had lost out in the distribution of land.

9. W. M. MACMILLAN, SOUTH AFRICAN SEGREGATION AND COMMONWEALTH RACE RELATIONS 1919–1938

1 Edgar Brookes, *The Colour Problems of South Africa* (Lovedale, 1934), p. 79.

2 For Macmillan's biography and intellectual formation, see Chapters 1 and 2 of this volume.

3 S. M. Molema, *The Bantu Past and Present* (Edinburgh, 1920), pp. 366–7.

4 W. M. Macmillan, *The South African Agrarian Problem and its Historical Development* (Johannesburg, 1919), p. 101.

5 Macmillan, *My South African Years*, (Cape Town, 1975), p. 146; see also John Marincowitz, 'From "Colour Question" to "Agrarian Problem"': reflections on the interim', Chapter 7 above.

6 Ernest Stubbs papers, Church of the Province Archives, University of the Witwatersrand, W. M. Macmillan to E. Stubbs, 4 August 1923.

7 W. M. Macmillan, 'Native land and the provisions of the Natives Land Act of 1913' in *European and Bantu: papers and addresses read at the conference on Native Affairs 27 to 29 September 1923* (Cape Town, 1924), p. 21.

8 Macmillan, 'Native land and the provisions of the Natives Land Act of 1913', p. 24; for the ideas and influence of Stubbs see Paul Rich, 'The origins of apartheid ideology: the case of Ernest Stubbs and Transvaal native administration, 1902–1932', *African Affairs*, lxxxix, 3–4 (1976), pp. 229–51.

9 W. M. Macmillan, *The Land, The Native and Unemployment* (Johannesburg, 1924), p. 5.

10 *Ibid.*, p. 11.

11 *Ibid.*, p. 4.

12 R. A. Lehfeldt, 'Labour conditions in South Africa', *South African Journal of Science*, xvii, 1 (November 1920), p. 92; see also Bruce K. Murray, *Wits: the early years* (Johannesburg, 1982), p. 142.

13 See, for example, Edgar Brookes, 'The economic aspects of the native problem', *South African Journal of Science*, xxi (1924), pp. 651–63.

14 J. D. Rheinallt Jones, 'Drift and danger in native affairs', *The South African Quarterly*, vii, 3 (June–November 1924).
15 Church of the Province Archives, University of the Witwatersrand, 'Minutes of the Meeting of the Joint Council held at the University, Johannesburg', 17 August 1923.
16 *Report of the Native Affairs Commission for the Years 1925 and 1926*, U.g. 17–'20, p. 3.
17 J. B. M. Hertzog papers, Union Archives, Pretoria, Box 27, J. B. M. Hertzog to Kennedy, 30 March 1925.
18 Ibid., Box 83, J. D. R J to J. B. M. Hertzog, 16 November 1925. For Rheinallt Jones's hopes for an African 'parliament' see Archives of the South African Institute of Race Relations, (ARSAIRR) University of the Witwatersrand, B72(a), undated memo. Howard Pim, however, was rather more cautious towards the proposals considering that the idea of seven elected native representatives would not be acceptable to white opinion and raised the same spectre of 'chaos' as in the period of Reconstruction after the American Civil War: ibid., Howard Pim to J. B. M. Hertzog, 1 January 1926 encl. 'Note on General Hertzog's Smithfield proposals'.
19 J. D. Rheinallt Jones, 'The land question in South Africa' paper presented to the European–Bantu Conference convened by the Federal Council of the Dutch Reformed Churches at Cape Town, 31 January–2 February 1927, p. 6. The paper was considerably shaped by Macmillan's 1919 work *The South African Agrarian Problem* and championed John Philip as 'a great segregationist' (p. 3). Rheinallt Jones's paper did much to win the financial backing from the Phelps-Stokes Fund and Thomas Jesse Jones promised Jones further 'financial co-operation' after being 'deeply impressed by the statesmanship of your analysis and recommendations', ARSAIRR, T. Jesse Jones to J. D. R J., 11 April 1927.
20 Patrick Duncan papers, Jagger Library, University of Cape Town, BC294 D2.31 W. M. Macmillan to Patrick Duncan, 16 May 1925.
21 W. M. Macmillan, 'Folly of the colour bar', *The Cape Times*, 29 January 1926, Macmillan, *My South African Years*, pp. 185–6.
22 W. M. Macmillan, 'At the roots II — crowded native areas', *The Cape Times*, 12 April 1926.
23 *Umteteli wa Bantu*, 20 November and 4 December 1926.
24 J. Howard Pim papers, University of the Witwatersrand, A88I/BM, A. Roberts to H. Pim, 15 January 1924.
25 Ernest Stubbs papers, E. Stubbs to McLeod, 25 November 1926.
26 ARSAIRR, 'Minutes of the meeting of the Joint Council held in the Exploration Buildings', 17 December 1925. However, Victor Selope Thema condemned the 'Sedition Clause' in the Bill as likely to 'rouse suspicion and to foment unrest among the Bantu people', *Umteteli wa Bantu*, 9 April 1927.
27 J. Howard Pim Papers, W. M. Macmillan to H. Pim, 17 December 1926.
28 Sydney Olivier, *The Anatomy of African Misery* (London, 1927), p. 61.
29 Martin Chanock, *Unconsummated Union: Britain, Rhodesia and South Africa, 1900–45* (Manchester, 1977), pp. 201 –2.

30 W. M. Macmillan, *The Cape Colour Question* (London, 1927), pp. 10, 287.

31 London, ILP, 1906. For an analysis of Olivier's thought see P. Rich, *Race and Empire in British Politics*, (Cambridge, 1986), pp. 72-6.

32 ARSAIRR, 'Minutes of the Joint Council meeting held in the Bantu Men's Social Centre', 4 August 1927.

33 W. M. Macmillan, '"Solving" the South African native problem', *New Statesman*, 9 June 1928; 'South African nationalism', ibid., 13 July 1929.

34 Margery Perham, *African Apprenticeship* (London, 1974), p. 138.

35 Macmillan, *My South African Years*, pp. 193-4; Sir Philip Mitchell, *African Afterthoughts* (London, 1954), p. 103.

36 W. M. Macmillan, *Bantu, Boer, and Briton: the making of the South African native problem* (London, 1929), pp. 200, 289.

37 Philip Mitchell Diaries, Rhodes House Library, Oxford, MSS Afr. 101, entry for 3 November 1929.

38 W. M. Macmillan, *Complex South Africa* (London, 1930), p. 8. Edwin Smith, in reviewing this book, criticized it for failing to study the economic condition of the African society in Herschel before the advent of the European 'culture contact' and 'before the great crisis in their life arrived' and also the change in African mental attitudes to this transformation, *Africa*, iv, 3, (1931), pp. 370-2.

39 I. Schapera, 'Economic changes in South African native life', *Africa*, i, 2 (1928), pp. 170-88.

40 Bronislaw Malinowski, 'The rationalization of anthropology and administration', *Africa*, iii, 4 (1930), p. 406. 'Practical anthropology'; *Africa*, ii, 1 (1929), pp. 22-38.

41 P. E. Mitchell, 'The anthropologist and the practical man', *Africa*, iii, 2 (1930), p. 220. See also Wendy James, 'The anthropologist as reluctant imperialist' in Talal Assad (ed.), *Anthropology and the Colonial Encounter* (London, 1972), pp. 41-69.

42 W. M. Macmillan papers, in the private possession of Mrs M. Macmillan, P. Mitchell to W. M. Macmillan, 2 November 1930.

43 Ibid., P. Mitchell to W. M. Macmillan, 17 June 1932.

44 J. Howard Pim papers, A881/CC44 H. Pim to F. A. W. Lucas, 9 September 1930. Pim was especially impressed by the empirical study of the Rev. James Henderson, Principal of Lovedale, in the Victoria East district, showing the decline of a peasant economy and dependency on the cash income from labour migration.

45 Howard Pim, *Introduction to Bantu Economics* (Lovedale, 1930), p. 5.

46 A. W. Hoernlé, 'An outline of the native conception of education', *Africa* iv, 2 (1931), p. 163. For Winifred Hoernlé's importance in the development of anthropological studies at the University of the Witwatersrand see Murray, *Wits*, pp. 137-8.

47 A. W. Hoernlé, 'New aims and methods in social anthropology', *South African Journal of Science*, xxx (1933), pp. 76-7.

48 P. Rich, *White Power and the Liberal Conscience* (Manchester, 1984), pp. 58-60.

49 J. Howard Pim papers, BL4/123, R. F. Alfred Hoernlé and J. D. Rheinallt

Jones, Report on Behalf of the University of the Witwatersrand and the South African Institute of Race Relations to the President, Rockefeller Foundation, 1930.

50 *Native Economic Commission*, Minutes of Evidence, King Williams Town, 26 June 1931, ev. Marmaduke Gwynn Apthorp, C. N. C. Cape Province, p. 4476. See though, W. M. Macmillan, 'Overcrowded native reserves' *The Star*, 6 August 1932. Apthorp's views do not appear to have been accepted at the local level in Herschel where the Native Commissioner wrote in 1930 that the district was 'so hopelessly eroded that it is very difficult to tackle the position on a small scale. To do any good a great deal of expenditure would be involved, which would hardly be equal to the good done', NST 9496 138/400(i) N. A. King, N. C. Herschel to C. N. C. King Williams Town, 9 October 1930.

51 *Imvo Zabantsundu*, 13 September 1932.

52 Saul Dubow, '"That Curious Native Administration Bill" of 1927, and the native Administration Department', ICS seminar paper (London, 1985).

53 Perham, *African Apprenticeship*, pp. 51–2.

54 *Umteteli wa Bantu*, 6 October 1928, 25 May 1929, 28 June and 30 September 1930, 24 June and 1 July 1933. Rheinallt Jones denied that the Joint Council was trying to usurp African political activity, arguing that the Joint Council was no substitute for a 'strong and healthy' Congress — *Umteteli*, 13 October 1928. Eventually the Joint Council arranged in 1933 for a motion to be moved by D. D. T. Jabavu in response to 'Enquirer's' attack that the Joint Council had 'among its principles of policy, the encouragement of Bantu leadership through Bantu organisation for self upliftment'. The motion was accepted unanimously. 'Minutes of a Meeting of the Johannesburg Joint Council', 11 September 1933.

55 *Umteteli wa Bantu* 5 June and 23 October 1926.

56 'Minutes of the Joint Council Meeting held in the Bantu Men's Social Centre', 4 August 1927.

57 Peter Walshe, *The Rise of African Nationalism in South Africa* (London, 1970), p. 218.

58 'Minutes of a Meeting of the Joint Council in the Bantu Men's Social Centre', 11 February 1935.

59 ARSAIRR B71(a) J. J. G. Garson (Aliwal North) to J. D. R J, 9 December 1932; Sec. Ladybrand Joint Council to Adviser, SAIRR, 26 August 1932; Winifred Holtby papers, Hull Public Library, W. G. Ballinger to W. Holtby, 18 January 1933.

60 ARSAIRR (4) H. Pim to J. D. R J, 3 October 1930.

61 Ibid., Joint Council Mss, 1931–34, J. D. R J to R. Dunlop, 16 April 1931.

62 'Minutes of a Meeting of the Johannesburg Joint Council held at the Bantu Men's Social Centre', 14 November 1932.

63 'Minutes of a Meeting of the Johannesburg Joint Council held at the Bantu Men's Social Centre', 9 February 1931.

64 Martin Legassick, 'Liberalism, social control and liberation in South Africa', unpublished seminar paper, University of Warwick, 1976.

65 *Umteteli wa Bantu*, 16 September 1933. On the Joint Councils, Macmillan

later recollected, 'Perhaps I didn't like to admit that they were politically of so little use', *My South African Years*, p. 228.

66 ARSAIRR (4) J. D. R J to S. B. Theunissen, 18 November 1932.

67 *The Midland News*, 13 January 1934; Walshe, *The Rise of African Nationalism*, p. 218.

68 *Umteteli wa Bantu*, 29 September 1934. Ironically 'Enquirer' upheld Seme as standing 'for the genuine African race leadership as against the hybrid Euro-Bantu leadership under the Joint Council', *Umteteli wa Bantu*, 17 February 1934.

69 For Macmillan's relationship to the SAIRR and the development of Bantu Studies at Wits see H. Macmillan 'Paralyzed conservatives', Chapter 2 above and above p. 204.

70 Macmillan, *My South African Years*, p. 242.

71 For Cripp's writings on South African segregation, see Arthur Shearley Cripps, 'An Africa of the Africans', *International Review of Mission*, 10 (1921), pp. 99–109 in which a plea is made for an enlarged African reserve on lines earlier suggested by Maurice Evans in *Black and White in South East Africa*. See also Arthur Shearley Cripps, *An Africa for Africans* (London, 1927).

72 Leonard Barnes, *The New Boer War* (London, 1932); Chanock, *Unconsummated Union*, pp. 202–3.

73 Lionel Curtis papers, Bodleian Library, Oxford, 91, W. M\ Macmillan to L. Curtis, 16 May 1935.

74 M. Perham and L. Curtis, *The Protectorates of South Africa* (Oxford, 1935).

75 London Group on African Affairs papers, Rhodes House, Oxford, Mss Afr. S 1427 1/B L. Barnes to F. Livie-Noble, 11 July 1933.

76 Lionel Curtis Papers, 91, L. Curtis to W. M. Macmillan, 30 May 1935.

77 W. M. Macmillan, 'Colour and the Commonwealth', *New Statesman*, 1 June 1935.

78 W. M. Macmillan, *Warning from the West Indies* (Harmondsworth, 1936). Gordon Lewis has noted that Macmillan's 'exposé of West Indian social disorganisation and economic retardation' in the book served as 'an effective antidote to the Bloomsbury cult of the simple and healthy savage that infected so much thinking even of the British Left, and which was largely responsible for the cult of peasant ownership in the more liberal-minded of British officials in the Caribbean area from Sir Henry Norman to Lord Olivier', G. Lewis, *The Growth of the Modern West Indies* (New York and London, 1968), p. 93.

79 W. M. Macmillan in the 'Discussion' following Margery Perham, 'Some problems of indirect rule in Africa', *Journal of the African Society*, xxxiv, cxxcx (1935), pp. 16–17. See also *New Statesman*, 26 September 1936.

80 W. M. Macmillan, *Africa Emergent* (London, 1938), p. 184.

81 Ibid., p. 181.

82 London Group on African Affairs, *Memorandum on Rights and Liberties of Africans: No 2 South African native policy* (London, 1937), p. 18.

83 R. F. Alfred Hoernlé, *South African Native Policy and the Liberal Spirit* (Cape Town, 1939). For an analysis of Hoernlé's thought see Paul Rich, 'R.

F. A. Hoernlé, idealism and the liberal response to South African segregation', paper presented to the South African History Workshop, Wesleyan University, Conn., April 1986.

84 R. Shepherd papers, Cory Library, Rhodes University, Grahamstown, MS16, 322, R. F. A. Hoernlé to R. H. W. Shepherd, 10 October 1940. For Hoernlé's thinking in the context of a wider South African debate on ethnic pluralism see Paul Rich, 'Ethnic pluralism, apartheid and the crisis of the South African state', ICS seminar paper (London, June 1986).

10. MACMILLAN AS CRITIC OF EMPIRE: THE IMPACT OF AN HISTORIAN ON
COLONIAL POLICY

1 This term is used to embrace the central tenets of British colonial policy in the tropical colonies at this time, that colonies should live entirely from their own financial resources. Revenues had to pay for all expenditures. Given the poverty of colonial economies this meant that 'development' was limited to public works of transport such as could increase trade, and therefore customs revenues. The number of officials and services was kept to the minimum which revenues could bear, hence systems of indirect rule in West Africa and reliance upon settlers in East and Central Africa, which kept costs to a minimum. It was axiomatic that the British taxpayer should not be called upon to subsidize colonial governments; where this was unavoidable because revenue did not balance expenditure the system of 'Treasury control' came into operation, with the purpose of removing the need for 'grants-in-aid' as soon as possible by the practice of strict economy. For a detailed study of the system, and of the nature of 'development' in these years see S. Constantine, *The Making of British Colonial Development Policy, 1914-40* (London, 1984).

2 There was a fourth, the Marxists, but these played no role in the colonial reform movement because they had no programme for constructive reform of the system of colonial rule. For them, imperialism was incapable of reform, being simply a higher stage of capitalism designed to extract wealth from the colonies in order to postpone the crisis of capitalism in the metropole and thereby obscure the inevitability of class struggle. Colonial rule, by its very nature, could only intensify 'backwardness'. 'Progress' would only come to regions like Africa through the working out of a revolutionary dialectic. For a characteristic Marxist view of the time see H. Rathbone, 'The problem of African independence', *Labour Monthly*, 18 (1936), quoted in Penelope Hetherington, *British Paternalism and Africa, 1920-1940* (London, 1978) an excellent analysis of writings about Africa in the inter-war period.

3 My use of this word is in no way meant to be pejorative, but indicates the sense of rebellion and frustration which runs through this type of writing, as well as the reception which it received at the hands of pro-imperialist sentiment. The vast majority of former colonial officials who wrote memoirs or commentaries on their experiences appear to have accepted an

unwritten code that such writing should not contain any serious criticism of colonial policy or practice.

4 N. Leys, *Kenya* (London, 1924) and *Last Chance in Kenya* (London, 1931).

5 Leys, *Last Chance in Kenya*, p. 72.

6 William McGregor Ross, *Kenya from Within* (London, 1927).

7 Frank Melland, 'Our colonial complacency', *Nineteenth Century*, 118 (1935), pp. 151-62. Melland wrote a large number of articles between 1920 and 1938, which are listed in Hetherington, *British Paternalism*, pp. 173-4.

8 Oldham worked these techniques to powerful effect in the Kenyan crisis of 1921-23, mobilizing the support of the Archbishop of Canterbury and other bishops in the House of Lords. It was Oldham who suggested the 'native paramountcy' concept to the Duke of Devonshire, then Colonial Secretary. Thereafter, missionaries constantly stressed the literal wording of the declaration as a kind of *magna carta* of African rights. See Roland Oliver, *The Missionary Factor in East Africa* (London, 1952). Oldham was appointed member of the Hilton Young Commission of 1928-29 and supported the majority report which rejected responsible government for Kenya and proposed the 'Central Authority' system to unify 'native policy' in the East African territories under imperial control without settler participation.

9 Hetherington, *British Paternalism* pp. 71-2, 175-6, lists Oldham's long list of writings on African questions, concerned with the impact of missions on society, education, labour and race relations.

10 For example, J. H. Harris, *Slavery or 'Sacred Trust'?* (London, 1926), p. 109. For a list of Harris' writings, see Hetherington, *British Paternalism*, pp. 166-7.

11 Partha Sarathi Gupta, *Imperialism and the British Labour Movement, 1914-1916* (London, 1975), p. 399 and index, p. 440.

12 Hetherington, *British Paternalism*, p. 16.

13 W. M. Macmillan, *The Road to Self-rule: a study in colonial evolution* (New York, 1959), p. 206.

14 Gupta, *Imperialism and the British Labour Movement*, pp. 225-31.

15 J. A. Hobson, *Imperialism: a study* (London, 1899).

16 H. N. Brailsford, *The War of Steel and Gold* (London, 1914). Brailsford joined the staff of the *New Statesman and Nation* in the 1930s and remained a leader writer there until 1946.

17 *Labour and the Nation*, 1928, p. 44, quoted in Kenneth Robinson, *The Dilemmas of Trusteeship: aspects of British colonial policy between the wars* (London, 1965), pp. 57-8.

18 Hetherington, *British Paternalism*, pp. 67-73 and 96-8 shows how writers on the left feared the impact of industrialization and the destructive effects of the formation of 'class' in Africa and appeared to believe that development of social services could be accomplished through African peasant proprietorship in predominantly agricultural economies.

19 When Malcolm MacDonald, on the eve of the war, summoned a meeting in the Carlton Hotel to discuss the 'future of Africa' all those invited, other than his attending officials, were historians, with the exceptions of Lord

Lugard and Julian Huxley, the biologist.

20 Quotations from Ronald Robinson, 'Oxford in imperial historiography' in F. Madden and D. K. Fieldhouse (eds), *Oxford and the Ideal of the Commonwealth: essays presented to Sir Edgar Williams* (London, 1982), p. 36.

21 Coupland posed the rhetorical question at the end of a passage which argued that African colonies would follow India in the process of development of self-governing institutions 'smoothly to its end'. Coupland, *Empire in these Days* (London, 1935), p. 179.

22 Madden and Fieldhouse, *Oxford and the Ideal of the Commonwealth*, p. 13.

23 On the Round Table movement see John E. Kendle, *The Round Table Movement and Imperial Union* (Toronto, 1975). For Curtis' career in its Oxford setting see Deborah Lavin, 'Lionel Curtis and the idea of the Commonwealth' in Madden and Fieldhouse, *Oxford and the Ideal of the Commonwealth*, p. 97-119.

24 Lavin, 'Lionel Curtis', p. 113.

25 For details of the planning of what became the *African Survey* see Lavin, 'Lionel Curtis', pp. 114-15; Stephen King-Hall, *Chatham House* (London, 1937); Lucy Mair, 'The social sciences in Africa', *Human Organisation*, xix, 3 (1960), pp. 98-106; and Lord Lothian's foreword to Hailey, *African Survey*, 1938 edn.

26 There is some irony in the fact that the promoters of a 'Durham Report' for Africa should have looked to US philanthropy as the source of their funds but this too was a symptom of 'minimal government'. By this time they had little hope that the Colonial Office would, or could, pay for research about Africa. Colonial Office files in the CO 847 series after 1935 contain numerous requests for financial support for research proposals from academics, especially from Oxford. Coupland was pressing for financial support for a history of Africa, there were proposals for studies of land tenure, social relations, educational problems and labour questions, but nothing came of these until Malcolm MacDonald became Colonial Secretary and threw his support behind the advocacy of a massive research effort expounded in Hailey's *African Survey*.

27 Curtis to Keppel, of the Carnegie Foundation, 20 July 1931, quoted by Lavin, 'Lionel Curtis', p. 114.

28 See note 35 below.

29 Hailey was born in 1872 and after taking a first class honours degree in Litt. Hum. at Oxford, joined the Indian Civil Service in 1895. In 1907 he became Secretary of the Punjab government, and in the following year a Deputy Secretary in the Government of India. After serving as Chief Commissioner of Delhi from 1912 to 1918, Hailey became a Member of the Governor-General's Executive Council, Finance and Home Departments, from 1919-24. From 1924-28 he served as Governor of the Punjab, and from 1928-30 and, again, from 1931-34 as Governor of the United Provinces.

30 Quotations from Jean van der Poel, *Selections from the Smuts Papers*, vi (Cambridge, 1973), p. 490, Smuts to M. C. Gillett, 24 January 1940.

31 Coupland later accused Macmillan of 'rocking the boat' on the issue of the

High Commission Territories of South Africa in 1935; see W. M. Macmillan, *My South African Years* (Cape Town, 1975), p. 247.

32 Macmillan, *My South African Years*, pp. 223-30.

33 W. M. Macmillan, 'Southern Rhodesia and the development of Africa', *Journal of the African Society*, xxxii, (1933) pp. 294-8; 'The development of Africa', *Political Quarterly*, iii (1932), pp. 552-69; 'Position of native education in British Africa', *United Empire*, new series, xxv (1934), pp. 137-42; 'The importance of the educated African', *Journal of the Royal African Society*, xxxiii (1934), pp. 137-42; 'Colour and the Commonwealth', *New Statesman and Nation*, 1 June 1935.

34 Macmillan, *My South African Years*, p. 224.

35 Macmillan discovered thirty-seven years later that his own candidacy had failed for political reasons, when a friend of his son unearthed in the Lothian papers a letter from Curtis to Carr Saunders of 27 June 1933 stating that Macmillan 'was of course one of the people whose names have been thought of in the last two years [for the Survey]. But had we given him the job we should have had against us the Union Government in South Africa, and all the settler elements in East Africa.' It seems also that the same considerations cost Macmillan a Leverhulme Fellowship, for which he was turned down later. Macmillan, *My South African Years*, p. 224.

36 Mona Macmillan, *Champion of Africa*, p. 108. Hetherington, *British Paternalism*, p. 98, notes that *Africa Emergent* and the *African Survey* both ultimately stress the same theses but she does not comment on the fact that Hailey had prior access to Macmillan's draft.

37 W. M. Macmillan *Warning from the West Indies: a tract for the Empire* (Harmondsworth, 1938), p. 25. These were the first two sentences of the first edition of 1936.

38 Ibid., p. 37.

39 Ibid., p. 78.

40 ibid., p. 78.

41 Ibid., p. 85. The words were used in the context of landlessness and unemployment, but the theme runs implicitly throughout the whole book, and is of course implicit in the title.

42 Ibid., p. 173.

43 Ibid., pp. 171-2.

44 Ibid., Preface to 1st edn., p. 19.

45 Ibid., p. 25.

46 Ibid., p. 78.

47 Ibid., pp. 27-8.

48 Ibid., p. 30.

49 CO 318/422/71092, minutes by Clauson from 30 March to 1 May, 1936, cited in Gupta, *Imperialism and the Labour Movement*, p. 246.

50 Macmillan, *Warning from the West Indies*, p. 11, Preface to the 1938 Penguin edn.

51 Gupta, *Imperialism and the Labour Movement*, p. 229.

52 CO/96/758/31228, 'Notes ... made by Professor Macmillan', 20 January 1939. Macmillan was arguing that the Gold Coast was so different from

Nigeria that its next Governor should not be a man with Nigerian experience.

53 Macmillan *My South African Years*, pp. 244-5.

54 Macmillan's missionary background and research is clearly at the root of his thinking. Chapter 1 of *Africa Emergent* was entitled 'the mission of civilization in backward Africa', a phrasing which could have been taken from almost any work of the nineteenth-century evangelical writers. The theme of the chapter, however, is that private missionary zeal and resources were inadequate and that the 'civilizing mission' was now to bring development to Africa of the minimum social conditions expected in a modern welfare state. This could only be accomplished by the imperial state itself, which at last must assume the mission it had always claimed but never exercised.

55 W. M. Macmillan, *Africa Emergent* (London, 1938), p. 23.

56 *Parliamentary Debates*, HC, ccvli, 14 June 1938, debate in supply committee, Colonial Office, cols. 80-96.

57 See ibid., speeches of Morgan Jones, cols. 96-108; Josiah Wedgewood, cols. 137-44 and Creech Jones, cols. 150-61.

58 For an account of MacDonald's role in establishing a colonial reform policy in these years see my article, 'Planned decolonization and its failure in British Africa', *African Affairs*, lxxxii, 328 (July 1983), pp. 389-411.

59 H. Laski (ed.), *Programme for Victory: a collection of essays prepared for the Fabian Society* (London, 1941). Macmillan was in very distinguished company — other contributors included Harold Nicholson, G. D. H. Cole, Herbert Read and Ellen Wilkinson.

60 Ibid., p. 85.

61 Ibid., p. 91.

62 Ibid., p. 103.

63 Ibid., p. 105.

64 Ibid., pp. 109, 115.

65 Ibid., p. 106.

66 C. K. Meek, W. M. Macmillan, E. R. J. Hussey, *Europe and West Africa* (London, 1940), pp. 103-4.

67 Laski, *Programme for Victory*, p. 95.

11. MACMILLAN, INDIRECT RULE AND *AFRICA EMERGENT*

* This account is drawn largely from Mona Macmillan's *Champion of Africa. W. M. Macmillan. The Second Phase* (Long Wittenham, 1985), ch. 2. We are grateful to Professor Michael Crowder for suggesting that this could fill an important gap in the collection and for his editorial advice. We are also grateful to Mona Macmillan for allowing us to make use of this material. Unless otherwise stated, the original correspondence cited is all from the Macmillan papers in the possession of the author.

1 Macmillan, *Africa Emergent* (Harmondsworth, 1949), p. 18.

2 Ibid., p. 17.

3 Ibid., p. 40.

4 W. McCulloch, *Dietaries of Hausas and Town Fulani* (Lagos, 1930).
5 Leys to Macmillan, 12 May 1936, and elsewhere.
6 Macmillan, *Africa Emergent*, p. 107.
7 Mitchell to Macmillan, 2 November 1930.
8 *The Political Quarterly*, October-December, 1932.
9 Ibid., p. 558.
10 Ibid., p. 567.
11 Leys to Macmillan, 9 September 1930.
12 Mitchell to Macmillan, 2 November 1930.
13 Oldham to Macmillan, 2 September 1930.
14 Mitchell to Macmillan, 2 November 1930.
15 Leys to Macmillan, 19 January 1931.
16 Public Records Office, DO 35, 452/20283/75.
17 Ibid.
18 Ibid.
19 Ibid.
20 W. M. Macmillan to Mona Tweedie (later Macmillan). Further quotations are from the same source.
21 Thomas to Macmillan, 27 February 1934.
22 The Kumasihene, Prempeh II, who became Asantahene, on the restoration of the Ashanti Confederacy in 1935. See M. Crowder, *West Africa under Colonial Rule* (London, 1968), pp. 230–3.
23 Macmillan, *Africa Emergent*, p. 166.
24 Ibid. pp. 360–1.
25 Sir James Currie, 'The educational: experiment in the Anglo-Egyptian Sudan, 1900–1933', Part II, *Journal of the Royal African Society*, xxxiv (1955), p. 55.
26 Ibid. p. 54.
27 Macmillan, *Africa Emergent*, p. 395.
28 Lewin to Macmillan, 13 March 1938.

12. PROFESSOR MACMILLAN GOES ON SAFARI: THE BRITISH GOVERNMENT OBSERVER TEAM AND THE CRISIS OVER THE SERETSE KHAMA MARRIAGE, 1951

1 Public Records Office (PRO), Dominions Office (DO) 35/41341 W. A. W. Clark, minute, 4 July 1951.
2 Ibid., G. H. Baxter, minute, 4 July 1951.
3 PRO, DO 35/4140, Clark to Miss Emery, 6 July 1951.
4 Ibid., Emery to Secretary of State, 6 July 1951.
5 Personal communication from Hugh Macmillan.
6 Colin Legum, the *Observer*, 30 July 1951.
7 The original of this letter is in the Botswana National Archives [BNA]. S 599/14 'Judicial enquiry re: Chief Seretse Khama'.
8 BNA S. 169/15/1 : 'Seretse, Chief: marriage of': Lawrenson, District Commissioner, Serowe to Nettelton, Government Secretary, Mafeking, (?)19 November 1948.

9 BNA, DCS. 37/12: 'Seretse, confidential': Nettelton to Priestman, High Commissioner's Office, 5 November 1948.

10 BNA, S. 169/15/1: 'Seretse, Chief: marriage of': 'Transcript of notes of the closing speeches in the Kgotla at Serowe, 19 November, 1948'.

11 BNA S. 170/1/1: 'Seretse, Chief: marriage of': 'Report on tribal meeting held at Serowe ... from 20th to the 25th June, 1949, in connexion with the Bamangwato Succession'.

12 Information from Mr M. J. Fairlie, an administrator in Serowe at this time, Edinburgh 26 April 1986.

13 PRO, DO 35/4114, Baring to Liesching, 11 July 1949.

14 PRO CAB 128/16, Cabinet Conclusions, 21 July 1949, p. 115.

15 Kenneth O. Morgan, *Labour in Power 1945-1951* (London: 1984), p. 416.

16 Ibid., p. 198.

17 Ibid., p. 199.

18 PRO DO 35/4118, *Report of the Judicial Enquiry re Seretse Khama of the Bamangwato Tribe*, 1 December 1949, p. 16.

19 Ibid., p. 17.

20 PRO CAB 128/17, 'Cabinet Conclusions', 31 January 1950, p. 14.

21 Ibid., p. 14: the words are those of the Secretary of State for Colonies, J. Griffiths.

22 Ibid., p. 34.

23 Cmd 7913. *Bechuanaland Protectorate: Succession to the Chieftainship of the Bamangwato Tribe* (CRO, London, 1950).

24 PRO DO 35/4136, Territories Department, 'Summary and analysis of Bamangwato affairs: 1948 – September 1951', 29 October, 1951.

25 The pressure was not only placed on the Labour government by the South African government, but also by Smuts who made his own fears of the consequences of Seretse's recognition clear not only to Attlee but to Churchill as Leader of the Opposition, which had been using the Seretse affair as a stick with which to beat the beleaguered government. See University of Cape Town Libraries Ms Collection, Smuts Letters, 95, 16 March 1950, Draft of letter to Churchill. Smuts had been prompted to write to Churchill as a result of a letter he had received from Leif Egeland, the South African High Commissioner in London, (93, 1950, 11 March 1950) warning him: 'The Seretse [sic] affair has taken a very ugly turn, both Beaverbrook and Winston having gone off the deep end....' Smuts cabled Churchill on 15 March informing he was sending a letter 'which advised caution from Commonwealth viewpoint'. His letter stressed the risk involved in recognition of Seretse as strengthening Republican sentiment in the National Party and demands for annexation of the High Commission Territories.

26 Tshekedi Khama Papers (TKP) Pilikwe, 58. 'History of Tshekedi Khama's case' ts, 2 June 1951.

27 TKP, Pilikwe, 54. For instance Arthur Creech-Jones, the former Labour Secretary of State for the Colonies congratulated him on his 'resource and skill in keeping the Bechuanaland problem alive' (Creech-Jones to Tshekedi, 12 July 1951). Peter Calvocoressi wrote to Sir Andrew

MacFadyean that Tshekedi had a 'cast iron case' that was 'a traditional and real Liberal issue'. 'Incidentally if the Liberal Party is in the last stages of dissolution let it be recorded in the chronicles that in extremis it still attached greater importance to righteousness than to electoral arithmetic or petty personalities' (11 June 1951).

28 Tshekedi employed a press-cutting agency in London and assiduously filed all news items concerning himself and Seretse, whether favourable or hostile. He was much more skilled than Seretse in lobbying the press and would have made a highly successful public relations officer.

29 DO 35/4136, 'Summary and analysis of Bamangwato Affairs', p. 7. This had been the conclusion of Patrick Gordon-Walker, the Secretary of State for Commonwealth Relations, after his own visit to Serowe in February. 'The simple fact that we must accept is that Tshekedi is intensely disliked in the Reserve' DO 35/4132, Gordon-Walker to Liesching, telegram. 7 February 1951.

30 DO 35/4/4133, Acting High Commissioner to CRO, telegram, 13 April 1951:

As you know my hope last year was successfully to prosecute a policy of bringing Tshekedi back to a position of power in the Bamangwato Reserve. For the time being it is necessary to abandon that policy. The only alternative is a policy of strict adherence to the White Paper... If by allowing Tshekedi to visit the reserve we provoke serious trouble there we will destroy our chances of establishing a reformed or indeed any type of native authority, Tshekedi's prospect of calming feeling against him will be lessened, and his position among the Bamangwato worsened and we will consequently have fallen between two stools.

31 These are well covered in Mary Benson, *Tshekedi Khama* (London 1960), ch. 18.

32 Ibid., p. 236; also *Manchester Guardian*, 23 June 1951; also *Observer* 24 June 1951.

33 Benson, *Tshekedi Khama*, p. 237; also *The Times*, 27 June 1951.

34 PRO DO 35/4134, Baring to Secretary of State, telegram, 28 June 1951.

35 Ibid., Barron, Rogers and Nevill to Under-Secretary of State, 29 June 1951.

36 BNA DCS 38/2 'Ngwato affairs', High Commissioner to Secretary of State, telegram, 17 July 1951.

37 BNA S536/2, Tergos [Territorial Gossip], News Report on the High Commission Territories, July 1951.

38 PRO DO 35/4134, High Commission to CRO, telegram, 23 July, 1951. The report is based on the opinion of the head of the South African Press Agency. This was also the fear of local administrators. See BNA DCS 38/1 'Ngwato Affairs', Beetham, Resident Commissioner to Chief Secretary, Turnbull, Secret, Personal, 8 July 1951 in which he expresses the fear that if Tshekedi returned he would 'be bumped off'.

39 Ibid. Statement issued by Seretse on 18 July 1951 after his meeting with Gordon-Walker at which 'He said he would stake his future on being able to restore order, arrange a Kgotla with a fair hearing for Tshekedi and

institute a system of councils' (CRO to High Commissioner, South Africa, 17 July 1951).

40 Ibid., Baring to Liesching, telegram, Secret, Personal, 18 July 1951.

41 DO 35/4140, Secretary of State to High Commissioner, telegram, 21 July 1951.

42 BNA DSC 38/2, 'Ngwato affairs', 'Reply of tribe to invitation to hold joint kgotla', nd.

43 'Professor lost in bush', *Scottish Daily Express*, 10 August 1951.

44 BNA DCS 38/2, K. A. Lowry, OC Security Camp Mahalapye to OC Security Camp Serowe enclosing reports of Trooper Koosenye.

45 PRO DO 35/4142, 'Note of a meeting between the representatives of the Bamangwato tribe and the three independent observers at Mahalapye on 3rd August 1951'.

46 Ibid., note of an informal meeting between Bamangwato tribal representatives and independent observers at Palapye ..., 29 July 1951.

47 Mona Macmillan, 'Biography of W M Macmillan', ts p. 215. W. A. W. Clark used a similar phrase of Lipson 'who seems to show tendencies to walk alone' in his letter to the Acting High Commissioner (PRO DO 35/4135, Clark to Acting High Commissioner, 3 August 1951).

48 M. Macmillan, 'Biography of W M Macmillan', p. 215.

49 Macmillan papers, 'Meeting at Rakops held on 6th August 1951: about 250 men present'.

50 M. Macmillan, 'Biography of W. M. Macmillan', p. 217.

51 BNA DCS 38/2 'Ngwato affairs', Cardross-Grant to District Commissioner, Serowe, 15 August 1951.

52 Ibid.

53 *Observer*, 4 August 1951.

54 TKP (Pilikwe) 55: 'TK's Case July–December 1951 incl. observers', Tshekedi to B Steinberg, Ernest Blackbeard, T Watson, 22 July 1951 wrote of Legum as 'one of the good people who had helped to make my stay in London possible and comfortable'.

55 Ibid., Tshekedi to Legum, 6 August 1951 forwarding him a letter to Lipson 'which I have opened for you to read and then seal up and hand to the bearer.... Any influence you can exert discreetly on the lines suggested in my letter to Mr Lipson will be appreciated'. He also asked Legum to give a lift to his cousin Mathiba, 'the gentleman I am sending to assist in collecting my sympathisers to attend the meeting'.

56 Mary Benson papers, Legum to Michael Scott and Mary Benson, 28 July 1951, p. 1.

57 Ibid., Legum to Astor, telegram, 31 July 1951:

Observers today informed officially by Keaboka on behalf Serowe headmen that they refuse to hold full tribal kgotla with Tshekedi present. Full statement is following urgently. Please advise William Clark for transmission friends this message in view rumoured debate Parliament today. Sending message two parts second part will come through first strong reasons suggest this tribal decision not in fact proper decision in terms tribal custom for making such decisions.

58 Mary Benson papers, Legum to Michael Scott and Mary Benson, 28 July 1951, p. 7.
59 TKP, Pilikwe, 55, Legum to Tshekedi, 2 September 1951: 'David will want another story for next Sunday.'
60 Another fiercely pro-Tshekedi journalist was Douglas Brown of the *Daily Telegraph*.
61 Macmillan papers, despatch from A. H. Mapleson: newspaper clipping but source unidentified.
62 Ibid.
63 PRO DO 35/4142, 'Report by Government Secretary on meeting between observers and Tshekedi Khama and his followers at Rametsana, 13.8.51'.
64 Macmillan papers, Mapleson's despatch; see also BNA DCS 38/3, 'Ngwato affairs', telephone conversation with Mr Dashwood relaying Reuter and *Rand Daily Mail* reports of 15 August 1951 (16 August 1951).
65 *The Times*, 27 June 1951.
66 BNA DCS 38/2 'Ngwato affairs', 'Meeting held at Sefhare on Tuesday 7th August 1951'.
67 DCS 38/3, 'Ngwato affairs', 'Meeting of Bamangwato held on Thursday 16th August, 1951'.
68 PRO DO 35/4142, 'Note of meeting held at Serowe on the afternoon of Thursday, the 16th August, 1951, between the independent observers and the women of the Bamangwato tribe'.
69 Rhodes House Library, Fabian Colonial Bureau Papers, Mss. Brit. Emp. S 365, Box 91, File 1, K T Motsete to Marjorie Nicholson, 10 September 1951; see also his second letter to her of same date.
70 PRO DO 35/4135. See correspondence in this file relating to the drafting of the report.
71 PRO DO 35/4135, High Commissioner to Secretary of State, telegram, 17 August 1951.
72 Ibid.
73 Ibid., Turnbull to Liesching, telegram, 20 August 1951; also DO 4140, High Commissioner to Secretary of State, 22 August 1951.
74 Ibid.
75 PRO DO 35/4136, High Commissioner to CRO.
76 Colin Legum, 'Tribal chieftains accuse Britain' *Observer*, 2 September 1951.
77 Ibid.
78 PRO DO 35/4135, Minute by G. H. Baxter, 3 September 1951 *et passim*.
79 DO 35/4136, Sir S. Holmes to Prime Minister, 12 September 1951: most of the chiefs have 'partially, disavowed their signatures'.
80 BNA DCS 38/3, 'Ngwato affairs', Government Secretary, Mafeking to Dashwood, T J R, High Commission, 31 August 1951.
81 'Reports of observers on the attitude of the Bamangwato tribe to the return of Tshekedi Khama to the Bamagwato Reserve' (1951), reprinted in 'Joint report by Mr H. L. Bullock and Professor W. M. Macmillan', *Botswana Notes and Records*, x, nd. pp. 137–45.
82 Ibid., pp. 145–8.
83 PRO CAB 128/20, Cabinet, 27 September 1951, p. 235.

84 PRO DO 35/4136, Liesching, to High Commissioner, telegram, 20 September 1951.
85 Ibid., telegram to CRO based on report by Germond.
86 TKP, Pilikwe, 46^B, 'Case v. Keaboka'.
87 PRO CAB 129/47, 'Cabinet papers', CP (51) 250, 'Bamangwato affairs: Tshekedi Khama', memorandum by the Parliamentary Under-Secretary of State for Commonwealth Relations, 22 September 1951, pp. 3–4.
88 Benson, *Tshekedi Khama*, pp. 251–2.
89 University of Cape Town Libraries, Manuscript Collection, Smuts papers, private letters 95, telegram to Churchill 15 March 1950.

Should the British Government ignore this sentiment [against the marriage] in South Africa, public opinion here would harden behind Malan's claim for the annexation of the Protectorates to the union, and in case this claim were refused, the extreme course of declaring South Africa a Republic would at once become a live issue.... I think it would be a mistake to exploit British feeling in favour of Seretse to an extent which may damage the relations of South Africa to the Commonwealth and the Commonwealth itself.

90 PRO CAB 128/23, 'Cabinet conclusions', pp. 48, 54; PRO CAB 129/48, 'Cabinet papers', C(51) 21, 19 November 1951 'Bamangwato affairs', memorandum by the Secretary of State for Commonwealth Relations.
91 For instance, Benson, *Tshekedi Khama*, p. 253.
92 BNA DCS 38/1, 'Ngwato affairs', District Commissioner, Serowe to Government Secretary, Mafeking, 29 June 1951: a deputation of 21 headmen led by Keaboka asked for the removal of Rasebolai from Serowe since 'being the senior to Keaboka [he] is dangerous'.
93 TKP, Pilikwe, 86, 'Correspondence with Rasebolai' translated by Bandie Ramothibe.
94 See Michael Crowder, 'Resistance and accommodation to the penetration of the capitalist economy in Southern Africa: Tshekedi Khama and mining in Botswana 1929–1959', seminar paper, Institute of Commonwealth Studies (University of London, October 1985).
95 This was the view of Sobhuza, Paramount Chief of Swaziland, when he was interviewed by the observers.
96 'Report by Bullock and Macmillan', p. 144.
97 Ibid., p. 143.
98 Bullock and Macmillan, p. 144.
99 National Archives of Zimbabwe, S482 145/48, 'Natives: removal of Mswazi from Bechuanaland Protectorate'. The Prime Minister, Godfrey Huggins, wrote to the Governor of Southern Rhodesia describing Tshekedi's techniques as 'somewhat Russian and rough' (Huggins to Kennedy, 5 November 1947). On 12 January 1948 he informed the Governor that, in the area of Matabeleland where the refugees were settled, 'the question is being openly asked as to whether Tshekedi or George VI is King'.
100 'Report by Bullock and Macmillan', p. 144.

101 Ibid., p. 143.

102 Neil Parsons, 'The Bangwato political crisis 1948–53: another stab at Botswana social history', paper presented at the University of Botswana, Department of History, Workshop on Bangwato Politics under Colonial Rule, November 1984 argues that Tshekedi's ban on beer brewing was an important factor, since beer-brewing was a woman's occupation. Theophilus Mooko, 'The role of royal women in Bangwato politics under the regency of Tshekedi Khama, 1926–1949', BA Research Essay, History Department (University of Botswana, 1985), p. 16, contests this.

103 Parsons 'The Bangwato political crisis'.

104 PRO DO/4135, private handwritten notes from Bullock to Gordon-Walker dated 15 August and 16 August 1951.

105 Macmillan papers, Macmillan to Mrs Macmillan, 12–13 August 1951.

106 'Report by Bullock and Macmillan', p. 145.

107 Macmillan papers, Peter Cardross-Grant to Macmillan, nd.

108 Parsons, 'The Bangwato political crisis'.

109 PRO DO 35/4136, 'Notes on the Bechuanaland Protectorate suggested by tour in July–August 1951 by Professor W. M. Macmillan', 1 October 1951.

110 W. M. Macmillan, *My South African Years: an autobiography*, (Cape Town, 1975), p. 237.

111 PRO DO 35/4136, Minute by ? to G H Baxter, nd.

W. M. MACMILLAN: CHRONOLOGY

1885	Born Aberdeen, Scotland, 1 October.
1891	Approximate date of move to Stellenbosch, South Africa.
1900	Elder brother killed in action near Krugersdorp. Matriculated from Stellenbosch Boys' High School.
1901	Enrolled at Victoria College, Stellenbosch.
1902	Passed intermediate exams.
1903	Elected one of first Rhodes scholars. Enrolls at Merton College, Oxford.
1906	Graduates with Second Class Honours in Modern History. Enrols for Divinity course at United Free Church College, Aberdeen.
1907	Visits South Africa. Enrols for Education courses at University of Aberdeen.
1909	Abandons Divinity course at Aberdeen. Teaches at prep. school in Kent, and for two terms at Llandovery School, Wales.
1910	Summer semester at University of Berlin. Resumes Divinity studies at United Free Church College, Glasgow. Appointed lecturer in History and Economics at Rhodes University College, Grahamstown.
1911	Takes up appointment in Grahamstown. Visits Bloemfontein, Basutoland, Johannesburg, and northern Transvaal for first time. Joins Fabian Society.
1914	Begins work on 'Poor Whites'.
1915	Visits Britain. Meets Sidney Webb. Decides not to enlist.
1916	Visits Johannesburg. Applies for professorship in History at School of Mines. Attends Cradock conference on 'Poor Whites'.
1917	Takes up appointment in Johannesburg.
1919	Gives series of public lectures in Johannesburg on the South African Agrarian Problem.
1920	Begins work on the papers of Dr John Philip. Visits Britain. Meets R. H. Tawney. Produces memorandum on South Africa for British Labour Party.
1922	Rand Strike. Writes first of series of articles for *New Statesman and Nation*. Joins Johannesburg Joint Council.
1923	Attends first conference on Native Affairs organized by the Dutch Reformed Church. Makes first public statement on Native Affairs. Probable date of election as President of Workers' Education Association.
1924	Series of articles for *The Star*, later published as *The Land, the Native and Unemployment*.
1925	Lobbies with some success against the Colour Bar Bill.
1926	Completes sample survey of Herschel district and submits report.

Publishes series of articles in *Cape Times* under the title 'At the roots'. Attends conference on Christian Missions in Africa at Le Zoute, Belgium. Visiting Associate Member All Souls' College, Oxford.

1927	Publishes *The Cape Colour Question*. Gives evidence to the Select Committee on the Native Bills.
1929	Publishes *Bantu, Boer, and Briton*.
1930	Publishes *Complex South Africa*. Elected chairman of Johannesburg Joint Council. Travels through the Rhodesias, Congo, Tanganyika, Kenya and Uganda.
1931	Meets Mona Tweedie. Visits Southern Rhodesia and Nyasaland. Papers of Dr John Philip destroyed by fire. Begins work on book on British policy in Africa as a whole.
1932	Publication of Natives Economic Commission. In conflict with Pirow and Jansen. Leaves South Africa for sabbatical in Britain. Travels via the Rhodesias, Congo and Angola.
1933	Visits West Africa for first time. At All Souls' College, Oxford. Resigns from Johannesburg chair in September.
1934–35	Visits USA and West Indies.
1936	Publishes *Warning from the West Indies*.
1938	Publishes *Africa Emergent*. Second visit to West Africa.
1939	Gives Heath Clark Lectures at London School of Hygiene and Tropical Medicine.
1940	Gives lecture to Fabian Society on 'Freedom for colonial peoples'. Appointed member of Colonial Office Advisory Committee on Education.
1941	Empire Intelligence section, BBC.
1943	Senior Representative, British Council, West Africa.
1947	Director, Colonial Studies, University of St Andrews, Scotland. Colonial Labour Advisory Committee.
1949	Visits South Africa. Gives Hoernlé Memorial Lecture in Durban.
1950	Visits South and East Africa.
1951	Observer mission to Bechuanaland.
1952	Visits central and southern Africa.
1954	Retires. Acting professor of History, University College of the West Indies.
1955	Returns to Britain.
1957	Honorary D. Litt., University of Oxford.
1958–9	Visits central and southern Africa.
1962	Honorary D. Litt., University of Natal. Lectures at South African Universities.
1973	Last visit to southern Africa.
1974	Honorary D. Litt., University of Edinburgh. Died 23 October.

W. M. MACMILLAN: SELECT BIBLIOGRAPHY

Books

1919   *The South African Agrarian Problem and its Historical Development*, Johannesburg. Reprinted Pretoria, 1974, with a preface by F. A. van Jaarsveld.
       A South African Student and Soldier, (ed.), Johannesburg.

1927   *The Cape Colour Question, A Historical Survey*, London. Reprinted Cape Town, 1968, with a foreword by C. W. de Kiewiet.

1929   *Bantu, Boer, and Briton; the making of the South African native problem*, London. Revised and enlarged edn., Oxford, 1963. Reprinted Westport, USA, 1979.

1930   *Complex South Africa, an economic foot-note to history*, London.

1936   *Warning from the West Indies; a tract for Africa and the Empire*, London. Revised and enlarged edn., Harmondsworth, 1938.

1938   *Africa Emergent*, London. Revised and enlarged edn; Harmondsworth, 1949.

1959   *The Road to Self-rule, a study in colonial evolution*, London.

1975   *My South African Years*, Cape Town, with a preface by Dame Lucy Sutherland.

Pamphlets

1915   *Sanitary Reform for Grahamstown*, anon., Grahamstown.
       Economic Conditions in a Non-industrial South African Town, Grahamstown.

1916   *Poverty and Post-war Problems*, Grahamstown.

1918   *The Place of Local Government in the Union of South Africa*, Johannesburg.

1924   *The Land, the Native and Unemployment*, Johannesburg.

1941   *Democratise the Empire! a policy for colonial change*, London.

1949   *Africa Beyond the Union*, Johannesburg.

Contributions to books

1923   'Native land and the Land Act', in *European and Bantu, being papers and addresses read at the conference on Native Affairs*, Cape Town.

1926 'Black and white in South Africa' In E. Smith (ed.), *The Christian Mission in Africa, a study based on the proceedings of the international conference at le Zoute,* London.

1936 'Political development, 1822–34'; 'The problem of the coloured people'; 'The frontier and the Kaffir Wars, 1792–1836'; 'South Africa after the union: the High Commission Territories' in E. Walker (ed.), *The Cambridge History of the British Empire,* viii, 'South Africa', Cambridge. Revised edn., 1963.

1940 'African development, (a) by external capital: mining enterprise and the labour problem'; 'African development, (b) the negative example of Sierra Leone, (c) by African enterprise: Gold Coast cocoa industry'; 'Political and social reconstruction: the peculiar case of the Gold Coast colony' in C. K. Meek, W. M. Macmillan and E. R. J. Hussey, *Europe and West Africa,* London.

1941 'Freedom for colonial peoples' in Fabian Society, *Programme for Victory,* London.

Articles

1908 'South Africa revisited', (unsigned) *The Aberdeen Free Press,* 1 March.

1916 'The study and teaching of history', *The Educational News of South Africa,* July.

1919 'The strike and unrest. Some thoughts on present discontents' (unsigned) *The Rand Daily Mail,* 19 April.

1921 'The future of the land', *The Rand Daily Mail,* 2 May.

1922 'War on the Witwatersrand', *The South African Quarterly,* March. 'The truth about the strike on the Rand', *The New Statesman and Nation,* 13 May (first of a series signed 'M').

1923 'The Commonwealth and the parish pump', *The New Statesman and Nation,* 15 September.

1924 'The land, the native and unemployment' *The Star,* August (5 parts). 'Politics in South Africa', *The New Statesman and Nation,* 10 May. 'South Africa after the elections', *The New Statesman and Nation,* 9 August.

1925 'Party politicians and the colour bar', *The New Statesman and Nation,* 4 April. 'The South African situation', *The New Statesman and Nation,* 12 September. 'Are whites being swamped', *The New Statesman and Nation,* 11 November. 'The missionary as scapegoat', *The Star,* 24–25 March (2 parts).

1926 'Squatting', *The Cape Times,* 3–5 March (3 parts). 'At the roots', *The Cape Times,* from 12 April (10 parts).

1927 'The political ideals of the backveld', *The New Statesman and Nation,* 23 July.

1929 'Shadow and substance in native policy', *The Cape Times*, 19–22 July (3 parts).
'Nationalism and its dangers', *The Rand Daily Mail*, 15 October.
'South Africa's "white" problem', *The New Statesman and Nation*, 21 December.

1930 'Tropical Africa and the Union', *The Star*, from 5 June (5 parts).

1931 'East Africa as seen from the South', *The Manchester Guardian*, February (3 parts).
'South Africa and its sacred trust', *The New Statesman and Nation*, 22 August.

1932 'The development of Africa: impressions from Rhodesia', *The Political Quarterly*, October.
'From bad to worse in South Africa', *The New Statesman and Nation*, 23 April.
'Overcrowded Native reserves', *The Star*, 6 August.

1933 'Southern Rhodesia and the development of Africa', *Journal of the African Society*.
'Taking counsel together', *Umteteli wa Bantu*, 16 September.
'Some African contrasts', *The Star*, 11 November.
'The real moral of the Tshekedi case', *The New Statesman and Nation*, 20 September (unsigned editorial).
'Our African task', *The Glasgow Herald*, September (2 parts).

1934 'The importance of the educated African', *Journal of the Royal African Society*.
'The Protectorates', *The New Statesman and Nation*, 2 June.
'How we "play the game" in Kenya', *The Daily Herald*, 11 July.

1935 'Colour and the Commonwealth', *The New Statesman and Nation*, 1 June.

1936 'Last chance for justice' *The Daily Herald*, 11 June.
'Imperialism – old style and new', (unsigned editorial) *The New Statesman and Nation*, 20 June.
'Black and white in South Africa', *Overseas* (Journal of the Overseas League), July.
'Changing Africa — new nationalisms', *The Manchester Guardian*, 2 July.
'Africa and the West Indies', *The African Observer* (Bulawayo), August.

1939 'An unusual colony — the Gold Coast — a Native middle class', *The Manchester Guardian*, 24 April.
'Neglected outposts of empire', *The New Statesman and Nation*, 6 May.
'Native labour in Africa', *The Manchester Guardian*, 24 May.
'The new imperialism', (unsigned editorial) *The Economist*, 2 December.

1940 'What about the colonies?', *The New Statesman and Nation*, 10 February.

1946 'Juggernauts in the colonies', (unsigned editorial), *The Economist*, 21 December.

1950 'Race policies and politics', *The Listener*, 29 June.

1951 'East African outlook', *The Listener*, 28 June.

1953 'African growing pains', *United Empire*, May–June.
1959 'The economics of African politics', *The Sunday Times*, 22 March.
'Federation after six years — higher production the key to greater stability', *The African World*, June.
'Boer and Briton revisited', *The Sunday Times*, 29 October.
1960 'South Africa revisited', *The Rand Daily Mail*, 7–8 January (2 parts).
'African growing pains: a second assessment', *African Affairs*, January.

INDEX

Hailey, Lord, 33, 218, 221–9, 232–3, 252–3
  An African Survey, 33, 221–4, 228–9, 252–3
Haldane, Robert, 135
Hammond, J. L., and Barbara, 68, 74
Hancock, Sir Keith, 177
Hardy, Thomas, 53, 113
Harris, Sir John, 215
Hauasa-speaking people, 236
health, 26, 48, 107–108, 116, 123, 217, 226, 229, 235, 244
Heath Clark lectures, 23, 232
Hebrides, 44
Hellman, Ellen, 85, 180
Herbst, J. F., 199
Herschel districts,
  alleged isolation, 184–6
  alleged lack of cohesion, 184–6
  cattle, 181
  chiefs, 186
  opposition to District Councils, 186–7
  opposition to state intervention, 187–8
  political movements, 185–8
  production and consumption, 181–3
  'progressives', 176, 178, 185, 187–90
  reactionaries, 188
  remittances, 183
  'sample district survey', 20, 69, 179–91, 198, 205
  statistics, 182–3
  see also reserves
Hertzog, J. B. M., 8, 69, 72, 83, 97, 105, 196–8, 201, 233
High Commission Territories, 83, 209, 233, 242–3, 255, 269, 277; *see also* South Africa
Hill, Polly, 24

Hintsa, 12, 137
historians,
  African, 103
  Africanist, 99–100
  Afrikaans-speaking, 103, 168
  Afrikaner Nationalist, 153
  Asian, 103
  British, 40
  Coloured, 103
  English-speaking, 103, 168, 177
  liberal, 9, 12, 153
  radical, 9, 173, 190
  settler, 97–8, 101–102, 141
  Whig, 102
historians and colonial policy, 219
historical
  analogies, 21, 24, 174–5
  imagination, 33
  materialism, 101–102
  methodology, 13, 76–8, 86
  reconstruction, 77
  sources, 153
historiography
  American, 133–4
  Cape, 133, 153
  radical, 20, 168, 190
  settler, 106
  South African, 8, 13, 91, 99, 125–6
history, schools of, British social, 74
  South African Liberal, 14, 100–102
history, 33–4, 72, 74, 87
  African, 13, 89
  agrarian, 168–9
  Afrikaner, 84
  Cape, 138
  colonial, 219
  contemporary, 72
  economic, 10, 99
  and ideological bias, 31
  imperial, 12, 93, 99, 220

INDEX

Ngubane, Jordan, 89
Nguni, (Cape), 154–5, 161
Nicholson, Marjorie, 268
Nicolaus, George, 260
Nigeria, 219, 243–7
Nkrumah, Kwame, 29
Non-European Unity Movement,
  11
Northern Rhodesia, (Zambia), 82,
  214, 249–50
nutrition, 26, 225, 229, 236
Nyasaland, (Malawi), 214

Observer, The, 266, 269
Office of Censuses and Statistics,
  179
Oldham, J. H., 214, 221, 237, 241
Olivier, Lord, (Sydney), 22, 199–
  201, 208, 210–11;
  The Anatomy of African Misery,
  200
  White Capital and Coloured
  Labour, 201
Oppenheimer, Franz, 16–17
Orange Free state, 184–5, 196
Orange River Sovereignty, 98
Ordinance, 50, 140, 148, 150–52
ostriches, 53, 109, 117
Oudtshoorn, 163
Overberg, 160, 165
Oxford University, 38–9, 42–4, 96,
  208, 219–24, 232–3, 248
  All Souls College, 208, 232–3
  Mansfield College, 39
  Merton College, 39, 44
  Ruskin College, 42
The Oxford History of South
  Africa, 12

'Pact' government, (1924), 197
Palestine, 220, 239
Pslapye, 266–7
parallelism, 85

Parker, J., 250
parliamentarism, 65
  see also British: Parliament
Parsons, Neil, 275
'partnership' 29
pastoralism, 119, 122, 174
Paton, Alan, Towards the
  Mountain, 103
peasant proprietorship, 26
peasant societies, 178
peasantry
  Scottish, 43
  South African, 55, 119
peasants, 69, 157, 161, 166, 188
  and settlers, 238–9
  see also bywoners, crofters,
  share-croppers
Peires, J. B., 12–13
  The House of Phalo, 12–13
Penguin books, 28, 228, 252
Perham, Dame Margery, 201,
  209–10
petite bourgeoisie, 28, 198
Phelps-Stokes Fund, 73, 169, 178,
  200, 224
  lectures, 211
Philip, Dr John, 8–12, 78, 92, 135–
  52, 194, 199–201, 223
  American influence on, 133–4
  and 'civilization', 135, 137, 145
  and James Cropper, 140–52
  and Khoisan, 145–7
  and Liberalism, 126, 133, 135–6
  and Ordinance 50, 148
  and political economy, 143–6,
  149–50
  and politics, 8, 141
  and press freedom, 144–5
  and racial equality, 126, 128–30,
  134
  and radical evangelicalism,
  132–5
  and the Reads, 126–8

Scottish Daily Express, 263
Scottish
'enlightenment', 143–4
Highlands, 55, 132; 'clearances',
24, 43–5, 203, 237
Searle, Thomas, 112
Sebina, 263
Second World War, 8, 27, 69,
211–12
segregation, segregationism, 8, 15,
21, 23, 27, 53, 69, 72–4, 79,
84–5, 102, 111–13, 115, 172,
205, 207–10
liberal segregationism, 9, 13, 15,
176, 178–9, 188–9, 192–3, 196
see also apartheid, racism
Sekgomas, the, 260–61
Selection Trust group, 250
self-government, 29, 216–18, 222,
224, 226–9, see also
decolonization
Seme, Pixley, 207
serfdom, 75, 201
settlers, white, 29, 136–7, 208, 213,
214, 217–18, 226–7, 238–9
settler
colonies, 29, 226
dominions, 177
expansionism 13
share-croppers, share-cropping,
18, 52–5, 118–19, 162, 164–6
shop-keeping, 109–10
Sierra Leone, 249
Simons, Jack, 237
slave
labour, 174
trade, 75, 148
slavery, 140–52, 153, 201
and abolition, 133–4, 150, 225
and capitalism, 148–51
and emancipation, 10, 153–4
slums, 55, 58, 81
Glasgow, 46–7, 106

Grahamstown, 109–10
Johannesburg, 51–3, 110, 114,
180
Lagos, 247
Smith, Adam, 147, 149–50, 233
The Wealth of Nations, 149–50
Smith, A. L., 43, 46, 105
Smith, Edwin, 86
Smith, Gerrit, 133–4
Smith, Sir Harry, 138, 156
Smith, T. L., 134
Smithfield, 197
Smout, T. C., 131
Smuts, J. C., 72, 95, 105, 197, 201,
220, 222, 271
Sobhuza II, Paramount Chief, 268
Social
Darwinism, 20–21, 130, 135–6
Democratic Party, (German), 17
'social' economics', 110
Social
change, 86–8, 224
control, 78
democracy, 17, 173
engineering, 76
socialism, 17, 105, 122
international, 18
middle class, 41
see also Communism,
Fabianism, Labour movement,
Labour Party
Socialist Labour Party, 46
society, African, 99–100, 169, 172,
176–7, 237
sociology, 16, 33, 74, 77, 97, 103,
110
Soga, J. H., 15
Sombart, Werner, 74
Somerset, Lord Charles, 143–5
Sorin, G., 133–4
South Africa, passim
as a 'common' or single society,
7, 14–15, 19–20, 32, 72–90,